REPRESENTATIONS OF THE SELF FROM THE RENAISSANCE TO ROMANTICISM

In this volume a team of international contributors explore the way modern conceptions of what constitutes an individual's life-story emerged in the seventeenth and eighteenth centuries. The Enlightenment idea of the self – an autonomous individual, testing rules imposed from without against a personal sensibility nourished from within – is today vigorously contested. By analyzing early-modern "life writing" in all its variety, from private diaries and cor-respondences to public confessions and philosophical portraits, this volume shows that the relation between self and community is more complex and more intimate than supposed. Spanning the period from the end of the Renaissance to the eve of Romanticism in Western Europe, a period in which the explosion of print culture afforded unprecedented opportunities for the circulation of life-stories from all classes, this book examines the public assertion of self by men and women in England, France, and Germany from the Renaissance to Romanticism.

Patrick Coleman is Professor of French at the University of California, Los Angeles. His books include *Rousseau's Political Imagination: Rule and Representation in the "Lettre à d'Alembert"* (1984) and *The Limits of Sympathy: Gabrielle Roy's "The Tin Flute"* (1993). He edited Rousseau's *Discourse on Inequality* (1994) and co-edited *The Swiss Enlightenment: Reconceptualizing Nature, Science, and Aesthetics* (1998).

Jayne Lewis is Associate Professor of French at the University of California, Los Angeles. She is author of *The English Fable: Aesop and Literary Culture 1651–1740* (1996), *Mary Queen of Scots: Romance and Nation* (1998) and *The Trial of Mary Queen of Scots: Sixteenth Century Crises of Female Rule* (1998).

Jill Kowalik is Associate Professor of Germanic Languages at the University of California, Los Angeles. She is author of *The Poetics of Historical Perspectivism: Breitinger's Critische Dichtkunst and the Neoclassic Tradition* (1992).

REPRESENTATIONS OF THE SELF FROM THE RENAISSANCE TO ROMANTICISM

EDITED BY

PATRICK COLEMAN, JAYNE LEWIS, AND
JILL KOWALIK

CAMBRIDGE
UNIVERSITY PRESS

#4231600

PUBLISHED BY THE PRESS SYNDICATE OF THE UNIVERSITY OF CAMBRIDGE
The Pitt Building, Trumpington Street, Cambridge, United Kingdom

CAMBRIDGE UNIVERSITY PRESS
The Edinburgh Building, Cambridge CB2 2RU, UK http://www.cup.cam.ac.uk
40 West 20th Street, New York, NY 10011-4211, USA http://www.cup.org
10 Stamford Road, Oakleigh, Melbourne 3166, Australia

© Cambridge University Press 2000

First published 2000

Printed in the United Kingdom at the University Press, Cambridge

Typeset in Monotype Baskerville 11/12¼ pt. [SE]

A catalogue record for this book is available from the British Library

Library of Congress cataloguing in publication data

Representations of the self from the Renaissance to Romanticism /
edited by Patrick Coleman, Jayne Lewis, and Jill Kowalik.
p.   cm.
Includes bibliographical references and index.
ISBN 0 521 66146 3 (hardback)
1. Literature, Modern – 18th century – History and criticism.
2. Self-presentation in literature.   3. Enlightenment – Europe.
I. Coleman, Patrick.   II. Lewis, Jayne Elizabeth.   III. Kowalik,
Jill Anne.
PN751.R47 2000
809'.93353–dc21   99-30728 CIP

ISBN 0 521 66146 3 hardback

Contents

Illustrations

Contributors

FELICITY BAKER (University College, London) is the author of numerous essays on Rousseau. She has also translated Claude Lévi-Strauss's *Introduction to the Work of Marcel Mauss* (1987).

PATRICK COLEMAN (University of California, Los Angeles) is the author of *Rousseau's Political Imagination: Rule and Representation in the "Lettre à d'Alembert"* (1984), *The Limits of Sympathy: Gabrielle Roy's "The Tin Flute"* (1993) and *Reparative Realism: Mourning and Modernity in the French Novel 1730–1830* (1998). He is the editor of Rousseau's *Discourse on Inequality* (1994), and co-editor of *The Swiss Enlightenment: Reconceptualizing Nature, Science, and Aesthetics* (1998).

ROBERT FOLKENFLIK (University of California, Irvine). His publications include *Samuel Johnson, Biographer* (1978) and *The Culture of Autobiography* (1993).

JULIE CANDLER HAYES (University of Richmond, Virginia). Her books include *Identity and Ideology: Diderot, Sade, and the Serious Genre* (1991) and *Reading the French Enlightenment: System and Subversion* (1999).

ANTHONY J. LA VOPA (North Carolina State University, Raleigh). His publications include *Grace, Talent, and Merit: Poor Students, Clerical Careers, and Professional Ideology in Eighteenth-Century Germany* (1988) and a forthcoming biography of Fichte.

BENOÎT MELANÇON (University of Montréal) is the author of *Diderot Epistolier: contribution à une poétique de la lettre française au XVIIIe siècle* (1996), and has edited several collections of essays on French and Quebec literature.

ANNE K. MELLOR (University of California, Los Angeles). She is the author most recently of *Romanticism and Gender* (1993) and the editor (with Richard E. Matlock) of *British Literature 1780–1830* (1996).

PETER N. MILLER (University of Maryland, College Park) is the author of *Defining the Common Good: Empire, Religion, and Philosophy in Eighteenth-Century Britain* (1994).

MARY O'CONNOR (McMaster University, Ontario) is the author of *John Davidson* (1987) and of numerous essays on British and American women writers.

TIMOTHY REISS (New York University). His many books include *The Meaning of Literature* (1992) and *Knowledge, Discovery, and Imagination in Early Modern Europe: the Rise of Aesthetic Rationalism* (1997).

DEBORA SHUGER (University of California, Los Angeles). Her publications include *The Renaissance Bible: Scholarship, Sacrifice, and Subjectivity* (1994) and *Religion and Culture in Renaissance England* (1997, with Claire MacEachern).

RICHARD WENDORF (Boston Athenaeum). His publications include *The Elements of Life: Biography and Portrait-Painting in Stuart and Georgian England* (1990) and *Sir Joshua Reynolds: the Painter in Society* (1996).

STEPHEN WERNER (University of California, Los Angeles). His books include *Socratic Satire: An Essay on Diderot and the Neveu de Rameau* (1987) and *Blueprint: A Study of Diderot and the Encyclopédie Plates* (1993).

Acknowledgments

This book emerged from a year-long series of conferences sponsored by the UCLA Center for Seventeenth and Eighteenth Century Studies and the William Andrews Clark Memorial Library on the theme "Life Studies: Autobiography, Biography, and Portrait in the Seventeenth and Eighteenth Centuries." We are deeply grateful to Peter Reill, the Director of the Center, for the support and encouragement he has so generously given us from the very beginning of the project and throughout its development into this volume. The Center's staff (Lori Stein, Candis Snoddy, Marina Romani, and Nancy Connolly) made the whole process of running the conferences an easy and most agreeable one. Together, along with Bruce Whiteman, the Clark Librarian, they make the Center a uniquely creative resource and an exceptionally congenial venue for interdisciplinary studies in this period. We wish to thank all the conference participants and regret we were unable to include all their papers here. All the chapters here have been specially revised and edited for this volume. For helping prepare them for publication, we thank Ellen Wilson, whose contribution goes far beyond the patient and scrupulous editorial work she has done on the texts. Her insightful suggestions and critical acumen have been invaluable. We are also indebted to Marina Romani for suggesting the illustration on the dust jacket. Finally, our thanks to our editor, Ray Ryan, of Cambridge University Press, for helping us through the publication process. The chapter by Anne K. Mellor, in a slightly different version, has already been published in the journal *Nineteenth-Century Contexts*. We extend thanks to the editors of this journal for permission to include Professor Mellor's paper in our volume. Thanks also to the museums and other institutions which have graciously given permission for art reproduction: The British Museum, The Wallace Collection, The National Trust Waddesdon Manor, and The Courtauld Institute, for illustrations in the chapter by Anne K. Mellor; to The British Library, Victoria and Albert Picture

Library of the Victoria and Albert Museum, National Gallery, London, and Hazlitt, Gooden, and Fox, London, for the illustrations in the essay by Richard Wendorf; and to The Los Angeles County Museum of Art for the cover illustration.

Introduction: life-writing and the legitimation of the modern self

Patrick Coleman

The chapters in this book explore conceptions of the self as they emerge from the biographical and autobiographical writing of seventeenth- and eighteenth-century Europe. Standard accounts of the period do, of course, discuss the rise of individualism as a key factor in the genesis of modern states. Governments were legitimized, to an increasing degree, by the consent of autonomous citizens, and cultures judged by how well they accommodated the free expression of personal desires. In recent years, however, we have become more aware of the complexities of that history, and, in particular, of how the different and often contradictory experiences of women and other marginalized groups have been glossed over. But beyond the need to recover the past more fully, there are other reasons for re-examining early modern notions of the self as they appear in life-writing. This volume arose in particular from reflection on two features of the contemporary world which we believe can be illuminated by such an investigation.

The first is the ubiquity of "life-writing" itself as a cultural form. Associated a century ago with documentary or chronicle-like accounts of a famous career, this term is now used to encompass the whole range of the autobiographical and biographical narratives which have become so pervasive a phenomenon in our time. Alongside conventional literary works, we find journals, memoirs, diaries, and oral histories of all kinds, from the "witness literature" produced by survivors of totalitarian regimes to television talk-show spin-offs and the scandal-focused biography that Joyce Carol Oates has called "pathography."[1] This proliferation of life-writing has provoked widespread debate about the culture and especially the media that have fostered it. Historical perspective, however, is often missing from the argument. A closer look at the relationship between the first major wave of life-writing which accompanied the explosion of "print culture" in the early modern period may lead to more nuanced judgments about the contemporary scene. Conversely, our own increased sensitivity to the power of the media should help us modify our often idealized views about the representations of the self put forward by the canonical writers of the Age of Reason.

The neutral pairing of the two words "life-writing" highlights a second important feature of contemporary (auto)biography: the dissolution of preconceived notions about the relationship between the work and the circumstances of which it speaks. The authenticity, consistency, or expressive power of the writing, it would seem, need not depend on the ontological or even chronological priority of the life. Autobiographies and biographies used to portray lives that had run enough of their course for their ultimate significance to be assessed, but today the techniques of life-writing are employed as pedagogical devices to encourage children to imagine lives they might potentially live, or to help adults overcome the restrictive "scripts" of their past.[2] Nor should one make any assumptions about the kind of coherence one should expect of any particular instance. On the contrary, generic distinctions and traditional narrative conventions are often subverted, as in the deliberate refusal of closure in witness accounts of events like the Holocaust, which shake our confidence in the power of any narrative to frame them.[3] Even the apparently basic difference between one's own point of view and that of another may be blurred, as in some memoirs of mental disturbance.[4] In short, today's "life-writing" reflects a postmodern emphasis on the particulars of experience at the expense of generalizing explanatory patterns. The chapters in this volume show that such experimentation with form was a feature of life-writing from very early on, and that the relation between the critique and the construction of normative images of the modern self is, in fact, much more intimate than is often supposed.

This extension of life-writing's scope has prompted contemporary students of the subject to rethink the boundaries of their own disciplines: not just how to interpret the evidence, but what counts as relevant evidence of identity formation. Good historians have always been attentive to the information conveyed by style, genre, and tone, while good literary scholars have never neglected the circumstances of a text's composition and circulation, but what distinguishes the new interdisciplinary approach to life-writing is its willingness to reconsider at every stage the implications of these various elements. Thus, while the chapters in this book begin from a variety of disciplinary starting points, in the practice of each author the aesthetic or architectonic concerns of the critic are not always easy to distinguish from the archival curiosity of the historian. Certainly both perspectives are essential for anyone attempting to write the life of yesterday's life-writer.

Changing assumptions about the self have not been limited to the forms in which that self is expressed. The very possibility of a "self" in the paradigmatic Enlightenment sense – an autonomous individual, testing rules imposed from without against a sensibility nourished from within, demanding as a matter of right to flourish in his or her own way – has been called into question. This is the second reason why we believe it important to look again at early modern representations of the self. What is new in the current debate is not skepticism about the self's inner coherence. In its modern formulations, the idea of the self has always been colored by skeptical attitudes, from Descartes and his doubts to the ironies of Pascal and Hume. What is now at stake is the legitimacy of focusing on the self as a foundational idea, however conceived. To be sure, Marxists and post-Nietzschean philosophers such as the writers of the Frankfurt school had earlier questioned celebratory accounts of the self's apotheosis as the embodiment of modern freedom in the form of the bourgeois subject. They identified nonetheless with the emancipatory thrust of what Alisdair MacIntyre has called the "Enlightenment project."[5] Today, some postmodern and postcolonial theorists go much further. The Enlightenment project itself, they argue, in the abstract (but in fact Eurocentric) universalism of its concept of human nature, cannot accommodate true respect for difference in a multicultural world. This politics of difference is in turn denounced by conservative thinkers such as MacIntyre (himself a former Hume scholar) who believe it undermines the ideal of a common civic discourse. Yet, far from advocating a return to the Enlightenment, "communitarian" thinkers such as MacIntyre want to repair the damage it caused by reabsorbing the self into the stabilizing web of community and tradition. A postmodern theorist such as François Lyotard would in turn reply that "tradition" is only another story, invented to mask the contingency of the particular.[6] Both sides point to the proliferation of life-writing as a sign of the times that proves their case. But while they disagree in their politics, they share the view that by exploring the multiple determinations of gender, or race, or class, contemporary life-writing presents personal experiences as not just unique, but incommensurable. They cannot be judged by any common standard.

These claims, and the historical assumptions behind them, need to be questioned. Does the postmodern diversification of life-writing really mean the early modern self has been superseded? A closer look at the life-writing of that past might lead one to argue that what we see now are in fact further manifestations of the latter's protean energy. And is the communitarian critique of the modern self not a by-product of the very Enlightenment it rejects? As Charles Larmore has pointed out, there is something self-contradictory about identifying with unreflective tradition on the basis of a systematic critique of the past.[7] And yet, this gesture, too, is part of our tradition. It occurs most starkly in some of the thinkers, such as Rousseau, Burke, and Herder, who mark the transition between the Enlightenment and Romanticism, and who were well aware of its ambiguities. A similar awareness of the ambiguities of modernity as a whole informs the chapters gathered here. Skeptical about teleological histories of the self – including postmodern narratives of the end of teleology – the contributors to this volume show how a new look at the past can help us rethink the relationship between self and community in today's decentered world.[8]

The chapters included here span the period from the end of the Renaissance to the eve of Romanticism in Western Europe. For our purposes, this period may be defined in terms of three interrelated developments. The first, of course, is the spread of "print culture," that is to say the circulation of mechanically produced texts and images (newspapers, broadsheets, cartoons, and prints, as well as books), beyond the small clerical and humanistic elite of the Renaissance to a broader, unspecialized public. Second, in the wake of the Reformation and various civil and confessional wars, the force of religious and political tradition began to be supplemented by more explicit recognition of the need to legitimize authority through arguments based on premises independent enough of particular traditions to win common consent. Although in practice such consent, whether articulated through political participation or through informal networks of communication, remained the privilege of a small minority, it rested on a theory of universal rationality to which those excluded from participation could appeal. Finally, with the growth of those networks, there emerged, alongside the court and corporations that traditionally represented the community to itself, the domain we now call civil society. With this development came new ways of distinguishing between the "private" and the "public" spheres of life. If in earlier times the lives of kings, warriors, and priests carried exemplary significance by virtue of their roles in the old order, similar value could be claimed for persons whose lives exemplified the importance of unofficial action, as distinct from visible public function, in the life of civil society. Eventually, any life could be seen as invested with general significance irrespective of its "inherent" social importance. For what was the "public" itself, if not the domain constituted by the self-representations of private individuals in print and other media?[9]

The growth of the publishing industry offered, among other things, greater facility for the anonymous production and underground distribution of all sorts of printed material, and men and women of different social classes were quick to exploit these media in order to test, revise, sometimes reinvent their social, cultural, and sexual identities. The enlightened *Bürger*, the man of feeling, the *salonnière* who figure in traditional cultural history were only a few among many roles imagined and imitated in the writing of the age. At all levels of literate society, from court to coffee-house, new means became available for generating and capitalizing on various forms of personal distinction through the circulation of new fashions of dress or speech, and, also, for integrating individuals of different origins into an ideal community of "civil conversation" based on standards of polite discourse anyone could adopt, and behind which, given an increasingly rapid rhythm of circulation of people and print in major urban centers, anyone could hide.

Given this complexity, it is often difficult to separate creativity from conformity as we study modes of characterization in the early modern period. As the sources of authority became more diffuse, the boundary between authorized representations and the free interaction of individuals asserting or exploring identities of their own devising, and replicating them through a variety of media, became harder to draw. To take a crucial example, new standards of "politeness" applicable to all who wished to participate in civil society came to play a central role in the Western European culture of the late seventeenth and early eighteenth centuries.[10] Were these standards intended as ways of disciplining behavior according to a more thoroughgoing inspection of manners, or were they designed to protect the privacy of one's "real" opinions from intrusive inquisition? In some measure, of course, both answers are correct, but finding that measure is a delicate matter. Pinpointing the relationship between institutional and individual agency is an especially challenging task, whether we are considering an event, a text, or the peculiar combination of the two in writers' accounts of their own experiences. Textual analysis needs to be supplemented by other insights, such as those that emerge when we look at the images and objects through which subjectivity is portrayed or projected. This kind of anthropological approach has long been used to study cultures remote from us in space or time and to reconstruct the imaginative world of an individual when other evidence is unavailable.[11] We are discovering how fruitful it can be to apply a similar approach to a period of European culture until recently considered familiar and commonly interpreted as the period in which the self, in its modern sense, took articulate shape.

The writings discussed here are presented in chronological order, but the various chapters of the book form a number of distinct historical and thematic clusters. A first group of chapters examines the kind of self that is asserted in three important early seventeenth-century contexts of communication: the educational institutions established by the Jesuits; the political arena of court and Parliament in late Renaissance England; and the networks of epistolary correspondence among the members of an emerging international Republic of Letters. Contrary to some recent claims in Renaissance scholarship about a radical break in the concept of the subject around 1600, the authors show how the idea of the self is articulated within a broader picture of social ties. Thus, in his opening chapter, Timothy Reiss shows how Descartes, the emblematic figure of the modern individual, was shaped by an education at the Collège of La Flèche based on rhetorical ideals of communicative interaction. He argues that Descartes's notion of the self was a provisional ideal, a "passage" concept designed as a way station on the path toward a reconstituted political community whose nature Descartes could only glimpse amid the violence of the Thirty Years' War.

Debora Shuger focuses on the ways potentially violent encounters between powerful men in early Stuart England were deflected by the exercise of a wit finely poised between the acknowledgment of subordination and the *parrhesia* of speaking truth to power. Against those who assert the sudden appearance at this time of a self defined by its interiority, Shuger emphasizes how the ethos or character of a man was defined, his "life" epitomized, by what he revealed in speech, and not by a domain of feeling divorced from the externalized expression. Warning us against the temptation to apply anachronistic notions about the coherence of a single "self," she points out in the second part of her chapter that while the word "soliloquy" was used at this time in reference to a kind of private speech, it was in the specific context of communication with God. The interpenetration of this sphere of self-examination and the proud aristocratic self-representation evidenced in the social world would be a slow and complicated process.

Peter Miller's chapter on the erudite antiquarian Peiresc illustrates another aspect of the complexities of the relationship between life-writing and the notion of the self. Peiresc is the first scholar to be awarded the honor of a biography, but he himself published nothing and gained fame primarily by his tireless efforts to facilitate communication among other scholars across Europe. At the same time, he offered, in the discretion and moderation of his self-assertions (evidenced by his willingness to engage, in an atmosphere of continuing tension following the religious wars in France, with correspondents of different faiths and philosophies), a new model of the self-governing man inherited from the Stoics. Knowledge rather than will was the key to self-government and personal independence, and Miller argues that we find here a crucial source of the ideal of informed politeness which spread in the following century to the citizenry of the Enlightenment public sphere.

The next two chapters offer complementary perspectives on the relationship between public and private concerns articulated in the life-writings of three English women. Mary O'Connor argues that we need to modify the very distinction between private and public if we wish to capture the peculiar situation of aristocratic seventeenth-century women such as Anne Clifford or Anne Dormer. Their domestic lives as bearers of children and managers of households cannot easily be separated from their role in the dynastic politics of their families. By studying these women's intimate relationship with familiar objects of their work and leisure – the sewing needles and cups of chocolate mentioned in passing in their account books, letters, and diaries – O'Connor helps us understand more clearly how women participated in wider networks of production and consumption and how they created spaces of resistance to outside pressures. One might say that O'Connor offers a feminist twist on the idea of "technologies of the self" as defined by Michel Foucault in his last works, based on models of self-mastery used by the leisured men of antiquity.[12]

With the eighteenth-century actress Charlotte Charke, whose autobiography is the subject of Robert Folkenflik's chapter, the challenge of recovering the subjectivity within the represented self is very different. The *Narrative of the Life of Mrs. Charlotte Charke* is written in a thoroughly extroverted way. It is a public attempt to placate her father, Colley Cibber, himself a man of the theatre, and at the same time it is a farcical "advertisement for myself," as Folkenflik aptly notes. Charke was famous for her cross-dressing on and off the stage, and yet this play with disguise, far from disclosing a secret connection between subjectivity and gender, highlights the speculative nature of any attempt to establish such a connection except at the level of the genre and style of the text itself.

The importance of genre as a framework within which subjectivity can be articulated is a recurring theme in the next three chapters, which illustrate the search, in mid eighteenth-century France, for new ways of defining the individual's experience of time and memory in relation to family or other genealogical connections. This period has long been identified with an emerging cult of sensibility, but, as Benoît Melançon and Julie Candler Hayes point out, French scholarly investment in the role of "les grands hommes" in the cultural history of their country has too often predetermined the kinds of questions that are asked. Beginning instead by wondering why Diderot did *not* write the autobiography one might have expected from the author of so many personal letters, Melançon compares the formal characteristics of diaries, letters, and autobiographical narrative in order to show how the position of these genres at a given moment define a range of sometimes incompatible options for the writer. This is especially important for France, where generic constraints were felt more strongly than in England, and where stylistic choices were closely linked to questions of cultural status. Diderot's letters verge on autobiography, but he is too attached to the implied presence of a personal addressee to abandon the epistolary mode. Rousseau did, of course, write an autobiography, but he planned to include within, or alongside it, a substantial corpus of letters, and although only some letters were ultimately incorporated in the final version, they underscore the author's preoccupation with evidence and direct communication as defenses against misunderstanding. This reluctance to abandon the link to the other is also found among less literary writers. Elisabeth Bégon, for example, wrote to her son-in-law, away in America, every day during the winter months, when mail service was interrupted. Piling up one next to the other until they could be sent in the spring, the letters almost become a diary, but not quite. A full explanation for the French hesitation on the verge of autobiography will depend on further investigation of other non-canonical texts, but focusing on the tension between generic options in well-known works allows us to glimpse the self in the process of its construction.

Stephen Werner offers another original approach to Diderot's protean self-representations. He contrasts the lyrical mode of personal reminiscence that finds expression in the *Essai sur les règnes de Claude et de Néron* with the innovative comic form of life-writing represented by *Le Neveu de Rameau*. If Diderot preferred speaking to others to the self-enclosure that for him may have disqualified autobiography, it was by "speaking through others" that he could draw his self-portrait. While the letters to Sophie Volland present an image of Diderot as a thinking and desiring subject, ironically it seems that only in the satirical dialogue of the Nephew and the Philosopher, where the lyricism is no longer that of a "moi" or self but a universal music of nature, could Diderot depict that self.

The Abbé de Sade's biography of Petrarch is best known for claiming the poet's Laura as an ancestor of the Sades and thus of the abbé's nephew, the infamous marquis. But as Julie Candler Hayes shows, the three long volumes of erudite commentary (a form not subject to the generic constraints of more literary writing) provided ample room for the abbé's self-representation, in the course of writing the life, not of a reprobate "other," but of the archetypal poet of love. The work shows the abbé as the author of a sprawling family romance, but also as a man of letters for whom the manipulation of the driest documents is invested with his own dreams and desires. Insisting that his work is not a "Life" but only "Memoirs" toward a Life – in this respect, the work differs markedly from such works as Johnson's *Lives of the Poets*, with which it might in some respects be compared – the abbé reveals his reluctance to bring the project, and its opportunity for fantasy, to closure.

Felicity Baker's chapter on Rousseau's affair with Madame de Warens and Anthony La Vopa's account of Fichte's adoption of Kantian philosophy probe the relationship between life-writing and what Baker calls the "crisis in symbolic relations" in the last decades of the eighteenth century. Rousseau and Fichte were talented but poor young men, unable to benefit from the patronage networks of the time and looking for alternative means of self-promotion. But they also felt very keenly the need to overcome a deeper alienation from societies which seemed to them to have lost grasp of that elusive "good object," that locus of value which, whether located in a personal God or a moral ideal, could be transmitted as a legacy from teacher to student or from parent to child, and which is vital to the renewal of culture. Understanding what is involved in such transmission in a secular, post-Revolutionary world would become a central issue in Romantic literature and may be one of the driving forces of life-writing since that time. Works like Rousseau's or Fichte's are particularly valuable because they illustrate the challenge of finding appropriate terms in which to undertake such reflection without falling into the nostalgic sentimentality that sometimes overwhelms the writers of a later period.

Looking back on his youth, Rousseau confesses his puzzlement in trying to convey just what it was that made his relationship with Madame de Warens so precious. By accepting Rousseau's account as an

effort to be faithful to an elusive reality and not as evidence of a neuro-
sis all too easily labeled, Baker is also able to recover the exceptional personality of Françoise-Louise de Warens herself. Where Baker focuses on
Rousseau's retrospective narrative in the *Confessions*, La Vopa's essay on
Fichte follows the young philosopher as he tries to define, in letter,
sermon, and essay, the link between his calling and his career – his vocation, in other words, in the full sense of the term. Fichte's endorsement
of Kantian solutions to the problem of freedom and necessity, and to the
relation between head and heart in matters of belief, needs to be seen in
the context of his personal situation in Enlightenment Germany. As La
Vopa writes, "there was something intensely personal about Fichte's
commitment to an impersonal determinism," and the biographer of
such a philosopher must do equal justice to the logic of the personality
and to the rigor of the arguments.

The volume concludes, fittingly enough, with two chapters on the
ways individual life-stories are rewritten by friends, disciples, the public
at large – and by the subjects themselves in their own defense. Anne
Mellor studies the competing narratives developed to explain the behavior of Mary Robinson (1758–1800), an actress and poet whose love affairs
with the Prince of Wales and then with army colonel Banastre Tarleton
were public knowledge. The witty verbal thrusts with which Debora
Shuger's Renaissance noblemen defended their reputation would be of
no use to a late eighteenth-century woman obliged to conform to bourgeois standards of modesty and confronted, not by a small court audience, but by the manifold productions of the press, by polemics and
cartoons freely circulating to a large and varied readership. As Mellor
says, Robinson was a celebrity, "a set of visual and verbal public texts."
The self-representations she developed in response to her critics are
equally complex. Her adoption of numerous pseudonyms suggests that
she began to view her identity as itself a kind of performance. How
much this was the result of external pressure and how much it might
have been a liberating response to that pressure must remain an open
question, for the later biographer herself is confined to what evidence
the conflicting texts provide.

A painter's life, as Richard Wendorf points out in his study of Sir
Joshua Reynolds's posthumous reputation, is written not only in his pic-
tures but in the tools of his trade. Picking up a theme articulated in Mary
O'Connor's discussion of domestic objects, and alluded to in Peter
Miller's references to the antiquities dear to Peiresc's heart and in Felicity
Baker's treatment of Madame de Warens's medicinal plants, Wendorf

emphasizes the need to take objects and accessories into account in the theory as well as the practice of life-writing. These objects can be invested with both psychic and socio-economic significance. Sometimes, as in the case of Reynolds's palette inscribed with the names of successors wishing to write themselves into the artist's "afterlife," or the cenotaph erected in Reynolds's memory, with its inscriptions by Wordsworth and by Constable, these objects form part of the continuum of media – from full-scale narratives to letters and diaries, and from philosophical treatises to account books – through which life-stories are written and read.

With the image of the cenotaph as a self-conscious exploitation of the remembered self's absence from the scene, we come to the threshold of a different cultural era. That representations of the self are, for better and for worse, detachable from their origin and ostensible object had become a familiar theme by the end of the early modern period. It can be argued that a new period begins when, to the focus on the self in or behind the circulation of representations, is added a fascination with the absent self, that is, with the self as the name for the absent spiritual or moral center around which the whole symbolic field of cultural representations revolves. Wordsworth, of course, plays a key role here, along with Chateaubriand, the title of whose *Mémoires d'outre-tombe* captures an outlook which Rousseau had already articulated in his last work, the *Rêveries d'un promeneur solitaire*. But this would be the subject of another book.

We began with the questioning of the Enlightenment project by contemporary postmodern and traditionalist writers suspicious of the autonomous self as a cultural ideal. The chapters in this volume show how early modern representations of that self do not emerge in isolation from their material and cultural contexts but as reflection of and on the communal discourses and practices in which they are embedded. Yet the particular value of life-writing lies in the way this process of reflection, through which the subject positions himself or herself in relation to these conditions, comes to us through the articulation of individual voices. The fact that, in the past, discussion of this individuality has been colored by idealized views of the autonomous modern self should not lead us to downplay its enduring value. The Russian literary critic Mikhail Bakhtin, who experienced at first hand the ideological and spiritual upheavals of twentieth-century Russia, devoted much of his work to exploring how the subject's self-positioning, especially in its most aestheticizing mode, could be integrated into an ethical perspective that avoids the temptation of a false or hollow universalism. Bakhtin's early essays on the "answerability" of the individual subject to the situation in which he finds himself offer possible ways in which the study of life-writing might take us beyond the quarrel over the Enlightenment project. I will conclude by suggesting very briefly how the chapters in this book may be seen in that light.

For Bakhtin, moral responsibility is not enshrined in a set of rules but rather is embodied in a response or answer, whose expression is what Bakhtin calls the "personally uttered word." This word is a kind of action through which the subject determines or "finalizes" himself as self. Indeed, for Bakhtin, "the self is partially brought into being by the commitment of the act itself."[13] The other to whom the answer is directed (it could be another person, or another point of view within the subject) forms an image of the subject which he then can bestow on him as a unifying or "finalizing" definition.

This return action may be oppressive in many cases, but it can be a vital gift, since no subject can be fully aware of himself as he acts, can see himself "from behind." Rousseau's expressions of gratitude toward Madame de Warens, as analyzed by Felicity Baker, offer a striking acknowledgment of a such a gift. At the same time, however, through this "personally uttered word" the subject, to the extent that he moves beyond the given situation, resists or breaks free of obsolete or fossilized finalizations. Rousseau's paranoid anxieties, which stand in such stark contrast to his expressions of love, offer pathetic examples of such an effort. The variety of discourse genres Benoît Melançon sees deployed in the *Confessions* invites analysis along Bakhtinian lines, as do the women's diaries discussed by Mary O'Connor. Anne Mellor's analysis of how Mary Robinson's narrative of her own life compares with those proposed by others illustrates the ambiguity of "finalization" with particular clarity. Mellor emphasizes the ambiguous role played by Robinson's daughter, who completed her mother's unfinished memoirs. By highlighting Robinson's maternal behavior, the daughter provides her mother with what she no doubt considered to be the most positive of finalizing images. But Robinson's own writings, in which she embraces a multiplicity of roles and voices, reject even this sympathetic image as too narrow.

In his essay "Author and Hero in Aesthetic Activity," Bakhtin suggests that different genres of life-writing can be distinguished according to the different relationship between two aspects of utterance embodied in confession and autobiography. In confession, finalization can only come from God, and so the text itself cannot be completed. "Confessional self-accounting is precisely the act of noncoinciding with oneself in principle and actuality"; its justification lies "in the unpredetermined, risk-fraught future of the actual event of being."[14] Augustine's *Confessions* offer the paradigmatic articulation of this idea, but one can see it work in the social context of seventeenth-century England, in the oral performances of religious testimony analyzed by Debora Shuger. Autobiography, which, in contrast with confession, Bakhtin puts in the same category as biography,[15] includes a finalizing point of view (one's own or another's) within the text. The presence of that point of view may be crucial to what Bakhtin calls the "aesthetic of lived life," an expression we may connect with Michel Foucault's aesthetic of the self shaped by its techniques and exercises.[16] Bakhtin stresses, however, that the subject of this aesthetic, inasmuch as it is constituted as an inner principle of unity, "is not suited to biographical narration: my *I-for-myself* is incapable of *narrating* anything."[17] That is, he cannot open up the story to that "excess of seeing" which in confession may be attributed to God, but which in secular forms of life-writing (as well as in novels) belongs not to the "hero" of the life being told, but only to the "artist" who remains skeptical about the "hero's life" and all predetermined meanings or standards.

Who is this artist? Or rather, how can any life-writer – biographer or autobiographer – take on such a role? The question is (or should be) faced by anyone setting out to compose a life-story. While there can be no definitive answer, we can find examples, as well as warnings, in early modern Europe, when for the first time such stories no longer sought to invoke the sanction of religious or political authority, but appealed instead to the free exercise of a publicly sharable memory. Peter Miller gives us a thought-provoking example of such a gesture in Gassendi's "Life" of Peiresc, a man who, devoted as he was to a far-ranging correspondence with other scholars, never thought of writing a book himself, let alone narrating his own life. Fichte's letters, on the other hand, as Anthony La Vopa show us, offer poignant expressions of the subject's own attempt to escape the constraints of moralistic and socially prejudiced notions of character while respecting the spirit of the Pietist ethic in which he was raised.

Fichte found in his struggle to comprehend and then champion Kantian philosophy an indirect way of rewriting the terms of his mental itinerary. By contrast, the Abbé de Sade's personal investment in his biography of Petrarch suggests that in this case the writer is attempting less to acknowledge the split between the hero's finalized vision and the artist's "excessive" seeing than to blur the boundary between the two by assimilating the one to the other through the life-writing enterprise. This is perhaps the greatest temptation for the life-writer, and one which was apparent enough to the most lucid minds of the period. Diderot's *Neveu de Rameau* is perhaps closest to Bakhtin in its comic awareness of the impossibility of fusing the two perspectives of life-writing distinguished by the Russian critic. Diderot also reminds us that while any good writer cannot be indifferent to the prospect of such a fusion, pursuing it too single-mindedly undermines the ethical value of the undertaking itself. The portrait of Rameau's immoral nephew ("He") is also an affectionate questioning of "Myself's" complacent self-image as the "answerable" man. This ironic awareness is not least among the reasons for rereading the life-writing of the Enlightenment.

NOTES

1. Shirley Neuman claims credit for introducing this self-conscious use of the term to encompass the whole range of genres in "Life-Writing," in *Literary History of Canada: Canadian Literature in English*, ed. W. H. New, vol. IV, 2nd edn. (Toronto: University of Toronto Press, 1990), 333–70. See her "Introduction: Reading Canadian Autobiography," *Essays in Canadian Writing* 60 (1996): 5. The need to find a broader term was felt perhaps most immediately by critics of marginal colonial and postcolonial literatures.
2. See Philippe Lejeune, *On Autobiography*, ed. Paul John Eakin (Minneapolis: University of Minnesota Press, 1989) and Jean Poirier, *Les Récits de vie: Théorie et pratique* (Paris: Presses universitaires de France, 1983). "Self-help" sections of North American bookstores include numerous guides to writing one's journal.
3. See Shoshana Felman and Dori Laub, MD, *Testimony: Crises of Witnessing in Literature, Psychoanalysis, and History* (New York and London: Routledge, 1992).
4. A number of autobiographies, such as *The Education of Henry Adams*, have been written in the third person, but Gertrude Stein took a radical new step in writing and signing *The Autobiography of Alice B. Toklas*. It is now common to see books, such as Susanna Kaysen's *Girl Interrupted* (New York: Turtle Bay, 1993), in which the author writes in the first person about another person within her. For an analysis of the different forms of the "autobiographical pact," see, in addition to Lejeune, Peggy Kamuf, *Signature Pieces: On the Institution of Authorship* (Ithaca, N.Y.: Cornell University Press, 1988).
5. Alisdair MacIntyre, *After Virtue: A Study in Moral Theory*, 2nd edn. (Notre Dame: University of Notre Dame Press, 1984), 39. The term refers to attempts to provide a "rational justification for morality" independent of

theological, legal, and aesthetic traditions. But the expression is now often used as a metonym for modernity itself.

6. François Lyotard, *La Condition postmoderne: Rapport sur le savoir* (Paris: Minuit, 1979).

7. Charles Larmore, *The Morals of Modernity* (Cambridge: Cambridge University Press, 1996).

8. For an attempt to think through the political dimensions of this problem using the categories of Lockean philosophy, see James Tully, *Strange Multiplicity: Constitutionalism in an Age of Diversity* (Cambridge: Cambridge University Press, 1995).

9. For a stimulating new perspective on these issues, see Michael Maschuch, *Origins of the Individualist Self: Autobiography and Self-Identity in England, 1591–1791* (Stanford, Calif.: Stanford University Press, 1996).

10. See Lawrence E. Klein, *Shaftesbury and the Culture of Politeness: Moral Discourse and Cultural Politics in Early Eighteenth-Century England* (Cambridge: Cambridge University Press, 1994).

11. The history of methodological debates within classical scholarship can, in fact, shed valuable light on the outlook of the most forward-looking aspects of the Enlightenment, as J. G. A. Pocock has shown in his studies of Gibbon. Of particular relevance, also, are recent efforts to reconstruct the imaginative world of individuals expressing themselves through the often conventional vocabularies of religious discourse in early modern Europe. See for example Nathalie Zemon Davis, *Women in the Margins: Three Seventeenth-Century Lives* (Cambridge, Mass.: Harvard University Press, 1995).

12. See *Technologies of the Self: A Seminar with Michel Foucault*, ed. Luther H. Martin, Huck Gutman, and Patrick H. Hutton (Amherst: University of Massachusetts Press, 1988).

13. Gary Saul Morson and Caryl Emerson, *Mikhail Bakhtin: The Creation of a Prosaics* (Stanford, Calif.: Stanford University Press, 1990), 216.

14. M. M. Bakhtin, *Art and Answerability: Early Philosophical Essays*, ed. Michael Holquist and Vadim Liapunov, trans. and notes Vadim Liapunov, supp. trans. Kenneth Brostrom (Austin: University of Texas Press, 1990), 143.

15. *Ibid.*, 150; see also Morson and Emerson, *Mikhail Bakhtin*, 217.

16. Mikhail Bakhtin, "Author and Hero," in *Art and Answerability*, 152. Foucault's work was influenced by that of Pierre Hadot, whose *Qu'est-ce que la philosophie antique?* (Paris: Gallimard, 1995) provides an excellent presentation of the *souci de soi*.

17. Bakhtin, "Author and Hero," 155 (italics in text).

CHAPTER ONE

Revising Descartes: on subject and community

Timothy J. Reiss

That the modern Western idea of the self-possessive, centered, and willful "subject" has its philosophical foundation in Descartes's cogito is a commonplace of our culture.[1] People in the Western street take subjective individualism for granted. Philosophers deploy as much energy against this Cartesian "error" as they do against its counterpart that divided subjective mind from objective body. They defend it with equal fervor. That the same thinker put the new "subject" to its earliest psychological analysis in his *Passions de l'âme* is probably less widespread a commonplace, only because that analysis has seemed more closely tied to contemporary doctrine and discussion. I want to question these commonplaces.

I shall not, of course, make the foolish claim that the highly intelligent people who have seen such a foundation in Descartes's work have been wrong for three and a half centuries. The *Discours de la méthode*, the *Meditations*, and the *Principia philosophiae* certainly did elaborate the grounds of a "subject" defining itself in terms, as many put it at the time, of *savoir*, *vouloir*, *pouvoir*, and *faire*: reason, will, power, action. Indeed, the very establishment of such a concept of the "subject" required that it be the source of knowledge and action, the site of a "new beginning." Descartes himself, on occasion, said as much, even as he faced the necessity to set aside history and memory that such a beginning implied,[2] and as he confronted the problem of the multiplicity of "subjects" – what I am calling *community* – although that term will actually have two meanings: a society grounding "subjects" and one grounded *in* "subjects." To establish such a source and site was to suppose that the particular history of their development had no importance, for they composed a universal by definition out of history. One could not fully adopt the concept, even less be such a "subject," that is to say, without assuming such isolation. There lies much of the dilemma: blindness was presupposed; the "subject" so defined had to be its own universal origin.

If one supposes for the sake of this argument that Descartes and others *argued* themselves to such a claim about the "subject," then the importance of the idea's own history becomes evident. At the same time, it displaces the "subject" from its axiomatically central position. Furthermore, Descartes's difficulties with questions of history and community, to which he alludes when writing of a scientific community in the sixth part of the *Discours* and when analyzing political relations in his correspondence with the Princess Elisabeth, can be better understood when we replace them in the context of his developing arguments, and in that of his education and the debates in which he was involved.[3] We begin then to see that this powerful "subject" may well best be characterized as what I call a *passage technique*: a philosophical – or other – means to get from one way of thinking about things to another, using, reordering elements present in that earlier way to respond to new exigencies of context and practice; a means, not an end.

We are, in fact, familiar with such techniques in Descartes: the most immediately obvious is the celebrated *morale par provision*. I argue that these techniques were actually a constant device of Descartes's thinking, crucial to its development. I also suggest that he found them precisely where we would most expect him to have done so: in that neoscholastic training which he so often praised. In the 1616 dedication to his law theses, even though he regretted its ultimate inadequacy, he first noted how legal training had allowed him to travel across "the vast waters of the sciences and all the rivers that flow from them so plentifully." More familiar to us is the similar praise of the breadth of his Jesuit education in the "Première partie" of the 1637 *Discours*.[4]

How seriously he took that education is shown by his plans in the early 1640s to make the *Principia* a textbook response to scholastic theses. Indeed, while he agreed that he held many views opposed to those of his Jesuit teachers, he maintained theirs was the best education available. "Philosophy," he wrote on 18 September 1638 to his close friend, the mathematician Florimond Debeaune, who had sought advice on his son's schooling, "is the key to the other sciences," and a good course in the subject should be taken. "There is nowhere in the world," he added, "where I judge it better taught than at La Flèche."[5] We should start, then, with some idea of that education.

I want to note how the idea that a private, self-reflexive "subject" could think, act, and exist in isolation had no tradition behind it. Quite to the contrary: one would have to look hard to find anything of the sort before the European seventeenth century. Certainly Descartes's teachers held no such view. Their history of constant theological debate and political dispute, a pedagogical practice founded on oral exchange, and an intellectual style embedded in commentary, controversy, and public intercourse, made all their work intensely communal.

Such notions as authorial sovereignty, individual primacy, or pure inquiry held neither for them nor for those whose work they took as the necessary ground of learning. In Aristotle's practice, for example, meaning arose from a dialogue with predecessors and contemporaries. Inquiry itself was the principal element in a life of eudemia, the ground and necessary context of which was social intercourse. The "subject" was a social "subject," not a private one. The concept of *zóon politikón* made community the ground of being. Aristotle's *Rhetoric*, central to Jesuit pedagogy, was held by its author and his followers to teach techniques foundational of the polis. Its vital object was to enable "rational discourse about the intelligible reality of politics." His *Ethics* spoke wholly to communal life.[6] Reading Cicero's letters, dialogues, and speeches, as the Jesuits' pupils did from earliest school days, shows how that Athenian ideal lived on in Roman form.

Ideas of subjective authority and individual inquiry did not hold for Augustine either, for whom meaningful concepts were a recapturing of seeds put in the mind by God, and inquiry a path to the Divine. Nor did they hold for Aquinas, who sought to put these powerful traditions together, and whose concerns were furthered by Descartes's Jesuit teachers at the Collège of La Flèche. They did so by using the extensive Aristotle exegeses generated at Coimbra, Salamanca, Alcalá, and the Collegio Romano, as well as the lay commentaries issuing from Padua, Florence, Rome, and elsewhere. Knowledge and meaning were sought in past agreement and present debate. The first condition of inquiry lay in dialogue and exchange. Such was the age's general style of learning, from conversation to altercation and polemic (at its least edifying, to theft and calumny).

We must be ready to take these forms of pedagogy, *scientia*, and *sapientia* as seriously as Descartes himself did. He made them his constant sounding board partly because he did think neoscholastic Jesuit scholarship, embodied in the Coimbran commentators, in Pedro Fonseca, Francisco Toleto, Antonio Rubio, and above all Francisco Suárez, the most powerful philosophy of his day, and partly because an initial vesting of conceptual authority in the individual cogito was a main novelty of his own thought. (I stress *initial*: it was, as I say, one of his passage techniques.) To this last, Jesuit pedagogy afforded a striking contrast of method, form, and content. Prælection, repetition, disputation, explanation and defense of opinions, above all the *concertatio*, were the basic pedagogical exercises. The 1599 *Ratio studiorum*'s first explanation of *concertatio* is revealing:

The concertatio, which is usually conducted by the questions of the master or the corrections of rivals, or by the rivals questioning each other in turn, must be held in high esteem and used whenever time permits, so that honorable rivalry, which is a great incentive to studies, be fostered. Some may be sent individually or in groups from each side especially from the officers; or one may attack several; let a private seek a private, an officer seek an officer; or even let a private attack an officer, and, if he conquers, let him secure his honor or some other award or sign of victory, as the dignity of the class and the custom of the place demand.[7]

The military metaphors are particularly interesting. The "officers" and "privates" in question were pupils who had been separated into two sides for purposes of debate. *Concertatio* was used not just in rhetoric, the highest of the five "lower classes," but from the earliest grammar class.[8] Exchange and fierce debate grounded knowledge of authority and the opinion essential to understanding. That was why and how such contemporaries of Descartes as Jean Duvergier de Hauranne, François Garasse, Marin Mersenne, Gabriel Naudé, François Ogier, and his good friend Jean de Silhon put such exhaustive effort into refuting deists and arguing about stoics, Rosicrucians, skeptics, and others in the 1620s. And with respect to Descartes himself, we may well wonder what it could mean to wish to refute the neoscholastics, if the full meaning of one's work lay only, as so many have asserted, in the work itself and in the lone questing mind. The refutation would be unnecessary and confusing.

What, more importantly, could we then make of his determined collecting of "Replies" and "Objections" to the *Meditations;* of his earlier efforts to do the same for the *Discours* and its "Essais"? How could we understand his "Replies" (1640–42) to them? Their very existence belies any notion of self-sufficiency. Their purpose was surely to create the community of thinkers and doers described in the *Discours*. It was also to enable the elaboration of thought itself. How else could we fathom the widely accepted idea that Descartes's career itself was at least partly the result of an impromptu interjected disquisition at a late 1628 Paris gathering, provoking Pierre de Bérulle to urge him to dedicate himself to philosophical research and make his talents of service "au genre humain" (to humankind)?[9] In the same light we may better grasp Descartes's bitter dispute (1641–45) with Ghisbert Voet and Martin

Schoock, as well as his attempts to engage the entire Jesuit Society by reacting in print to Pierre Bourdin's criticisms (1640 and 1642) of the "Essais" and of the "Seventh Set of Objections" to the *Meditations*.[10] Even more in this light should we view the making of the *Passions de l'âme* in dialogue with the Princess Elisabeth from 1645 to 1647. Lastly, of course, Descartes elaborated much of his thinking via the vast correspondence pursued with so many important intellectual and political figures in the Low Countries, England, Sweden, and France.

Descartes did not draw these procedures as conclusions from his own work. They composed, I am suggesting, the atmosphere people breathed. In his case, they were made precise by eight years of Jesuit schooling. When Isaac Beeckman first met him in Holland in 1618, he noted in his *Journal* that this Poitevin was deeply versed in the work of many Jesuits and of other learned and scholarly people: "cum multis Jesuitis alijsque studiosis virisque doctis versatus est."[11] But what was in question was not simply a style of thought and its content. The air breathed also lay over action and event. The Jesuits were profoundly alive to their role in these. Indeed, participation in worldly life was an essential goal of all their thinking and teaching.

So it was for Descartes. In the preface to the 1647 French translation of the *Principia*, he was clear that the final goal of any philosophy had to be "the highest and most perfect moral system, which, supposing a complete knowledge of the other sciences, is the ultimate level of wisdom."[12] Adrien Baillet only echoed Descartes himself in suggesting he had been thinking about this in one way or another all his life.[13] This ethics would enable "not just prudence in worldly matters but a perfect knowledge of everything humans can know, as much for the conduct of life as for the conservation of health and discovery of all the arts."[14] Two years earlier, Descartes had expounded to the Princess Elisabeth the human condition such a *morale* addressed: "One is really one of the parts of the universe, and yet more particularly one of the parts of this earth, one of the parts of this State, of this society, of this family, to which one is joined by one's home, one's oath, one's birth. And the interests of the whole of which one is a part must always be preferred to those of one's own particular person."[15] In this light we may better understand the end of philosophy as public "douceur et concorde" (gentleness and harmony).[16]

This posed a nice dilemma. By the sixteenth century's end, the European world was everywhere felt to be in a state of irresolvable disarray.[17] The very inadequacy of the finest of all educations was itself evidence that something had gone wrong; it could no longer provide analysis of and consequent action in the world and society. The problem was how to achieve a new instauration, as Bacon put it. Descartes's new grounding of thought in the cogito led him directly to the individual "subject." The dilemma, then, was the apparent conflict between that "subject" and the multitude of "subjects" that community necessarily became. To define the "subject" as an isolated self-centered thinking essence seemed to mean that community was inconceivable save as ubiquitous confrontation: Hobbes's state of nature. That is, indeed, how later thinkers took it. Hobbes's covenant became its settled solution.

Some other solution might have been possible, had Descartes's "subject" been taken as the means it was, rather than as the end it became. Then community could still have been considered the origin and end of political thinking. As it was, claim based on community yielded to claim based on the individual. Duties and obligations gave way to freedoms and rights. These are but two of the drastic changes that later thinkers have since taken to characterize the period and have found most clearly embodied in Descartes's thinking, when they do not actually make it the source of such transformations. *That* is wrong simply because debates grounding such changes long predated Descartes. But it is assuredly the case that cogito and Cartesian "subject" could be taken to give them particularly solid foundations. I am suggesting that Descartes himself had something else in mind.

Just as the idea and practice of community were fundamental in assumption, style, and content to Jesuit education, so was the use of pedagogical or philosophical *bridges* to get from one level of thinking and training to another. The first step in education, for example, was that of learning to speak and write Latin. For three years, pupils in grammar worked their way from the simplest parsing to complex verse-making and prose dispute. Gradually, they read ever harder Latin texts. Having started with Cicero's *Familiar Letters*, they were, by the third year, reading his *Paradoxa Stoicorum*, *De senectute*, *De amicitia*, *Somnium Scipionis*, and, in the fourth, that of humanities, his speeches like *Pro lege Manilia* and *Pro Archia*: students eventually would have read most of his works. His writings were deeply embedded in issues of community, society, and politics. One could not possibly escape them – certainly not in the oral expository and debating techniques used by the Jesuits. I would note, too, that grammar itself was presented, not just as a means to language use, but as essential to concordant social community. Emmanuel Alvarez's standard grammar made the point at its outset, and major Jesuit educators like Pedro de Ribadeneyra, Suárez, and Juan de Mariana insisted on it elsewhere.

Grammar did not just ground later learning. It was the bridge to a clearer idea of living in community *concordissime*, as Alvarez had it.[18]

In the second semester of the second year of grammar, pupils studied an immensely popular text, one used everywhere in schools throughout the Renaissance – and indeed into the nineteenth century. Cebes's *Tabula* offered an allegory of the road to the true and the good, a reply to the very question Descartes would later draw from Ausonius: "Quod vitae sectabor iter?" Stoic in emphasis (although its philosophical ties have provoked much controversy), it described a painting depicting three, or maybe four (it is difficult to interpret the text precisely) enclosures through which humans passed on their way to wisdom. Two things are especially relevant here. The first is a character who stands just outside the first gate – Suadela (Deceit) – serving a goblet of varied amounts of error and ignorance to humans as they enter life (opposed here to Genius, who simultaneously offers right guidance). Suadela was a figure of mischief whose malign influence the successful sage would at last bypass and transcend. The second thing is the text's commentary on *doctrina*, the divers disciplines that composed familiar knowledge. These were actually *falsa disciplina* that, even so, provided a *lingua*, a language the sage could use to reach true wisdom and the good.

My first example, from grammar, was of a standard pedagogical device. The second two seem to have given Descartes and others actual models for thinking from the false to the true. Suadela had several dramatic counterparts, among them the *deus maleficus* of Book Two of Plato's *Republic*, on which Jean de Serres embroidered at length in the margins of the great 1578 Stephanus edition of Plato. De Serres asserted that before the city's magistrate could achieve any rectitude, justice, and wisdom of thought, the mere idea of such a *deus maleficus* had to be expelled.[19] A similar idea could be found in the work of Duvergier de Hauranne, a friend of Descartes's family, whose 1609 *Question royalle* asked whether in peacetime, any conditions obliged a subject to save a sovereign's life, knowing it would mean loss of one's own. Duvergier wrote of the need of a "sens clair & net," without impediment from a change of medium or "Devil's illusion."[20] I mention these, not as having anything to do with irrelevant issues of "originality" or such, but as being familiar markers on a road to knowledge, an *iter* or *hodos* (as in "method"), from uncertainty to certainty: passages to wisdom. Not for nothing, no doubt, did Leibniz later call the moral allegory offered by Cebes's *Tabula* not itself conclusive, but as serving "to waken the mind": a comment recalling Descartes's own *morale par provision*.[21]

The notion of drawing a rational *lingua* even from false doctrine is still more striking. Cebes's allegory may almost be thought here to have named a stable device of Jesuit education, one that Descartes specifically adopted as early as the *Regulae*. Each stage of education was carefully presented as a way to use what had preceded even while going beyond it. Each provided, as it were, a "language" needed to pave a way to its own supersession (I almost said *Aufhebung*). The clearest rapid example may be taken from a student's fifth year, that of rhetoric. For many this was their last year. Those like Descartes, it prepared for three subsequent years of philosophy, divided into logic, natural philosophy, and ethics and metaphysics. The rhetoric year was built around Cyprian Soarez's *De arte rhetorica*, which pupils actually began studying in the second semester of humanities: another bridge. In the second semester of rhetoric, similarly, some distinctly new questions were broached. Along with rhetoric proper, students were to explore such matter as "hieroglyphics, Pythagorean symbols, apothegms, adages, emblems and enigmas."[22]

The questions indicated by this phrase were popular among many Jesuits and others. The *Ratio studiorum*'s rule referred teachers and students to at least two areas of study of very broad significance, the one rooted in the humanist past, the other with shoots pushing toward a different kind of future. The first was the study of chronology, which thought to find there an ark holding the one unified knowledge of humanity. Among its techniques were computation of astronomical and astrological data, examination and comparison of calendars and temporal cycles from all known cultures and theologies, exegesis of historical and chronological works of equally wide range, and interpretation to this end of such things, precisely, as "hieroglyphics . . . emblems and enigmas." History, then, was not simply to be found in written documents. Its elements were held to be subject to precise calculations, dependent on the physical world.

This connected to the second area of study I mentioned: that of the "magical" and "scientific" aspects of symbols and enigmas. Some aspects of their treatment tended to query the weight placed on the very rhetoric being studied, to raise questions about the relation between the true and the probable, fact and mere opinion. Modern scholars have begun to show that much of what was written about "natural" magic adumbrated what we now think of as science. Natural magic "aimed . . . at producing changes in the physical environment desired by the operator," by mechanical or illusionary device; and tested such effects "experimentally" against expectations.[23] No less importantly, its practitioners questioned claims made for the occult effects of words, tokens, symbols, incantations, spells, charms, and such.

If an effect had neither natural nor rhetorical explanation, it should be considered a superstitious figment. Such was the aim of the Jesuit Martin Antonio Delrio in the first book of his famous and hugely influential *Disquisitionum magicarum libri sex* of 1600: to apply rational analysis to worldly effect. The study of symbols and the like took the student from the humanities to problems of rational logic. It also made a passage from rhetorical analysis to mathematical studies and scientific questions, which were introduced in the second semester of the logic year, even though natural philosophy did not formally begin until the next year. Similarly, questions of free will and necessity were raised in the final year, but not fully debated until the theology years, open only to those who were to enter the Society itself. Descartes would, of course, raise them constantly in later writings.

What we see here is something not at all unlike the *lingua* of the false doctrine confronted in Cebes's *Tabula*. Each stage of education did not actually treat preceding ones as false, but it certainly showed that they had to be superseded. So when Descartes urged the insufficiency of poetry, history, rhetoric, and familiar mathematics, he was repeating what he had learned. False doctrine, the *Tabula* had said, lay in the letters and mathematical studies of the trivium and quadrivium, to say nothing of medicine, law, and the rest. Yet these were needed to bridle the young. They did not themselves improve one. They provided the *lingua* to guide toward the true. Descartes would write in the second "Regula" (late 1619):

Yet I certainly do not condemn the way of philosophizing that others have hith-erto devised, nor those war machines that are scholastic probable syllogisms, excellent for [oratorical] battles. For they exercise the minds of the young, pushing them to rivalry. It is far better their minds be formed by opinions of this sort – even if they are evidently uncertain since they are disputed among the learned – than they be left free and to their own devices. Without guidance they might run upon precipices, but so long as they stay in their master's footsteps, they may occasionally stray from the truth, but will take a path safer at least in that it has already been tested out by more expert heads.[24]

Echoing the Jesuit handbooks, Descartes drew from his education the idea of a *raison par provision*. It would let one think even as one worked toward a permanent, more accurate rational method. It would avoid but learn from the errors of those "exceptional minds" who had "almost all copied those travelers who, having left the high road to take a short cut,

remain lost among thorns and precipices."[25] Passage techniques
responded to the tensions and dramatic shocks of an age obscurely
aware of being in transition. They allowed familiar tools to be forged
into new ones. In the Jesuit rhetoric class, symbols, hieroglyphs, and
enigmas were brought in to let a reformed Aristotelian logic reply to
them, just as, in a next step on a student's path, masters used mathematics to reply to the logic. Each step was a provisional reason on a way to
full wisdom and that *summum bonum* with which Descartes and his correspondents were still to be preoccupied at mid century.

Method itself was just such a passage to right reason, full knowledge,
and always revisable praxis. That is why its presentation gave way to
three "Essais" – not applications but trials providing patterns for exploration. They moved toward a goal whose shape was not wholly foreseeable. So Daniel Garber is quite right to argue that the "Method"
presented in 1637 differed from what Descartes would apply later: a
method adequate to cope with all problems seen as separate and individual but interconnected became insufficient to treat the interconnec-
tions themselves.[26] In his "Replies" to the "Second Set of Objections"
(by Mersenne) to the *Meditations*, we can trace how Descartes actually got
from neo-Aristotelian analysis and synthesis to "Method" – itself, too,
always a *raison par provision*, always a becoming.[27]

It has taken some time to get from showing how fundamental were
the assumptions about idea and practice of community to demonstrating the ubiquity of passage techniques and, especially, the importance of
raison par provision. But we are already well launched into dilemmas of
cogito and "subject"; for rational "Method" assumed security of the
thinking self. The leaning, stumbling, windblown, sinister subject of
Decartes's November 1619 dreams sought provisional security in reliance on the rational *iter* of neoscholastic masters: the text cited from the
second "Regula" seems to date from the same time. But the *Regulae* as a
whole proposed a more precise *mathesis*, based on breaking down the elements of a physical dilemma to find a first intuition (or more than one)
from which a mathematical analysis could then reconstruct the complex
dilemma. What such a *mathesis* could not explain was how one could trust
the first intuition. The *Discours* likewise simply took for granted the
power of the historical "I" with which the first parts began, and drew
from it the "we" of the scientific community with which the last two
parts ended. Such a passage from "subject" to community needed a far
more substantial grounding. The *Meditations* gave it.

As we know, the "First Meditation" elaborated a retreat from the

outside world and from the senses in a new search for the right road to
security of reason, culminating in the now-familiar "genium . . . malig-
num." The "Second Meditation" concluded that even were there such
a "malign deceiver," yet the very ability to suppose so proved "ego sum,
ego existo; certum est." I must at least be "res cogitans."[28] This "something thinking" could as yet rely on nothing at all but its awareness of
itself as thinking process. We remain pretty much in the realm of an
illustrious predecessor of Descartes, Montaigne, for whom the thinking
"subject" had to remain strictly private, taking no part in the public
arena of the citizen subject fixed in public hierarchies precisely because
of thought's instability, its characteristic "branloire perenne" (perennial
seesaw).[29] But, in this regard, we need to look much more closely at "res
cogitans," a concept that I think no modern vernacular can really echo.

Descartes reached it by means of a process remarkable (to modern
Western exegetes) in the way it objectified the expression of anything
like personal being. For we must remember that Latin could, and did,
express the site of thinking and saying by a first-person verb that did
not involve any separate expression of "selfness." Having dismissed possible attributes of personal being as unreliably knowable, he asked
whether, nonetheless, these things could in fact differ "ab eo me quem
novi" (from this "me" that [I] know). For the moment, he noted, he
could say nothing about that; he could simply assert that something (the
present thinking process) existed: "Novi me existere" ([I] know the "me"
exists). But he had to ask "what may be that 'I' that I know" (quaero
quis sim ego ille quem novi).[30] This led to "res cogitans," an expression
much misunderstood because largely untranslatable. In medieval and
Renaissance Latin, *res* could mean "thing" in pretty much all its modern
senses. Equally typically, it could mean the referent of any word or
concept, without regard to ontological status. Descartes used the latter
sense when he asked about the object or referent of thought that this
"I" is: "Sed qualis res? Dixi, cogitans" (But what sort of thing/referent?
I have said a thinking).[31] To translate the phrase combining the two
terms as "thinking thing" or "chose pensante" is inevitable. It is also
entirely misleading, as Descartes's separation of them in the just cited
passage suggests:

Sed quid igitur sum? Res cogitans. Quid est hoc? Nempe dubitans, intelligans,
affirmans, negans, volens, nolens, imaginans quoque, & sentiens.
(But what am [I] therefore? [This "thinking" thinks of it as] a thinking something. What is this? Certainly [a process of] doubting, conceiving, affirming,
denying, willing, not willing, imagining, as well, and feeling.)[32]

What, he asked, if all these acts could be separated from this present act of thinking – of being conscious: "Quid est quod a mea cogitatione distinguatur?" Could any of these activities be separated from what must be referred to as "me ipso," the source of these thinkings? That from this "source" came the activities of doubting, conceiving, and willing was clear, Descartes claimed. Yet the clarity is undermined by the dubitative subjunctives he employed to affirm it:

Nam quod ego sim qui dubitem, qui intelligam, qui velim, tam manifestum est, ut nihil occurrat per quod evidentius explicetur.
(For what "I" may be who doubts, conceives, wills, is so evident that nothing may be found to explain it more clearly.)[33]

An obvious problem existed here: how to establish something like the place from which thinking happened. This was just the question to which Descartes sought to respond in the "Third Meditation." There he began by making clear that the process of thinking was not agent, but "passible subject," reactive to "something": "ut, cum volo, cum timeo, cum affirmo, cum nego, semper quidem aliquam rem ut subjectum meae cogitationis apprehendo" (as, when [I] wish, fear, assert, deny, [I] always understand something like the subject [the lying-under] of my thinking).[34] "Ego" and its cognates were not, at this stage – it bears repeating – any sort of agent, any more than was "res cogitans." These were names given to the place where thinking (as any form of mental activity) occurred; or, better still, as Descartes expressed it, they were simply the referents *subjected* to that thinking process. This was why the "Third Meditation" proceeded to seek a sure God, and the "Fourth Meditation" to distinguish the true and the false: they had to provide grounding. But we must be aware that in this exercise, something had already changed in this thinking process: it had become an internal agency.

Before we get to know how Descartes worked this out, we need to glance briefly at how the process of thinking could itself be offered as necessitating a thought of a perfect thinking process – or, as Descartes put it, of "God." The "Third Meditation" addresses this question as Descartes teases out of this "present process of thinking" some process (and reliability) that would transcend it. We need to be clear that, at this point, Descartes is trying to draw the potentially greater certainties of such a "higher" process from the very act of thinking. Evidently, he wrote, if this present thinking could conceive (have an idea of) a think-ing process more perfect than the one it was using, then this idea must come from somewhere "prior" to this present thinking, since a lesser cannot precede a greater, just as "non potest calor in subjectum quod prius non calebat induci" (heat cannot be produced in a subject[ed] that was not previously heated).[35] Here again, Descartes emphasized the *subjected* nature of the thinking process. The continuing arguments of the "Third Meditation" depended on this assertion: one had to find an "ideam . . . primam" (first idea) that was like an "archetype" making lesser ideas.[36]

This idea was one of a thinking that was "more perfect" than this thinking that was happening right now in "me," an idea that was in itself "clear and distinct." Indeed, as the idea of absolute clarity and distinctness, it was of necessity the clearest and most distinct idea that "my" present thinking could have.[37] "God" was first of all the idea of a thinking process whose perfection could not derive from this here-and-now process whose imperfection was evident. For this "I" that was "cogitans" had to be aware of its "own" ability (and concern/interest/desire) gradually to increase in knowledge.[38] By definition, perfect thinking would not be subject to such increase: it would already have full knowledge. Behind this argument hovers the ghost of the "impassible" universal soul of Aristotle's *De Anima* set against the "passible" soul incorporated in the human body. For Descartes, when this "I"-process-of-thinking thought perfection, it could only think a perfect "rem cogitantem."[39] "God" was thus, first of all, the "idea" produced from "my" thinking of this perfect thinking process.[40] In fact, Descartes was always to hold this view of the soul as "a thinking" subjected to passions coming to it through the senses, or innately, or "by prior dispositions in the soul," or by "movements of the will." As he wrote to the Jesuit priest Denis Mesland in 1644:

I make no difference between the soul and its ideas, other than that between a piece of wax and the various shapes it can take. And just as it is not an action, properly speaking, but a passion in the wax to receive various shapes, it seems to me that it is also a passion in the soul to receive such and such an idea, and that only its volitions are actions; and that its ideas are put in [the soul] partly by objects that touch upon the senses, partly by impressions that are in the brain, partly, too, by the dispositions which preceded [a given idea] in the soul, and by the movements of its will.[41]

To transform, however momentarily, this ever-moving passible process of thinking into an agent – cogito or ego cogito – exemplified a trope with which Descartes's studies in rhetoric certainly familiarized him: "personification, the preeminent rhetorical figure of agency," as

Victoria Kahn has put it.[42] For Descartes, as for his teachers, rhetoric was *always* a road to something else, a passage. Here, it enabled a particular sort of passage. As the thinking process became an agent, not only reasoning (which included doubting, imagining, denying, affirming) but also willing had to characterize it. As an agent, the cogito's own contents were converted and became its ground. As an agent it also conceived the idea of agency more complete than its own, capable, indeed, of everything. This idea of something perfect and greater than itself cannot have been created by the cogito, argued Descartes, for a lesser cannot make a greater, and my current dilemmas of thinking show "me" to be not perfect and so not self-created. Perfection by definition includes existence: that perfection we call God.

Agency's willfulness became abstract absolute will. But cogito was, perhaps, above all grounded in an idea of *recta ratio*, a right reason whose foundations could not be deceptive. It could, of course, reach wrong conclusions if based on wrong information, but that was wholly distinct from the rectitude of the rightly organized process itself. It is then not surprising that after the personification of supreme agency, as he returned in the "Fourth Meditation" to further exploring its foundations (in issues of reason, freedom, matters indifferent, truth, and falsehood), Descartes made this a definition of the human's secure relation with God: "I recognize it to be impossible that he should ever deceive me; for in every fraud or deception is to be found some imperfection."[43] The same held true for the faculty of judgment that such a God placed in one, since a perfect being could not *set out* to falsify.

Truth was the identified ground and end not only of Method but also of the "subject," as well as of reason, morality, and a communal ethics – what we more usually choose to call politics. And truth was being approached here by means of arguments whose familiarity is now largely lost to us, but which were then altogether familiar both in theology and in rhetoric. These were arguments about "things indifferent." In Christian debate these were matters of worldly knowledge or action having nothing to do with salvation. The concept came primarily from Stoic argument, where *adiaphora* referred to a class of *indifferentia*, morally neutral things to be preferred or rejected according to one's purpose and situation.[44] For the Stoics, the material world itself was wholly composed of such *adiaphora*. There is no question as to Descartes's familiarity with the work of neo-Stoic thinkers like Justus Lipsius (himself trained by Jesuits, who used his writings in their schools), Pierre Charron, Guillaume du Vair, Errycius Puteanus, and others. Furthermore, students of the Jesuits were introduced to *indifferentia* through Cicero's *Paradoxica*.

Things concerning God were evidently not such – hence the need to try and ground truth there. For about everything else not only was there room for debate but perhaps, too, no way to determine a decision. To personify the cogito as willful agency and find its epitome in God explains why Descartes then insisted that it was "only the will, or freedom of choice, that I experience within me to be so great that I can grasp the idea of none greater; so much so that it is above all through the will that I understand myself to bear some image and likeness of God."[45] It also explains why God, will, and the ground of truth were virtually equated. Otherwise truth itself would fall into the realm of the indifferent and of mere rhetorical advantage: as Kahn puts it, some absolute truth was needed "as a check on the weakness of individual judgment and the indeterminacy of the rhetorical 'wars of Truth'."[46] But how could the mere assertion of such a truth serve to distinguish it from falsehood? There had to be a certainty and security of truth able to ground the willful self for right action *in the world*. We need not be surprised, therefore, that Descartes explored *indifferentia* in just this context:

For [the will, *or free will*] consists simply in our being able to do or not to do (that is, to affirm or deny, to pursue or flee), or rather, simply in that we are brought to affirm or deny, to pursue or flee what is proposed to us by the intellect in such a way that we sense we have been determined to it by no external force. For me to be free, I do not need to be able to be moved two ways: on the contrary, the more I lean in one direction, whether because I understand that truth and goodness lie in it, or because God so disposes my inmost thoughts, so do I choose the more freely. Neither divine grace nor natural knowledge ever diminishes freedom, but rather increases and confirms it.[47]

To hesitate between possibilities, Descartes added, to hold a choice "indifferent," was "the lowest level of freedom." To lack constraint was but license of anarchy: "not at all perfection of will, but defect of knowledge, or some negation: for if I always saw clearly what is true and good, I should never deliberate over what is to be chosen or judged; and so although I would evidently be free, I could never be indifferent." The will can only be indifferent, Descartes went on, in areas where its knowledge is insufficient. And there it should make no choice at all: there, "if I abstain from making a judgment, it is clear I am acting rightly and not erring."[48] Such are the conditions of *passages par provision* – a withholding of decision until certainty was possible: that is as much the reason for his not publishing *Le Monde* in 1633, as for the *morale par provision* in 1637. And we begin to see, I think, just how the "subject" itself needs to be seen as the provisional instrument it was: a rhetorical tool to ground new formations of truth and society. Not accidentally, in this light, did Descartes try to forge a rational community from the *Meditations* themselves: I mean of course through the "Objections" and "Replies."

Even more, to apply once theological argument to a citizen's life in community, or at least to know what was necessary for it, would not be overly hard. A moral yardstick was needed to direct a clear-sighted grasp of the true and good, that "highest and most perfect moral system" which Descartes would propose in the "Lettre-Préface" to the *Principia*. This yardstick would proffer the same bounds of control and sureties of truth in the realm of ethics and politics as God did in those of ontology and theology. Once found, it could rule that fine concord of public and private life which he also named there. So when Descartes took up the argument of the "Fourth Meditation" in the *Passions de l'âme* to apply it to relations between desire and truth, passion and goodness, freedom and order, he phrased it so as to combine theological, psychological, and political connotations: "I see in us only one thing able to give us legitimate reason to value ourselves, namely the use of our free will and the sovereignty we have over our volitions." This, he wrote, as he had nine years before, "renders us in some way like God, by making us masters of ourselves."[49] The *Passions de l'âme* began to present the requisite moral measure to the public. The two paragraphs after the one just cited defined "generosity" as knowledge and sharing of sameness among subjects.

In this way the cogito and the "subject" – whatever its initial individuality and self-possessiveness – was to be reinserted in community. The *Passions* here sought to generalize notions Descartes had started to advance in his September 1646 letter to the Princess Elisabeth about Machiavelli's *The Prince*. There, his context had been that of trying to understand how one could get from individual action, benefiting private interest in an imperfect society, by means of mask and morality provisional, to a new society where all acted to everyone's benefit. He put forward the good prince as guide: if only there were a leader who possessed all the qualities of one who had acquired the means of true knowledge, good judgment, and the use of methodical reason, and was thus able to direct the will to the common interest, then such change and a new establishment would be possible.

It is worth remembering that the letter began with the architectural metaphor of the second and third parts of the *Discours*. There it was used

of mind and method. Now it was used of the State to be founded on
method, knowledge of truth, and that habit of virtue which meant one
supported others' interests because one was attentive to one's own. The
good prince knew the wicked nature of man, but he also did everything
that right reason dictates. This good prince would be generalized to
everyone in the paragraphs of the *Passions* to which I referred, but in fact
Descartes already started to do that in the 1644 *Principia*: "The power
men have over each other was given so that they might employ it in dis-
couraging others from evil."[50] The will of the sovereign, we readily see,
was but the counterpart of the methodically rational individual made
particular. The word "prince" not seldom referred to sovereign authority, which could, of course, be embodied in more than one person.

"Conscience" and "inclination," Descartes wrote to Elisabeth on 6
October 1645, would necessarily make such people act to protect others'
interests with their own.[51] That, too, is the sense in which he constantly
wrote about friendship. Amity marked the obligation one owed as an
individual to others. The word "obligation" signaled an enlightened play
of everyone's interests allowing the proper working of the new society
based on method, will, and reason. To fail such friendship was to cause
the failure of all effort to build this new society. For the individual's interest, protected by this amity, was to be equated with the very thinking
"subject" whose will permitted the institution of "Method." To fail
friendship was thus to fail knowledge of truth, prudence, good judgment, and the thinking "subject" itself. It was to go against the cogito
and the essence of being human. Care was needed: "You must not
attempt to draw people abruptly to reason, when they are not accustomed to understand it; but you must try little by little, whether by public
writings, through the speech of preachers, or any other means, to make
them comprehend it."[52] So wrote Descartes in the letter on Machiavelli.

Clearly, here, the particular good prince was already becoming the
good, rational being of the *Passions*. Reason of State, properly considered, was reason. Community could now consist of individual selves,
each embodying a reason common to all, shared by all, and worked by
all. Each also embodied the play of will and necessity, reason and
passion, consent and coercion, intention and effect, freedom and necessity, that became the terms of civil association. The self/"subject"
embodying these terms was, to use a metaphor we can now readily
understand and expand, the personification of a particular locus of
turmoil, conjuncture of dismay. By this very personification, an agency
was formulated that made it possible to resolve those conflicts: in a way,

it eventually absorbed them. Gathering these elements of conflict into a solution, to change the metaphor, produced a new precipitate, a new compounded formation.

Metaphors are one thing, of course – decorative or banal. Facts on the historical ground are quite another. For theory, however, there was something new: the human, not as exemplary figure or divine instrument, but as typical and universal actor and knower in a rational universe, whose agency could intervene in and resolve the very sources of conflict.[53] Such views were at the root of the idea of progress and essential optimism of Enlightenment. In the realm of the political, not for nothing did Descartes's disciple, Pierre-Sylvain Régis, combine Hobbes's with his master's voice in his *Cours de philosophie*, treating formation of societies, cession of individual rights, duties of sovereigns and subject, mixing Cardin Le Bret, Descartes, Malebranche, and Hobbes, and explaining the need for a Cartesian society because, "in the state of nature, passions rule, war is perpetual, poverty inescapable, fear never leaves, etc."[54] Here, the personified Cartesian cogito united in civil community because in nature, the subject's life was, to quote Hobbes, "solitary, poore, nasty, brutish and short."[55]

Rejected into a state of nature before civil society as mere animals or even monsters, remembered in times of new constitutions and internal peace (more or less) as suffering victims of violent civil or religious wars, these unnecessary "zeds" had been replaced by the rational consenting subjects of a new establishment. This notion of consent, grounded in the legalism of contractual debate, further strengthened the personification of rational thinking: it gave the subject a title of judgment, a justification of will, a claim to decision. For Hobbes, writing in exile (1640–42), the moment of consent was hardly separate either from ongoing conflict or the civil association it was held to permit. Things would be a bit clearer ten years on, but never so clear as for Locke, who managed to make reason precede conflict and consent thus be its foreseeable rational resolution; or for Montesquieu and Rousseau, who invented increasing numbers of stages to separate an original rational "subject" from the eventual necessities of association.

Locke, too, added the idea of "concept" as the rational tool in the mind to mark a moment of passage from individual perception, *Vorstellung*, to communal meaning, *Sinn*. For a concept was not a "concept" unless it put my (and one can now even emphasize that *my*) perception in a context of sense that was publicly comprehensible. Late seventeenth-century debate in the realm of aesthetics did with the idea of "taste" what "concept" did in that of epistemology and "contract" did in that of politics: taste – "good taste" – signaled how my perceptions of the beautiful, the fine, and the good were adjusted to the norms agreed by the community. Taste might even play the same role in the domain of behavior, of ethics – as the reference to the "good" was meant to suggest.

All these terms – responses to and enabled by Cartesian passages and becomings – marked resolutions of conflicts in distinct areas of action and thought. Freedom and coercion, consent and control, reason and passion could now be understood as modes of the relations between the individual and society, the one and the many, the self and others. Descartes himself, I proposed, thought of something more tenuous, less resolved or resolute: a kind of constant give and take within a community whose priority still made duty and obligation primary for a willfully rational "subject." Maybe that was never practicable. Indeed, he would not go to the Palatinate in 1649, just because things there were still shifting and would only become "agreeable" after "two or three years of peace."[56] That was no doubt a different kind of shifting, and the decision to go to stable Stockholm was not wise either. The later sureties of possessive individualism and what I call authoritarian liberalism have proven hardly less drastic in their outcomes, as the primacy of community in political theorizing has yielded to that of the individual. Perhaps we may see that, too, as a historically necessary but perilous passage technique.

NOTES

1. I thank Patrick Coleman for his early editorial work on this essay, but above all Ellen Wilson for her exemplary care and generosity of attention to editorial (and intellectual) detail. Both have shown unusual patience and restraint.
2. On Descartes's struggle with questions of history and memory see my "Denying the Body? Memory and the Dilemmas of History in Descartes," *Journal of the History of Ideas* 57.4 (October 1996): 587–607.
3. The first has been discussed through Descartes's complex use of "I" and "we" in Sylvie Romanowski, *L'Illusion chez Descartes: La Structure du discours cartésien* (Paris: Klincksieck, 1974), the second in Timothy J. Reiss, "Descartes, the Palatinate, and the Thirty Years' War: Political Theory and Political Practice," in *Baroque Topographies: Literature/History/Philosophy*, ed. Timothy Hampton, Yale French Studies, 80 (New Haven: Yale University Press, 1991), 108–45.
4. Jean-Robert Armogathe, Vincent Carraud, and Robert Feenstra, eds., "La

Licence en droit de Descartes: un placard inédit de 1616," *Nouvelles de la République des Lettres* (1988:2): 123–45, here 126–27; "Discours de la méthode," in Descartes, *Œuvres*, ed. Charles Adam and Paul Tannery, new presentation, 11 vols. (Paris: Vrin, 1964–75), VI: 4–10; this edition cited hereafter as AT. Translations are my own, but I have referred to *The Philosophical Writings*, ed. and trans. John Cottingham, Robert Stoothoff, and Dugald Murdoch (with Anthony Kenny for vol. III), 3 vols. (Cambridge: Cambridge University Press, 1985–91). This is directly keyed to AT, so I do not give a reference. Where possible, I give references to Descartes, *Œuvres philosophiques*, ed. Ferdinand Alquié, 3 vols. (Paris: Garnier, 1963–73) (hereafter FA), on the assumption that most people may have more immediate access to this edition: here FA, I: 571–77.

5. AT, II:378; FA, II:89–90.

6. Larry Arnhart, *Aristotle on Political Reasoning: A Commentary on the Rhetoric* (De Kalb: Northern Illinois University Press, 1981), 3. Richard Bodéüs convincingly analyzes his ethical thought in this light: *The Political Dimensions of Aristotle's "Ethics,"* trans. Jan Edward Garrett (Albany: State University of New York Press, 1993).

7. "Rules Common to the Professors of the Lower Classes," Rule 31, in *The Ratio Studiorum of 1599*, trans. A. R. Ball, in *Saint Ignatius and the Ratio Studiorum*, ed. Edward A. Fitzpatrick (New York and London: McGraw-Hill 1933), 203, hereafter *Ratio studiorum*. I also refer to G. M. Pachtler, SJ, ed., *Ratio studiorum et institutiones scholasticae Societatis Jesu per Germaniam olim vigentes collectae concinnatae dilucidatae . . .*, 4 vols., in *Monumenta Germaniae Pedagogica . . .*, gen. ed. Karl Kehrbach (Berlin, 1887), II: 234–481, and Ladislaus Lukács, SJ, ed., Monumenta Paedagogica Societatis Jesu, new edn., 7 vols. (Rome, 1965–92), V: 355–454.

8. "Rules of the Professor of Lower Grammar Classes," Rule 9, in *Ratio studiorum*, 234.

9. Adrien Baillet, *La Vie de Monsieur DesCartes*, 2 vols. (Paris: Hortemels, 1691; facsimile reprint, Hildesheim and New York: Georg Olms, 1972), I: 160–66 (here: 165), cited hereafter as Baillet, *Vie*. The event occurred at the house of the Papal Nuncio Cardinal Francesco Bagno, gathering many scholars (including Mersenne) to hear the sieur de Chandoux present a new philosophy rejecting the scholastic. All approved except Descartes, who convincingly took it apart and gave examples of his own new method's power.

10. The first dispute is now available in French translation: René Descartes and Martin Schoock, *La Querelle d'Utrecht*, ed. and trans. Theo Verbeek (Paris: Impressions Nouvelles, 1988); for the second, see Baillet, *Vie*, II: 70–85, 162–65.

11. Isaac Beeckman, *Journal . . . de 1604 à 1634*, ed. Cornélis de Waard, 4 vols. (The Hague: Martinus Nijhoff, 1939–53), I: 244 (also excerpted in AT, x:52).

12. AT, ixb:14; FA, III:780.

13. Baillet, *Vie*, I: 115.

14. AT, ixb:2; FA, III:769.

15. Descartes to Princess Elisabeth, 15 September 1645, AT, IV:293; FA, III:607.
16. AT, IX:14; FA, III:785.
17. On this, see chs. 1–2 of my *Meaning of Literature* (Ithaca and London: Cornell University Press, 1992).
18. Emmanuel Alvarez, *De institutione grammatica libri tres* (Rome: Gulielmus Facciottus, 1595), 6.
19. *Platonis opera quae extant omnia*, trans. and ed. Joannis Serrani . . ., notes and emendations Henri Stephani, 4 vols. (n. p.: Henr. Stephanvs, 1578), II: 379.
20. [Jean Duvergier de Hauranne], *Question royalle et sa decision* (Paris: Toussainct du Bray, 1609), f. 17r–v.
21. Gottfried Wilhelm von Leibniz, "Nouveaux essais sur l'entendement humain [1703–5]," in *Philosophische Schriften*, ed. Leibniz-Forschungstelle der Universität Münster (Berlin: Akademie-Verlag, 1962), VI: 385.
22. "Rules for Professors of Rhetoric," Rule 13, in *Ratio studiorum*, 214.
23. Wayne Shumaker, *Natural Magic and Modern Science: Four Treatises, 1590–1657* (Binghamton, N.Y.: Medieval and Renaissance Texts and Studies, 1989), 3.
24. AT, x:363–64; FA, I:81–82.
25. AT, x:497; FA, II:1107.
26. Daniel Garber, "Descartes and Method in 1637," in *PSA 1988: Proceedings of the 1988 Biennial Meeting of the Philosophy of Science Association*, vol. II, "Symposia and Invited Papers," ed. Arthur Fine and Jarrett Leplin (East Lansing, Mich.: Philosophy of Science Association, 1989), 225–36.
27. I explore this in "Neo-Aristotle and Method: Between Zabarella and Descartes," in *Descartes' Natural Philosophy*, ed. Stephen Gaukroger and John Andrew Schuster (London and New York: Routledge, forthcoming).
28. AT, VII:27–28; FA, II:418–20.
29. Timothy J. Reiss, "Montaigne and the Subject of Polity," in *Literary Theory/Renaissance Texts*, ed. Patricia A. Parker and David Quint (Baltimore and London: Johns Hopkins University Press, 1986), 115–49.
30. AT, VII:27; FA, II:185.
31. *Ibid.*
32. AT, VII:28; FA, II:185–86.
33. AT, VII:29; FA, II:186.
34. AT, VII:37; FA, II:193.
35. AT, VII:41; FA, II:196.
36. AT, VII:42; FA, II:197.
37. AT, VII:46; FA, II:200.
38. AT, VII:47; FA, II:201.
39. AT, VII:49; FA, II:203.
40. AT, VII:52; FA, II:205.
41. Descartes to Denis Mesland, 2 May 1644, in AT, IV:113–14; FA, III:70: " Je ne mets aucune différence entre l'âme et ses idées, que comme entre un morceau de cire et les diverses figures qu'il peut recevoir. Et comme ce n'est pas proprement une action, mais une passion en la cire, de recevoir diverses figures, il me semble que c'est aussi une passion en l'âme de recevoir telle

ou telle idée, et qu'il n'y a que ses volontés qui soient des actions; et que ses idées sont mises en elle, partie par les objets qui touchent les sens, partie par les impressions qui sont dans le cerveau, et partie aussi par les dispositions qui ont précédé en l'âme même, et par les mouvements de sa volonté. . . " My translation is less smooth than Anthony Kenny's in Cottingham, Stoothoff, Murdoch, and Kenny, eds. *The Philosophical Writings*, vol. III, because I have sought to keep the force of Descartes's active verbs in the final clause: signaling active events that are received by the passible soul. Kenny replaces the first "sont mises" by "it receives" and all the subsequent active verbs by noun phrases.

42. Victoria Kahn, "Revising the History of Machiavellism: English Machiavellism and the Doctrine of Things Indifferent," *Renaissance Quarterly* 46.3 (Autumn 1993): 526–61, here 554.
43. AT, VII:53; FA, II:456.
44. Jason Lewis Saunders, *Justus Lipsius: The Philosophy of Renaissance Stoicism* (New York: Liberal Arts Press, 1955), 104–10.
45. AT, VII:57; FA, II:460–61.
46. Kahn, "Revising the History," 555.
47. AT, VII:57–8; FA, II:209–10: "quia tantùm [voluntas, *sive arbitrii libertas*] in eo consistit, quòd idem, vel facere vel non facere (hoc est affirmare vel negare, prosequi vel fugere) possimus, vel potius in eo tantum, quòd ad id quod nobis ab intellectu proponitur affirmandum vel negandum, sive prosequendum vel fugiendum, ita feramur, ut a nullâ vi externâ nos ad id determinari sentiamus. Neque enim opus est me in utramque partem ferri posse, ut sim liber, sed contrà, quo magis in unam propendeo, sive quia rationem veri & boni in eâ evidenter intelligo, sive quia Deus intima cogitationis meæ ita disponit, tanto liberius illam eligo; nec sane divina gratia, nec naturalis cognitio unquam imminuunt libertatem, sed potius augent & corroborant."
48. AT, VII:59; FA, II:464.
49. Descartes, *Passions de l'âme*, §152 in AT, XI:445; FA, III:1066–67: "Je ne remarque en nous qu'une seule chose qui nous puisse donner juste raison de nous estimer, à savoir l'usage de notre libre arbitre, et l'empire que nous avons sur nos volontés." ". . . il nous rend en quelque façon semblables à Dieu en nous faisant maîtres de nous mêmes . . ." The discussion of the aforementioned relations is at §§ 144–48 in AT, XI:436–42; FA III:1059–64.
50. AT, VIIIA:19; FA, III:114: Pt. I, §38.
51. Descartes to Princess Elisabeth, 6 October 1645, AT, IV:316–17; FA, III:619.
52. AT, IV:491; FA, III:670.
53. Bernard Le Bovier de Fontenelle in the 1680s gave a startling instance of this in historiography: "Someone of considerable wit, simply taking account of human nature, could deduce all past and future history, although never having heard speak of any event"; in "Sur l'histoire," in *Textes choisis*, 1683–1701, ed. Maurice Roelens (Paris: Editions Sociales, 1966), 216–17. He was not being ironic. César Vichard de Saint-Réal held analogous views, to say nothing of Leibniz and others.

54. Pierre-Sylvain Régis, *Cours entier de philosophie, ou système général selon les principes de M. de Descartes, contenant la logique, la métaphysique, la physique, et la morale*, 3 vols. (Amsterdam: Huguetan, 1691), III: 493. "Dans l'état de nature, les passions règnent, la guerre est perpetuelle, la pauvreté est insurmontable, la crainte n'abandonne jamais, &c":

55. Thomas Hobbes, *Leviathan*, ed. C. B. Macpherson (Harmondsworth: Penguin, 1968), pt. I, ch. 13, 186.

56. AT, v:283; FA, III:891.

CHAPTER TWO

The "man of learning" defended: seventeenth-century biographies of scholars and an early modern ideal of excellence

Peter N. Miller

A new ideal of individual excellence was articulated in the seventeenth and eighteenth centuries. The "best" man was deemed the one most truly self-governing, liberated by the rule of reason from the tyranny of the passions. Freedom was expressed in the ability to choose, and choice was believed to be fortified by learning. Politics and religion each claimed to be able to assure that individuals made the "correct," that is, moral choice. From the later sixteenth century some argued that following the choices made by others, however civic-minded or pious, could not guarantee that the choice was correct. Conformity to others' choices also deprived the individual of the experience of choosing. To this way of thinking, knowledge became the necessary prerequisite for choosing well, and the individual's capacity to freely make this choice was designated the highest human freedom. Kant's *sapere aude* transformed this ideal into the watchword of Enlightenment.

As sixteenth-century European empires and monarchies descended into civil wars triggered by political and religious conflicts, the "citizen" and the "saint" – the "best" of men from a political or religious perspective – lost some of their appeal. The ideal of the constant, self-controlled, freely judging hero emerged under these conditions. Justus Lipsius's *De constantia* (1584) was a text that helped define this goal and its wide European diffusion testifies to the power of "neo-Stoicism." Montaigne's *Essais* (1580, 1588) was another of these European books that took responsibility for moral choice away from both polity and church and sought to teach individuals to find the answers from their own resources. For both Lipsius and Montaigne, friendship grounded on reason and manifested in acts of reciprocity emerged as the ideal interpersonal relation and an expression of the free, well-ordered soul. Neo-Stoicism and *libertinage érudit* have provided scholars with useful categories for describing the focus on the individual that both Lipsius and Montaigne, to keep to familiar examples, encouraged.[1]

In this chapter, I want to examine the way in which a man of learning could have been presented as the embodiment of this ideal, and I
want to do so by looking at biographies of scholars. The scholar's knowledge was believed to liberate him from the conventions, prejudices, and
superstitions that constrained from the outside, even as his self-control
and rationality freed him from the sway of the passions within. The
appeal of the scholar reflected a fascination with his combination of self-
governance and governing of others. With other sorts of communities
disintegrating, the learned world attracted the attention of those who
thought about politics. A third great European book of this epoch also
spoke to this audience. Stefano Guazzo's *Della conversatione civile* (1574,
1579) emphasized the role of conversation and beneficence in creating
and maintaining communities bound only by elective affinities. The
academy, like the one described by Guazzo, was a model community
whose rules and style were reflected on an international scale in the
Republic of Letters.[2]

The genre of "biographies of scholars" was new in the seventeenth
century and reflects the fascination of contemporaries with the scholar
as an individual and colleague.[3] It is precisely because biography, in a
culture shaped by classical rhetoric, was intended and understood as an
extended exemplary presentation, that it can be used as evidence for
what that particular time and place thought worth emulating or avoid-
ing.[4] A good way to discover what the seventeenth century thought an
excellent man looked like would be to turn to an explicitly exemplary
creation, like biography. These lives painted ideal types for the education of other members of the learned world but also for the wider
society. Moreover, these biographies represent an explicit and self-conscious attempt to ascribe the aristocratic virtues of the hero to a new
social type, the scholar. Their proliferation mirrors the diffusion of aristocratic ideas that marks the making of civil society in Europe and so
provides historians of civil society with a useful tool.

In *The Advancement of Learning* (1605), Francis Bacon had treated biography as one of the three types of "perfect" history, the others being
studies of an age or a particular event. The genre of "Lives" took a single
person as the subject "in whom actions both trifling and important, great
and small, public and private, must needs be united and mingled."
"Perfection" followed from the natural integrity and coherence of a
single life. Reflecting on his own time, Bacon observed that, though there
were few rulers or heroes to compare with antiquity, "yet there are many
worthy personages (even living under kings) that deserve better than dispersed report or dry and barren eulogy."[5]

Despite the continued prominence of rulers and generals as subjects of biography, there is some indication that Bacon's counsel was heeded. For in *Polyhistor*, a guide to the world of learning published near the century's end, Daniel Morhof included a chapter on biographies of scholars, "De vitarum scriptoribus."[6] Morhof defended the value of studying "private" men by declaring that lives of literary individuals, like political greats, could teach prudence. In some respects they were even better teachers since they showed how the little details of living, not generally celebrated in heroic and martial biography, also offered opportunities for the exercise of virtue. Moreover, the quotidian and the ordinary, far from being superfluous, were essential to painting an accurate portrait. Above all, Morhof wrote, three subjects had to be addressed in biographies of intellectuals: their learning, their mores and conversation, and the whole, rather than partial, course of their lives.[7]

Among the many modern lives of scholars listed by Morhof, those of Peiresc by Pierre Gassendi, Gian Vincenzo Pinelli by Paolo Gualdo, and Paolo Sarpi by Fulgenzio Micanzio were given priority.[8] Gassendi's *Vita Peireskii* was the best example of this new genre because it was written by a biographer who had unparalleled access to the person and, later, to his literary remains.[9] Nicolas-Claude Fabri de Peiresc (1580–1637) was born and died in Aix, was trained as a lawyer, and served as a councilor in the Parlement of Provence. A polymath and antiquary, he was famous for a total dedication to learning and an unparalleled generosity that endeared him to Gassendi, Galileo, Rubens, Mersenne, Grotius, Campanella, Sarpi, de Thou, and Scaliger, among others.[10] His close friend, Girolamo Aleandro, described Peiresc as "the greatest and most happy man in the world."[11] In this chapter I hope to make clear what Aleandro meant.

Peiresc's role as "procureur-général" of the Republic of Letters, to quote from Pierre Bayle's article in the *Dictionnaire historique et critique*,[12] was marked by two posthumous publications. The first, the *Monumenta Romanorum* (Rome, 1638), contained orations delivered at a memorial meeting of the Roman Accademia degl'Umoristi and an extraordinary collection of multilingual elegiac poetry called *Panglossia*. The second, Pierre Gassendi's *Viri illustris . . . Nicolai Claudii Fabricii de Peiresc . . . vita* (Paris, 1641), presented him as an ideal man in the terms of the contemporary literature on comportment and sociability.

It is as if Gassendi framed his work as a reply to Bacon. He claimed to have set pen to paper so "that Posterity should understand, that Nature was not therein worn out and barren, but that she was able to produce a great and rare Man, fit to be propounded as an Example to other Ages." How much more explicit could Gassendi have been about the didactic purpose of his biography? As for those who would object that Peiresc was an unlikely subject, being neither a martial nor political hero, Gassendi replied, in a further echo of Bacon, "Those men deserve abundantly to be commended, whom though fortune has not raised to the greatest Wealth and Dignities; yet bear the greater minds, are of a more generous Virtue, and undertake far greater Designs, than any man could expect from men of their Condition."[13] If, certainly, not a life of Everyman, the *Vita Peireskii* did seek to broaden the category of the heroic.

Before turning directly to Gassendi's account, it is worth pondering the extent to which the *Vita Peireskii* approaches Bacon's example of biography as perfect history. Gassendi called the book "Commentaries" as distinct from history because his chronicle of names, dates, and events was not given a stylish finish.[14] Elegance aside – and there is some reason to believe Gassendi's statement to be an example of rhetorical self-deprecation since Bayle used this very adjective, "composée élégamment," to describe it[15] – anyone reading this book is also reading a history of the study of antiquities, natural history, astronomy, botany, and politics in Europe. The range of Peiresc's friendships and interests make this "Life" also a cultural and intellectual history of the age. It still makes fascinating reading.[16]

The first five books of the *Vita* are arranged chronologically from Peiresc's birth to death. In the sixth, Gassendi stepped back to give an account of "the habit of the Body, the manners of his mind, and the studies in which he exercised his Wits."[17] This was a picture of the scholar as the early modern *happy man*. Like the ideal, Peiresc emerged as one who exchanged benefits for gratitude, creating friendships whose flourishing was nurtured by conversation and preserved by a self-governance in which reason ruled the passions.[18] Like the virtuous republican citizen described in Cicero's *De officiis*, Peiresc demonstrated his loyalty to family, *patria*, and cosmopolis. Yet, although Peiresc's loyalties are amply attested by Gassendi, it is the dependence of Gassendi's account on Seneca's rough and ready guide to life under a single ruler, *De beneficiis*, that is most striking. The emphasis was on Peiresc's excellence as a friend, not as a citizen. While the community of citizens was held together by law and justice, that of friends was linked by acts of beneficence and conversation.

The leading and most commented upon of the Peireskean virtues was, in fact, beneficence. "Who is there," Gassendi wrote, "that knows not how much he was inclined to Beneficence? Doubtless there was never man gave more chearfully, liberally, or frequently." His exemplars were God and Nature, "who do not lend, but freely give all things."[19] Like *De beneficiis*, which began with the assertion that "What we need is a discussion of benefits and the rules for a practice that constitutes the chief bond of human society," [20] Gassendi's *Vita Peireskii* is a guide to virtuous giving and all that followed from it. The learned and deserving were given gifts to support activities that promised great benefit to the world; the poor were given charity with no expectation of recompense.[21] If Peiresc was himself given a gift he immediately "would return to the value of what he received, with use."[22] In fact, his greatest pleasure was "in a gift well bestowed." A day in which he failed to exercise this liberality was accounted lost.[23]

Specifically, Peiresc sought to advance learning by helping learned men. Mostly, he acted as a clearing-house for information; but sometimes, as with Campanella and Galileo, serving scholars came at a high financial and political price.[24] In his Roman eulogy, Jean-Jacques Bouchard proclaimed that Peiresc was driven by a liberal, "perpetual and constant desire to adorn and set forth learned men."[25] Bayle may have had this in mind when commenting that "never has any man rendered more service to the Republic of Letters."[26] But beneficence, as Seneca emphasized, was symbiotically linked to gratitude. "It is gratitude," Peiresc himself wrote, "that secures and defends the bonds of human society."[27] It was for this reason that nothing angered him more than ingratitude. Only this was capable, he admitted, of making him "forget" his philosophy.[28]

In its classical and early modern Senecan forms, "beneficence" was perceived as the fundamental means of binding individuals together.[29] Seneca and, by extension, Gassendi, offered an alternative to other accounts that made common political or religious beliefs the basis of community.

Conversation was another means of building relations between men. Peiresc was said to delight more in conversation "than any other thing in the world." [30] He possessed the ability to know how to talk to different types of people. The description of Peiresc's practice amounts to a set of rules for the aspiring conversationalist. Peiresc first ascertained the interests of his guests and then discussed only those matters about which they had some knowledge. With scholars or travelers he asked detailed questions about what they knew best and then shared some of his own learning with them.[31] The prudence he displayed in managing his conversation directly parallels Seneca's insistence that the giver gauge his benefits according to "the when, wherefore, and where of the gift," and its sweetness was so winning that interlocutors often pressed him not to stop.[32] Gassendi's narrative was transformed, by the end of a century in which conversation became a formal art, into the clearly defined set of rules offered in Morhof's *Polyhistor*.[33]

Nor was conversation limited by the constraints of physical presence, for correspondence, following a tradition established by Erasmus, was seen as the conversation – more fixed but no less intimate – of absent friends.[34] Peiresc was one of the century's great letter writers; his "Commerce and Correspondence of Letters," Gassendi wrote, enabled him "more abundantly to unite all Mankind" and to better supply the needs of the learned around the world.[35] Thousands of his letters survive, countless others having been lost to the depredations of time and carelessness.[36] The letters present the person at work in the most immediate way. Because Peiresc never published anything his erudition was made "public" chiefly through this correspondence. Gassendi presents Peiresc's system of writing letters as yet another set of rules for aspiring members of the Republic of Letters.[37]

Since nothing, according to Gassendi, gained friends "so much as Beneficence and friendly Offices; it is no wonder that he had so many, so good and so illustrious, all the world over."[38] Peiresc literally "made" friends by performing services and kindnesses; as Seneca claimed, "from benefits friendship arises."[39] In accord with Seneca's dictum, however, he never sought his own profit but acted only "for his friends's sakes."[40] Beneficence shown through conversation and correspondence made friends of other learned men, and, over time, a community of like-minded individuals coalesced around him.[41]

Peiresc's goal was the construction of an intellectual community that could serve "the advancement of learning" – a phrase used repeatedly by his English translators.[42] He supported people who were committed to learning regardless of their social status or wealth.[43] Some of his heirs, Gassendi wrote, were concerned about the management of his estate since "his expences seemed to exceed his Incomes; which they could judge by this one thing, that he sent to Rome yearly, three thousand pounds Tours, to be expended."[44] Spending around one-third of his income on scholarship caused him to be seen as a Maecenas who showered not only wealth but also information and personal assistance on those he wished to assist.[45] Gassendi acknowledged this by describing Peiresc as a worthy successor to the great early seventeenth-century patrons and brokers of learning, Vincenzo Pinelli, Marcus Welser, and Domenico Molino.[46]

The relation described by Gassendi between beneficence, conversation, friendship, and community can be found across learned Europe, from Seville to Breslau and from Padua to Edinburgh. Its prominence reflects, in part, the significance of friendship in a time of civil crisis, when conventional political communities were collapsing or being challenged. In the 1620s, in Venice, for example, a debate about the shape of political community was conducted in terms of differing notions of friendship.[47]

That learned culture was suffused with the language of friendship could be demonstrated through any number of sources. For example, a little-known collection of essays by the Paduan Professor of Philosophy Flavio Querenghi (*c.*1590–1647) addresses these themes. Its successful, and utterly self-conscious, emulation of Montaigne's *Essais* makes it an especially valuable bridge to the now unfamiliar world of provincial erudite sociability and its residually aristocratic conceptual vocabulary.[48] A nephew of the famous poet and secretary Antonio Querenghi, Flavio's circle included some of Peiresc's friends and acquaintances, such as Lorenzo Pignoria. His extraordinary *Discorsi morali politici et naturali* (1644) is, in equal and mutually reinforcing parts, autobiography, biography, learned and semi-learned essays.[49] It takes the form of a series of discourses, bracketed by letters to and from the author and his friends commenting on the contents.

The book exists because of friendship. In the preface, Querenghi explained that his reluctance to publish was overcome by the implorings of friends who wished to preserve for posterity through print what otherwise risked disappearing into the ephemera of a manuscript culture. The autumnal and elegiac tone of this old man's reflections captures a feeling for the relationship between friends and learning that was not uncommon at this time; in fact, the passage echoes Montaigne's preface to his own readers:

Nevertheless, now that I am so advanced in years, my friends wish me to change my mind, thinking me ill-willed to depart without leaving them some reminder of me. They urge that this small part of various Italian discourses also be printed (in addition to my Latin book just arrived from Holland) so that my fate is not like that of fish who leave no trace of themselves after passing through water. And if the *learned* will have no need for my discourses, at least my dear friends will desire a portrait of me from nature before my impending departure. It is for those who love me that I write . . . We are, indeed, happy to have many friends.[50]

The letters that surround the text drip with sentimental evocations of friendship's obligations.[51] When a friend, who was leaving Padua for Rome, asked for a copy of the *Discorsi*, Querenghi accompanied the text with a description of its relationship to him that trades on the common practice of using a visual representation of a friend as a stand-in for living presence.[52]

I leave you these few memories both to satisfy your requests and so that if we are separated by fate you will not, however, be entirely deprived of the conversation and counsel of your most loyal friend. You could, though the exchange is unequal, converse with my writings instead of me and take counsel, at times, with them. In this way the damage that is caused by distance will be less and less grave will be the sadness you will suffer whilst I am far away.[53]

Friendship was sustained by conversation, but also, as Gassendi had shown, by acts of beneficence. In an essay on the benefits exchanged by friends, Querenghi returned to the connection between friends and political patrons. In both relations pleasure was derived not from the action performed so much as from the spirit and "promptness of will" (prontezza della volontà) with which it was performed. Neither friend nor ruler could be satisfied by actions that did not emerge "dall'interno del cuore" (from within the heart). The ability to distinguish between sincere and insincere expressions was the task of the oracle within.[54]

Both friends and patrons were impressed more by the cause than the effect, by the soul than the utility of the action. It was, Querenghi suggested, "a natural law to give pleasure without waiting to be provoked."[55] His insistence that the true friend was the one who acted freely without reference to self-interest followed Seneca in making friendship the model for the independent thinking that alone preserved the individual from despair and the idols of tribe and market.[56]

The society of friends was, first and foremost, a community of reason. This was why sober, sensible friendship was preferred to love, with its ecstatic and uncontrollable transports. The ability to rule over the passions was one of the achievements of the excellent man since it guaranteed freedom from internal bondage. Peiresc claimed to have learned to "rule his passion" and curb his anger after observing the combat between a louse and a flea through a microscope. The blood pulsing through the louse led him to marvel at "how great a Commotion of Humors and Spirits, and what a disturbance of all the faculties, anger must needs make and what harm that man avoids, who quits that passion."[57] The strength of mind that he learned was displayed over the course of a sickly life. His "custom of suffering was perfected and assisted by Reason, which told him; that, what cannot be avoided, must be suffered patiently and gently."[58]

Gassendi's account of Peiresc's final illness, like those in other biographies, is evidence of the fashion for depictions of graceful and self-controlled demise that made paintings of the death of Seneca so immensely popular in the seventeenth century.[59] Gassendi's long account of the great discomfort endured by Peiresc, first from the kind of urinary tract problems that were then so common, and then, from the fever and acute pain caused by the disintegration of his bladder, make for exceedingly gory reading. But that only worked to enhance the dignity with which Peiresc bore his end and lived his philosophy.[60] This was the kind of extreme self-control that contemporaries learned from the stories of any number of ancient heroes like Seneca, Mucius Scaevola, and Attilius Regulus. That Gassendi located this strength in the mind of a modern rather than a famous ancient is part of the transformed definition of the heroic that this biography sought to effect.[61]

The work of the contemporary Aragonese Jesuit Baltasar Gracián helps us to understand this shift. Writing for and about the inhabitants of Baroque courts, Gracián sketched the outlines of the ideal man in a series of works entitled *El heroé* (1636), *El discreto* (1646), and *Oracolo manuál y arte de prudencia* (1647). He did this by weaving together biography, fashionable philosophy, and courtesy literature, creating a hybrid hero who showed "the way to eminence and perfection," according to Sir John Skeffington, the English translator of *El heroé* (1652).[62]

For Gracián, like Querenghi, the crucial attribute was self-control. It made thought, the only freedom that could be secured by the individual himself, possible. Gracián's first rule was that "it is a Masterpiece to make one's self known, but not to be comprehended . . . If he that comprehends, commands, then he that keeps concealed, never renders himself."[63] Where Alexander tarnished his achievements by "rendring himself to the weakness of his Passions" the true hero was able "to suppress his Passions, or at least to dissemble them, with so much dexterity, that no countermine find a way to uncipher his will."[64] In a Tacitean world, whether of state or courtly politics, the only freedom that remained was freedom of thought. It was attained by the difficult practice of self-mastery and had to be jealously guarded.

The *Discreto*, marvelously rendered into eighteenth-century English as *The Compleat Gentleman*, was said by its translator to provide a model for the "Man of Sense" who could be perfected by "Genius," "Learning," "Virtue," and "Politeness."[65] The most powerful weapon in the *discreto*'s arsenal – as in that of Lipsius, Guillaume du Vair, and any number of early modern writers who sought to fashion a modern, Christian stoicism – was reason.[66] It alone enabled people "to apprehend, to penetrate

into the most abstruse Things and to unravel their secret Principles."
But, in a telling caveat, "this noble Superiority" was said to be impossible to obtain "without great Application."[67] Ferdinand the Catholic, a
frequent example elsewhere in Gracián's corpus, was the subject of *El
político* (1640). His personal heroism was assimilated to the modern stoic's
detachment and rational self-control. To be learned in prudence so as
"always to govern according to the occasion, this was the great aphorism of his politics."[68] And this was none other than the skill required by
the *discreto*. With Gracián, the virtues of self-governance are completely
assimilated to those demanded of rulers. His is another way of addressing Bacon's suggestion that public and more private lives could be
equally worthy of examination.

Gracián's insistence on self-control recurs in the lead essay of
Querenghi's *Discorsi*, "Alchimia delle passioni dell'animo overo Modo di
convertire i nostri dispiaceri in diletti" (The Alchemy of the soul's passions or, The way to convert our dislikes into delights). The examples of
emotional turmoil are the common ones: loss of friends and defeat in
interest-laden court intrigue.[69] Querenghi's counsel was that friends lost
so easily could hardly have been worth much to begin with. In the end,
neither wealth nor sweetness of behavior could alter the iron law that
even the greatest of successes "cannot endure for a long time."
Consolation came with the knowledge of that impermanence. "You
have not lost anything because from the beginning things were as they
are now, but you did not notice." Learning, wrote Querenghi, always
brought benefit, and "to be undeceived even once is not without useful-
ness."[70]

As with Gracián, *desengaño* is a necessary part of the therapy for
someone living in the world despite the cost of such disenchantment.[71]
"To escape even once from ignorance," wrote Querenghi, "must be
counted amongst the happiest of successes," and until one learns this
"one will not know how to accommodate one's soul to the change in this
friend, or that prince, whom you once loved without guile."[72] Only an
honest acknowledgment of the reality that all things human were "naturally mutable" made it possible to live a stable, happy life.[73]

Self-knowledge is paramount for both Querenghi and Gracián. But,
since knowledge did not necessarily lead to practice, its acquisition could
only be considered a first step toward the self-control that was really
decisive. Nothing else in this world was so worthy of praise. "If one has
the ambition to be a ruler, why not command the passions, which are
powerful, and rebellious, vassals?" Without the ability to dominate the

passions the individual, like the ruler of a kingdom, would lose control. The solution offered by Querenghi was a moderation as much Aristotelian as Middle Stoic and which sought to use the passions to do the bidding of reason.[74]

Like Lipsius and Montaigne, Querenghi offered a philosophy for those committed to a worldly life and thus at risk from the world. In his own mind, and those of his friends, the *Discorsi* constituted an epitome of all that was needed by a seventeenth-century man of the world. "I have sought," he wrote Cardinal Capponi, "to formulate a compendium of compendia and with two short and simple precepts to instruct men in *commercio* and *conversatione civile*. For not everyone can give himself to the study of philosophy and the reading of history in order to furnish himself with prudence and learn how to comport himself, his household, *patria* and friends."[75]

The *Vita Peireskii*, however, offered a more specific vision of the end and the means to attain it. The goal was a tranquillity born of the ability to ignore unworthy disturbances. Peiresc frequently affirmed, as in a late letter to Gabriel Naudé, that there was nothing "more certain and sweet" than to live with "as little disturbance to tranquillity as we can hope for in our condition."[76] This was not to be attained by a withdrawal from the world. Peiresc's close friends, such as Paolo Sarpi, Jacques-Auguste de Thou, Hugo Grotius, and John Selden, belonged to that circle of European thinkers who played an active role in the political life of their polities. These men were also, not coincidentally, defenders of civil jurisdiction and the representative bodies that exercised this sovereignty. Their minimally doctrinal Christianity and rejection of divisive ecclesiological politics, whether Catholic or Calvinist, linked them in an arc that bent from Venice through Paris and from Leiden to London.[77]

Peiresc belonged to this world. Like his close friends, he did not insist on conformity, according to Gassendi, as long as "the Statutes of Religion; and Laws of the Countrey were not meddled with." He believed that the authority of law had to be protected "for as much as in the observation thereof, consisted the safety of the Commonwealth; so that such as are not very just, may be more useful for publick good, than juster, provided they be religiously observed."[78] This same sentiment lay behind Sarpi's characterization of the Torah as the ideal law and Hobbes's conceptualization of the state as a Leviathan.[79]

Travel was one way to gain this breadth of perspective. Its importance as an intellectual phenomenon in early modern Europe is now recognized.[80] In a famous letter to Joseph Scaliger in 1604, for example, the encyclopedic historian Lancet Voisin de la Popelinière explained that more perfect knowledge of the world could not be attained by study but only by traveling.[81] Peiresc agreed that seeing how other people lived and recognizing that for them their customs and manners were as compelling as one's own could lead a man "to elevate his mind above the vulgar condition."[82]

Inevitably, with so much attention paid to the critical impact of travel on the intellectual orthodoxies propagated and perpetuated in books, it has been easy to overlook the skeptical, prejudice-smashing power of *reading* about the world.[83] Antiquaries like Peiresc, or Poggio Bracciolini two centuries earlier, were often responsible for transforming travelers' accounts into the texts that were then widely disseminated – with these revolutionary consequences. By integrating the travelers' reports into the existing body of knowledge, stay-at-home scholars helped create new world histories. Study of "the Laws and customs of sundry Nations" and comparison with one's own, Peiresc thought, should be part of the necessary education of the modern European. It reflected his profound confidence that "an ingenuous man might lay aside that prejudice, which makes the vulgar sort of men account the Customs of their own Country to be the Law of Nature, and that nothing is well done, which is not setable to their waies and manners."[84] Not everyone could travel, but anyone able to read could reap its benefits.

The goal of learning about the world was nothing less than the ancient injunction to self-knowledge. When men mistook the "true ends" of life and made destructive choices, it was because they knew too little about what these choices entailed. If only men could be taught not to covet "superfluous things," it would be possible for "humanity, honesty, and moderation" to survive in the world.[85]

The education represented in the person and practice of Peiresc aimed to create a modern Socrates who was "a citizen, not of one country only, but of the whole world," possessing the equanimity that enabled him "to enjoy the greatest tranquillity possible, and consequently, the greatest good."[86] As the popularity of Lipsius's *De constantia* makes plain, the ideal of self-control was so important and its resulting equanimity so sought-after precisely because its readers were men unable to extricate themselves from the world. Those in positions of authority or responsibility, like Grotius, Sarpi, and Peiresc, or even John Eliot, who wrote the stoic *Monarchy of Man* in the Tower of London (where he received a gift of *De constantia* from Peiresc's friend, Sir Robert

Cotton), were the ones who needed this lesson in comportment, not those living far from the threatening shadows of power.

In his praise of Peiresc, Gassendi only alluded to Montaigne, who, when awarded honorary Roman citizenship, had been hailed as the "French Socrates." But some of Querenghi's friends actually equated Querenghi and Montaigne. The historian Enrico Davila, who had lived in France, wrote to Querenghi in 1620, that "Montaigne had a bit of learning, but nothing profound. He had his own style, but it was plain. He was, in the end, more soldier than learned. But your Lordship, that brings forth learning and letters from the heart of the sciences, that aids and perfects nature with art, surpasses him by a great distance."[87] Another correspondent, Guillaume Sohier, a Fleming at the Barberini court, in returning an Italian translation of Montaigne's *Saggi* to Querenghi, offered the following judgment: "I predict that our descendants, considering the conformity of your genius and this worthy writer, will say one day: either Montaigne Querenghizes or Querengho Montaignizes."[88]

The co-opting of Montaigne into a seventeenth-century discourse of sociability and self-study, if not always self-control, shows how the scholarly Republic of Letters provided itself with a genealogy. With the emphasis on sociability in the new community came the insistence on self-knowledge and self-control as the measure of an individual's excellence.

The reception of Gassendi's *Vita* in England is documented in the front matter of the 1657 translation and helps us see how contemporary readers articulated these themes.[89] First, the translation was entitled *The Mirrour of True Nobility and Gentility*. The English perceived that the mirror for princes had finally found its complement. That only they saw fit to translate the text does, I think, say something significant about the self-conscious creation of a national intellectual culture in the midst of a great political upheaval. That this was the only complete translation into any modern language until 1992 is striking.[90] The Latin text was adequate for Europe's cosmopolites and learned men. But if the "Peireskean virtues" were to have any broader extension, they had to be put in the vernacular.

The English translation was executed at the suggestion of Samuel Hartlib and one of his collaborators, Benjamin Worsley, and it was dedicated to John Evelyn. Peiresc had captured the attention of precisely those who were seeking to organize for "the advancement of learning." The translator, William Rand, hoped that from Peiresc

Englishmen could learn "that knowledge, which is the highest perfection of Man, by which he differs from Beasts, must needs be the principal accomplishment of a Gentleman."[91] Where Gassendi used Peiresc as a model for behavior in the learned republic, the English adapted his virtues for the existing political society. In drawing an explicit contrast between the subject who hunted and hawked – fine exercises for the body – and one who learned, Rand described hunting as breeding "an humor inclinable to Tyrany, like that of Nimrod the mighty Hunter, and *Proto-Tyrant* [original emphasis] of all mankind." From Peiresc, the "English Gentry" would learn a better use of their leisure and become more fit to serve "the Common-wealth in the most weighty concernements thereof."[92]

Elaborating on the contrast between tyranny and commonwealth – surely no idle antithesis in a work achieved during the years of Civil War and Interregnum – Rand argued that the gentry had become fodder for tyranny precisely because they did not think for themselves. Forced "to see with the Eyes of others," they had to rely on the dictates of others suitable "to their own Interests, Factions and Trades, instead of following their own well-informed, unbiassed and generous understandings."[93] The preservation of the polity was best given over to the care of an educated citizenry. Evelyn himself urged a friend traveling in France to visit Peiresc's home in the countryside, "for, certainly though the curiosities may be much dispersed since the tyme of the most noble Peireskius, yet the very genius of that place cannot but infuse admirable thoughts into you."[94]

In *The Learned Man Defended and Reform'd* (English translation, 1660), Daniello Bartoli asserted that "to know the world is to possess it."[95] Bartoli's book defended the ideal projected by Gassendi, that the scholar was the best man because his knowledge of the world made possible the greatest self-knowledge and so the wisest moral choices. Biographies of scholars like Peiresc offer us a remarkably coherent picture of what the seventeenth century believed to be the best way to live. It is the combination of self-perfection through training of the mind and collegial sociability that made the ideal of excellence embodied by Peiresc so powerfully alluring.

The readers of the *Vita Peireskii* and *Mirrour of True Nobility and Gentility* were shown how learning made for true freedom and how a community linked by friendship would also be able to defend itself more effectively against tyrants whose primary aim was control of information. This is the first part of a story whose continually widening social horizon transformed what began as an aristocratic ideal of comportment and community into the civil foundation of political community. What was first adapted for the Republic of Letters in the earlier seventeenth century was further transformed by the third Earl of Shaftesbury and essay journals like *The Spectator* in the early eighteenth century into *politeness*, a lifestyle appropriate for a post-revolutionary and commercial British state.[96] The history of the gradual extension of this ideal from the aristocratic to the polite is also the history of the beginnings of civil society.[97] Many of the tensions in modern political thought result from this progressive democratization of an aristocratic ideal of excellence. But the belief that learning about the world was necessary for self-knowledge and that this alone made for true freedom also offered a means of easing this tension. In the work of Friedrich Schiller, Wilhelm von Humboldt, and their nineteenth-century American disciples, this early modern ideal of individual excellence based on learning became *Bildung* and inspired others who argued that the corrosive effects of commerce on sociability could be neutralized, if not reversed, by thorough and early exposure to the liberal arts.

NOTES

Earlier versions of this were presented to audiences at the William Andrews Clark Memorial Library of the University of California, Los Angeles; the East–West Seminar meeting in Münster, Germany; and the Renaissance Seminar at the University of Chicago. I thank all those whose questions gave me pause and, in particular, Peter Reill, Robert Darnton, and Richard Strier, whose kind invitations made these possible. I want also to thank Anthony Grafton and Joan-Pau Rubiés for reading drafts of this essay. It is dedicated to the memory of an exemplary scholar and teacher, Judith Shklar.

1. For neo-Stoicism, see Gerhard Oestreich, *Neostoicism and the Early Modern State*, ed. Brigitta Oestreich and H. G. Koenigsberger, trans. D. McClintock (Cambridge: Cambridge University Press, 1982); Morris W. Croll, *Style, Rhetoric, and Rhythm*, ed. J. Max Patrick and Robert O. Evans (Princeton: Princeton University Press, 1966); Nannerl O. Keohane, *Philosophy and the State in France: The Renaissance to the Enlightenment* (Princeton: Princeton University Press, 1980); Mark Morford, *Stoics and Neostoics: Rubens and the Circle of Lipsius* (Princeton: Princeton University Press, 1991); Richard Tuck, *Philosophy and Government 1572–1651* (Cambridge: Cambridge University Press, 1993); Jacqueline Lagrée, ed., *Le Stoicisme aux XVIe et XVIIe siècles*, Cahiers de philosophie, politique et juridique de l'Université de Caen (Caen: Université de Caen, 1994). For libertinism, see René Pintard, *Le Libertinage érudit dans la première moitié du XVIIe siècle* (Geneva: Slatkine Reprints, 1983; 1st

edn., Paris: Boivin, 1943); Giorgio Spini, *Ricerca dei libertini: La teoria dell'im-postura delle religioni nel seicento italiano* (Rome: Editrice Universale di Roma, 1950); A.M. Battista, *Alle origini del pensiero politico libertino: Montaigne e Charron* (Milan: Dott. A. Giuffre, 1966); Sergio Bertelli, ed., *Il libertinismo Europeo* (Milan: R. Ricciardi, 1980); T. Gregory et al., *Ricerche su letteratura libertina e letteratura clandestina nel Seicento* (Florence: La Nuova Italia, 1981).

2. See the work of Françoise Waquet, "Qu'est-ce que la République des Lettres? Essai de sémantique historique," *Bibliothèque de l'Ecole des Chartes* 147 (1989): 473–502; and *Le Modèle français et l'Italie savante: Conscience de soi et perception de l'autre dans la République des Lettres, 1660–1750* (Rome: Ecole Française de Rome, 1989); and Anne Goldgar, *Impolite Learning: Conduct and Community in the Republic of Letters, 1680–1750* (New Haven and London: Yale University Press, 1995).

3. These lives are nearly always of men. However, Christian Gryphius, *Vitae selectae quorundam eruditissimorum ac illustrium virum* (Breslau: C. Bauchius, 1711), which begins with a citation of Morhof's discussion of lives of scholars, does include the lives of two women, Helena Cornara and Cassandra Fedele.

4. For the intellectual utility of the study of biography, see Arnaldo Momigliano, *The Development of Greek Biography* (Cambridge, Mass.: Harvard University Press, 1971, 2nd edn., 1993) and Marc Fumaroli, "From 'Lives' to Biography: The Twilight of Parnassus," *Diogenes* (1987): 1–27. On forms of early modern biography, see Thomas F. Mayer and D. R. Woolf, eds., *The Rhetoric of Life-Writing in Early Modern Europe: Forms of Biography from Cassandra Fedele to Louis XIV* (Ann Arbor: University of Michigan Press, 1995) and Orest Ranum, "Men of Letters: Sixteenth-Century Models of Conduct," ch. 1 in *Artisans of Glory: Writers and Historical Thought in Seventeenth-Century France* (Chapel Hill: University of North Carolina Press, 1980). The link between biography and rhetoric is central to Timothy Hampton, *Writing from History: The Rhetoric of Exemplarity in Renaissance Literature* (Ithaca, N.Y.: Cornell University Press, 1990), esp. ch. 1; John D. Lyons, *Exemplum: The Rhetoric of Example in Early Modern France and Italy* (Princeton: Princeton University Press, 1989); and Thomas M. Greene, *The Light in Troy: Imitation and Discovery in Renaissance Poetry* (New Haven: Yale University Press, 1982).

5. Francis Bacon, "De Augmentis Scientiarum," in *The Works of Francis Bacon*, ed. James Spedding, Robert Leslie Ellis, and Douglas Denon Heath, vol. IV (London: Longman and Co., 1858), bk. 2, ch. 7:307.

6. Daniel Georg Morhof, "De vitarum scriptoribus," in *Polyhistor* (Lübeck: P. Bockmann, 1708, 1st edn., 1688), bk. 1, ch. 19; cited hereafter as Morhof, *Polyhistor*. The older genre of lives of "illustrious men" does not approach the fully rounded biographies discussed by Morhof. For a discussion of the implications of thinking in terms of *hommes illustres*, see Patricia Eichel-Lojkine, "Les Vies d'hommes illustres," *Nouvelle revue du seizième siècle* 12 (1994): 63–77. I thank Raia Zaimova for bringing this to my attention. In Vasari's *Lives*, one encounters a different phenomenon: the life used to explain an age, rather than an individual mind.

7. Morhof, *Polyhistor*, 234–36.
8. Gualdo's biography was a model for Gassendi, just as Pinelli had been for Peiresc. So was – or, at least, could have been – Micanzio's of Sarpi, which though published only in 1646, had circulated in manuscript from 1633, when Peiresc obtained a copy from the Dupuy brothers in Paris.
9. "Plane in hoc labore exercuit ingentium suum Gassendus . . . Optandum esset, ut simili diligentia illustrium Virorum memorabilia consignarentur, quod fieri non potest, nisi ab amicis & familiaribus, vel nisi ipsi auctores vivi rerum suarum Commentarios scripserint, ut fecit Thuanus & alii nonnulli, vel saltem lineamenta ejus duxerint, unde perfectum deducere opus Viri harum rerum periti possint," Morhof, *Polyhistor*, 239–40.
10. Scholarly discussion of Peiresc is found in Arnaldo Momigliano, *The Classical Foundations of Modern Historiography* (Berkeley and Los Angeles: University of California Press, 1990), 54–57; Cecilia Rizza, *Peiresc e l'Italia* (Turin: Giappichelli, 1965); Sydney Aufrère, *La Momie et la tempête: N.-C. F. de Peiresc et la "Curiosité Egyptienne" en Provence au début du XVIIe siècle* (Avignon: Editions A. Barthélemy, 1990); *Peiresc: Lettres à Claude Saumaise et à son entourage*, ed. Agnès Bresson (Florence: L. S. Olschki, 1992) with a superb bibliography. See also the essays of David Jaffé: "Peiresc – Wissenschaftlicher Betrieb in einem Raritäten-Kabinett," in *Macrocosmos in Microcosmo*, ed. Andreas Grote (Opladen: Leske + [*sic*] Budrich, 1994), 301–22; "Peiresc and New Attitudes to Authenticity in the Seventeenth Century," in *Why Fakes Matter: Essays on Problems of Authenticity*, ed. Mark Jones (London: British Museum Press, 1993), 157–73; "Aspects of Gem Collecting in the Early Seventeenth Century: Nicolas-Claude Peiresc and Lelio Pasqualini," *Burlington Magazine* 135 (1993): 103–20. The best biography remains that by Gassendi.
11. Jean-Jacques Bouchard, "Prayse of Peireskius," in Pierre Gassendi, *The Mirrour of True Nobility and Gentility* (London: 1657), 255.
12. Pierre Bayle, *Dictionnaire historique et critique*, 4th edn., 3 vols. (Amsterdam: P. Brunel, 1730), III:638.
13. Gassendi, *Mirrour*, sig.a1v.
14. "Others may, if they please, with a more elegant pen, polish and reduce into the form of an History, such Commentaries as I shall only digest as loose materials, after the way of Annals, and according to the course of years," Gassendi, *Mirrour*, sig.a1r.
15. Bayle, *Dictionnaire*, III: 639.
16. Indeed, as Momigliano has argued, "it is difficult to separate antiquarianism from biographical research." *Bios* made no distinction between individuals and nations and the reconstruction of a person's life, like a given past, required no justification. Momigliano, *Classical Foundations*, 155. See also, Momigliano, *Development of Greek Biography*, 13. That Gassendi immediately went on to write another biography, that of Epicurus, has to raise doubts about Lynn Sumida Joy's assertion in her fascinating *Gassendi the Atomist* (Cambridge: Cambridge University Press, 1987), ch. 3, that Gassendi viewed the antiquarian encyclopedic project, embodied by Peiresc, as having failed.

17. Gassendi, *Mirrour*, bk. 6, 157. All references are to Book Six unless otherwise indicated.
18. The following offer points of entry to the political, philosophical, and cultural worlds characterizable in this way: M. Røstvig, *The Happy Man* (Oslo: Oslo University Press, 1954); Marc Fumaroli, *Héros et orateurs: Rhétorique et dramaturgie cornéliennes* (Geneva: Droz, 1990), *L'Ecole du silence: Le sentiment des images au XVIIe siècle* (Paris: Flammarion, 1994), and "Rhétorique et société en Europe (XVIe–XVIIe siècles)," summarized in Collège de France, *Annuaire* (1986–87 to 1992–93); Keohane, *Philosophy and the State in France*, chs. 3–6; Iain Fenlon and Peter N. Miller, *The Song of the Soul: Understanding "Poppea"* (London: Royal Musical Association, 1992), chs. 3–6; *Stefano Guazzo e la civile conversazione*, ed. Giorgio Patrizi (Rome: Bulzoni Editore, 1990); Hugh Trevor-Roper, "The Great Tew Circle," in *Catholics, Anglicans, and Puritans. Seventeenth Century Essays* (Chicago: University of Chicago Press (1992), 166–230. For a view of the political uses of "friendship" and its cognate concepts, see Sharon Kettering, *Patrons, Brokers, and Clients in Seventeenth-Century France* (New York and Oxford: Oxford University Press, 1986), esp. 13–16.
19. Gassendi, *Mirrour*, 169.
20. Seneca, *De beneficiis*, trans. John W. Basore (Cambridge, Mass.: Loeb Classical Library, 1989), i. iv.2.
21. Gassendi, *Mirrour*, 170.
22. *Ibid.*, 171.
23. *Ibid.*, 172.
24. For Peiresc's relationship with these men and their tormentors, see Rizza, *Peiresc e l'Italia*.
25. Gassendi, *Mirrour*, 246.
26. "Jamais homme ne rendit plus de services à la République des lettres que celui-ci"; Bayle, *Dictionnaire*, III:638.
27. "C'est la gratitude qui assure et boucle le lien de la société humaine"; Peiresc to Dupuy, October 1636, in Tamizey de Larroque, ed., *Lettres de Peiresc*, 7 vols., Collection de documents inédits sur l'histoire de France (Paris: Imprimerie nationale, 1888–98), III:589.
28. Gassendi, *Mirrour*, 170.
29. Seneca, *De benef.*, IV.xviii.1–2
30. Gassendi, *Mirrour*, 164.
31. *Ibid.*, 176.
32. Seneca, *De benef.*, II.xvi.1.
33. Morhof actually presents systematic rules for conversation in *Polyhistor*, ch. 15: 167–79. On conversation as a cultural style, see Marc Fumaroli, *La Diplomatie de l'esprit de Montaigne à La Fontaine* (Paris: Hermann, 1994) and his "La Conversation," in *Les Lieux de mémoire*, ed. Pierre Nora, vol. III, *Les France*, pt. 2, *Traditions* (Paris: Gallimard, 1992), 679–743.
34. Paul Dibon, "Communication in the Respublica Literaria of the Seventeenth Century," *Res publica litterarum* 1 (1978): 43–55; Marc Fumaroli,

"Genèse de l'épistolographie classique: rhétorique humaniste de la lettre, de Pétrarque à Juste Lipse," *Revue de l'histoire littéraire de la France* 78 (1978): 886–905; H. J. M. Nellen, "La Correspondance savante au xviie siècle," *XVIIe siècle* 178 (1993): 87–98; Giuseppe Olmi, "'Molti amici in varii luoghi': Studio della natura e rapporti epistolari nel secolo xvi," *Nuncius* 6 (1991): 3–31; Hans Bots and Françoise Waquet, eds., *Commercium litterarium, 1600–1750: Forms of Communication in the Republic of Letters*, Conférence des colloques tenu à Paris 1992 et à Nimègue 1993 (Amsterdam: APA-Holland University Press, 1994).

35. Gassendi, *Mirrour*, 236.

36. The mass of Peiresc's surviving manuscripts are in the Bibliothèque Nationale, Paris (Fonds Français, Dupuy, and Nouvelles Acquisitions Françaises) and the Bibliothèque Inguimbertine, Carpentras. Copies of selected material are in the Bibliothèque Méjanes, Aix-en-Provence. A fairly comprehensive finding list is provided by Francis W. Gravit, *The Peiresc Papers*, University of Michigan Contributions in Modern Philology, no.14 (Ann Arbor: University of Michigan Press, 1950).

37. Gassendi, *Mirrour*, 216–17.

38. *Ibid.*, 173.

39. Seneca, *De benef.*, ii.xviii.5.

40. Gassendi, *Mirrour*, 174; Seneca, *De benef.*, v.xi.5.

41. Gassendi, *Mirrour*, 174.

42. *Ibid.*, year 1610:147, year 1616:172, year 1635:135; and bk. 6:172. We know him to have been a careful reader of Bacon's programmatic writings on science, allegory, and political history, and he was instrumental in the French translation of Bacon's *History of the Reign of King Henry VII* (see, for example, Peiresc's letters to Dupuy of 28 April 1624, 4 January 1627, 29 January 1627, early February 1627, 10 February 1627, and 17 July 1627 in Tamizey de Larroque, ed., *Lettres de Peiresc*, i: 32, 121, 133, 142, 293.

43. Gassendi, *Mirrour*, 178–79.

44. *Ibid.*, 172.

45. Gassendi referred to Peiresc as a Maecenas in *Mirrour*, sig.ar, as did Balzac in a letter quoted by Bayle in the *Dictionnaire*, iii:639, n. A. For the figure, see the biographical material reprinted in *L'Eté Peiresc. Fioretti II*, ed. Jacques Ferrier (Avignon: Aubanel, 1988), 93

46. Gassendi, *Mirrour*, 216.

47. I discuss this episode in my forthcoming *Peiresc's Europe: Learning and Virtue in the Seventeenth Century* (New Haven: Yale University Press).

48. For particular studies, see Jonathan Dewald, *Aristocratic Experience and the Origins of Modern Culture: France, 1570–1715* (Berkeley: University of California Press, 1993); David G. Halsted, *Poetry and Politics in the Silesian Baroque: Neostoicism in the Work of Christophorus Colerus and his Circle* (Wiesbaden: Harrassowitz, 1996); Otto Brunner, *Adeliges Landleben und Europäischer Geist* (Salzburg: O. Mueller, 1949); Hugh Trevor-Roper, "The Great Tew Circle," 166–230; James Amelang, *Honored Citizens of Barcelona: Patrician Culture and*

Class Relations, 1490–1714 (Princeton: Princeton University Press, 1986); Paula Findlen, *Possessing Nature: Museums, Collecting, and Scientific Culture in Early Modern Italy* (Berkeley: University of California Press, 1994).

49. For Querenghi, see Emilia Veronese Ceseracciu, "La biblioteca di Flavio Querenghi, professore di filosofia morale (1624–1647) nello studio di Padova," *Quaderni per la storia dell'università di Padova* 9–10 (1976–77): 185–213; and Lucciano Stecca, "Montaigne e Flavio Querenghi," in *Montaigne e l'Italia* (Geneva: Slatkine, 1991), 83–101. I thank Warren Boutcher for bringing these to my attention.

50. Querenghi, *Discorsi morali politici et naturali* (Padova, 1644), sig.a2r, hereafter cited as Querenghi, *Discorsi:* "Tuttavia hor, ch'io sono molto avanti ne gli anni, gli amici mi fanno mutuar parere, perche vedendomi essi malvolontieri partire senza che resti qualche memoria di me, laudano, che si stampi (oltre il mio libro latino, venuto d'Olanda ultimatemente) anco questa particella di varii Discorsi volgari, che mi trovo; perche io non faccia come i pesci, che non lasciano impresso nell'acqua alcun vestigio dopo di loro. E se i letterati non havranno bisogno de' miei Discorsi, havranno desiderio almeno i miei cari amici d'un mio ritratto del naturale in questa mia vicina partenza. A questi che mi amano, io scrivo . . . Noi contentiamci d'haver molti compagni." Montaigne, *Essays*, trans. and ed. M.A. Screech (Harmondsworth: Penguin, 1991), lix: "To the Reader: I have not been concerned to serve you or my reputation: my powers are inadequate for such a design. I have dedicated this book to the private benefit of my friends and kinsmen so that, having lost me (as they must do soon) they can find here again some traits of my character and of my humours. They will thus keep their knowledge of me more full, more alive."

51. In a letter to Monsig. Barisoni, the Arciprete of Padova, Querenghi writes that he is sending his writings for approval and to satisfy the obligations of the "amore hereditario passato da' nostri Zii in noi." Moreover, of such "vera Amicitia" there was said to be nothing "in questo Secolo, che s'accosti alle Antiche, certo è questa, che mi viene lasciata dal Zio" (Querenghi, *Discorsi*, b4r). In response, Barisoni affirmed that "l'amicizia e la fede anche fra di noi dovessero durare eterne" (*ibid.*, c1r). He wrote that the *Discorsi*, and their author, were full of prudence and learning and, what was "so rare in our century," "una sincera, e ferma amicizia" (*ibid.*, c2v).

52. See Carlo Dionisotti, "La galleria degli uomini illustri," *Lettere Italiane* 33 (1981): 482–92 and David Jaffé, "Peiresc's Famous Men Picture Gallery," in *L'Eté Peiresc*, 133–49.

53. Querenghi, *Discorsi*, 362: "Vi lascio queste poche memorie; e per sodisfare alle vostre dimande, e perche se ci divide la sorte, non siate però affatto privo della conversatione, e consiglio del vostre fedelissimo amico. Potrete, sebene è disuguale il cambio, conversare in mia vece con questi miei scritti, e consigliarvi talhora con essi, & in questo modo sarà minore il danno, che vi è per arrecare la mia lontananza, e men grave il dispiacere, che siete anche voi per sentire, mentre io vi starò lontano."

54. *Ibid.*, 22–23: "Che habbiamo tutti dentro di noi un' Oracolo, il quale ci può sicuramente, & facilmente ammaestrare nella conversatione civile."

55. *Ibid.*, 26–27: "Che i beneficii, che ci può far l'amico senza esser richiesto, & avvisato da noi, non meritan alcuna lode ò ringratiamento, se aspetta, prima d'operare, le nostre preghiere, & gli avvisi."

56. *Ibid.*, 30: "Che i beneficii . . ."

57. Gassendi, *Mirrour*, 169.

58. *Ibid.*, 168.

59. See the inventory prepared by Andor Pigler, *Barockthemen: Eine Auswahl von Verzeichnissen zur Ikonographie des 17. und 18. Jahrhunderts*, 2 vols. (Budapest: Verlag der Ungarischen Akademie der Wissenschaften, 1956), II:409–10.

60. In Busenello and Monteverdi's *L'Incoronazione di Poppea* (1643), Seneca declares, after deciding to commit suicide, "Hor confermo i miei scritti, / autentico i miei studi" (II:i).

61. Elie Diodati invoked these same popular attributes when conveying the news of Peiresc's death to Galileo. He urged him to bear the tidings with "your usual constancy in moderating sadness," with the hope that "reason will triumph in you over the excess of emotions"; Galileo Galilei, *Opere*, 20 vols. (reprinted, Florence: Edizione Nationale, 1966), XVII:130.

62. My focus on courtesy literature as a source for defining an ideal of personal excellence rather than a means of enforcing absolutism differs in principle, as I hope will be clear, from Orest Ranum's seminal argument in "Courtesy, Absolutism, and the Rise of the French State, 1630–1660," *Journal of Modern History* 52 (1980): 426–51.

63. Baltasar Gracián y Morales, *El heroé*, published in English as *The Heroe of Lorenzo, or the way to Eminence and Perfection*, trans. Sir John Skeffington (London: John Martin and James Allestrye, 1652), 1, 3; hereafter Gracián, *The Heroe.*

64. *Ibid.*, 11–12.

65. Gracián, *The Compleat Gentleman: or, a Description of the several qualifications, both natural and acquired, that are necessary to form a Great Man*, trans. T. Saldkeld (London: T. Osborne, 1730), translator's pref: sig.A4v.

66. Anthony Levi, *French Moralists: The Theory of the Passions, 1585–1659* (Oxford: Clarendon Press, 1964).

67. Gracián, *The Compleat Gentleman*, 4.

68. Gracián, "El político" in *Obras completas*, ed. Miguel Batllori and Ceferino Peralta (Madrid: Ediciones Atlas, 1969), I:287. On page 288, Gracián proceeded to uphold the time-honored distinction between this kind of prudence and low astuteness. Cf. Dante, *Il Convivio*, IV:27.

69. Querenghi, "Alchimia," in *Discorsi*, vol. II, cited hereafter as Querenghi, "Alchimia."

70. *Ibid.*, 3: "Non facesti perdita alcuna, perche fin dal principio le cose eran quali son hora; ma tù non te n'accorgervi . . . Il disingannarsi una volta non è senza utilità."

71. On *desengaño*, see Otis H. Green, "Desengaño," in *The Literary Mind of*

Medieval and Renaissance Spain (Lexington: University Press of Kentucky, 1970), 141–70. I thank Timothy J. Reiss for bringing this to my attention.

72. Querenghi, "Alchimia," 6.

73. *Ibid.*, 7. Confusion was precipitated by the unprecedented explosion of information. A subsequent essay, "Contra la multitudine de' libri," argues that the proliferation of printed books has drowned out the thinking individual: "La confusion dell'ingegno, e la sovversion della memoria non nasce, se ben consideri, da altra cagione che dalla multitudine hormai infinita de' Libri, introdotta in questo secolo dalla vanità de gli huomini con l'inventione delle stampa." Rather than follow the fashions and applause of the multitude "è necessario, che tù faccia dentro di te qualche concetto, che sia tuo" (Querenghi, *Discorsi*, 128).

74. Querenghi, "Contra l'adulatione," in *Discorsi*, 57–58; "Se s'hà ambitione d'esser Signore, perche non si comanda à gli affetti, che sono vassalli potenti, e ribelli?"; "Così io non intendo d'estirpar dalla radice gli affeti, che questa sarebbe una Stoica crudeltà. La ragione, che la parte divine tiene di nostra natura, e'n cima siede; di che sarebbe Regina, se le mancassero i sudditi? Gli affetti sono i guerieri della ragione... La modestia ne gli honori, & nelle ricchezze; la giustitia, e la fede; la mediocrità di tutte le perturbationi, sono la vera grandezza." Albert Hirshman, *The Passions and the Interests* (Princeton: Princeton University Press, 1978) remains the standard account of this argument.

75. Querenghi, "Utilità del precedente discorso," in *Discorsi*, 17; my italics in the English translation. "Hò cercato di formare un compendio de i compendi stessi, & con due soli precetti facili, & brevi mi sono affaticato, d'istruir l'huomo nel commercio, & nella conversazione civile. Non può ogn'uno darsi allo studio della Filosfia, & alla lettione dell'historie, per fornirsi di prudenza, & per saper, come debba portarsi, & con se stesso, & con la casa, & con la patria, & con gli amici."

76. Peiresc to Gabriel Naudé, 3 January 1635, in *Peiresc: Lettres à Naudé (1629–1637)*, ed. Phillip Wolfe (Paris, Seattle, Tübingen: Papers on French Seventeenth-Century Literature, 1983), 32; "Le plus seur et le plus doulz, est de jouyr le plus doucement qu'on peult et avec moins de bruict de la tranquillité que nous pouvons trouver en nostre condition . . ." A year later, writing to Cassiano dal Pozzo in Rome, Peiresc seemed to blame the circumstances of public life. "La quiete domestica gli poteva prolongar la vita molto più che la vita delle corte con li disaggi che l'accompagno"; Peiresc to Cassiano dal Pozzo, 3 October 1636, in *Nicolas-Claude Fabri de Peiresc: Lettres à Cassiano dal Pozzo, 1626–1637*, ed. Jean-François Lhote and Danielle Joyal (Clermont-Ferrand: Adosa, 1989), 252.

77. For this world, see the essays Gaetano Cozzi collected in *Paolo Sarpi: Tra Venezia e l'Europa* (Turin: G. Einaudi, 1979); see also Enrico De Mas, *Sovranità politica e unità Christiana nel seicento Anglo-Veneto* (Ravenna: Longo, 1975) and *L'Attesa del secolo aureo, 1603–1625: Saggio di storia delle idea del secolo XVII* (Florence: L. S. Olschki, 1982); Hugh Trevor-Roper, *Renaissance Essays* (London: Secker and Warburg, 1985) and *Catholics, Anglicans, and Puritans*,

and Marc Fumaroli, *L'Age de l'éloquence: Rhétorique et "res literaria" de la Renaissance au seuil de l'époque classique*, pt. 3 (Geneva: Droz, 1980).

78. Gassendi, *Mirrour*, 210.

79. See Paolo Sarpi, *Pensieri naturali, metafisici e matematici*, ed. Luisa Cozzi and Liberio Sosio (Milan and Naples: Riccardo Ricciardi, 1996), nos. 403, 405, 407, 413, 414, 423.

80. For references see Joan-Pau Rubiés, "New Worlds and Renaissance Ethnology," *History & Anthropology* 6 (1993): 157–97, and "Instructions for Travellers: Teaching the Eye to See," *History & Anthropology* 9 (1996): 139–90.

81. La Popelinière to Scaliger, in *Epistres françaises des personages illustres et doctes à Joseph-Juste de la Scala*, ed. Jacques de Reves (Harderwijk, 1624), 303–06; reprinted in the appendix to George Huppert, *The Idea of Perfect History: Historical Erudition and Historical Philosophy in Renaissance France* (Urbana: University of Illinois Press, 1970).

82. Gassendi, *Mirrour*, 210.

83. For the clash between the authority of books and observation, see Anthony Grafton, *New Worlds, Ancient Texts: The Power of Tradition and the Shock of Discovery* (Cambridge, Mass.: Harvard University Press, 1992).

84. Gassendi, *Mirrour*, 210.

85. *Ibid.*, 212.

86. *Ibid.*, 211.

87. "H. D." [Enrico Davila] to Querenghi, in Querenghi, *Discorsi*, 347: "Montagna: era tinto di lettere, ma non profonde; haveva quella sua maniera di scrivere, ma naturale: era finalmente più soldato che letterato. Ma V.S. che porta eruditione et lettere dal centro di tutte le scienze, che aiuta e lima la natura coll'arte, supera di gran lungo."

88. Guillaume Sohier to Querenghi, in Querenghi, *Discorsi*, 348: "Prevedeo ch'i posteri nostri considerando la conformità dell'ingegno di V.S. e di quel degno scrittore, diran un giorno: O Montagnes Querengheggia, ò Querengo Montagneggia."

89. For more on the English context, see Richard W. F. Kroll, *The Material Word: Literate Culture in the Restoration and Early Eighteenth Century* (Baltimore: Johns Hopkins University Press, 1991), ch. 3.

90. Gassendi, *Peiresc, 1580–1637: Vie de l'illustre Nicolas-Claude Fabri de Peiresc*, trans. Roger Lassalle with the collaboration of Agnès Bresson (Paris: Bélin, 1992).

91. Gassendi, *Mirrour*, A4r.

92. *Ibid.*, A4v.

93. *Ibid.*, A5r.

94. Evelyn, *Familiar Letters*, quoted in Linda Van Norden, "Peiresc and the English Scholars," *Huntington Library Quarterly* 12 (1948–49): 389.

95. Daniello Bartoli, *The Learned Man Defended and Reform'd. A Discourse of singular Politeness and Elocution; seasonably asserting the Right of the Muses; in opposition to the many Enemies which in this Age Learning meets with, and more especially those two IGNORANCE and VICE*, trans. Thomas Salusbury (London: R. and W. Leybourn, 1660), 32.

96. For this English story, see Lawrence E. Klein, *Shaftesbury and the Culture of*

Politeness: Moral Discourse and Cultural Politics in Early Eighteenth-Century England (Cambridge: Cambridge University Press, 1994).

97. This theme has stimulated some of the most provocative postwar European historiography, including Reinhart Koselleck, *Critique and Crisis: Enlightenment and the Pathogenesis of Modern Society* (Cambridge, Mass.: MIT Press, 1988); Jürgen Habermas, *The Structural Transformation of the Public Sphere* (Cambridge, Mass.: MIT Press, 1989); J. G. A. Pocock, *The Machiavellian Moment: Florentine Republican Thought and the Atlantic Republican Tradition* (Princeton: Princeton University Press, 1975); Franco Venturi, *Settecento riformatore*, 5 vols. (Turin: G. Einaudi, 1969–90); and François Furet, *Penser la révolution française* (Paris: Gallimard, 1978).

CHAPTER THREE

Life-writing in seventeenth-century England

Debora Shuger

The memoirs, diaries, epistolary collections, hagiographies, character sketches, and royal lives that constitute seventeenth-century life-writings do not, as this catchall label suggests, add up to a genre; they neither belong to a single literary genealogy nor establish an intertextual order among themselves. Treating "life-writings" as a coherent rubric thus presents difficulties. There is a natural temptation to approach them as early experiments (along the lines of Homo Erectus or Neanderthal Man) in the evolution of modern psychological portraiture, but seventeenth-century life-writings seem particularly resistant to even vaguely Freudian analyses. Typically, on the rare occasions when these texts avert to what we would consider "private" matters, the intimate revelations turn out to be "public" signifiers. In particular, sex in seventeenth-century life-writings has a curious tendency to dissolve into politics. Thus in his *The Court and Character of King James*, Anthony Weldon describes a farewell scene between the King and the Earl of Somerset:

The King hung about his neck, slabboring his cheeks; saying, for Gods sake when shall I see thee againe? On my soule, I shall neither eate, nor sleep, untill you come again; the Earl told him, on Monday (this being on the Friday,) for Gods sake, let me, said the King, shall I? shall I? Then lolled about his neck; then, for Gods sake, give thy Lady this kisse for me: in the same manner at the stayres head, at the midle of the staires, and at the stayres foot.[1]

Weldon depicts this bathetic farewell with evident disgust – not, however, because the scene reveals the King's homosexuality but because at the same time that James slobbers over Somerset, he has already decided to ruin the Earl. The point of the episode, so far as Weldon is concerned, is that it shows "how perfect the King was in the art of dissimulation."[2] the incident demonstrates the King's political duplicity, not his closeted sexuality.

A few life-writings – for example, Francis Bacon's *Henry VII* – attempt to probe their subject's hidden self, but the visage behind the mask belongs to a Tacitean master-strategist guarding "privy secrets" rather than to a subjectivity repressing primal scenes. These texts do not explore the subconscious underpinnings of identity. It may be worth noting that in Locke's account of personal identity, a "subconscious self" is impossible; for John Locke, a self is "that conscious thinking thing," a "person" or "personality" that "extends *itself* beyond present existence to what is past, only by consciousness," whereby it imputes its past actions to itself and becomes accountable for them.[3] While earlier writers do not use Locke's terminology, his identification of self-hood with the conscious subject of moral judgment (rather than the subconscious subject of psychological analysis) approximates that implicit in most seventeenth-century life-writings.

These texts characteristically maintain an obdurate silence on matters of absorbing interest to modern biographers and autobiographers, several thousand pages yielding barely a handful of phobias, fantasies, perversions, or traumas – and these often just barely visible between the lines. Conversely, early modern life-writings display an abiding interest in rhetorical performance, recording verbatim their subjects' *obiter dicta*, *bon mots*, repartee, aphorisms, epigrams, and orations. Pivotal episodes repeatedly climax in verbal confrontations. These texts, it would seem, locate the *haeceitas* – the individuating "thisness" – of a life in the spoken word rather than unspoken or unconscious depths.

John Foxe's eloquent martyrs may stand behind the seventeenth-century fascination with "sayings." But the assumption that speech manifests ethos pervades early modern rhetorical theory, especially its anti-Ciceronian and ecclesiastical branches. Late Renaissance theories of language presuppose the expressive semiotic of Politian's anti-Ciceronian manifesto – "non enim sum Cicero. Me tamen (ut opinor) exprimo";[4] or as Ben Jonson puts it, "language most shewes a man."[5] Seventeenth-century life-writings, at times, comment explicitly on this non-referential and anti-formalist semiotic shaping their own narrative practices: James Howell thus notes that language "represent[s] . . . the inward man"; Richard Baxter describes his writings as "a transcript of the heart"; in his *Life and Death of Mrs. Jane Ratcliffe*, Samuel Clarke relates how "when time, company, and occasion did invite" the saintly lady

to communicate to others the good matter which her *heart* had *indited* of God, she used her *Tongue as the pen of a ready writer* . . . And when she had that great King for the subject of her speech, she spake of him . . . with such an affectionate force, as if her soul were ready to leap out at her lips into the ears of others.[6]

To claim that language expresses ethos does not, rather obviously, imply that all speakers tell the truth but that moral character determines rhetorical praxis in the same sense that it determines all voluntary behaviors. Hence, seventeenth-century life-writings generally disallow the opposition between social persona and "that within," although they clearly differentiate between the two. But the relation of outer to inner is not that of mask to face but symptom to syndrome, for "the tongue will speake according to the passions of the heart – as a Rat running behinde a painted cloth, betrayeth her selfe."[7]

Most late Renaissance rhetorical theory regards language as an expressive medium. In the life-writings, however, verbal self-expression tends to take unexpectedly politicized and aggressive forms. The speech acts they record (except those addressed to God) seem, by and large, tactical maneuvers – strategies for holding one's own against power. The scenes of verbal contestation fall into various stereotypic patterns, often based on prior literary models: Foxe, Plutarch, Diogenes Laertius, saints' lives, etc. Of these patterns, I will discuss only two – one more characteristic of religious, the other of secular aristocratic lives.

An eloquent example of the first type forms the climax to George Carleton's 1629 *Life of Bernard Gilpin*, the "apostle to the North" during the first half of Elizabeth's reign. Gilpin, having fallen into disfavor with his corrupt bishop, is ordered to deliver a sermon in his presence – a command designed to entrap and discredit the preacher; although reluctant, Gilpin obeys the bishop's summons and preaches a fierce diatribe, explicitly charging the prelate with injustice, chicanery, and nepotism; he then waits for the axe to fall. Instead, however, the bishop invites Gilpin to his home, where he "upon a sodaine caught Mr. Gilpin by the hand, and used these words upon him: 'Father Gilpin, I acknowledge you are fitter to be bishop of Durham, then my selfe to be parson of this church of yours. I aske forgiveness for errours passed; forgive me, father'."[8] Like the early Christian narratives of Ambrose's confrontation with Theodosius in 390, or the monk Macedonius facing down the Imperial troops in 387, after the Riot of the Statues at Antioch, this episode exemplifies the *parrhesia* (bold speaking) of the holy man – a *parrhesia* that succeeds in disciplining and reforming the exorbitancies of power.

Half a century later, Samuel Clarke's *Life and Death of Mr. Ignatius Jurdaine* extols the power of lay *parrhesia*.[9] Jurdaine (1561–1640), a fiercely Puritan Norwich merchant, had gained notoriety for his zealous

endeavors to reform public morals; the *Life* thus describes his fulmina-
tions against Sabbath-breaking, his practice of interrogating hapless
passersby on the state of their souls, his attempts to whip and stock
"swearers, drunkards, unclean persons, and such like notorious
offendors."[10] But the episodes Clarke recounts with reverent circumstan-
tiality center on Jurdaine's compassion toward the poor and his defiance
of the powerful. Thus when the Norwich magistrates complain about
the cost of Jurdaine's "liberal" welfare proposal, he informs the horrified
city fathers, "rather than the poor shall want, let us sell our Gowns";[11]
the bill apparently passed, although Clarke neglects to mention whether
the aldermen had to sacrifice their civic regalia. In another episode, the
Bishop of Exeter, who had arrested "some godly persons" for holding an
illegal conventicle, also experiences Jurdaine's *parrhesia*. Hastening to
Exeter to intercede for these victims of episcopal rigor, Jurdaine confronts the prelate: "My Lord, Do you think that the Lord Jesus Christ,
when he comes to Judgement, will say concerning these, and such like
poor Christians, Take them Devil, take them, because though they
sought me by fasting and prayer, yet they did not observe every circum-
stance with so much prudence as they might have done." The bishop,
like the Norwich magistrates, recognizes the voice crying in the wilder-
ness, and, Clarke notes, drops the case.[12]

The *Life* makes it evident that most of Jurdaine's fellow townsmen did
not share his Puritan commitments. One is, therefore, surprised to discover that the citizens of Norwich chose Jurdaine for their mayor and
parliamentary representative. They selected him, Clarke explains,
because "the ordinary sort of men [i.e., non-Puritans] were convinced
of his integrity, insomuch as carnal and vicious men at a time of election of *Burgesses* for Parliament would say one to another, If you choose
any, choose *Jurdaine*, he will be right for the commenwealth [*sic*], and will
do the City service."[13] They select him, that is, precisely because he exercises *parrhesia*, speaking the truth in high places without fear or favor.

The immense moral authority of Jurdaine's *parrhesia* irradiates even
his one great fiasco. Having been elected MP, he threw his energies into
making adultery a capital crime; but "when he made a motion for the
passing of that Bill; one, or more of the Members in the House cried
out, Commit it Mr. *Jurdain*, commit it; upon which a great laughter was
occasioned." On the verge of sinking from saint to schlemiel, Jurdaine
turned and "said unto them (in a zealous manner like himself) *Do you
laugh when a man speaks for Gods honour, and glory?*" For the next few minutes
"a more than ordinary silence" prevailed in the House. In the end,

Clarke seems to find the fact that Commons never approved Jurdaine's draconian legislation less significant than its hushed recognition that a new prophet had arisen in Zion.[14]

Moreover, except in this instance, Jurdaine, like Gilpin, wields his *parrhesia* successfully. Their bold words redeem the time because those in power have given them the right to speak the truths that condemn the givers. They have been designated – interpellated, if you will – as bearers of truth, as holy men. Hence, their narratives do not simply attest to the peculiar sanctity of two individuals; they configure the exemplary relation between the prophet and the social order – a relation neither subversive nor contained, since, in these texts, the powerful authorize their own indictment, and, yet, the indictment effectually reforms abuses of power. The sinful people whom the prophet denounces nevertheless acknowledge his prophetic authority and thus submit their wills to his word. Hence these scenes of triumphant *parrhesia* form the optimistic counterpart to the Protestant martyrologies, in which bold speaking fails and, by failing, exposes the diabolic foundations of state power. The narratives of sacred *parrhesia* simultaneously validate the holy man and the political community that both authorizes him and submits to his authority.

Seventeenth-century life-writings do not, however, yield many examples of *parrhesia*. As Hythloday warned Morus and as Archbishop Grindal discovered to his cost, the authorities usually refuse to acknowledge those who lay claim to *parrhesia* as, in fact, bearers of sacred truth. By the 1590s, the attempt to exercise *parrhesia* had become a specifically Puritan trait, one that generally failed because by the sixteenth century there no longer existed any social consensus on who counts as the Lord's prophet. As Peter Brown has recently pointed out, the ancient holy man is, by definition, one "uncompromised by political attachments" – usually a monk or hermit, whose disengagement from the polis allows him to be perceived as a spokesman for sacred truth rather than an ideological faction.[15] The latter half of Richard Baxter's *Autobiography*, in contrast, narrates the impossibility of locating oneself outside the political, and, hence, the erasure of the prophet as a cultural role. As Baxter repeatedly endeavors to position himself as a "catholic" Christian defending "primitive simplicity" against ideological faction, his opponents "said we did but thereby set up another party."[16] The majority of holy men celebrated in Tudor/Stuart lives – Andrewes, Donne, Herbert, Hooker, Ferrar, Whitgift – conspicuously do not denounce the abuses of power; Walton's saintly clerics are men of "quiet and meek spirits," who

overcome "their opposers by . . . a blessed Patience and long
Suffering."[17]

Throughout the seventeenth century, however, secular life-writings pay
tribute to another type of bold speaking. Aristocratic lives in particular
give striking prominence to their subjects' epigrammatic wit. Like *parrhesia*, these pointed "sayings" function as strategies for making power
back down; but in secular texts, such agonistic orality does not bear
witness to a higher truth but manifests the speaker's tactical intelligence
and what might be called strength of character. Both Edward Herbert
and Simonds D'Ewes thus regard speech as a version of combat maneuvering. A man should speak "ingeniously or wittily," Herbert remarks, to
give his words "vigour and force," it being

a general note, that a man's wit is best showed in his answer, and his valour in
his defence; that therefore as men learn in fencing how to ward all blows and
thrusts, which are or can be made against him [*sic*], so it will be fitting to debate
and resolve beforehand what you are to say or do upon any affront given you.[18]

George Puttenham's *Arte of English Poesie* presupposes the same "rhetoric
of combat," whose "strokes and parries," as Frank Whigham remarks,
"are specific to the courtly experience per se" precisely because they
function as modes of "self-defense against aroused anger and enmity."
Like Herbert, Puttenham seems to regard rhetorical figures as a species
of weaponry: *ironia* is thus "the dry mock; *sarcasmus*, the bitter taunt;
asteismus, the merry scoff or civil jest; *micterismus*, the fleering frump; *anti-
phrasis*, the broad flout; and *charientismus*, the privy nip."[19] These are
"*quotable* actions," intended not only to score an immediate triumph but
also to be repeated anecdotally – in one's memoirs, for example – thus
enhancing the speaker's longterm reputation.[20] For "honour that is
gained and broken upon another," as Bacon shrewdly notes, "hath the
quickest reflection; like diamond cut with fascets."[21]

    In seventeenth-century life-writings, these bouts of verbal sparring
typically cluster at the moments when the demands of aristocratic
hauteur and political (usually royal) prerogative threaten to collide. Thus
Herbert relates how, when the French king Henri IV tried to pressure
the Duke of Montmorency to "donate" his castle to the crown, the
nobleman managed to retain both the castle and royal favor by responding, "'Sieur, la maison est à vous, mais que je sois le concierge'; which in
English sounds thus: 'Sir, the house is yours, but give me leave to keep it
for you'."[22]

Toward the end of his *Life*, Herbert records an episode in which he himself outmaneuvers the notoriously smooth-speaking Spanish ambassador, Count Gondomar. Hoping to disrupt Anglo-French relations, Gondomar pays a visit to Herbert, who has recently been appointed English ambassador to France; "looking merrily" upon Herbert, Gondomar announces: "I will dine with you yet; I told him, by his good favour, he should not dine with me at that time, and that when I would entertain the ambassador of so great a King as his, it should not be upon my ordinary, but that I would make him a feast worthy of so great a person." At this juncture, Herbert casually invites the gentlemen accompanying Gondomar to stroll about his kitchen, where they find "three spits full of meat," large numbers of stews, pies, poultry, tarts, and "sixteen dishes of sweetmeats, all which was but the ordinary allowance for my table." The Spaniards, suitably impressed, relay what they have seen to Gondomar, whereupon Herbert again declines to invite his visitors to dinner, claiming that such food would be unworthy of the Spanish ambassador. "Gondomar hereupon coming near me, said, he esteemed me much . . . and that he thought that an Englishman had not known how to avoid handsomely a trick put upon him under show of civility." His "blows and thrusts" having been parried, Gondomar manages a dignified retreat, promising Herbert "that I ever should find him my friend, and would do me all the good offices he could in England."[23]

Izaak Walton describes a similarly tense diplomatic episode in which Sir Henry Wotton, who had been sent as ambassador to the Imperial court to resolve the Bohemian crisis, gave an "*Italian* Lady" a valuable diamond, which the Emperor had previously bestowed on him "as a testimony of his [the Emperor's] good opinion." The Emperor, not surprisingly, interprets Wotton's act as a "high affront." Faced with the dangerous stirrings of royal wrath, Wotton responds with a bold gallantry worthy of Sir Gawain, informing the Emperor "that though he received" the jewel "with thankfulness, yet he found in himself an indisposition to be the better for any gift that came from an Enemy to his Royal Mistress the Queen of Bohemia"[24] – a response which both insinuates that the Emperor's gift was a bribe (and hence rightly refused) and somehow manages to make bestowing the jewel on an Italian lady appear a romantic gesture of homage to his King's daughter. Even clerical lives, on occasion, pay tribute to their subjects' deft management of power. Waller thus preserves Bishop Andrewes's response to an ominous royal query: James had asked Andrewes and

Neale (Bishop of Durham), "Cannot I take my subjects' money when I want it without all this formality in parliament?" To which Neale abjectly responded, "God forbid, sir, but you should . . . you are the breath of our nostrils." Andrewes, however, elegantly deflects the loaded question: "I think it lawful for you to take my brother Neale's money, because he offers it."[25]

Although seventeenth-century life-writings associate this epigrammatic dexterity primarily with aristocratic self-assertion, it shapes the negotiations of power across class lines. Howell thus recounts a wonderful episode in which "a very abusive satire" attacking King James is recited in the royal presence:

as the passages were a reading before him he often said, that if there were no more men in England the rogue should hang for it, at last being come to the conclusion, which was (after all his railing):
> "Now God preserve the King, the Queen, the peers,
> And grant the author long may wear his ears."
This pleased his majesty so well that he broke into a laughter, and said, 'By my soul, so thou shalt for me; thou are a bitter, but thou are a witty knave.'[26]

At the other end of the social hierarchy, Thomas Fuller's character of Elizabeth consists mostly of scenes exemplifying the Queen's consummate tactical wit in diplomatic negotiations: her ability, for instance, to outface the Spanish ambassador, who had delivered his master's insulting demands in Latin hexameters, by responding, in the same learned tongue, with an apt and extempore monostich.[27]

The point, presumably, of these verbal fencing matches is that the speakers successfully hold their own, obtaining their ends without having to stoop to what Puttenham terms "prince-pleasing." Their epigrammatic wit allows a resistance to authority that does not, in turn, ruffle royal feathers – a real and ever present danger. Untempered by wit, aristocratic freedom of speech could have disastrous consequences. The Lord Deputy of Ireland, Sir John Perrot, an old soldier of signal "courage and height of spirit," lost his life for what Sir Robert Naunton calls "exorbitancies of the tongue" – in particular, his more blunt than witty comment on Elizabeth's reaction to a threatened Spanish invasion: "Lo, now she is ready to bepiss herself for fear."[28]

While not all tactical "sayings" contest royal authority, they always deflect an equal or superior power, as in Elizabeth's discomfiture of the Spanish King's emissary. The elegance and wit of these "sayings" acquire strategic value in such perilous contestations because the display of rhetorical skill allows the challenge to authority to be read as evidence of the speaker's courage, intelligence, and grace under fire. That is, the formal excellence of the speech ambiguates the nature of the speech act; simultaneously political critique and self-expression, the saying licenses the former by drawing attention to the latter.

Tactical "sayings" bear witness to a cultural ideal of self-hood in which resistance to authority signifies ethos and conversely ethos operates as a political praxis. Their rhetorical mode is characteristic of late Renaissance Senecanism, whose pregnant laconisms and epigrammatic point were understood to signify their user's moral and intellectual independence, marking him as an *auguste esprit* incapable of servile flattery or docile subjection.[29] Discussing "the wisdom of conversation" in *The Advancement of Learning*, Bacon thus maintains that "the sum of behaviour is to retain a man's own dignity, without intruding upon the liberty of others," but above all, a man "must take heed he not shew himself dismantled, and exposed to scorn and injury, by too much dulceness, goodness, and facility of nature, but shew some sparkles of liberty, spirit, and edge: which kind of fortified carriage, with a ready rescuing of a man's self from scorns . . . doth greatly add to reputation."[30] The Senecanism championed by Bacon, Lipsius, and their followers thus encodes a particular type of ethos inseparable from its political edge, since the *auguste esprit*, by definition, defends his autonomy, honor, and integrity against the "injury or insolence" of power.[31]

The name seventeenth-century life-writings give to this cultural ideal is most informative; in text after text, the term designating moral worth is "magnanimity" or its variants: "height of spirit," "greatness of heart," "noble spirit," "noble mind," "native majesty," "naturall greatness," "bravery of spirit."[32] Magnanimity (*megalopsychia*) is, of course, the preeminent Aristotelian virtue, although one that no longer exists; most modern English editions of the *Nicomachean Ethics* thus translate *megalopsychia* as "pride," apparently confusing this foremost classical virtue with the chief deadly sin.

The confusion is understandable since Aristotle's magnanimous man is one who not only merits but lays claim to "great things," above all, "honor . . . the greatest of external goods." This deep and deserved sense of personal worth produces a distinctive political bearing, it being the mark of the magnanimous man

to be dignified towards people who enjoy high position and good fortune . . . He must also be open in his hate and in his love (for to conceal one's feelings is a mark of timidity), and must care more for truth than for what people will think, and must speak and act openly; for he is free of speech because he is contemptuous, and he is given to telling the truth, except when he speaks in irony to the vulgar.[33]

Early modern life-writings record scene after scene of verbal sparring because the defining virtues of the magnanimous man – openness, courage, and personal dignity – are modes of self-assertion; in this profoundly aristocratic system of value, the ability to hold one's own against power by polishing a challenge into an aphorism gives luminous proof of "naturall greatness," unflinching self-expression being the key index of a free and august spirit.

If sayings imply political resistance – that is, resistance to the encroachments of power – they need not connote principled ideological opposition (which, however, does not mean they are merely self-promotional "sound bites"). Seventeenth-century life-writings represent the verbal *rencontres* of early modern public life because they exhibit a man's worth.[34] They do not, of course, constitute the only cultural measure of worth; spiritual autobiographies like John Bunyan's *Grace Abounding* lack both sayings and the ethics of magnanimity that gives them meaning. Yet, although at least since Nietzsche, this ancient aristocratic morality has been regarded as fundamentally unchristian, it remained the dominant paradigm of ideal male self-hood through the seventeenth century, central not only to secular texts like Naunton's *Fragmenta regalia* or Edward Herbert's *Autobiography* but to Lucy Hutchinson's deeply religious memoir of her husband, Colonel John Hutchinson – a Parliamentary officer, regicide, Anabaptist, and Leveller.

Hutchinson's account of the life and martyrdom of this revolutionary *miles Christianus* operates within an explicitly aristocratic and Aristotelian system of value; if she pays homage to the Colonel's "resignation and submission to God," she also celebrates his "heroique glorie," "greate heart," and "noble spiritt of government."[35] The character sketch with which the *Memoirs* open dwells with love and awe on the Colonel's classical virtues. His "amiable countenance" thus

carried in it something of magnanimity and majesty mixt with sweetenesse . . . Greatnesse of courage would not suffer him to put on a vizard to secure him from any . . . Nor was his soule lesse shining in honor than in love . . . [hence] he never regarded his life in any noble and just enterprize . . . I cannot say whether he were more truly magnanimous or lesse proud; he never disdain'd the meanest person nor flattr'd the greatest . . . [but] ever preserv'd himselfe in his owne rank, neither being proud of it so as to despise any inferior, nor letting fall that just decorum which his honor oblieg'd him to keepe up.[36]

The only time Colonel Hutchinson loses his temper occurs when, having been arrested shortly after the Restoration, his jailer "behav'd himselfe most insolently; whereupon the Collonell snatcht up a candlestick and lay'd him over the chaps with it," demanding to be treated as a "gentleman."[37] Such passionate assertion of gentility involves something more than pride of rank; to lay claim to honorable treatment, to maintain one's "noble spiritt" against the injustices and usurpations of power are moral virtues. In the *Memoirs*, "gentle" and "noble" still designate real intrinsic goods. For making sense of such an episode, Kant seems less helpful than the *Iliad*. It is easy enough to dismiss this aristocratic ethic as a mystified class ideology, more difficult (and more illuminating) to grasp its moral seriousness – to grasp the extent to which the *auguste esprit* of Achilles and Aristotle's magnanimous man (rather than anything we would consider "political" commitments) shapes the Hutchinsons' republicanism, their demand for religious and political liberty, their lofty integrity amid the Interregnum's frenzied power struggles and the vengeful persecutions of the Restoration.[38]

All this seems rather remote from our original topic, but tactical "sayings" are the outward and audible form of this intrinsically politicized ethic, which, like all premodern ethics, defines an ideal of moral self-hood (ethos) rather than a criterion of right action. In premodern cultures, politics, ethics, self-hood, language, masculinity, and class typically constitute overlapping and intertwined categories, which is why seventeenth-century life-writings depict "self-hood" as a political, moral, gendered, and ranked rhetorical performance. Both *parrhesia* and "sayings" – both, that is, the assertion of transcendent truth and the assertion of one's own dignity – presuppose the intimate conjunction of rhetorical performance and self-hood whereby agonistic orality comes to signify moral/spiritual eminence. The majority of seventeenth-century life-writings (except conversion narratives) operate in terms of a cultural paradigm that basically requires resistance to power by making bold speech signify moral worth.[39]

One final point seems worth making, albeit briefly. If seventeenth-century life-writings ascribe an ancient heroic sense of self to men of deep (or at least orthodox) piety, they *never* use this classical discourse to delineate their subjects' devotional life. The representations of spiritual communion draw on a different system of values and adumbrate a different figuration of ideal self-hood. In the presence of God, noble spirits become meek, passive, obedient, and lowly; in Puritan life-writings, times set aside for religious observance are called "days of humiliation."[40] But humility – like obedience, meekness, and passivity – is neither a classical nor aristocratic virtue. Aristotle's magnanimous man does not undertake days of humiliation.

Early modern life-writings maintain a strict partition between the forum in which men strut, shove, and butt horns, and the closet in which they kneel to beg forgiveness of their sins. Significantly, the usual seventeenth-century term for speech addressed to God is "soliloquy." In such contexts, the word clearly does not have the modern sense of "speaking to one's self" but rather means "speaking to God as opposed to other persons" – a usage that marks the contrast between social and supernatural, outward and inner, domains as the basic polarity organizing early modern representations of self-hood. This contrast structures seventeenth-century English life-writings; in particular, it governs their portrayal of speech acts, dividing and distinguishing language as social performance from the voice of the soul, the rhetoric of "sayings" from soliloquy.

Almost the only human relationship depicted as capable of being suffused by an intense piety is the bond between husband and wife. So Simonds D'Ewes and his bride, like Milton's unfallen pair, retire together to watch and pray.[41] So, too, as Colonel Hutchinson gropes toward the veiled millenarian subtext of Saint Paul's Epistle to the Romans during his final terrible weeks imprisoned in the damp cold of a ruinous castle, he bursts out, "I have . . . discover'd much more of the mistery of truth in that Epistle, and when my wife returns I will make her set it downe . . . I w'll have her in my chamber with me, and they shall not pluck her out of my armes."[42]

If, outside these domestic spaces, social and spiritual domains are incommensurate, they are not incompatible. Most life-writings (although not all) slip back and forth between classical and Christian moral frames; their subjects struggle to submit in patient humility to God's will while proudly asserting their "noble spiritt of government" in public life. These texts thus reproduce the dominant early modern conceptualization of the self as what William Perkins calls "a double person":

Every person is a double person and under two regiments. In the first regiment I am a person of mine own self, under Christ . . . [and must] humble myself, forsake and deny myself . . . In the temporal regiment, thou art a person in respect of another. Thou art husband, father . . . wife, lord, subject and there thou must do according to thine office. If thou be a father, thou must do the office of a father and rule.[43]

Perkins's division of a person of one's own self and a person in respect of another, with their respective humility and "spiritt of government," closely corresponds to that implicit in the life-writings between Christian inwardness and classical ethos.

To the extent that this configuration shapes early modern identity, it is by no means clear that the revolutionary upheavals of the mid-seventeenth century had much to do with either the emergence or transformation of "an interior subject."[44] In most early modern life-writings, inwardness remains largely devotional, untouched by the possessive individualism of the bourgeoisie. Before the end of the seventeenth century, English does not even have a word for the secular equivalents of "soul," "conscience," "heart," "inward man," "spirit"; and "soliloquy" still only refers to private devotional utterance.[45]

Yet insofar as the public verbal performances that signify a man's worth involve resistance to power, the political history of the subject, at least in early modern England, would seem to center on ethos rather than inwardness. Recent attempts to correlate subject-formation with radical politics have argued that a newly emergent sense of one's "inner reality" – as distinct from the inauthentic shows and seemings of public life – was what enabled detachment from and opposition to "the body politic which is the king's body."[46] But this separation of individual/inward from social/exterior seems strangely absent from the episodes of revolutionary or protorevolutionary contestation narrated in the life-writings. These episodes, like so many others, associate resistance with verbal courage and moral character; the "self" that matters, politically speaking, is public, rhetorical, ethical, and social.

Thus, in his "secret meditation," Jurdaine experiences a divine "sweetness" and "ravishings of spirit," yet when this pious merchant finds himself

summoned to appear in the *Star-chamber*, for an act of Justice, wherein it was supposed that he went somewhat beyond the strict letter of the Law, being there in the presence of some of his Judges, who were Noble men, and hearing them to swear divers Oaths, he told them, that they must pay for every oath that they had sworn, or otherwise he would make it farther known.[47]

This episode, charged with intimations of rebellions to come, most emphatically does not register a split between inner reality and social exterior. If Jurdaine has something within him that "passeth show," it is irrelevant. The narrative assumes that a person's public bearing and utterances disclose who he is – that Jurdaine's insubordinate *parrhesia* manifests his revolutionary ethos.

John Aubrey's biographical sketch of the regicide and republican Henry Martin focuses almost exclusively on his strategic *bon mots*. He had, Aubrey thus remarks,

an incomparable Witt for Repartes . . . His speeches in the House were not long, but wondrous poynant, pertinent, and witty . . . He alone haz sometimes turned the whole House . . . Oliver Cromwell once in the House called him, jestingly or scoffingly, Sir Harry Martin. H. M. rises and bowes; I thanke your *Majestie.* I always thought when you were a *King* I should be Knighted.[48]

It seems easy enough to discern the relation between this republican portrait and the classical/aristocratic paradigm that structures the majority of early modern secular life-writings, where what matters is not subjectivity but outspokenness, not "inner reality" but the public display of verbal (and, where necessary, physical) courage. Seventeenth-century life-writings do not represent social personae as limbs of the royal body but as self-poised noble spirits, careful of their honor and independence – which is why Civil War radicals like Martin, Hutchinson, and Milton betray startlingly aristocratic values. It is less Hamlet's habit of thinking out loud than his aristocratic disdain for servile courtiers, his resistance to royal injustice, and his fencing skills (both verbal and physical) that link his tragedy to the socio-political revolutions of the seventeenth century.

NOTES

1. A[nthony] W[eldon], *The Court and Character of King James* (London, 1651), 95.
2. *Ibid.*, 94.
3. John Locke, *An Essay Concerning Human Understanding*, ed. John Yolton, 2 vols. (London: Dent, 1965), II:27; 1:286, 291.
4. Politian [Angelo Ambrogini], *Politiani epistolae* (Amsterdam, 1642), 307, quoted in Rudolf Pfeiffer, *History of Classical Scholarship from 1300 to 1850* (Oxford: Clarendon Press, 1976), 43.
5. Ben Jonson, *Discoveries*, ed. Maurice Castelain (Paris: Libraire Hachette, 1906), 104; cf. Thomas Wright, *The Passions of the Minde in Generall* (1604), ed. Thomas Sloan (Urbana: University of Illinois Press, 1971), 105–06.
6. James Howell, *Familiar Letters or Epistolae Hoelianae*, 3 vols. (London: Dent, 1903), 1:254; Richard Baxter, *The Autobiography of Richard Baxter, Being the "Reliquiae Baxterianae" Abridged from the Folio (1696)*, ed. J. M. Lloyd Thomas (London: Dent, 1925), 95; Sa[muel] Clarke, *A Collection of the Lives of Ten Eminent Divines* (London: n. p., 1662), 427.
7. Wright, *Passions*, 78.
8. George Carleton, *The Life of Mr. Bernard Gilpin* (1629), vol. III of *Ecclesiastical Biography; or, Lives of Eminent Men, Connected with the History of Religion in England*, ed. Christopher Wordsworth, 3rd edn. (London: J. G. & F. Rivington, 1839), 428–30.
9. Clarke's account of Jurdaine reprints Ferdinand Nicholls's *The Life and Death of Mr. Ignatius Jurdain, One of the Aldermen of the City of Exeter* (1654) with only minor changes.
10. Clarke, *Jurdaine*, 464.

11. *Ibid.*, 483.
12. *Ibid.*, 485.
13. *Ibid.*, 484.
14. *Ibid.*, 477.
15. Peter Brown, *Power and Persuasion in Late Antiquity: Towards a Christian Empire* (Madison: University of Wisconsin Press, 1992), 62.
16. Baxter, *Autobiography*, 90–91.
17. Izaak Walton, *The Lives*, ed. George Saintsbury (London: Oxford University Press, n. d.), 46.
18. Edward Herbert, *The Autobiography of Edward, Lord Herbert of Cherbury*, ed. Sidney Lee, 2nd edn. (London: Routledge, 1906), 35–36; cf. Simonds D'Ewes, *The Autobiography and Correspondence*, 2 vols., ed. James Orchard Halliwell (London: n. p., 1845), 1:103.
19. Frank Whigham, *Ambition and Privilege: The Social Tropes of Elizabethan Courtesy Theory* (Berkeley: University of California Press, 1984), 139, 142.
20. *Ibid.*, 142.
21. Francis Bacon, *The Works of Francis Bacon*, 10 vols. (London: n. p., 1826), II:368.
22. Herbert, *Autobiography*, 55.
23. *Ibid.*, 127.
24. Walton, *Lives*, 125–26.
25. This anecdote can be found under "Lancelot Andrewes" in *The Dictionary of National Biography*.
26. Howell, *Familiar Letters*, 1:88–89.
27. Thomas Fuller, *Selections*, ed. E. K. Broadus (Oxford: Clarendon, 1928), 67.
28. Sir Robert Naunton, *Fragmenta Regalia, or, Observations on Queen Elizabeth, Her Times & Favorites*, ed. John Cerovski (Washington: The Folger Shakespeare Library, 1985), 67.
29. Marc Fumaroli, *L'Age de l'éloquence: Rhétorique et "res literaria" de la Renaissance au seuil de l'époque classique* (Geneva: Droz, 1980), 59–60, 90, 155–57.
30. Bacon, *Works*, 1:187, 203–04.
31. *Ibid.*, 203.
32. See, for example, Naunton, *Fragmenta*, 62, 65, 67, 79; Weldon, *King James*, 53, 110, 170; Lucy Hutchinson, *Memoirs of the Life of Colonel Hutchinson*, ed. James Sutherland (London: Oxford University Press, 1973), 3, 8, 11–12; *The Overburian Characters*, ed. W. J. Paylor, Percy Reprints 13 (Oxford: Blackwell, 1936), 13–14.
33. Aristotle, *Nicomachean Ethics* 4.3.1123b1–1125a34, trans. W. D. Ross, rev. J. O. Urmson, in *The Complete Works of Aristotle: The Revised Oxford Translation*, ed. Jonathan Barnes, 2 vols., Bollingen Series 71 (Princeton: Princeton University Press, 1984), II:1773–75.
34. Given this intimate link between agonistic orality and masculine ethos, it seems likely that the perceived aggressiveness of language, rather than (or along with) its sexual charge, lies behind early modern (and ancient) injunctions against female speech.

35. Hutchinson, *Memoirs*, 6, 8, 12.
36. *Ibid.*, 3–11.
37. *Ibid.*, 245.
38. The unwillingness to see this aristocratic system of values as anything more than mystifications of the *libido dominandi* seems to me the one serious weakness of Whigham's *Ambition and Privilege*.
39. These texts leave one with the distinct sense that the massive Tudor/Stuart campaign to inculcate the political virtues of obedience, submission, and childlike trust was not an overwhelming success.
40. D'Ewes, *Autobiography*, 1:353, 363.
41. *Ibid.*, 1:363.
42. Hutchinson, *Memoirs*, 270.
43. William Perkins, "A Dialogue of the State of a Christian Man," in *The Work of William Perkins*, ed. Ian Breward (Appleford, England: The Courtenay Library of Reformation Classics, 1970), 382.
44. Francis Barker, *The Tremulous Private Body: Essays on Subjection* (London: Methuen, 1984), 36.
45. According to the *Oxford English Dictionary*, Hamlet's speeches were not called soliloquies until 1873; the earliest use of "soliloquy" in its modern secular/theatrical sense occurs in Vanbrugh's *A Short Vindication*, published in 1698. See Raymond Williams, *Writing in Society* (London: Verso, 1983), 41.
46. See Barker, *Tremulous*, 31–36, 41; Catherine Belsey, *The Subject of Tragedy* (London: Methuen, 1985), 18, 33–35, 42. David Aers offers a devastating critique of this argument in his "A Whisper in the Ear of Early Modernists; or, Reflections on Literary Critics Writing the 'History of the Subject'," in *Culture and History, 1350–1600: Essays on English Communities, Identities and Writing*, ed. David Aers (Detroit: Wayne State University Press, 1992), 177–202.
47. Clarke, *Jurdaine*, 450, 457, 467.
48. John Aubrey, *Aubrey's Brief Lives*, ed. Oliver Lawson Dick, 3rd edn. (London: Secker and Warburg, 1958), 194.

CHAPTER FOUR

Representations of intimacy in the life-writing of Anne Clifford and Anne Dormer

Mary O'Connor

Anne Bradstreet's poem, "Upon the Burning of Our House July 10th, 1666," articulates a tension between the love of intimate material things and the love of God.[1] The burning of her house and all its contents gives her a metaphorical language for imagining a heavenly "wealth" and "Treasure," a house "Fram'd by that mighty Architect," while simultaneously meditating on the complex intimate values of domestic objects and places. The process of the poem is disciplinary, detaching oneself from and then shedding those material things one finds most precious:

> When by the Ruines oft I past
> My sorrowing eyes aside did cast
> And here and there ye places spye
> Where oft I sate and long did lye,
> Here stood that Trunk, and there ye chest
> There lay that store I covnted best
> My pleasant things in ashes lye
> And them behold no more shall I.
> Vnder thy roof no gvest shall sitt,
> Nor at thy Table eat a bitt.
> No pleasant tale shall 'ere be told
> Nor things recovnted done of old.
> No Candle 'ere shall shine in Thee
> Nor bridegroom's voice ere heard shall bee.
> In silence ever shall thou lye
> Adeiu, Adeiu, All's Vanity.[2]

At least one image here is produced from a sequence in the biblical Book of Revelation heralding the end of the world.[3] Nevertheless, Bradstreet's poem is exceptional for its evocation of the complexity of a woman's relation to her objects and her home. We are not dealing with a simplistic concept of consumerism or any notion of acquisitions for the sake of status. As she describes the intimate objects that have been lost, she inscribes a broader cultural practice that is the basis of social relations.

She reconstitutes her life in its specific relation to places and objects that defined her: "Where oft I sate and long did lye." The trunk and chest are placed "here" and "there" in the present, though they are no more than ashes. What is particularly lost is a set of social relations known and produced through the objects in this domestic space: the roof produces guests, and the table produces communal meals and culture, the passing on of stories and memories from generation to generation. The candle produces a bridegroom's voice.

These observations lead us directly to the subject of this chapter, an inquiry into the relation of seventeenth-century women to domestic objects and an examination of the manner in which women represent that relation. A great deal has been said about women being made into objects or about women and their consumption of commodities, but equally significant is the fact that women choose objects to be indicative of, or constitutive of, their identity. These objects are central to the activities of everyday life and the so-called private life; yet objects such as brewing vessels and spinning wheels, as well as fashionable bonnets and good linen, offer points of intersection between women and the economic and social forces that surround them. They situate women as consumers or producers within a larger economic and cultural system. Through their activities in the home, women are both producers of new and reproducers of existing social relations.[4] By analyzing women's responses to these self-constituting objects in their diaries, letters, wills, and account books, we can chart women's own agency within that system.

One particular form of deep attachment to domestic objects that may point to women's agency warrants attention. A modern-day example might be the relation to a special coffee mug or a tea cup in a woman's life – how that may stand for a refuge from service or abuse, or for some unalienated social relation. In a day that is filled with service to others, use of this object carves out a time and practice of one's own. The object itself takes on the meaning or attachment of that state, perhaps defined as peace, perhaps safety, perhaps re[-]creation, perhaps friendship. It may be linked to rest or to socializing, to a moment of understanding or laughter. These are intimate moments with oneself or another. That intimacy can, on the one hand, be a product of certain discursive practices (e.g., regulated time off within larger disciplinary confines), or it can be outside of and a critique of the practices and discourses demanded of women by their public or institutional function in the family. The object itself may eventually stand in for the experience. To look at it, to touch

it, or to remember it, may suffice in re-presenting the pleasure and resistance of the experience, or it may evoke a pained nostalgia for that space
and time.

The purpose of my inquiry is not to individualize or psychologize the
situation. The object exists within the larger system of production and
consumption, and the woman must be situated in the context of the
social relations available to her in the economic and social conditions of
her world. Women's personal attachments to objects are thus historical
and their representations of those attachments are both revealed and
constrained by the system of practices and range of critique available to
them.

Examining notions of intimacy presents problems for the modern
student of seventeenth-century women. Our documents and other
sources are limited and embedded in their own historical moment. Our
overlay of nineteenth-century notions of the separation between public
and private spheres prevents us from seeing the specificity of early
modern configurations of the private or public. Such critics as Patricia
Fumerton, Susan Dwyer Amussen, and David Cressy have pointed out
that the public/private dichotomy is actually misleading for any study of
early modern history:

> However much we may need to define the concepts as separate (or envision a
> culture *all* one or the other), "private" and "public" can only be conceived as a
> split unity divided along a constantly resewn seam that can never be wholly
> closed or absolutely parted. The history of subjectivity is the history of delicate
> shiftings between changing conceptions of private and public self.[5]

Perhaps the categories of public and private are too laden with prejudg-
ment. A shift to the category of intimacy should, with subtlety, allow us
more accurate perceptions of the complexity of early modern experience.

The intimate moments to which this chapter points will be constructed as private, but they are by no means unconnected to the public
realm. In fact, this chapter attempts to complicate the categories of
public and private, rendering a mere polarization of the two obsolete.
What *is* an intimate moment in the lives of seventeenth-century women
and in relation to what objects do women represent these moments?
How will we read the admission that a woman turns to drinking chocolate (if not coffee in a special mug) for consolation?

> I then divert my self with my two sweete children think of all my kind friends,
> and take a dish of chocalate, which I find the greatest cordiall and reviveing in
> the world . . .[6]

The diversionary acts of drinking chocolate and writing about it in a
letter are, for Anne Dormer, politically as well as psychologically motivated. Dormer's nervous condition, as we shall see, is produced out of
anxiety at her husband's abuse within the home and without. This
excerpt suggests that the concept of intimacy, commonly limited to
sexual intimacy, must be broadened to include a variety of possible relations – with friends, husband, lover, and even oneself. Dormer's
"think[ing] of all my kind friends" constructs an imaginary space of intimacy, secret and safe from her husband, an intimacy that counteracts
the "private" space of her husband's abuse. It constructs another voice
or series of dialogic voices to help her speak back to her husband. This
process is fully realized in the multiple voices she ventriloquizes in her
letters: hers, her husband's, her friends', her sister's. Dormer's diversionary practices, both with objects in the home and with her own version
of life-writing, in fact, as we shall see, offer political critique.

The diversionary possibilities of intimate objects, creature comforts,
and imagined or real protected spaces could be problematic for women
of the seventeenth century since they conflicted, it was believed, with a
properly spiritual life. Fundamental to one's salvation would be the
desire, as Mary Hurll put it, to be "wean'd from the things of Time."[7]
Women's religious diaries of this period reveal a constant struggle
against material things.[8] We have seen one solution to this tension in
Anne Bradstreet's *vanitas* poem with which this chapter opened. Another
solution was to transform a private space – a woman's closet – into a protected place of private devotions. That space of intimate prayer proved
both enjoyable and resistant to outside forces. Elizabeth Bury's diary
figures her private relation with God, often, as a retreat into the private
space of her closet for "secret prayer." On 18 October 1695 she writes:
"This Morning my Chamber has been sweeter to me, than a Thousand
elsewhere"; and on 9 March 1697, "The Lord drew near, and taught me
to Pray, and heard my Prayer, and made my Chamber his Presence-
Chamber."[9] With punning delight, Bury transforms her intimate domestic space into the semi-private chambers of the court where she is
allowed an audience with her King. By contrast, when neighbors invade
her space for communal secular visits, she is perturbed in being taken
away from Christ's sacred communion or "Table."[10]

The extensive documents left by two seventeenth-century women,
Anne Clifford and Anne Dormer, offer material for a complex discus-
sion of the relation between life-writing and domestic space and objects.
Clifford wrote from 1600 to 1676; Dormer from 1685 to 1691. The first

chose a number of genres in which to write out her own life and the lives of her family: diaries, account books, chronicles, letters. The second left a series of letters to her sister, Lady Elizabeth Trumbull, who was living in Paris and Constantinople during the time.

When Anne Clifford was ten years old, she purchased two notebooks, one for her catechism and one for her accounts.[11] As I have argued elsewhere, the account book suggests a remarkable strategy or technology for producing a certain kind of subjectivity in a child; it also offers interesting details about the material culture of a wealthy aristocratic child of 1600.[12] Anne constructs her identity in terms of objects – a looking glass, an ivory box in which to put a picture, an hour glass, shoes of Spanish leather – as well as in terms of services – tips to the man who found her miniature – and their monetary equivalents.[13] Coupled with the evidence of the later account books and diaries, the evidence of this youthful notebook strongly suggests the child saw herself as an accountable aristocrat. Her writing is a public document making her responsible for her expenditures while simultaneously inscribing her as private owner of these possessions. That is, we are witnessing the young girl in the act of constructing herself and knowing herself as an aristocrat in the world through a series of objects. What is interesting about the notebook is that it includes, in a more eclectic than selective way, a series of objects for which money has been paid. The self-representation here is of one who makes transactions: an economic subject, not just a cultural one.

When Anne turns to the diary form during her marriage, noting events, thoughts, movements, and objects, she is also taking up a regulating practice. She charts her relations with the court and her husband, along with seemingly trivial details of her domestic activities such as sewing. The diary also offers cryptic moments of intimacy. Anne's absence from the court often produces her most personal writing, referring frequently to being alone at home, doing needlework or reading. Does a description of sitting quietly sewing while her husband reads beside her constitute a moment of intimacy: "Upon the 28th [August 1616] we made an end of Dressing the House in the Forenoon, & in the Afternoon I wrought [Irish] Stitch Work and my Lord sat and read by me"?[14] And do we read the account of games on the lawn followed by her husband's coming to sleep with her as representations of intimate scenes: "After Supper we played at Burley Break upon the Green. This night my Lord came to lie in my Chamber"?[15]

It is far from clear what these scenes represent about the intimacy between husband and wife. The diary entries offer intimate moments of

Anne's response to her husband, to Knole, its rooms, and the activities in which she engages while there. There are references to where she slept, whether Richard slept with her in her chamber or not, whether they had had a fight and slept separately. Anne confides to her mother on 25 November 1615 that her husband is both commendable and is "as violent as is possible . . . I have lived in fear and terror daily."[16] The principal dispute between Anne and her husband was over Anne's legal battles to secure an inheritance. George Clifford, Earl of Cumberland, left all his lands to his male cousin rather than to Anne, his only surviving child. Anne and her mother sued for a reversal of the inheritance, claiming that an early deed entitled the heir, whether male or female, to the land. Anne's husband, Richard Sackville, Earl of Dorset, was interested in her renouncing the suit and settling for money since he would then have it to spend. Anne gives accounts of being pressured by the King, the Archbishop, and many others, including her husband, to give up her suit. The Knole diaries recount the long battle Anne waged. The battle had its public dimensions, but it also affected the quality of Anne's domestic life. Her husband banished her from public life, canceled her jointure house, and took their young child away from her for a period of time. In the end, though she never won the suit, she outlived all male heirs and, in 1634, finally inherited all her father's lands.[17]

Clifford's material conditions – her status as only heir to one of the largest estates in the land, her subsequent disinheritance, and her mother's suit on her behalf – produced a subjectivity that knew itself primarily but not exclusively as an agent in history.[18] Whether as the accountable ten-year-old aristocrat or the mature writer of family chronicles, Anne knows herself as a Clifford. Noting whether Sackville slept with her or not may have been motivated by her sense of herself as a Clifford and a Sackville, that is, as the possible producer of an heir and as the suitable, active wife of the Earl of Dorset.[19] Katherine Acheson points out that Clifford seems to have known when she was fertile and that she noted whether or not her husband slept with her on those nights.[20] It is possible that the scene of husband and wife sitting together, he reading and she sewing, is a public tableau of aristocratic union. As such the scene would go beyond any extant Renaissance and Jacobean portraits, for they do not include such homely details as the "Irish Stitch" so lovingly reported by Anne.

Anne's narrative in the diary encodes sitting silently and alone with sewing and reading as indicative of her troubles at the court and with her husband. As a gendered activity, sewing also provides a challenge to her skills in embroidering. She notes when she starts an embroidery project and when she finishes it. She had long been interested in and good at needlework, as all aristocratic women were supposed to be at the time. The portrait representing her at the age of fifteen shows silk threads of many colors.[21] Her account book kept at ten years of age shows she acquired silkworms and slea silk.[22] Her Irish stitch also, at times, reminds her of friends and intimacies, for example someone with whom she started the project at an earlier time. Yet Anne's Irish stitch functions in the diary not only as a reference to the everyday, or to gendered domestic activity; it comes to act almost as a trope, a synecdoche, for her sadness and her troubles:

(1616)
November.
Upon the 4th I sat in the Drawing Chamber all the day at my work.
    Upon the 9th I sat at my Work & heard Rivers and Marsh read Montaigne's *Essays*, which Book they have read almost this fortnight.
    Upon the 12th I made an end of my cushion of Irish Stitch[23] which my Coz. C. Neville began when she went with me to the Bath, it being my chief help to pass away the time to work . . .[24]
(1617)
June.
    The 30th still working and being extremely melancholy & sad to see things go so ill with me, & fearing my Lord would give all his land away from the Child.
July.
The 1st. Still working & sad.[25]

The diary entry of 28 August 1616 occurs in the midst of Anne's mourning for her mother. She and her husband are in the North, at one of her father's former castles (her mother's jointure house in which she died). After her mother's death, there is a short reconciliation between Anne and her husband, since she hands over her inheritance claims to him in return for his promise to provide for their child. The diary entry, then, has Anne settling into a castle that does not, at this point, belong to her. She and her husband have "dressed the house," have settled in, taking her mother's and father's place. They are hoping that possession will, in the eyes of the law, translate into legal ownership. The diary entry documents, or notes, not only that they have positioned themselves in the castle but also that they have comfortably, domestically placed themselves "at home." I am not trying to paint Anne Clifford and the third Earl of Dorset with prototypical bourgeois subjectivities, but I am trying to find the interdependence that makes these acts simultaneously intimate and public. I am trying to articulate the complexity of this moment and of its notation in a diary. How did she experience this moment and how does she represent it for herself and others?

    As a "notation" of the event, the process of life-writing is the process of placing or positioning a life in a system of meaning and equivalents (as in musical or mathematical notation). The signifying subject, here, presents itself as a part of both a domestic scene – husband and wife in conjugal activity, the act of dressing the house, and the congruent, gendered activity of reading and sewing "by" each other's side – and a public scene, "at home" in the publicly disputed property of the barony. The 28 August 1616 entry appears as a momentary relief from the usual juncture of isolation and needlework. Anne's accomplishment is to place her gendered work on public display as integrated into her court disputes. Intimacy here entails both bringing your Lord into the realm or sphere of influence of homely activity and placing that domestic activity within a larger public sphere. Furthermore, the keeping of a diary, the process of registering events, places multivalent moments into a public – that is, potentially meaningful – configuration. This entry in her diary is at one and the same time a record of an intimate moment with her husband and a public display of power and right.

The 1616 diary begins: "Upon New Year's Day I kept to my chamber all day, my Lady Rich and my Sister Sackville supping with me, but my Lord and all the Company at Dorset House went to see the Mask at the Court."[26] This private space of her chamber is produced as it were by her husband's distancing himself. What Anne does with this space is write about it, in the process mapping out a new identity that transcends that of a publicly active member of court. This early diary is engaged with both the expression of confidences – the disappointments, pain, and secrets she might share with a friend – and with a process of monumentalizing her experiences. She *writes about* her life, claiming it as history, making it into history. Ultimately, her technique will be to write out her activities and her rooms as history; the diary itself becomes a part of a larger history or set of chronicles that reinforce her claim to the northern lands and her Clifford lineage.[27]

As time passes, Anne's relation to things has more and more to do with her sense of herself as a Clifford, with her sense of history and where she fits into a lineage that must be continued, remembered, and written. Rooms, that is, spaces within her properties, hold memories of relatives and important events in their lives (or deaths) and, what is more, Clifford insists on writing out not only these memories but also her commemorative visits to these rooms. The process becomes a *mise en abyme* of writing/being history. In the meantime, the objects she encounters are often gifts that fit into an aristocratic economy: family, friendship, and court relations solidified, or clothes her child wears for the first time – a sort of ritual passage into aristocratic stages of life.

When, in later years, she turns to writing or adding further notes to earlier texts, Clifford monumentalizes the events.[28] This sculpting of events and space lifts them out of time at the same moment that it attempts to place them in time, that is, in history. Notice how multiple scenes from family and history are grafted on to any one event:

> Upon the 24th, being Friday, between the hours of 6 and 9 at night died my dear Mother at Brougham, in the same Chamber where my father was born, 13 years and 2 months after the death of Queen Elizabeth and ten years and 7 months after the death of my Father. I being 26 years and five months, and the Child 2 years wanting a month.[29]

This monumentalizing tendency becomes more strident in later diaries or chronicles. Once she gains her lands, she moves from one property to another, making her presence felt and tending to her various castles. The chronicling of these movements, one might argue, is itself a performative act that makes the lands hers, stamping her seal on to them:

> And the same 30th July [1673] being Wednesday in the forenoon, after I had layen in Brougham Castle in Westmerland in ye chamber wherein my Noble father was born and my Blessed Mother dyed, for about half a yeare, viz: ever since ye 28th of January last, did I goe for a while out of it into the middle room in ye great Pagan Tower, there where my old servant Jane Bricknell dyed, and then came into my owne chamber againe, where, after a short stay I went from thence through ye little passage room and the painted chamber and great chamber and the Hall down into ye Court of that Castle, where I went into my Horslitter in which I rid (being attended by my women in my Coach drawn with 6 Horses, and my menservants on horsback) along by ye Pillar I erected in memory of my last parting there with my Blessed Mother, and through Whinfield Park and by ye Hartshorn Tree, the brother tree, and Julian Bower, and through the entry and so, out of ye Park crossing ye Rivers of Lyvennett and Eden, I went through Kirbythure, Crackenthorp, Battleburgh and over Appleby Bridge and through ye Town, into Appleby Castle, whither I came well, thank God about 3 in the afternoon, having bin accompanyed most part of ye way by many of ye chief Gentry of the County and others, and by Neighbours and Tenants hereabouts; and so after I was now alighted in the Court of this Appleby Castle I came through the Hall and upstairs to ye Chappell, and great chamber, and from thence up ye green stairs and through ye Withdrawing Room into my owne chamber where I formerly used to lye, and where I had not bin since ye 28th of January last till now; and where I now continued to lye till the 2nd of March following that I removed with my family to Pendraggon Castle to lye there in it for a time.[30]

An extreme version of her monumentalizing appears in the diaries of her last months in 1676. Again and again she notes how "I went not out of this house nor out of my Chamber today." Her late diary may mention those who come to visit her in her chamber but the real events of the day are the ones she rereads in a ritual act of remembering:

> I remembered how this day was 59 years [since] I went with my first Lord to the Court at Whitehall, where in the inner withdrawing chamber King James desired & urged mee to submitt to the Award which hee would make concerning my Lands of Inheritance, but I absolutly denyed to do so, wherein I was guided by a great Providence of God for the good of mee & mine. And that day also had my first & then only childe a dangerous fit of her long Ague in Knowl house in Kent, where shee then lay.[31]

The intimate care and worry over her sick child is recalled in its historical context – the two dimensions becoming one. Retrospectively, we can read the early diary through this consciousness, the consciousness of one who sees herself as the aristocrat, the one who belongs to, or even *is*, the space she inhabits: I am Cumberland. Even the references to her "fits of wind" that punctuate the accounts of the last days are perhaps the notations of a public body. As we have seen, it is not only the later chronicles that recuperate intimate relations as historical or economic transactions. Clifford's life-writing was always a public act: a making of history and a confirming of lineage.

If life-writing for seventeenth-century women was a process of self-fashioning, it was also a process of criticism. Since the diary of Anne Clifford allowed for the critical contemplation of her husband and others, we might argue that the practice of intimacy was also a critical practice.[32] Anne Cotterell Dormer, writing as Francis Barker says of Pepys, "at the moment when the very division between the public and the private is constructed in its modern form," is quite aware of her writing as a practice in criticism.[33] She is particularly aware of an inside and an outside, of intimate writing and writing for show: "I contrive to write when he [her husband] is from home that I may spare my self and my friends the trouble of hatching a formall letter, he watches to read those I receive but now he is almost continually abroad I write when I can have most liberty to speake my thoughts."[34]

Dormer articulates her intimate relation with her sister as the ability to "tell thee all my joyes and all my sorrows."[35] Friendship, she argues, "requires a communication of all concerns without reserve . . ."[36] This need for intimacy, for the telling of all without reserve, grows out of constraints placed on her by her husband, but she also sees her particular form of intimacy (letters/writing) as a function of class: "a poore woman that lives in a thatched house when shee is ill or weary of he[r] work can step into her Neigh: and have some refres[h]ment but I have none but what I find by thin[k]ing writing and reading . . ."[37] The upper-class woman, then, turns to writing as the vehicle for intimacy because she is prohibited from entering the public sphere, not, in this case, the market place or political arena, but one of easy access to other women.

To be in the private realm does not mean that a woman is out of the political. Feminist theory has taught us that the personal is political – that is, that there are systemic means of control and oppression within the institutions of the time: the family, the law, the church. It is interesting that the one use of the word "intimate" in Dormer's letters is in refer- ence to her husband being intimate with neighbors during the political strife leading up to the Glorious Revolution. The implication of her use of the term is that her husband is actually in some kind of intrigue with the papist neighbors. In other words, the meaning is political. Dormer also speaks of her husband as a censorious spy and of "the insupport- able Tyranny I live under."[38] Her understanding of her relation with her husband is political. The events of her century and the immediate polit- ical instabilities are felt in her everyday life and used as an analogy for her marital relations. Her life-writing in the letters to her sister is a form of intimate intrigue that resists her husband's total oppression.

That is not to say that Dormer does not see her retreat from the active political sphere as gendered. From within her domestic world she feels herself to be out of the circuit of politics and public action. After the Glorious Revolution, she writes:

it is not for me my deare sister to give you any account of the wonderfull revo- lutions in this Kingdom and Gods most miraculous power which has beene once more shewed in the preservation of this church but tho I am too much out of the world to attempt the giving you a relation of such extraordinary things; as greate as my retirement is, no bodys joy can exceed mine upon the generall account, and as to my owne particular nothing could have brought me out of so many straites as this change has done . . .[39]

Her "owne particular" refers to the fact that she has been caught between her husband and her father in the struggle over the monarchy. If the larger political realm has had its intrigue and struggles over who should be the king and what religion should be dominant, Dormer herself has had to live out that struggle in her family life. Her husband has been courting the papists and her father has remained loyal to the two Charleses under whom he had served. The letters, in fact, indicate an integral relation between public politics and the so-called private space of the home.

Dormer seeks the privacy and safety of her chamber, away from her

abusive husband and the dangerous political times that surround her in
the 1680s. She sometimes turns to an intimate relation with God in
prayer. Yet even that space is not secure: she needs to be careful what she
says amongst her neighbors and "alone in my chamber where my Lord
was ever a sensorious spie upon me but now he often shews him self a
fury."[40] She resolves never to go out beyond the garden because of the
way her husband humiliates her in front of others; she retreats to her
room.[41] Yet, still, her room is not entirely safe: on one occasion her
husband broke down the nursery door when he thought she was in
there.[42] The letters reveal just how private this domestic sphere can be,
and just how political.

The letters also show what activities and materials are used to construct that privacy – how domestic objects can be used both to construct
the dangerous privacy of an abusive relationship and the ways Dormer
is able to, or the extent to which she is able or unable to, resist the oppression. Gloves, for instance, which are usually only marked in women's discourse of the time as gifts or commodities (Anne Clifford buys four
dozen at a time to give as gifts), show up in Dormer's letters as a signifier
of some perverse sexual action on the part of Dormer's husband: "here
lies one of my inexpressible torments . . . he still continnues his way of
kissing a durty glove of mine and saying he loves me extreamly and then
he will hang about my neck . . ."[43] The incident is referred to twice as an
example of the sexual advances that often accompanied his habitual
abuse.

Stimulant drinks, cordials, and the utensils used to consume them
offer Dormer a possible space of resistance: "I take the Kings dropps
and drink Chocalate and when my soul is sadd to death I run and play
with the children after I have prayed and almost read my eyes out . . ."[44]
Yet even her choice of medicinal drink is riddled with public discourses
about what and how much a woman should drink:

I thank God I do for all this gett ground of that languishing kinde of illness for
I am stronger then when you saw me which is owing to chocal[a]te wh[ich I]
take and have done constantly every day this winter it gives me spirits and
strength I thank God with cheerfulness to tugg through, and I would not for a
greate sum of mony have found so much good from sack, for it would have
beene a continuall torment to my mind if I had; but instead of that I am so
weary of it I can take that no longer, but now every day after my meate I take
sherry with nutmett and sugar and now have obtained to take it in my Lds sight
and that gives me one pleasure to see he begins almost to beleive I may be
trusted with it, I have a little dish for the purpose holds just three spoonfulls,
which is my usuall dosse, and somtimes I take five, as I find it best; and more I
would not take, if I were a Wine Coopers Wife . . .[45]

That "little dish for the purpose" holds a story, not only of the obvious master discourse about the control and shaping of women but also of a process of choosing, purchasing, or recycling an object for the specific practice of both relief from and reinscribing of her husband's abuse: who bought it, who suggested its use, where it has been kept out of his sight and then used in front of him. This letter holds an additional piece of evidence on gender and the ideology of stimulant drinks, seen from the perspective of a woman of the time.[46]

While her husband was alive, Anne Dormer had to negotiate daily interactions with him, always conscious of his power. In trying to deal with his affair with another woman, she says, "I have spoken my mind with very greate calmness, but with greate freedom to him, I must not exasperate him for I and my poore children are in his power."[47] But what is more astounding, even after the husband dies she remains tied by his habit of passionate control. The objects in the home that are now legally hers still carry the ideological force of his disciplinary actions, and she feels the attachment to him long after his death through her relations to these domestic objects. Dormer feels remorse looking in the trunks and boxes he kept locked, "and using such things as he would scarce suffer me to look upon I am I think like one ha[u]nted with an evill spirit or who has comitted some crime . . ."[48]

It is easy to read Dormer's letters as an example of the internalization of ideological discourses that have exploited and contained women, and yet the letters themselves are "an agent of resistance."[49] Dormer's taking of chocolate or her contriving to write in secrecy produce moments that are, if not free from dominant discourses, at least poised at an ironic distance. The subjectivity produced out of this writing of intimate relationships is, on the one hand, a kind of "depoliticized privacy"[50] and, on the other, an active political struggle. The reams of paper she covers in her letters suggest an ongoing, at times sarcastic critique.

Personal life-writing, then, in the cases of Clifford and Dormer, as well as others, provided a space in which to react to marital and political domination. The private spaces they sought or to which they were banished, like the privacy of religious devotion, were not only predetermined by existing hierarchical structures but were also the only available places for critique. The intimate sphere of domestic objects Clifford and Dormer chose to represent as constitutive of their identity is complex and multidimensional. Their chosen objects were not only objects of consumption or "relic-objects."[51] The women's life-writing engages with these objects, constructing a subjectivity through discourses they inherit and rewrite. If, as Francis Barker insists, they are writing in the century

of the "bourgeois man . . . [f]orbidden to speak and yet incited to discourse, and therefore speaking obliquely in another place,"[52] then their
silence and the forms of writing they chose were unstable. Writing produces and is produced by intimacy, yet that intimacy is never only a
private process.

NOTES

1. My thanks go to colleagues who have read this paper and offered invaluable
   comments for revision: Sylvia Bowerbank, Sara Mendelson, and Lesley
   Douglass. Research for this paper was funded by the Social Sciences and
   Humanities Research Council of Canada and by the McMaster Arts
   Research Board. Grateful acknowledgment is made to the British Library
   Board for permission to cite from the Letters from Anne Dormer to her
   sister, Lady Elizabeth Trumbull, 1685–91, Add. MS. 72516, fols. 156–243,
   cited hereafter as Dormer MS. Unless specifically noted, all quotations
   within this paper preserve original spellings and emphases.
2. Anne Bradstreet, "Upon the Burning of Our House July 10th, 1666," lines
   21–36, in *The Complete Works of Anne Bradstreet*, ed. Joseph R. McElrath, Jr.
   and Allan P. Robb (Boston: Twayne, 1981), 236–37.
3. Rosamond R. Rosenmeier, " 'Divine Translation': A Contribution to the
   Study of Anne Bradstreet's Method in the Marriage Poems," in *Critical
   Essays on Anne Bradstreet*, ed. Pattie Cowell and Ann Stanford (Boston: G.K.
   Hall, 1983), 200–01.
4. Amanda Vickery, in "Women and the World of Goods: A Lancashire
   Consumer and Her Possessions, 1751–81," in *The World of Goods*, ed. and with
   an intro. by John Brewer and Roy Porter (London: Routledge, 1994), 278,
   has shown that new theorizing about consumption in which it is seen "as a
   positive contribution to the creation of culture and meanings" has "pave[d]
   the way for the historical reclamation of the female consumer in particular
   . . ."
5. Patricia Fumerton, *Cultural Aesthetics: Renaissance Literature and the Practice of
   Social Ornament* (Chicago: University of Chicago Press, 1991), 109–10. Cressy
   takes the position that "all life was public in early modern England. . . .
   [A]gainst the demands of family, community, and society, the early modern
   world allowed no separate private sphere (in the modern sense), no place
   where public activity did not intrude. Even within the recesses of domestic
   routine, every action, every opinion, was susceptible to external interest,
   monitoring, or control. Walls had ears, and everybody's business was a
   matter of credit, reputation, or common fame." See David Cressy,
   "Response: Private Lives, Public Performance, and Rites of Passage," in
   Attending to Women in Early Modern England, ed. Betty S. Travitsky and Adele
   F. Seeff (Newark: University of Delaware Press, 1994), 187. Cressy cites
   Susan Dwyer Amussen, *An Ordered Society: Gender and Class in Early Modern
   England* (Oxford: Oxford University Press, 1988) and Martin Ingram, *Church*

Courts, Sex and Marriage in England, 1570–1640 (Cambridge: Cambridge University Press, 1987). The evidence of the defamation suits in church court records or of gossip at the time, as well as that of countless conduct books and devotional guides, suggests that public discourses and practices acted as strong disciplinary forces in the most private aspects of women's lives. Nevertheless, any attempt to characterize "*all* life" (my italics) as public or private risks simplifying the evidence. Amussen insists on the importance of the domestic realm since it acts as a formative model for civic and church structures.

6. Anne Dormer to Lady Elizabeth Trumbull, 10 September (1687?), Dormer MS, fol. 167v. I am indebted to Patricia Crawford for sharing with me her knowledge of Dormer's manuscript letters.

7. Mary Hurll, *An Account of the Remarkable Conversion and Experience of Mary Hurll, as taken from her own Mouth*, 2nd edn. (London: n. p., 1708), 21.

8. See Elizabeth Jocelin, *The Mothers Legacie, To her unborne Childe* (London: Printed by John Haviland, for William Barret, 1624); Elizabeth Stirredge, *Strength in Weakness Manifest: in the Life, Various Trials, and Christian Testimony of that faithful servant and Handmaid of the Lord, Elizabeth Stirredge, Who departed this Life, at her House at Hempstead in Hertfordshire, in the 72d Year of her Age. Written by her own Hand. Shewing her pious Care and Counsel to her Children, and according to their Desire, made Publick: Also for the Instruction and Benefit of many other Parents and Children concerned*, 3rd edn. (London: Mary Hinde, 1772); and Mary Rich, Countess of Warwick, *Autobiography*, ed. T. C. Croker (n. p.: Percy Society, 1848), xxii, and "Daily Spiritual Diary and Occasional Meditations, 1666–78," British Library Add. MSS. 27351–56.

9. Elizabeth Bury, *An Account of the Life and Death of Mrs. Elizabeth Bury, who died May the 11th, 1720. Aged 76. Chiefly collected out of her Own Diary. Together with Her Funeral Sermon, Preach'd at Bristol, May 22, 1720. By the Reverend Mr. William Tong, and her Elegy by the Reverend Mr. J. Watts* (Bristol: J. Penn, 1720), 136, 140.

10. *Ibid.*, 92.

11. Accounts of the notebook, which is now lost, can be found in Thomas Dunham Whitaker, *History of Craven* (n. p., 1823); Joseph Whiteside, "Some Accounts of Anne, Countess of Pembroke," *Transactions of the Cumberland and Westmorland Antiquarian and Archaeological Society* NS 5 (1905): 188–201; and George C. Williamson, *Lady Anne Clifford Countess of Dorset, Pembroke & Montgomery, 1590–1676. Her Life, Letters and Work. Extracted from all the original documents available, many of which are here printed for the first time* (Kendal: Titus Wilson, 1922). It is unclear whether the accounts were kept in Anne's hand or another's.

12. "Aristocratic Possessions," paper presented at the Rocky Mountain Medieval and Renaissance Association Conference, Banff, Alberta, May 1997.

13. Williamson, *Lady Anne Clifford*, 58–60.

14. Anne Clifford, *The Diaries of Lady Anne Clifford*, ed. D. J. H. Clifford (Stroud: Alan Sutton, 1990), 40. As I will be working with both the early and late

Clifford diaries and chronicles, I have chosen to cite from D. J. H. Clifford's edition, which includes the later writings. An excellent critical edition of the Knole diary (1616–19) using the Portland MS. now exists in *The Diary of Anne Clifford, 1616–1619: A Critical Edition*, ed. Katherine O. Acheson (New York: Garland, 1995). Substantial differences between the D. J. H. Clifford and Acheson editions will be noted. Here, the Portland MS. says "wrought Irish stitch" instead of "wrought Stitch Work" (Acheson, *Diary*, 58). Irish stitch, according to the *Oxford English Dictionary*, is "embroidery done in white thread upon a white ground."

15. Clifford, *Diaries*, 54.
16. Williamson, *Lady Anne Clifford*, 152.
17. For extensive discussions of these biographical matters, see Acheson's introduction in Acheson, *Diary*; Barbara Kiefer Lewalski, *Writing Women in Jacobean England* (Cambridge, Mass.: Harvard University Press, 1993); and Williamson, *Lady Anne Clifford*.
18. As such, my argument is similar to that of Mary Ellen Lamb in her article "The Agency of the Split Subject: Lady Anne Clifford and the Uses of Reading," *English Literary Renaissance* 22 (1992): 347–68, which identifies gender and class as contributing determinants of Anne's subjectivity.
19. In an autobiographical summary, Clifford begins with the exact time and place of her own conception: she "was, through the mercifull providence of God, begotten by my valiant father, and conceived with child by my worthy mother, the first day of May in 1589 in the Lord Wharton's house in Channell Row in Westminster" (Acheson, *Diary*, 1).
20. *Ibid.*, 163.
21. Commissioned by Anne in 1647 as part of "The Great Picture of the Clifford Family," attributed to Jan van Belcamp and displayed in the Great Hall at Appleby Castle, owned by the Abbot Hall Art Gallery, Kendal, Cumbria, and reproduced in Acheson, *Diary*, Clifford, *Diaries*, and elsewhere.
22. Slea or sleave silk is silk thread capable of being separated into smaller filaments for use in embroidery. As its citation the *Oxford English Dictionary* uses Bishop Rainbow's funeral sermon for Anne Clifford: "A Prime Wit [Dr. Donne] is reported to have said of this Lady – That she knew well how to discourse of all things, from Predestination to Slea-silk."
23. The Portland MS. says "the long cushion of Irish stitch" (Acheson, *Diary*, 60).
24. Clifford, *Diaries*, 41.
25. *Ibid.*, 59.
26. *Ibid.*, 28.
27. Margaret P. Hannay, in " 'O Daughter Heare': Reconstructing the Lives of Aristocratic Englishwomen," in *Attending to Women in Early Modern England*, ed. Travitsky and Seeff, 35–63, argues similarly: "by researching her father's voyages in the 'sea papers' while ill, she had discovered a vocation as a scholar and a writer . . . she had begun to create an identity based on accom-

plishment, not on gender" (35); however, she "sought to define herself as a Clifford, not as a writer; she seems to have written not because of religious devotion or literary aspirations, but to preserve her family heritage" (51). My emphasis would be that even as early as the 1600 account book, Anne had begun to write herself as a landed aristocrat. The diary and the later chronicles are further modes (or technologies) for constructing that subjectivity.

28. As such her writing is similar to her commissioning of stone monuments to the memory of her mother, her young cousin, and even of the poet, Spenser. See Alice T. Friedman, "Lady Anne Clifford as a Patron of the Visual Arts," *Quarto: Quarterly Bulletin of Abbot Hall Art Gallery* 28 (1990): 9, for Clifford's "deep feeling for the past and her sense of her own role as one who should preserve it" through her support for the arts.

29. Clifford, *Diaries*, 35.

30. *Ibid.*, 218–19.

31. *Ibid.*, 240.

32. As Sara Heller Mendelson, in *The Mental World of Stuart Women: Three Studies* (Amherst: University of Massachusetts Press, 1987), 101–05, has pointed out, Mary Rich, Countess of Warwick, provides an exemplary case of a woman whose intimate devotional space of prayer and diary writing allowed for a critical assessment of her husband.

33. Francis Barker, *The Tremulous Private Body: Essays on Subjection* (London: Methuen, 1984), 14.

34. Dormer to Lady Elizabeth Trumbull, 28 September (1688?), Dormer MS., fol. 186v. Anne Dormer is known in the historical accounts only as a footnote or minor detail in the lives of her father and son, both of whom have entries in the *Dictionary of National Biography*. Her father was Charles Cotterell, Master of Ceremonies to three kings, who resigned under James II in favor of his son. He was knighted and may be known to some as the one who encouraged Katherine Philips to write and publish. He himself had translations published as well as a historical account and a religious book. Anne's famous son was James Dormer, who had a successful military career and is known as a friend of Swift. Her husband Robert Dormer was a second son of an aristocratic family from Dorton and Rousham in Buckinghamshire and Oxfordshire. Anne writes most of her letters from Rousham. The other historical figure in Anne's life is William Trumbull, the husband of her sister Elizabeth to whom she writes these letters. They were written first to Paris where Trumbull was sent as extraordinary envoy during the time of the revocation of the Edict of Nantes and then to Constantinople while he was ambassador there. Anne had eleven children, eight of whom lived to be adults, seven of them boys and many having military careers. When the letters start she has just had her last child, while her eldest is only sixteen.

35. *Ibid.*, 10 September (1687?), fol. 167.

36. *Ibid.*, 29 November (1688?), fol. 194.

37. *Ibid.*, 5 April (1688?), fols. 176v–77.

38. *Ibid.*, 22 June (1687?), fol. 165v.
39. *Ibid.*, dated January the 2d 1688 (1689 by modern dating), fols. 198v–99.
40. *Ibid.*, 6 March (1688?), fol. 171.
41. *Ibid.*, 10 September (1687?), fol. 168.
42. *Ibid.*, 3 November (1688?), fol. 193.
43. *Ibid.*, 22 June (1687?), fol. 165v. On Clifford's use of gloves as gifts, see Whiteside, "Some Accounts," 193.
44. Dormer to Lady Elizabeth Trumbull, 24 August (1687?), Dormer MS., fols. 163–63v.
45. *Ibid.*, 5 April (1688?), fols. 177–77v.
46. Dame Sarah Cowper, Daily diary, 1700–16, Hertfordshire RO, Panshanger MSS, D/EP/F29–35. Dame Cowper speaks of her husband's disapproval of her consumption of stimulant drinks, mostly on the grounds of expense. She itemizes her use of tea, chocolate, coffee, and wine, all of which she takes for "Sustenance." Yet "Comes Sr W and wrangles at the Expence I make for my Breakfast and Supper, saying he did not think it was to be a Crown a week . . . The base inhumane Expressions that burst out upon this occasion are not fitt, nor possible to write, but in my Memory" (16 January 1701 [1702 by modern dating]). For a more general discussion of gender and stimulant drinks, concentrating on tea in the eighteenth century, see Beth Kowaleski-Wallace, "Tea, Gender, and Domesticity in Eighteenth-Century England," *Studies in Eighteenth-Century Culture* 23 (1994): 131–45.
47. Dormer to Lady Elizabeth Trumbull, 20 July (1688?), Dormer MS., fol. 181v. Anne has eight but her husband has one older son from his first marriage.
48. *Ibid.*, St. James's Day, 1689, fol. 202.
49. Sidonie Smith, *A Poetics of Women's Autobiography: Marginality and the Fictions of Self-Representation* (Bloomington: University of Indiana Press, 1987), 393.
50. *Ibid.*
51. *A History of Private Life*, ed. Philippe Ariès and Georges Duby, vol. III., *Passions of the Renaissance*, trans. Arthur Goldhammer (Cambridge, Mass.: The Belknap Press of Harvard University Press, 1989), 207.
52. Barker, *The Tremulous Private Body*, 9.

CHAPTER FIVE

Gender, genre, and theatricality in the autobiography of Charlotte Charke

Robert Folkenflik

At the outset of her *Narrative of the Life of Mrs. Charlotte Charke* (1755), in a conventional eighteenth-century gesture, Charke identifies her auto-biography as "the Product of a Female Pen" and, therefore, subject to possible dismissal on that ground alone, but the claim gives her an imme-diate gender identity that the text itself will call into question.[1] Charlotte Charke was best known in the eighteenth century for her cross-dressing on and off the stage. She represents herself in her autobiography by theatricalizing the genre in a way that embodies her identity as cross-dressing woman and actress.

Cross-dressing was more culturally familiar during this period than we may at times recognize.[2] The actual cross-dressers of early modern Europe were joined by representations in drama, poetry (especially in popular forms), and fiction. Shakespeare's plays, which enabled boys to play girls who played at being boys, took a new turn when actresses arrived on stage at the Restoration. At the outset of the seventeenth century, *Don Quixote* contains an episode in which the beautiful Dorothea disguises herself as a boy, and Cervantes's fiction includes a total of four female and two male cross-dressers. Defoe's Moll Flanders dons men's clothing at one point, and like Charlotte Charke later, makes a female conquest. Still more to the point, Fielding's *Female Husband* (1746), written after Charlotte joined his company, could hardly have been unknown to her, and she was certainly well known to him. It has even been argued that Fielding partially based his fictional version of the Mary Hamilton case on Charke herself.[3]

Literary examples of cross-dressing are sometimes dependent on cul-tural changes. Although there is a tradition, going back at least to the Elizabethan period, of the "roaring girl" whose mannishness is often reprehended, and women warriors also turn up in broadsides and popular songs,[4] the introduction of actresses on the English stage changed the stakes. Actresses from the Restoration period forward were accustomed to putting on men's clothing for "breeches" parts, which provided some sort of equality with the rake-heroes of comedy and a chance to show off their legs to the audience: poems of the time make clear the female attractiveness of these women dressed as men.

The actual cross-dressed woman is frequently encountered in Europe during the seventeenth and eighteenth centuries.[5] In England a range of cross-dressers, from Mrs. Christian Davies (known as Mother Ross) to the Chevalier d'Eon, who dueled in a dress, appeared throughout the century.[6] Actual male cross-dressers tended to be upper class; female, to be lower class. Charke, after being left by her husband, disowned by her father, and outcast from the legitimate stage, was *déclassée*.

The appeal of one version of the stage type and a rough model for some of Charke's self-construction can be seen in Aphra Behn's comedy *The Rover*, where Hellena, who is introduced as "wild," masquerades first as a gypsy and later "*dressed in man's clothes*." This is done under the aegis of carnival, but her original urging catches something of the spirit. She wants to "be as mad as the rest and take all innocent freedoms . . . Come, put off this dull humor with your clothes, and assume one as gay and as fantastic as the dress my cousin Valeria and I have provided, and let's ramble."[7] Freedom, a change of role and attitude, mobility: these are certainly some of the overdetermined elements of Charlotte Charke's cross-dressing.

In this connection Charlotte's identification of herself as "mad" and "madcap"[8] may be part of an attempt to register her behavior as that of a "young woman of lively and impulsive temperament"[9] rather than as a maniac, though she does seem to identify somewhat with an uncle who went mad,[10] and, from 1742, Alexander Pope's *Dunciad* would remind her that her grandfather Caius-Gabriel Cibber's stone statues of *Raving Madness* and *Melancholy Madness* above the gates of Bedlam were "Great Cibber's brazen, brainless brothers."[11] Her emphasis on "mad pranks" links her at once to picaresque novels and joke books, but also to the "mad" and "wild" heroines like Hellena in Restoration comedy.[12]

According to John Harold Wilson, almost a quarter of the new plays between 1660 and 1700 had breeches parts.[13] Nell Gwynn, Susannah Mountfort, and Peg Woffington played such roles in the Restoration, early- and mid-eighteenth century. Charke has been characterized as a specialist in breeches roles.[14] She certainly played a number, such as Sylvia, the attractive heroine who loves Captain Plume in *The Recruiting Officer*. And when a newspaper letter, likely written by Charke herself, congratulated her on returning to playing female characters, the role in question was the eponymous Pope Joan in *The Female Prelate*, a breeches part. Yet, when we restrict the term to roles written for women who cross-dress as men, even if we include whole roles designed for a woman to play a man (Wilson cites over a dozen in the Restoration), we still do not hit her specialty precisely. Charke was best known as a performer in male roles written for men.[15] She played only two such roles before 1734 – Roderigo in *Othello* at Drury Lane (1732) and the eunuch Haly in Rowe's *Tamerlane* (1733) – but she gained fame and notoriety in the summer of 1734, when she took over the Haymarket Theatre after its customary closing date and performed in over a dozen. In contrast, her first dozen roles included only one breeches role, Clarinda in her father's *Double Gallant*, before she began playing men's roles. In 1737, when Fielding cleverly and cruelly obtained her for his Haymarket company, he featured her (frequently cross-dressed) in farces whose satire was sometimes aimed at Colley Cibber – Charke's father and the most important "Other" in her autobiography. These performances led to a rift that will be considered later.

Actresses in male (and actors in female) roles were far from unknown. All-woman casts and totally cross-dressed casts appeared in the Restoration and eighteenth century. Colley Cibber highly praised Susannah Mountfort not just in breeches but in male roles:

Nor was her Humour limited, to her Sex; for while her Shape permitted, she was a more adroit pretty Fellow, than is usually seen upon the Stage: Her easy Air, Action, Mien, and Gesture, quite chang'd from the Quoif, to the cock'd Hat, and Cavalier in fashion. People were so fond of seeing her a Man, that when the Part of *Bays* in the *Rehearsal*, had, for some time, lain dormant, she was desired to take it up, which I have seen her act with all the true, coxcombly Spirit, and Humour, that the Sufficiency of the Character required.[16]

The major motivation given by Rudolf M. Dekker and Lotte van de Pol for the 119 examples of actual female cross-dressing discussed in *The Tradition of Female Transvestism in Early Modern Europe*, that of following a husband or lover into the military, does not apply to Charlotte Charke, but some of her traits, circumstances, and behavior fit into a pattern. Like Charke, some cross-dressers were actresses who possibly had played breeches roles or men's roles on stage. Bodily freedom, with its promise of other sorts of freedom, may have appealed to them. Many of these cross-dressers cited poverty as a reason for their behavior. Charke herself claims that her wearing of men's clothes enabled her to escape the attentions of creditors and bailiffs who hounded her, though at one point she fears her attractive male hat will cause her to be recognized. Moreover, such clothes clearly enabled her to enter a number of professions that she could not otherwise have entered as a woman. As "Mr. Brown," an identity probably drawn from the name of her hated elder sister's husband, she also was less apt to suffer robberies or rapes. This combination of family conflict, abandonment by a husband, work as an actress, poverty, and need for an occupation resembles the range of conditions and characteristics Dekker and van de Pol find typical of Dutch cross-dressers of the early modern period, though like Charke, the Dutch cross-dressers on trial were unlikely to confess that sexual desire for a woman was a reason for their actions.[17] Cases of female cross-dressing are less well documented in England than in the Netherlands because they were characteristically prosecuted in the latter as violations of the male prerogative. In England women brought to trial were usually those who attempted to marry other women, and they were, therefore, prosecuted for fraud rather than for a specifically sexual crime or breech of sumptuary laws.[18]

The strength of the interest in such cases can be gauged from the way they show up as the subject of articles in the mid-century *Gentleman's Magazine*, including an abridged, third-person version of Charke's *Narrative*. In 1745, the *Gentleman's Magazine* ran an essay on Mary Hamilton, who married another woman and was satirized in Fielding's *Female Husband*. *"Some Account of Hannah Snell, the Female Soldier"* appeared in 1750, the same year as two versions of Snell's biography; she soon went on stage with a military drill. In 1755, the *Gentleman's Magazine* published an essay based on *The True History and Adventures of Catharine Vizzani, a Young Gentlewoman a Native of Rome, who for many years past in the Habit of a Man; was killed for an Amour with a young Lady; and found on Dissection, a true Virgin. With curious Anatomical Remarks on the Nature and Existence of the Hymen*. The author of the original Italian version, Giovanni Bianchi, was a professor of anatomy at Siena.

Charlotte is quite mysterious about her reasons for cross-dressing: she does several times say things that imply she is not desirous of sex with women, but the story she tells indicates that from the first she is comfortable with male activities, not with female. Dekker and van de Pol suggest plausibly that, in the early modern period, some women who fell in love with women thought of themselves as men, and dressing as men not only facilitated but also "made it possible to legitimise a sexual relationship with another woman."[19] Certainly the absence of a social niche for the lesbian during the period might have encouraged such a constructed identity, though Terry Castle's study of Anne Lister in *The Apparitional*

Lesbian and other work suggests that such thinking may be based on limited evidence rather than early modern realities.[20] This solution, however, clearly would not apply to Charke, who married at seventeen and again at thirty-three, though the question of her sexuality is difficult to determine, as are some aspects of her motivation. It is suggestive, for example, that she played the male role of Lovegirlo in her own comedy *Tit for Tat* (1743), which went unpublished.

Modern psychologists seem to have difficulties determining the sexual orientation of female transvestites, and some would regard all as homosexual while a majority of male transvestites turn out to be heterosexual. The most likely position is that female cross-dressing does not provide grounds for establishing sexual practices in the early modern period. Marjorie Garber's suggestion that the cross-dresser is a "third term," not resolvable into heterosexual or homosexual, is attractive, as is Judith Butler's emphasis on multiple "sexualities."[21]

Throughout her *Narrative* Charke foregrounds that "singularization" which John Sturrock claims lies behind all autobiography.[22] Charke encourages the notion of her "oddity."[23] She is "a NONPAREIL OF THE AGE," and "universally known to be an odd Product of Nature."[24] Her emphasis on oddness parallels the biographies of some of her cross-dressing contemporaries: for example, the epigraph to the biography of Catharine Vizzani proclaims "What Odd fantastic things, we Women do!" and the shorter of two 1750 biographies of Hannah Snell speaks of "the oddity of her conduct."[25] In these biographies, the keynote use of the term "odd" codes it as a reference to cross-dressing. Charke's linkage of herself to George Alexander Stevens, however, suggests that a broader range of marginal behavior can be brought under its rubric: "Nor can you [second person because this is part of Charke's dedication 'The Author to Herself'] be match'd in Oddity of Fame, by any but that celebrated Knight-Errant of the Moon, G[eorg]e A[lexande]r St[even]s; whose Memoirs and yours conjoin'd, would make great *Figures in History* . . ."[26] I will return to Stevens later, but here I would like also to draw attention to Charke's father's *Apology for the Life of Colley Cibber, Comedian*, which stresses his "odd fate,"[27] and to her sense of herself as spectacle: she will "claim a Title to be shewn among the Wonders of Ages past, and those to come."[28] The "wonder" is the eighteenth-century equivalent of the exhibition in a "freak" show.

Charke's earliest remembered episode – it reads like a first memory – epitomizes a number of the themes of her life to come, and serves both as a prelude to the whole narrative and as wish-fulfillment. Indeed,

Jerome Bruner claims that in the oral autobiographies he collects the first five minutes of what tend to be thirty-minute self-representations contain the whole in miniature.[29] Charke introduces the anecdote, which dates from when she was four years old, in partial fulfillment of her promise "to conceal nothing that might raise a laugh," and as "a small Specimen of my former Madness":

Having, even then, a passionate Fondness for a Perriwig, I crawl'd out of Bed one Summer's Morning at *Twickenham*, where my Father had Part of a House and Gardens for the Season, and, taking it into my small Pate, that by Dint of a Wig and a Waistcoat, I should be the perfect Representative of my Sire, I crept softly into the Servants-Hall, where I had the Night before espied all things in Order, to perpetrate the happy Design I had framed for the next Morning's Expedition. Accordingly I paddled down Stairs, taking with me my Shoes, Stockings, and little Dimity Coat; which I artfully contrived to pin up, as well as I could, to supply the Want of a Pair of Breeches. By the Help of a long Broom, I took down a Waistcoat of my Brother's, and an enormous bushy Tie-wig of my Father's, which entirely enclos'd my Head and Body, with the Knots of the Ties thumping my little Heels as I marched along, with slow and solemn Pace. The Covert of Hair in which I was concealed, with the Weight of a monstrous Belt and large silver-hilted Sword, that I could scarce drag along, was a vast Impediment in my Procession: And, what still added to the other Inconveniences I laboured under, was whelming myself under one of my Father's large Beaver-hats, laden with Lace, as thick and as broad as a Brickbat.

Being thus accoutred, I began to consider that 'twould be impossible for me to pass for Mr. *Cibber* in Girl's Shoes, therefore took an Opportunity to slip out of Doors after the Gardener, who went to his Work, and roll'd myself into a dry Ditch, which was as deep as I was high; and, in this Grotesque Pigmy-State, walked up and down the Ditch bowing to all who came by me. But, behold, the Oddity of my Appearance soon assembled a Croud about me; which yielded me no small Joy, as I conceived their Risibility on this Occasion to be Marks of Approbation, and walked myself into a Fever, in the happy Thought of being taken for the 'Squire.

When the Family arose, 'till which Time I had employ'd myself in this regular March in my Ditch, I was the first Thing enquir'd after, and miss'd; 'till Mrs. *Heron*, the mother of the late celebrated Actress of that Name, happily espied me, and directly call'd forth the whole Family to be Witness of my State and Dignity.

The Drollery of my Figure rendered it impossible, assisted by the Fondness of both Father and Mother, to be angry with me; but, alas! I was borne off on the Footman's Shoulders, to my Shame and Disgrace, and forc'd into my proper Habiliments.[30]

The male clothing, the acting in the role of her father, her inability to fit properly into her father's clothes – a burden she willingly assumes – the

"Oddity of [her] Appearance," the mixed effect of the spectacle on the audience and especially her father's ambiguous response, the ditch as stage (a nice psychoanalytic touch for what seems to have the quality of dream), the precocity, the forced return to appropriately gendered clothing ("my proper Habiliments"), the ludicrously staged performance – all lead to "Shame and Disgrace," and yet, can we miss the note of pride as well? This scene of cross-dressing substitutes burden (with its Freudian emphasis on sword and wig – the latter also gendered male, of course) for lack. Later, when as a grown woman she is compelled to exchange her silver-laced hat for the huge and smoky hat of a bailiff, she claims that she "was almost as much incommoded as when I marched in the Ditch, under the insupportable Weight of my Father's."[31] Here her lack leads her to take a broom and obtain a bushy wig for her primal theatrical scene in which, as small phallus substitute, she goes back and forth in the ditch.

Above all there is the theatrical sense of self: the girl makes a spectacle of herself. The episode is represented, she would have it, not to inquire into her selfhood or explain the dynamics of her relation to her father, but to entertain her audience (that is, the buyers of her autobiography) and "raise a laugh." Her theatricality and her autobiography consist at once of exposing and hiding. This episode is also the first of a number in which she attempts to be "the perfect Representative of my Sire." It is to the point that Cibber, as Sir Fopling Flutter in George Etherege's *The Man of Mode*, made his first entrance in a huge full-bottomed wig, supported by a footman on either side. Charke is also aware, here as elsewhere, of her father as primary audience for her performance. In another early anecdote, when she stages a parade on a "young ass" with an entourage of lower-class children, "I perfectly remember, young as I was then, the strong Mixture of Surprize, Pleasure, Pain and Shame in his Countenance, on his viewing me seated on my infantical *Rosinante*."[32]

The outcome of Charlotte's marriage to the profligate composer-musician Richard Charke – a love match according to her – and her crossdressing served to alienate her father, as did some other aspects of her career, especially her performing with Henry Fielding.[33] The autobiography is meant, among other things, as a contrite performance that will win him back. Charlotte is identified on the title page as the "Youngest Daughter of Colley Cibber, Esq." The original serial publication of the book not only enhanced its value as a begging letter but also as blackmail, a strategy she might have derived from the publication in parts of the scandalous *An Apology for the Conduct of Mrs. Teresia Constantia Phillips* (1748). Although Charlotte represents herself as a dutiful daughter – Cordelia to Cibber's King Lear – who only wants his "BLESSING, and his PARDON," the subtext suggests that unless Cibber came through with cash, he could look forward to an increasingly unflattering presentation of himself, while he was offered the sort of role as forgiving father that he wrote in his own sentimental comedies.[34] Here, however, he was not to be drawn into dialogue. This desire of Charke's is certainly one key to the book, which is imagined from the beginning as a defendant on trial: "I . . . humbly move for its having the common Chance of a Criminal, at least to be properly examin'd before it is condemn'd: And should it be found guilty of Nonsense and Inconsistencies, I must consequently resign it to its deserved Punishment."[35] The crime here proceeds from being a woman writer, not from transgressive behavior. The book consists of confessions, but it also contains a good deal of defense and special pleading, especially extenuating circumstances. In an early installment Charlotte indicates that she hopes to be able to tell her readers by the following installment that she and her father have reconciled, but, instead, she reveals that the letter on which she placed her hopes was returned to her in a "blank," an empty page signifying receipt and a refusal to communicate.

The autobiography as blackmail failed. Charke's attempt to get back in her father's good graces was certainly doomed. He had disowned her after she took part in Fielding's entertainments in which she portrayed once again, as in her earliest memory, her father as actor. Colley Cibber was not likely to be swayed. He was, after all, the man whose imperturbability (or impenetrability) kept him for a long time from responding to the provocations of Pope. Several letters from Cibber to Charlotte that unequivocally cut her off are extant:

I am sorry I am not in a position to assist you further. You have made your own bed and therein you must lie. Why do you not dissociate yourself from that worthless scoundrel, and then your relatives might try and aid you. You will never be any good while you adhere to him, and you most certainly will not receive what otherwise you might from your father . . .[36]

The scoundrel in this undated letter was very likely Henry Fielding (from Cibber's perspective), though he might as easily have been her shadowy second husband, John Sacheverell. This letter expounds the position of many an eighteenth-century father, but Cibber was notorious for his love of gambling and neglect of his family. One anecdote of his early marriage tells of his leaving the gambling table after heavy losses with the

exit line, "Now I must go home and eat a child!"[37] In his own *Apology*,
Cibber makes a statement about his plays and his children that has
gained a certain immortality through the aegis of *The Dunciad*: "It may
be observable . . . that my Muse, and my Spouse were equally prolifick;
that the one was seldom the Mother of a Child, but in the same Year the
other made me the Father of a Play: I think we had a Dozen of each
Sort between us; of both which kinds, some died in their Infancy, and
near an equal Number of each were alive, when I quitted the Theatre
. . ."[38] The man who wrote this was not a good bet to prove sensitive to
his daughter's plight. His will cut Charlotte and another sister off with
£5 a piece, though he was generous to his eldest daughter (his main heir)
and two granddaughters. Charlotte was, as she puts it, "an Alien from
the Family."[39] But initially, even if this late and last child was an "unwel-
come Guest" and an "impertinent Intruder" among her numerous sib-
lings, she sees herself as loved by her father and mother.[40]

According to Charke, some of her interest in "masculine" activities
stemmed from her well-meant miseducation. She received the tuition
proper for a young man and "was never made much acquainted with
that necessary Utensil which forms the houswifely Part of a young
Lady's Education, call'd a Needle . . ."[41] She goes on to protect her
family from imaginary burglars with a gun (she gathers a small arsenal),
to ride unlike a girl, to become a volunteer gardener and groom, to set
up as an apothecary, a foretaste of the variety of occupations she tries in
the wake of the Licensing Act. It is likely that she was more the victim
of the Licensing Act (1737), which crushed many an acting career, than
of her father.[42] During the nine years she spent cross-dressed prior to
writing her autobiography, her occupations included valet, higgler, hog-
merchant, oil-merchant, typesetter, journalist, waiter, innkeeper, pastry
chef, and prompter. Charke's book is full of masculine gestures both in
her narrated past and her narrating present. She thinks of herself as a
cuckold, cocks her hat, beats the man who had spread false rumors
about her. Her emphasis on occupation in this life might lead some to
see its structure as that of masculine autobiography, but it is, at the same
time, as non-linear and other-directed as could be desired of any feminine self-representation.[43]

Charke's repudiation of two notorious occupational stories told about
her displays the psychological dynamics at work in her writing of the
Narrative. The first story alleged that she had dressed as a highwayman
and held up her father. A comparison of the version attributed by
Charke to an unsuccessful writer-actor with the account printed in a

contemporary newspaper suggests a kind of wish-fulfillment shaping her narrative. The newspaper story claims:

The amazing Mrs. Charke equipped herself with a horse, mask and pistols, made herself up as a highwayman and waylaid her father in Epping Forest. Poor Cibber handed over his money, making only the rueful reproof: "Young man, young man! This is a sorry trade. Take heed in time." "And so I would," replied his disguised daughter, "but I've a wicked hunks of a father, who rolls in money, yet denies me a guinea. And so a worthy gentleman like you, sir, has to pay for it!"[44]

This reads like something from the contemporary Joe Miller's *Joke Book*. The ironic punch line could only derive from Charke, were it true, and it has all the earmarks of fiction. So does Charke's own version of the story that she retells and disclaims. The supernumerary, whom she claims to have beaten with an oaken cudgel for his lie, spreads the rumor that:

I hired a very fine Bay Gelding, and borrowed a Pair of Pistols, to encounter my Father upon *Epping-Forest*; where, I solemnly protest, I don't know I ever saw my Father in my Life: That I stopp'd the Chariot, presented a Pistol to his Breast, and used such Terms as I am ashamed to insert; threaten'd to blow his Brains out that Moment, if he did not deliver——Upbraiding him for his Cruelty in abandoning me to those Distresses he knew I underwent, when he had it so amply in his Power to relieve me: That since he would not use that Power, I would force him to a Compliance, and was directly going to discharge upon him; but his Tears prevented me, and, asking my Pardon for his ill Usage of me, gave me his Purse with threescore Guineas, and a Promise to restore me to his Family and Love; on which I thank'd him, and rode off.[45]

The Lady doth detail too much. The tale of the highwayman shifts in her telling from repartee to sentimental comedy complete with a rehearsal of the wrongs done her, forgiveness, and cash. Like her "first memory" this is a story of wish-fulfillment, a textual enactment of desire.

The second story maintains that Charke was "selling some Flounders one Day, and, seeing my Father, stept most audaciously up to him, and slapt one of the largest I had full in his Face."[46] She denies that she was ever a fishmonger, and claims that the crowd would have taken justice on her if her father were unable to. But she tells the short, alliterative anecdote very well. Both stories dramatize a working out of hostility toward her father that she officially disowns. These are textual roles that she plays, and we may examine the sources of a range of others.

Charke apologizes for her constant recourse to allusion and quotation from plays when illustrating her situation: "I apprehend I shall be called in Question for my Inability, in conveying Ideas of the Passions which most tenderly affect the Heart, by so often having Recourse to abler Pens than my own, by frequent Quotations . . ."[47] Yet this tendency aestheticizes and shifts the tonalities of the events narrated. These allusions are a series of mini-roles that she slips on and off in her text.

From the very beginning her project to win over her father is compromised by overtones which she does not control. Both the dedication and the epigraph drawn from Gay would have displeased Cibber. The epigraph, which will be discussed later, would bring the Scriblerians to mind, and though Cibber himself had performed in Gay, Pope, and Arbuthnot's *Three Hours After Marriage*, he had long since become an enemy to the group and, in the preceding decade, had been enthroned by Pope as the archdunce, son of the Goddess of Dullness, in *The Dunciad*. Pope may not have written any part of *The What D'ye Call It*, but Cibber certainly thought he had.

Charke's autobiography is many things. I have suggested it is in part a begging letter, but we also might think of it as her *Advertisements for Myself*, for it is full of references to her projects as things her audience may support in the future – the novel *Henry Dumont*; an Academy for Actors; a new puppet theatre – and it also contains a series of mentions of those who have or have not been financially generous toward her.[48] She is quite literally selling her self in this book, an intensification of the commodified relation of the actress to her audience and an alternative to prostitution, that selling of the self forced, as she recognizes, upon too many women in her position.[49]

Yet the consistency of her characteristic way of representing her life deserves attention. One episode in particular may demonstrate at once the tonality of much of the work and its aesthetic registration. While living as a man she returned to her rented rooms and sick daughter, whom she had left "to prog for her and myself":

But, Oh! Heaven! how vast was my Grief and Surprize when I entered the Room, and found the poor little Soul stretched on the Floor; in strong Convulsion Fits; in which she had lain a Considerable Time, and no Mortal near to give her the least Assistance.

I took her up, and, overcome with strong Grief, immediately dropped her on the Floor; which I wonder did not absolutely end her by the Force of the Fall, as she was in Fact a dead Weight. My screaming and her Falling raised the House; and, in the Hurry of my Distraction, I run into the Street, with my Shirt-Sleeves dangling loose about my Hands, my Wig standing on End,

"*Like Quills upon the fretful Porcupine,*"

And proclaiming the sudden Death of my much-beloved Child, a Crowd soon gathered round me, and, in the Violence of my Distraction, instead of administring any necessary Help, wildly stood among the Mob to recount the dreadful Disaster.

The Peoples Compassion was moved, 'tis true; but, as I happened not to be known to them, it drew them into Astonishment, to see the Figure of a young Gentleman, so extravagantly grieved for the Loss of a Child. As I appeared very Young, they looked on it as an unprecedented Affection in a Youth, and began to deem me a Lunatick, rather than that there was any Reality in what I said.[50]

The shift from pathos to "astonishment" and the ludicrous comes about when the crowd perceives her as "the Figure of a young Gentleman" (we may have forgotten she is cross-dressed) whose response goes well beyond the gendered behavior they expect. The disparity between the audience reaction and her sense of her performance, here and in the episode when the four-year-old Charlotte marches cross-dressed as her father in the ditch, models Charke's willingness to accept diverse and even inappropriate responses. Some of her qualifications (for example, her reference to those "who had been employed in the Care, as I then thought, of my expiring Infant") prepare us for the non-tragic dénouement, as does her quotation of a line from *Hamlet* (1.5.19–20) to claim that the hairs of her wig stood on end. Introduced by a melodramatic apostrophe, this remains a "Scene of Sorrow" but the mistaken gender turns the episode into a mixed genre, one that approaches "travesty," a form that gains its effect from lowering or shifting the attitude to a work in a high genre. Johnson defines it in his *Dictionary*, also published in 1755, as "Dressed so as to be made ridiculous; burlesqued." It is literally a "changing of the clothes," and Charke's change of clothes leads to a shift in response both from the crowd in the story and from her reading audience.

Her strong sense of such effects is also observable in her reference to her escape from the bailiffs, who harassed debtors even in the theatre,

those Assailants of Liberty, who constantly attend every Play-Night there, to the inexpressible Terror of many a Potentate, who has quiveringly tremored out the Hero, lest the sad Catastrophe should rather end in a Spunging-House, than a Bowl of Poison or a timely Dagger – The want of which latter Instrument of Death, I once saw supplied with a Lady's Busk; who had just Presence of Mind sufficient to draw it from her Stays, and end at once her wretched Life, *and more wretched Acting*.[51]

Both instances here, the first generalized and the second specified, report travestied situations. Both turn tragedy into something ludicrous: the first with its oxymoronic trembling hero, the terrified potentate; the second with its murder weapon (a whalebone corset stay) that could

come straight from Pope's mock-heroic *Rape of the Lock.* Both self-con-
sciously juxtapose the stage and its fictions with the reality of life and its
contingencies. To take a somewhat different example, when a dog steals
the last three pounds of sausage off her table, leaving Charke and her
child to face a future as grim as that in any sentimental novel or play, she
begins a sentence, "After having sighed away my Senses for my departed
Pork . . ."[52]

Charke's sense of self, stage, and life, whatever their overdetermined
sources in her life, are registered in her autobiography through an
awareness of genre that relates directly to her theatrical background.
She wrote three plays, all farces, and, when she joined Fielding, she spe-
cialized in performing farces. Her one extant play is a metadrama, a
satire on theatre, and her epigraph to Gay's *The What D'ye Call It* could
be considered an attempt to deal with the generic problems of life's
"plot." Gay was the foremost author of farce before Fielding. In its full
title, he identifies *The What D'ye Call It* as a "Tragi-Comi-Pastoral," as
does her epigraph, which Charke misquotes, from Gay's Prologue:

> This Comic Story or this Tragick Jest,
> May make you laugh, or cry, as you like Best.[53]

The notion of her life as a "Tragick Jest" may have been a bit too close
to the bone, so she reversed the adjectives. The comparison of life to
farce can be found elsewhere in the eighteenth century in formulations
by Lady Mary Wortley Montagu. Gay proclaimed in his epitaph that
"Life is a Jest," while George Alexander Stevens, to whom Charke compares herself as an oddity, claims in his *Distress upon Distress: or, Tragedy in
True Taste. A Heroi-Comi-Parodi-Tragedi-Farcical Burlesque* (1752):

> Life is but a Joke – and our Art at the best
> Is solely in making the most of the Jest.[54]

Only in Charke's case, however, is the idea of life as farce used to structure an autobiography.

Charke's understanding and employment of farce has much in
common with her contemporaries and is easy to establish. Her book is
filled with references to farces and mixed generic forms: *The Comical
Humours of the Moor of Venice*, for example. When she drives a hard bargain
to perform in the comedy *The Recruiting Officer*, she says the play was "A
FARCE TO ME."[55] Her account of the strolling players includes an
instance where, having played Scrub in *The Beaux' Stratagem* a few nights
before, she was encouraged by a spectator in the pit to intersperse a few
of Scrub's speeches while "tragedizing in the part of *Pyrrhus*, in *The*

Distress'd Mother."[56] Similarly, in John Gay's *Rehearsal at Goatham*, Sir Roger explains his jumbling a number of plays together by claiming "You know my Neighbours never saw a Play before; and d'ye see, I would shew them all sorts of Plays under one."[57]

Earlier Charke and another actress had blown their lines in Farquhar's comedy, and, as Scrub and Mrs. Sullen "we both took a Wild-goose Chase through all the dramatic Authors we could recollect, taking particular Care not to let any single Speech bear in the Answer the least Affinity; and, while I was making Love from *Jaffier* [*Venice Preserved*], she tenderly approved my Passion with the Soliloquy of *Cato*."[58] Here we have two tragedies mixed in the midst of a comedy, but the lover is "tenderly approved" by a Stoic sage. The indecorums Charke specifies register as travesty: "I have seen an Emperor *as drunk as a Lord*, according to the old Phrase, and a Lord as elegant as a Ticket-Porter: A Queen with one Ruffle on, and Lord *Townly* without shoes, or at least but an Apology for them."[59] A cross-dresser on and off-stage, she was highly aware of the transgression of boundaries of genre as well as gender.

In this connection, it is worth noticing that farce was particularly at home with cross-dressing: Fielding's *Tom Thumb* was played at one point with all the gender roles reversed, and Tom was typically played by a woman. This reversal was also used for Gay's *Beggar's Opera*, a mock-opera in which Charke played Macheath at the Haymarket. Opera itself has been consistently receptive to cross-dressing, and some of its most celebrated eighteenth-century performers were the sexually ambiguous castrati. Charke's delight in oxymoron ("disgracefully exalted," "inexhaustible Fund of Poverty" "unneighbourly Neighbours," "happy Rags") is the stylistic equivalent of her own sexual transgression of gender boundaries and her literary employment of farce to transgress boundaries.[60] Oxymoron, like Garber's theory of cross-dressing, gives us not one thing or the other, but a third term.

Charke's links to cross-genre theatre abound. John Kelly's *The Plot*, in which Charlotte appeared in 1734, identifies itself on the title page as "A new tragi-comi-farcical operatical grotesque pantomime." Her own *The Art of Management* (1735) is a theatre satire in which she played herself as "Mrs. Tragic" (the subtitle is *Tragedy Expelled*). Envisioning herself as tragic within a farce – her Prologue was said by a reviewer to draw tears[61] – she virtually predicts her self-representation in her autobiography. Her undiscoverable *Tit for Tat* is subtitled *The Comedy and Tragedy of War*. Fielding's *Eurydice Hiss'd* (1737), in which Charke played the male role of Spatter, opened with her saying: "My lord, I am extremely obliged to you for the honor you show me in staying to the rehearsal of my tragedy. I hope it will please your lordship as well as Mr. Medley's comedy has, for I assure you it is ten times as ridiculous." Spatter explains that "a tragedy had better be ridiculous than dull, and that there is more merit in making the audience laugh than in setting them asleep."[62] This is at once foolish art and seen as such by the play, yet it is fairly close to Charke's own position in her *Narrative*. Sourwit later refers to Pillage's play within the play as a "merry tragedy." The "Nonsense and Inconsistencies"[63] that Charke fears will be found in her book are the very stuff of farce with its irregular plot, and they are the subjects of her satire in *The Art of Management*. In her autobiography, she describes herself as "the Principal in this Tragedy" when an "Orphan Heiress" makes her "as I may most properly term it, the unhappy Object of Love."[64] She clearly regrets the loss of the fortune and considers herself an "improper Object" of the young lady's love. But the event is hardly presented as tragic, though it does cost Charke a job.

Certainly there are a number of ways in which her autobiography can be seen as the replication of her father's odd if important *Apology for the Life of Colley Cibber, Comedian* (1740). There is no earlier pair of English father–daughter autobiographers and very little in the way of a secular tradition of autobiography before. As her father's is very much the auto-biography of an actor, hers is the first autobiography of an actress in England. She plays her father in her narrative, on the stage, and in her life. We have seen the inception of her role as "the perfect Representative" of Colley Cibber as her first memory. When she joined Fielding's company, she began by playing Lord Place, a character in *Pasquin* who is partially based on Cibber. In *The Historical Register for the Year 1736* (1737) she played Mr. Hen, a parody of the auctioneer Christopher Cock, though the major target of the play was Colley Cibber. *Biographia Dramatica* claims that Charlotte played the role of the character (Fopling Fribble) who satirized her father in "The Battle of the Poets," a scene added to Fielding's *The Author's Farce*, probably by Thomas Cooke.[65] Cibber was already attacked in the play itself as Marplot. Late in her career Charke speaks of rehearsing Cibber's prime role of Lord Foppington but being stopped, presumably because her brother Theophilus had enjoined the theatre manager from letting her play that role. In her autobiography, Charlotte allusively presents her father as King Lear to her Cordelia and her eldest sister's Goneril. Like Cibber, she insists on her oddness, and like him she cannot spell "para-phernalia." Like Cibber, Charke writes an autobiography that is also a history of the stage though hers is significantly observed from below, thereby presenting a low equivalent of his more dignified history. She seems to play her father to get his attention; he continues as her audience, though becoming a pointedly unresponsive one.

Whatever the impetus for her writing the *Narrative* of her life, Charke is unquestionably once again playing her father as she writes this apology (in both senses). Remembering her exchange of hats with the Falstaffian bailiff that leaves him with a small, elegant, laced hat perched upon his head, while she is smothered beneath his huge coachman's hat (an oxymoronic "smoaky Conveniency"), we should see this scene as an epitome of her *Narrative*.[66] Content and style come together in *A Narrative of the Life of Charlotte Charke*. Charlotte Charke's farcical form is autobiography as travesty.

NOTES

I am grateful to the University of California at Irvine for a grant which enabled me to conduct research at the British Library, the Print Room of the British Museum, the Theatre Museum, London, the Victoria and Albert Museum, and other locations. I am also grateful to Claudia Thomas at Wake Forest University, Karl Zender and Max Byrd at the University of California, Davis, and Deborah Payne and Jonathan Loesberg at American University, Washington, DC, for inviting me to give papers on Charlotte Charke. When I gave a version of this essay at the American Society for Eighteenth-Century Studies in Seattle, Marshall Brown's remarks were particularly useful.

1. There is no satisfactory modern edition. I am currently completing an annotated edition with the important variants noted. While I have utilized the two book editions of 1755 and that of 1759, as well as the extra-illustrated copies at the British Library and the University of California, Davis, references in the text are to Charlotte Charke, *A Narrative of the Life of Mrs. Charke, Written by Herself*, 2nd edn. (London, 1755, facsimile, ed. Leonard R. N. Ashley, rev. edn., Gainesville, Fla.: Scholars Facsimile and Reprints, 1989), here p. 11; hereafter cited as Charke, *Narrative*. The Bristol serial edition of 1755 is not extant. Charke's topos of the inability of the woman writer was long familiar.

2. The language for describing cross-dressing in this period often goes unnoticed. In 1687, Aphra Behn uses " en chevalier," nearly the same phrase as Charke's later "en cavalier." See Aphra Behn, *Love Letters between a Nobleman and his Sister*, ed. Maureen Duffy (New York: Penguin Books–Virago Press, 1987), 249, and Charke, *Narrative*, 78. The Abbé de Choisy, roughly Behn's French contemporary, speaks of dressing "en femme" or of talking the young women in whom he is interested into dressing "en garçon," though he also uses "en cavalier" (the same version of the term as Charke), perhaps

in its more restricted sense; see François Timoléon, Abbé de Choisy, *Transvestite Memoirs of the Abbé de Choisy*, trans. R. H. F. Scott (London: Peter Owen, 1973), 39.

3. Jill Campbell, "'When Men Women Turn': Gender Reversal in Fielding's Plays," in *The New Eighteenth Century: Theory, Politics, English Literature*, ed. Felicity A. Nussbaum and Laura Brown (New York: Methuen, 1987), 286 n. 7. For Fielding's fiction, see Terry Castle, "'Matters not Fit to be Mentioned': Fielding's *The Female Husband*," *A Journal of English Literary History* 49 (1982): 602–22; this journal will be cited hereafter as *ELH*.

4. See, for example, Dianne Dugaw, *Warrior Women and Popular Balladry, 1650–1850* (Cambridge: Cambridge University Press, 1989).

5. See Rudolf M. Dekker and Lotte van de Pol, *The Tradition of Female Transvestism in Early Modern Europe* (New York: St. Martin's Press, 1989).

6. Both of whom were also autobiographers. See Christian Davies, *The Life of Mrs. Christian Davies* (London, 1740). For d'Eon, see the biography by Gary Kates, *The Chevalier d'Eon is a Woman* (New York: Basic Books, 1996), which draws extensively on the as yet unpublished autobiography.

7. Aphra Behn, *The Rover* (1677), ed. Frederick M. Link (Lincoln: University of Nebraska Press, 1967), 1.1.41; 4.2.199; 1.1.181–87.

8. Charke, *Narrative*, 26, 33.

9. *Oxford English Dictionary*, s. v. "mad cap."

10. Charke, *Narrative*, 26.

11. Alexander Pope, *The Dunciad*, ed. James Sutherland, in *The Twickenham Edition of the Works of Alexander Pope*, ed. John Butt, vol. v (London: Methuen, 1965), bk. 1, line 32.

12. Charke, *Narrative*, 23, 271.

13. John Harold Wilson, *All the King's Ladies: Actresses of the Restoration* (Chicago: University of Chicago Press, 1958), 73; Pat Rogers, "The Breeches Part," in *Sexuality in Eighteenth-Century Britain*, ed. Paul-Gabriel Boucé (Towata, N.J.: Barnes and Noble, 1982), 248–58.

14. Rogers ("The Breeches Part," 251), claims "it would be safe to say that Mrs. Charke was the only specialist in breeches parts who publicly extended her cross-dressing to life outside the theatre"; but Dekker and van de Pol (*Tradition of Female Transvestism*, 8) instance the Dutch eighteenth-century actress Mietje de Bruin as such a specialist who cross-dressed at night outside the theatre, and they mention others. The playwright Susannah Centlivre may have cross-dressed before becoming (briefly) an actress, but the tradition is uncertain.

15. For an interesting account of Charke in the context of actors' and actresses' sexuality, see Kristina Straub, *Sexual Suspects: Eighteenth-Century Players and Sexual Ideology* (Princeton: Princeton University Press, 1992), esp. ch. 7, "The Guilty Pleasures of Female Theatrical Cross-Dressing and the Autobiography of Charlotte Charke."

16. Colley Cibber, *An Apology for the Life of Colley Cibber, Comedian*, 2nd edn. (London, 1740), 138.

17. See Dekker and van de Pol, *Tradition of Female Transvestism*, chs. 2–4.

18. Castle, "Matters," 604; and Lynn Friedli, "Passing Women: A Study of Gender Boundaries in the Eighteenth Century," in G. S. Rousseau and Roy Porter, eds., *Sexual Underworlds of the Enlightenment* (Chapel Hill: University of North Carolina Press, 1988), 234–60.

19. Dekker and van de Pol, *Tradition of Female Transvestism*, 55.

20. Terry Castle, *The Apparitional Lesbian: Female Homosexuality and Modern Culture* (New York: Columbia University Press, 1993).

21. Marjorie Garber, *Vested Interests: Cross-Dressing and Cultural Anxiety* (New York: Routledge, 1992); Judith Butler, *Gender Trouble: Feminism and the Subversion of Identity* (New York: Routledge, 1990). Charke's sexuality has been subject to much speculation, some of it based on little evidence. In *The Well-Known Trouble Maker: A Life of Charlotte Charke* (London: Faber and Faber, 1988), Fidelis Morgan elaborately and unconvincingly argues for Charke's heterosexuality. One detail, which she treats as evidence that Charlotte Charke and her companion slept separately, may demonstrate some of the complications involved. Morgan quotes Charke as saying she "consulted my pillow what was best to be done and communicated my thoughts to my friend" (205). While Charke actually says she "consulted on my Pillow," this is the least of the problems. First, Morgan is too literal-minded. Charke means that she thought things over before sharing her ideas. But what is lacking here is a sense of historical context. It is almost unthinkable that two poor eighteenth-century women would not share a bed at a time when even strange males might be asked to share a bed in an inn and women frequently were. I have no doubt that Charlotte Charke as Mr. Brown literally slept with "Mrs. Brown." The question of Charke's sexuality remains open. For a thoughtful brief account of this "longterm partnership between working women" which speaks of their affection and love, see Emma Donoghue, *Passions Between Women: British Lesbian Culture, 1668–1801* (London: Scarlet Press, 1993), 164–67 and 97–100.

22. John Sturrock, "Theory vs. Autobiography," in *The Culture of Autobiography: Constructions of Self-Representation*, ed. Robert Folkenflik (Stanford, Calif.: Stanford University Press, 1993), 21–37.

23. Charke, *Narrative*, 19, 86.

24. *Ibid.*, iv, 271.

25. *The Female Soldier; or the Surprising Life and Adventures of Hannah Snell* (London, 1750), reprint, Augustan Reprint Society, no. 257 (Los Angeles: William Andrews Clark Memorial Library, University of California, Los Angeles, 1989), iii.

26. Charke, *Narrative*, vi.

27. Cibber, *Apology*, 7.

28. Charke, *Narrative*, 13.

29. Bruner made this point in conversation. For his work on autobiography, see "The Autobiographical Process," in Folkenflik, *Culture of Autobiography*, 38–56.

30. Charke, *Narrative*, 17–20.
31. *Ibid.*, 95.
32. *Ibid.*, 20, 21–22. She sees herself as a child Don Quixote.
33. For Fielding's theatrical career see Robert D. Hume, *Henry Fielding and the London Theatre, 1728–1737* (Oxford: Clarendon Press, 1988).
34. Charke, *Narrative*, 14.
35. *Ibid.*, 11–12.
36. Quoted in Morgan, *The Well-Known Trouble Maker*, 87. The address in the original is Tavistock Street, not Tavistock Square, as Morgan has it. My text comes from the copy in the Theatre Museum, London, located on Tavistock Street.
37. Quoted in Leonard R. N. Ashley, *Colley Cibber*, rev. edn. (Boston: Twayne, 1989), 118.
38. Cibber, *Apology*, 217.
39. Charke, *Narrative*, 24.
40. *Ibid.*, 15–16.
41. *Ibid.*, 17.
42. For the Act, see Vincent J. Liesenfeld, *The Licensing Act of 1737* (Madison: University of Wisconsin Press, 1984).
43. For women's autobiography as structured differently from those of men, see Mary G. Mason in "The Other Voice: Autobiographies of Women Writers," in *Autobiography: Essays Theoretical and Critical*, ed. James Olney (Princeton: Princeton University Press, 1980), 207–35. I disagree with Sidonie Smith's judgment of Charke's autobiography as a "failure" in *A Poetics of Women's Autobiography: Marginality and the Fictions of Self-Representation* (Bloomington: University of Indiana Press, 1987), ch. 6.
44. Quoted in Morgan, *The Well-Known Trouble Maker*, 85, from an undated clipping. A "hunks" is a miser.
45. Charke, *Narrative*, 114.
46. *Ibid.*, 141.
47. *Ibid.*, 126.
48. For the novels, see Erin Mackie, "Desperate Measures: The Narratives of the Life of Mrs. Charlotte Charke," *ELH* 58 (1991): 841–65, who stresses their highly conventional morality, though some episodes in them, such as the homophobic baiting and beating of Billy Loveman by the hero, egged on by the heroine of *Henry Dumont*, need to be interpreted more problematically.
49. For Charke's awareness of this point, see Charke, *Narrative*, 139.
50. *Ibid.*, 97–99.
51. *Ibid.*, 103–04.
52. *Ibid.*, 143.
53. John Gay, *Dramatic Works*, ed. John Fuller, 2 vols. (Oxford: Clarendon Press, 1983), 1: 174.
54. "Dedication" to George Alexander Stevens, *Distress Upon Distress: or, Tragedy in True Taste. A Heroi-Comi-Parodi-Tragedi-Farcical Burlesque* (1752), iv.

55. Charke, *Narrative*, 105.
56. *Ibid.*, 208.
57. Gay, *Dramatic Works*, 1:180.
58. Charke, *Narrative*, 204–05.
59. *Ibid.*, 184–85.
60. *Ibid.*, 195, 207, 233, 105.
61. See Morgan's quotation from the *Daily Advertiser, The Well-Known Trouble Maker*, 56, which may be Charke's puff for herself.
62. Henry Fielding, *Eurydice Hiss'd* (London, 1737) in *The Historical Register for the Year 1736* and *Eurydice Hissed*, ed. William A. Appleton (Lincoln: University of Nebraska Press, 1967), 54.
63. Charke, *Narrative*, 11–12.
64. *Ibid.*, 106–07.
65. David Erskine Baker, *Biographia Dramatica* (London, 1812), vol. 1, pt. 1:104.
66. Charke, *Narrative*, 95.

CHAPTER SIX

Petrarch / Sade: writing the life

Julie Candler Hayes

"In a sense, I have always wanted my books to be fragments from an autobiography."

Michel Foucault[1]

Jacques François Paul Alphonse de Sade (1705–77) was best known to his intimates as an *abbé galant*, man of letters, and author of a three-volume biography of Petrarch, but he is best known to us as the uncle of the unruly marquis. Their relative importance was reversed in the eighteenth century. Madame du Deffand, regaling Horace Walpole with epistolary gossip about what biographers would later refer to as the "Rose Keller Affair," refers to the marquis as the "neveu de l'abbé auteur de *Pétrarque*."[2] Despite the marquis's twentieth-century preeminence, few of his biographers have been able to resist lingering on the figure of the abbé, libertine and erudite, who was, for five years or more, his nephew's guardian in a forbidding medieval chateau supposedly complete with underground torture chambers and sexual servants.[3] Although many have considered the effects on the marquis's literary imagination of the years spent with his uncle, I am more interested here in examining another family legacy, the Sade family's preoccupation with the poet Petrarch, his beloved Laura, and the particular form that interest takes in the abbé's *Mémoires pour la vie de François Pétrarque*.

Published anonymously in 1764 and 1767, the *Mémoires* represent an impressive scholarly achievement. Sade synthesizes previous work on Petrarch and carries out new archival research enabling him to contest earlier biographers and commentators. The *Mémoires* are not without a more intimate dimension, however. The abbé is at considerable pains throughout to argue that the Laura whom Petrarch loved was the historical Laure de Noves, wife of Hugues de Sade, the ancestor of an uninterrupted family line down to the abbé himself.[4] The *Mémoires* offer a covert family history and, to a certain extent, a family romance. A

serious work of scholarship containing provocative reflections on the art
of literary biography, the abbé's work is also a model for scholarship
become autobiography, in which erudition and interpretative acumen
are implicated in a system of self-projection, mythologizing, and desire.

I grew up believing in the truth of the precepts that were available to me: I
believed in the reality of space; I believed that distance separates, that it is a cor-
poreal substance; I believed in the reality of nations and borders; I believed that
across the border there existed another reality . . . And things which did not fit
my vocabulary were merely pushed over the edge into [a] chasm of silence.[5]

As the rhetorical drift of his past-tense credo suggests, the narrator of
Amitav Ghosh's 1988 novel *The Shadow Lines* gradually comes to doubt
the reality of certain divisions and exclusions, whether in the political
geography of India and Pakistan, or among the compartments of his
own memory. Events, ideas, recollections, feelings, and utterances
ineluctably permeate one another. Such is the structure of the abbé's
Pétrarque. An equivocal text, it would like to maintain and yet to undo the
dichotomies France/Italy, biographer/subject, but other things come
into contact here as well. For the contemporary reader, the work is a
textual "contact zone," shot through with not only the author's own
motives and ambitions, but also two centuries of reflections on the name
"Sade." As the allusion to Peter Weiss's *Marat/Sade* in my title suggests,
I will be discussing, if obliquely, the abbé's famous nephew, the marquis
de Sade. It would be disingenuous to pretend that a reading such as this
one could remain unaffected by considerations touching on the marquis,
in whose life and literary imagination Italy, in general, and Petrarch, in
particular, play significant roles.[6] The abbé's influence here is at least as
strong as in the development of his nephew's libertinism. Furthermore,
since the *Mémoires* are both a carefully crafted statement on the art of literary biography and a strong form of self-fashioning for their author,
they also provide a useful foil for considering recent biographies of the
marquis himself – biographies that bear an odd resemblance to the
abbé's project in its most personal, self-mythologizing moments. The
abbé's work becomes emblematic of the surreptitious desiring investments that infuse not only the productions of the various Sade biographers but other forms of scholarly writing as well.

Biographers have generally been in agreement in their accounts of the
abbé as a witty and refined man of letters. Most reflect on his worldly
connections and his friendship with Voltaire; all speculate on the degree

and nature of his influence on the marquis. The course of the relations between uncle and nephew is not entirely clear. Gilbert Lely cites an unpublished document indicating that the abbé took steps in 1775 to have the marquis imprisoned on a *lettre de cachet* following a number of public scandals, but Alice Laborde contests Lely's interpretation of the uncle's actions. Maurice Lever sees the abbé as becoming increasingly reticent in helping with his nephew's legal difficulties and the letters by the abbé included in Jean-Louis Debauve's recent collection of *inédits* point to a gradual eroding of their relationship as the marquis repeatedly seeks to excuse himself in his uncle's eyes following scandal after scandal.[7] Even such letters as these, however, testify to the depth and significance of their relationship, as we can see in the remarkably frank and psychologically acute letter that Sade wrote to his uncle in 1765, in which he analyzes his marriage: "Yes, I'd no doubt be happier if I loved my wife. . . ."[8] The relation between the abbé and his nephew has even inspired cinematic representation, the 1971 film *De Sade*, in which a rather confused young marquis (played by Keir Dullea) receives lessons in cynicism from the worldly abbé (John Huston). But whether or not the abbé's château Saumane should be seen as a small-scale model for the marquis's imaginary Silling, or the abbé understood as a prototype of Dom Séverino in *Justine*, readers of the marquis's writings – particularly such texts as the *Voyage d'Italie* or the dramatic prefaces – will recognize a certain rhetorical *air de famille* in the abbé's displays of erudition, his pitiless treatment of literary predecessors, his penchant for irony.

Let us consider the state and structure of the *Mémoires*.[9] The work is in three handsome quarto volumes of over 600 pages each. The author's name appears nowhere. The title page gives a false "Amsterdam" imprint; publication apparently occurred in Avignon. Of the two copies I have examined at the Bibliothèque Nationale and the University Research Library at the University of California, Los Angeles, the UCLA copy contained a tipped-in, non-paginated, unsigned dedicatory epistle to an Italian statesman, cardinal Torrigiani, suggesting a special "Italian edition." Volumes I and II have the same date, 1764, but, as the preface to Volume II emphasizes, eight months passed between the appearance of the two volumes (during which time, Sade explains, he had hoped that reviews and commentary would appear to which he could respond).

The first two volumes both end with an extensive, separately paginated section of "Notes," while Volume III closes with *Pièces justificatives* (documents such as Verger's early biography, letters, Laura's marriage

contract, and her will). Volume I begins with two prefaces, one addressed
to Italian men of letters and the other to their French counterparts;
Volume II addresses both groups together. These are rich texts, where
Sade considers the theoretical and polemical stakes of his enterprise and
reflects on his activity as a reader of archival material, previous secondary sources, and Petrarch's own letters and writings; he also discusses
translation problems and contrasts the literary cultures of France and
Italy. The main text, the "life" of Petrarch, follows a careful chronological narrative line and includes extensive quotations, translated into
French, from Petrarch's prose and poetry. The separately paginated
"Notes" are actually short essays on a number of topics, most of which
relate to either Laura or the Sade family.

The *Mémoires* are a complexly conceived text whose central narrative
thread is offset by alternative structures, some of which interact with one
another, some of which go in their own directions. Various documents
(*pièces*) follow the main narrative, which also contains extensive quotations from numerous sources. The heterogeneity of the textual materials and structures corresponds to the abbé's description of his project as
a "compilation." At the same time, there is a movement toward connection, whether in the linear narrative that occupies most of the space, or
in the cross-references (even verbatim repetitions) that draw prefaces to
notes and notes to main text.[10] As we shall see, Sade's reflections on the
art of biography similarly turn between two kinds of textual
configuration, the "compilation of memoirs" (*compilation de mémoires*) and
"a well-made life" (*une vie bien faite*).

Although the abbé's authorship may have been an open secret, he
maintains official anonymity. Even so, he reveals his personal stake
whenever his text touches on his family. Occasional cryptic remarks hint
that he might have private reasons to be "interested" in his subject, but
he maintains a fiction of detachment as he explains that the Sade family
archives have been "made available" to him.[11] Even as his recounting of
family history is ostensibly limited to setting down the simple facts of
who married whom, the abbé manages to inject a deeper resonance into
his account, first by insisting on the perfect state of the Sade family
archives extending back to the thirteenth century, and second by dismiss-
ing various illustrious and quasi-mythological versions of the family's
origins, one of which was reported by Nostradamus. In rejecting
affiliation with the princes de Baux or with the miraculous construction
of the Pont d'Avignon, Sade succeeds in reinforcing our sense of the
family's antiquity and fame, and strengthens his hold on the ancestor

he's interested in: Laura, emblematic and incomparable object of a poet's love.

It is important to Sade not only to prove that Laura is Laure de Noves, but also to present a particular image of her. He entertains the question of whether or not she wrote poetry and decides she did not: "Laura had considerable natural intelligence, without ornament or education. That is why Petrarch is content to praise the gentleness, the kindness, and the humanity of her words."[12] But although she does not produce writing of her own, she is supremely responsible for Petrarch's creations:

In a word, without Laura, without the desire to please her that spurred him on, not only would Petrarch never have written the poems that have made his name immortal, but he also would perhaps have sunk into debauchery, never to achieve the fame that we shall see him enjoy with such distinction, setting so to speak the tone for his age.[13]

Laura is the "author" of Petrarch; but she remains an image of gentle self-possession: she does not give herself to her lover, and she leaves us no concrete expression of her interior life, no poetry of her own. It is important to Sade to maintain this tension between affect or desire and self-possession. He makes the point explicitly in his final note, "On the Nature of Petrarch's Love" ("Sur la nature de l'amour de Pétrarque"), where he combats two common misconceptions about her: "One is that he never desired Laura's favors. The other is that he obtained them. Both are injurious to the lady."[14] Just as he had earlier argued that Laura was real, and no poetic figment or allegory, so now he proclaims that Petrarch's love was securely anchored in physical attraction. Laura remains an exemplary mother figure, both eroticized and chaste.[15]

In his prefaces, however, the abbé is mainly concerned with setting forth the principles of writing literary biography. He begins his account by detailing the shortcomings of all of Petrarch's previous biographers, whom he classifies chronologically. The first three biographers, who were contemporaries or near-contemporaries of the poet, fail to take advantage of their status as witnesses, but each fails in a significantly different way. Domenico Aretino (Dominique l'Aretin) recounts having spoken to Petrarch shortly before the latter's death, but he confesses that his emotion in recalling the encounter is so great that he cannot describe it. (Sade comments ironically on his "tender heart.") Next comes Coluccio Salutati de Stignano, a city administrator in Florence who might have revealed much about the poet's political career, but who, instead, restricts himself to writing "historical panegyrics" (*éloges historiques*) rather than "detailed lives" (*vies circonstanciées*).[16] And the third,

Pietro-Paolo Vergerio (Paul Verger), who knew Petrarch and his circle, simply repeats word for word Petrarch's own autobiographical letter to posterity.

Each of these fourteenth-century biographer-commentators appears to represent an aspect of the abbé's own project. Like Vergerio, he offers a life based on the works, a kind of *Pétrarque par lui-même*, in which he wants to "rassembler avec soin ces petits détails épars çà & là dans ses œuvres."[17] Second, and despite his disclaimer, "I am his biographer, not his champion," he will find himself, like Coluccio, in the position of furthering the poet's glory: response to Volume I of the *Mémoires* causes Sade to shift to a defensive mode in Volume II.[18] And, like Aretino, the abbé has a profound personal investment in setting forth the facts: aristocratic pride and self-assertion have as influential a role in his text as Aretino's "tender heart" had in his. Apparently sensing kinship with his fourteenth-century precursor, another ambitious intellectual, Sade cites Petrarch's advice to Aretino as if it were for himself: "Despoil every book, and by endless reading and rereading, let your name go forth to all posterity."[19] Thus Sade's detailed treatment and refutation of these three early figures serves the double purpose of prefiguring his own work and distinguishing his from theirs. Like Boswell, he establishes a sort of reciprocity with his subject, constructing himself as a man of letters through his biographical construction of a man of letters.[20]

The centripetal force of the figure of Laura is evident in the organization of the rest of the literature review, inasmuch as Sade tends to classify, even to judge periods of Petrarch scholarship based on their treatment of her – whether she was considered allegorical or real, for example, or whether the archival work took an interest in the facts of her life. Of Alessandro Vellutello's theory that Laura was the daughter of a different Provençal nobleman, Henri de Chabaud, Sade claims that it is nothing but a "novel" (*roman*) based on a faulty interpretation of a few lines taken out of context.[21] This description is dangerously close to the abbé's work as well, since he too emphasizes the close reading of Petrarch's poetry and prose for scraps of potential biographical information, ever in the interest of letting Petrarch "present himself."[22] Try as he will to let the text stand as transparent documentary evidence, "speaking for itself," Sade's complaints about the "obscurity" of certain verses or the poet's penchant for wordplay suggest the possibility that the ultimate truth may remain as inaccessible as Laura herself.

There is also a parallel between Sade's insistence on maintaining the tension between carnal desire and non-consummation in Petrarch's love and the account he gives of his own project, its methods and aims. His fullest statement of these comes in the first preface, following the literature review and various modest disclaimers in response to Christina of Sweden's remark that since Petrarch was a great philosopher, a great lover, and a great poet, then only someone possessing all these qualities could do him justice. In a sense, Christina's comment seals the fate of all the biographers Sade has discussed in his review, all of whom he found defective in understanding, sentiment, or interpretative skill. It is at this moment that the abbé chooses to tell his readers that he is not writing Petrarch's biography at all. I cite the passage in its entirety:

Thus it is not his life that I present to you, Messieurs; please note the title of my Book: *Memoirs for the Life of Petrarch*.

You know better than I; there is a great difference between a life and Memoirs. A life is a history: Memoirs should be considered as the raw materials for writing a history. More is required of a Historian than of a compiler of Memoirs. More discrimination in the choice of facts and a more stringent critique; more order and precision in narration; a more careful adherence to the subject and connection among parts; and especially a nobler, more precise, more pleasing style.

A life subject to the laws of history should have a regular pace, and the writer should not overly digress. In writing Memoirs, one has more elbow-room; one can take little excursions, emphasize various details, take up seemingly extraneous topics that would not fit in a carefully wrought history. I fear that some may accuse me of having abused this liberty: all I can say is that it takes more wit and talent to compose a life than to compile Memoirs. Compilation is an almost mechanical task; it is more wearisome and brings less honor.[23]

Of course, "compilation" as he accomplishes it, surpasses efforts such as Tomasini's *Petrarca redivivus*, a sixteenth-century anthology of source materials gathered with less "choice, order, and discernment."[24] I find Sade's distinctions between *Mémoires* and *Vie* all the more interesting inasmuch as I would defy anyone who reads the three volumes of chronological narrative interspersed with critical commentary and accompanied by copious notes and documents, to imagine she had read anything other than a biography, *une vie*. A related disclaimer that functions to affirm the significance and truthfulness of the project is Sade's insistence on his "plain style" and his inability to write in what he calls "le style à la mode."[25]

Why does the abbé refuse himself the honor, as he terms it, of writing a "life"? There is the question of how to avoid falling prey to the chain of critiques of previous biographies, several of which bore an uneasy resemblance to his own. Having set mercilessly high standards for others,

Sade excuses himself from the competition. On another level, the refusal to see the "life" as complete, however many facts may be adduced or materials compiled, is a way of assuming Petrarch's position with regard to the incomparable Laura. It is to permit oneself a certain material investment – in a book, the conditions of its production, distribution, and consumption – and to refuse completion, consummation, or closure. Without the benefit of stylistic polish or historiographical discipline, the abbé's work remains raw material waiting for some Italian scholar to "put to use,"[26] and the peculiar proleptic weight of the "*pour*" in the title *Mémoires pour la vie de François Pétrarque* becomes clear. The final goal, announced in a phrase so often repeated as to take on the value of a refrain, "at last to know Petrarch" (*enfin connoître Pétrarque*), can be felt as all the more profound and absolute as it remains unrealized.[27]

By insisting on the liberty of the compiler, Sade outdoes Petrarch, whose love for Laura, he speculates, owed its force to the constraining protocols of a particular historical context. Sade maintains his relation to the unrealizable, perfect *Vie de Pétrarque*, and retains his liberty as well, allowing himself "little excursions" without subjecting himself to "the laws of history."[28] In a move similar to Diderot's stance with regard to the *Encyclopédie*, Sade's assumption of the role of compiler allows him paradoxically greater creative liberty and authority than would that of author. The abbé injects his non-authorial authority in numerous ways. His manner of situating himself as the keenest judge of previous scholarship is a clear instance, and so is his method for constructing his audience, especially the Italian audience. Despite his humble posture as someone "who has not had the fortune to be born beyond the Alps,"[29] and his repeated assertions that many essential texts and archival sources can only be found in Italy, Sade constantly undermines Italian scholarship and even the Italians' understanding of their own poet. His references to the archival riches of Italian libraries are invariably accompanied by the remark that no Italian makes use of them, and he recounts in detail his own relations with curators and archivists such as the abbé Bandini of the Medici libraries.[30] Even as he modestly suggests that only an Italian could ever write the definitive *vie*, he describes it in terms that clearly reveal the balance of intellectual power: "a good life of Petrarch that at last will enable you to know this famous man whom you have admired for so long, but of whom your knowledge is so superficial."[31] Given his repeated insistence on the Italians' failure to understand their own poet or to make use of their own archives, the presumably modest request at the preface's end – "Faites-moi connoître mes erreurs" (Let me know my errors) – is sheer bravado.[32]

In the second of the two prefaces to Volume I, addressed to French men of letters, Sade speaks of France as "notre Nation," but he criticizes the widespread lack of appreciation in France for Petrarch and for the cultural products of the Italian Renaissance in general, a situation which he intends to rectify. Despite the acknowledgment of Italy as the birth-place of the Renaissance, the second preface, with its long disquisition on literary translation, appears to complete the work of cultural expro-priation begun in the first. Sade repeats textually the act of François I, removing (literally "translating") Italian art and artists from Italy. At the same time, however, Sade preserves an external, authoritative stance with regard to the northern French whom he will thus educate. In answer to the question of whether or not his work constitutes trespass-ing in others' territory, Sade first proclaims his internationalism: Petrarch belongs to the world. But he then redirects the argument entirely by noting that the poet was educated in Carpentras, Avignon, and Montpellier; that he was associated with the Sorgue and Vaucluse regions, and that ultimately as a man of letters he "belonged" more to the places where he was educated and where he wrote than to the country where he was born or died.[33]

This (non) authorial voice is authoritative, but unanchored from a fixed "national consciousness." If, on the one hand, the abbé appears to be constructing – or, as Benedict Anderson would say, "imagining" – a place, a faded lost origin called "Italy," and another place, "France," that might subsume that earlier place (and export its raw materials back to the *métropole*), I would nonetheless argue that, at a more profound level, neither "France" nor "Italy" quite function as secure and viable entities: both shift ground. This is in part because Sade addresses himself to both and identifies wholly with neither. In the preface to Volume II, Sade addresses a joint session of French and Italian literati, equalizing his dis-tance from both. This appeal to apparently stable national identities has the effect of calling our attention to their contingencies and blind spots. Like the narrator of *The Shadow Lines*, we come gradually to doubt "the reality of nations and borders" and to sense that other forms of affiliation – Sade's epistolary relations with librarians, fellow scholars, and potential readers, as well as his unacknowledged family ties – are more important. As Homi K. Bhabha has noted, "Designations of cul-tural difference interpellate forms of identity which, because of their continual implication in other symbolic systems, are always 'incomplete' or open to cultural translation."[34] The abbé's in-between status as south-erner – Provençal, *méridional* – traces itself into the text.[35] His awareness of his role as a stock speculator in the markets of cultural capital, his negative identity as not-Italian and not-quite-French, contribute to his ability to defamiliarize both the icon of the Florentine "good century" and the notion of Frenchness as centralized and homogenous. It is not anachronistic to see something of what Iain Chambers and others have described as a "trans-national" or even "migrant" identity in the abbé, who inscribes a shifting "I," an "I" in hiding, while writing in a language which, if no longer perceived in 1760 as that of the "colonizer," must nevertheless be known in relation to the alternative local language, Provençal.[36]

Thus Sade lays claim not only to Laura as ancestor, but also to Petrarch as spiritual compatriot and model. My point is not to minimize his achievement, nor to decry the years of effort put into research, translation, and writing, as so much self-mythologizing. Rather, I take the abbé's work as exemplifying the way in which many of us "involve ourselves in our work." As an instructive and particularly relevant example, consider the various biographies of the marquis de Sade. To pass from one to another is not to gaze upon a single distant planet through a variety of telescopes, but rather to come upon a conversation in which some participants are overtly eyeing one another and others serenely oblivious, but all are concerned with maintaining status, and each is affected by the others: more a Modern Languages Association cash bar than an "ideal speech situation."

Of the major Sade biographers since 1960, Gilbert Lely's relation to his predecessors seems the simplest at the outset, his ambitions little different from those of the abbé: he seeks to continue the "demythologizing" of Sade begun by Maurice Heine, to reclaim Sade from the popular imagination and to sculpt a new figure from the documentary evidence. The extent to which the others share in this project is exemplified by the significant role each gives to archival work and the continued excavation of *inédits*. But the documents are never entirely able to speak for themselves: however eloquent they may appear, their ambiguities call for elucidation. Lely alternates chapters of day-to-day enumerations of known "facts" with florid interpretative essays where his own passions – rabid anti-jacobinism, for example – are on display. Subsequent biographers must deal with Lely's own form of mythologizing and, to a lesser extent, with each other: they consult one another, snub one another.

Like Lely, each must come to terms with the iconicity of their subject and be concerned with his or her own role in maintaining or transforming the cultural role of "Sade." Thus Alice Laborde: "My intention is

not to make the marquis out to be an angel, but to rely on texts and documents and, to the greatest extent possible, avoid inflating the texts with
passages from his most 'sadistic' works in order to make up for the lack
of documents."[37] There is, of course, no escaping one's own implication
in that cultural space, whatever hopes one may profess of allowing
others to "enfin connoître Sade."[38] It would appear preferable to relin-
quish that dream of teleological progress toward the truth. Whatever we
choose to write about, we are writing about ourselves at some level, or
at any rate writing ourselves, because that writing becomes part of our
history. Jacques Derrida speaks of being able "to call just about anything
a self-portrait, not only any drawing ('portrait' or not), but anything that
happens to me, anything by which I can be affected or let myself be
affected."[39] It is the awareness that "self-writing" is a category susceptible of endless generalization that has led a number of critics to elaborate
further categories and distinctions: autography, autoscription, autosoci-
ography . . .[40]

The autographic dimensions of literary criticism or literary biography would seem obvious and scarcely worth emphasizing, were it not for
the number of calls over the past few years to "get personal" in scholarly
writing. In a well-known essay, Jane Tompkins refers to the conventions
of such writing as "the authority effect" and decides to jettison the lot:
"Well, I'm tired of the conventions that keep discussions of epistemology, or James Joyce, segregated from meditations on what is happening
outside my window or inside my heart. The public–private dichotomy,
which is to say the public–private *hierarchy*, is a founding condition of
female oppression. I say to hell with it."[41]

In discussing Tompkins's claim that her essay "turns its back" on literary theory, Nancy K. Miller argues that Tompkins offers an important
revisionary move, "turning theory back on itself."[42] What both miss, and
both leave intact, is the myth implicit in the "authority effect," a myth of
scholarly objectivity, neutrality, and power. But surely no discourse
deserves such a privilege. There is no end to the techniques of self-
inscription. "Identity is formed on the move,"[43] through non-linear and
irrecuperable processes of language, memory, resistance, desire, invention. In its unresolved tensions between self-affirmation and anonymity,
fixed identity and transient association, knowledge and an endless, iter-
ative will-to-truth, the abbé de Sade's project, for all its emphatic
"authority effects," carries on elements of the work of the *Canzoniere*.[44]

In my final look at the abbé, I will consider a moment when his
"public" and "private" projects collide dramatically. In the preface to

Volume II, Sade describes public reaction to his work as embarrassingly positive, but he feels compelled to respond to a letter published in the *Gazette littéraire* and identified by the *Année littéraire*'s critic as being by Voltaire. The letter is less a review of the abbé's book than a series of belittling reflections on Petrarch himself, claiming that his reputation is inflated and that Laura is a poetic figment. Sade denies that Voltaire wrote the piece, evincing unspecified "strong reasons."[45] Despite these denials, he finds himself cast into the role of defender.

The writer was, indeed, Sade's old friend Voltaire, whose correspondence from the summer of 1764 shows a flurry of letters to the *Gazette*, berating the editors for leaking his identity, and to the abbé, smoothing the ruffled feathers.[46] The point in mentioning this rather comic episode is that it foregrounds the tenuous fictions from which the prefaces are spun: Sade's official anonymity, his official disengagement from his subject, even his public dismissal of the idea that Voltaire wrote the *Gazette* article, are under considerable strain. Family allegiance, self-projection, authorial control, and friendship all tie the knot between textual and "extra-literary" drives.

As a kind of postscript, a note about textual and other desires, and the figure of Laura. One of the most powerful moments in the correspondence of the abbé's famous nephew speaks to an intense personal and familial investment in Laura. The marquis de Sade writes a letter from prison. He has been rereading the abbé's biography, and he tells his wife that he dreams constantly of Laura. In one of these dreams, she appears to him in his cell.

It was about midnight. I had just fallen asleep, [the abbé's] memoirs in my hand. Suddenly she appeared to me . . . I saw her! The horror of the tomb had not altered the brilliance of her charms, and her eyes still had as much fire as when Petrarch celebrated them. She was enveloped in black crepe and her beautiful blond hair fell on her shoulders. Love seemed to want to render her even more beautiful by softening the funereal appearance that she offered to me. "Why do you weep here on earth?" she asked me. "Come join me. No more ills, no more sorrows, no more disturbances, in the vast space where I live. Have the courage to follow me." At these words, I prostrated myself at her feet, I said to her, "O Mother! . . ." And sobs smothered my voice. She held out a hand to me and I covered it with tears; she shed tears as well. "When I still lived in this world that you hate," she added, "I was pleased to look in to the future; I extended my posterity as far as you and *did not imagine you so unhappy*."[47]

This piece has become an all-but-obligatory reference point for many Sade biographers and commentators. Maurice Lever ends his Prologue with the dream; Raymond Jean cites it in an introductory chapter;

Chantal Thomas relates it to a passage in *Juliette*.[48] Gilbert Lely returns to it at the end of the *Vie*, where he describes his own visit to chateau La Coste and claims quasi-ecstatically to have "seen the heart of the marquis de Sade."[49] Lely offers this reply to Laura's final phrase: "Enigmatic words that must have brought a bitter smile to Sade as he wrote! . . . But if the mediating ancestress had cast her gaze too far into the years to come? Perhaps the shade of Donatien-Alphonse-François is no longer *at present* so unhappy . . ."[50]

The marquis's brief consolation through the production of a dream, or the production of *une jolie phrase*, has become the vehicle for his biographer's desires, projections, and mythologizing. A new spiritual genealogy links Lely to Sade and the abbé to his poet; affiliation becomes appropriation and, finally, self-assertion.

NOTES

1. Cited by David Macey, *The Lives of Michel Foucault* (New York: Pantheon, 1993), xii.
2. Madame du Deffand to Horace Walpole, 2 April 1768; Du Deffand, *Lettres à H. Walpole, Voltaire et quelques autres* (Paris: Plasma, 1979), 46.
3. Maurice Lever sees parallels between the abbé's residence at Saumane and the marquis's imagined château de Silling in *Sade* (Paris: Fayard, 1991), 62–63. Lever's overt parallel is foreshadowed by Maurice Heine in *Le Marquis de Sade*, ed. Gilbert Lely (Paris: Gallimard, 1950), 331–33.
4. The matter remains unresolved. Morris Bishop accepts the abbé's identification and refers to the *Mémoires* as "a monument of Petrarchan scholarship." See his *Petrarch and His World* (Bloomington: University of Indiana Press, 1963), 65. Of two recent considerations, one rejects the Laura–Sade connection: Enzo Giudici, "Bilancio di una annosa questione: 'Maurice Scève e la scoperta della tomba de Laura'," *Quaderni di filologia e lingue romane* 2 (1980): 3–70 (cited in Lever, *Sade*, 662: n.12); another supports it: F. J. Jones, "Further Evidence of the Identity of Petrarch's Laura," *Italian Studies* 39 (1984): 27–46.
5. Amitav Ghosh, *The Shadow Lines* (New York: Penguin, 1990), p. 124.
6. The association with Laura plays an important rhetorical role in various denunciations of Sade. See Françoise Laugaa-Traut, *Lectures de Sade* (Paris: Armand Colin, 1973), esp. 27 (Dulaure), 78 (Villers), and 125–26 (Janin). Some of this attention may be due to the abbé's book, but that the story was already in circulation can be seen from its appearance in the *Mercure de France* (1733) writeup of the comte de Sade's wedding (Lever, *Sade*, 43).
7. See Jean-Jacques Pauvert, *Sade vivant*, 3 vols. (Paris: Laffont, 1987–90), I: 36. Lever, *Sade*, 64–67 describes both the abbé and his library, and cites a contemporary portrait of J. F. de Sade as "distrait" in the notes (672–73, n. 16). It also offers the text of the abbé's police record (673–74, n. 21). See also

Alice Laborde, *Le Mariage du marquis de Sade* (Paris: Champion-Slatkine, 1988), 78–96; and her *Les Infortunes du marquis de Sade* (Paris-Genève: Champion-Slatkine, 1990). For Gilbert Lely's portrait of the abbé, see his *Vie du marquis de Sade*, appearing as volumes I–II of his edition (hereafter abbreviated as *O. C.*) of Sade's *Œuvres complètes* (Paris: Cercle du livre précieux, 1966), I: 35–37. Lely addresses issues regarding the marquis's legal difficulties in I: 265–68, 270–71, 289–91, 300. Finally, see Marquis de Sade, *Lettres inédites et documents*, ed. Jean-Louis Debauve (Paris: Editions Ramsay/Jean-Jeacques Pauvert, 1990).

8. Marquis de Sade to the abbé de Sade, September 1765, in Marquis de Sade, *Lettres*, ed. Debauve, 75–77; "Oui je serais sans doute beaucoup plus heureux si j'aimais ma femme . . ." Unless otherwise indicated, all translations into English are my own.

9. [Abbé de Sade], *Mémoires pour la vie de François Pétrarque, tirés de ses œuvres et des auteurs contemporains, Avec des Notes ou Dissertations, & les Pièces justificatives*, 3 vols. (Amsterdam: Chez Arskée [*sic*] et Mercus, 1764–67), cited hereafter as [Abbé de Sade], *Mémoires*. Citations from the "Notes" sections will show "Notes" after the volume number.

10. For example, the same account of the Sade family origins appears both in the main text ([Abbé de Sade], *Mémoires*, I: 129–30) and in Note 7, "Sur Hugues de Sade" (*Ibid.*, I: "Notes," 40). Fragments from the same passage are also repeated verbatim in Lever's account of the family (Lever, *Sade*, 16).

11. The abbé's reticence in avowing his authorship carries over into his correspondence. Several letters mention an "homme d'esprit qui travaille chez moi à la vie de Pétrarque," which Laborde (*Mariage*, 81) reads as a way for the abbé to maintain his distance from a potentially controversial work. Pauvert (*Sade vivant* I: 34n) takes the same letter quite literally, calling the *Mémoires* "le fruit d'une collaboration dans laquelle l'abbé n'a pas le gros de la tâche." Given the polemical verve of much of the *Mémoires*, I incline to Laborde's view.

12. [Abbé de Sade], *Mémoires*, II: 470–72; "Laure avoit beaucoup d'esprit naturel, mais sans ornement & sans culture. C'est pour cela que Pétrarque se contente de louer la douceur, la gentillesse, & l'humanité de ses propos."

13. *Ibid.*, I: 114–15; "En un mot sans Laure, sans ce désir de lui plaire qui lui servit d'aiguillon, non-seulement Pétrarque n'auroit pas fait ces vers qui ont rendu son nom immortel; mais il auroit peut-être croupi dans la débauche, & il ne seroit jamais parvenu à cette considération personnelle dont nous le verrons jouir de la manière la plus flatteuse, & donner pour ainsi dire le ton à son siècle."

14. *Ibid.*, II: "Notes," 80; "L'une est de ceux que disent qu[e Pétrarque] n'a jamais désiré les faveurs de Laure. L'autre est de ceux qui soutiennent qu'il les a obtenues. L'une & l'autre sont injurieuses."

15. That this was a controversial position can be seen in the reaction of Edinburgh intellectual Alexander Fraser Tytler, who praises Sade's scholarship, especially in political history, but feels that the abbé takes too "French"

a view of love, in *A Historical and Critical Essay on the Life and Character of Petrarch* (Edinburgh: James Ballantyne, 1810).

16. [Abbé de Sade], *Mémoires*, I: viii.

17. *Ibid.*, I: 133;"carefully collect the small details scattered throughout the work."

18. *Ibid.*, II: vi; "Je suis son Biographe & non pas son Champion."

19. *Ibid.*, I: vi; "Eventrez tous les livres, & en lisant & relisant sans cesse, faites que votre nom aille à la postérité la plus reculée."

20. See Michael McKeon, "Writer as Hero: Novelistic Prefigurations and the Emergence of Literary Biography," in *Contesting the Subject: Essays in the Postmodern Theory and Practice of Biography and Biographical Criticism*, ed. William H. Epstein (West Lafayette, Ind.: Purdue University Press, 1991), 17–41.

21. [Abbé de Sade], *Mémoires*, I: xxxv. Lever, *Sade*, 662, n. 6 points out (although the abbé doesn't), that Henri de Chabaud's wife was a Sade, and thus Laura would still be related to the family – although no longer an ancestor to the main line.

22. [Abbé de Sade], *Mémoires*, I: xcvii; "se faire connoître lui-même." Sade discusses using poetry for biographical evidence in *Ibid.*, I: "Notes," 8, "On the Note Found in Petrarch's Virgil." Sade's interpretative techniques may appear arbitrary: he reads freely to support his own contentions, but denies that freedom to others. See his arch critique of another biographer's reading of "Nova angeletta" in *Ibid.*, I: "Notes," 56–57. He himself has little taste for Petrarchan allegory; of the famous sonnet "Una candida cerva," he remarks sourly that, like the prophecies of Nostradamus, it may be interpreted according to whim: "on explique comme on veut, parce qu'on n'y entend rien." See *Ibid.*, I: "Notes," 57.

23. [Abbé de Sade], *Mémoires*, I: lxv–lxvi (misnumbered; actually lxxiii–lxxiv); "Aussi n'est-ce pas sa vie que je vous présente, MESSIEURS; daignez faire attention au titre de mon Livre: *Mémoires pour la vie de François Pétrarque*. Vous le sçavez mieux que moi; il y a une grande différence entre une vie & des Mémoires. Une vie est une histoire: des Mémoires doivent être considérés comme des matériaux pour écrire l'histoire. On exige bien davantage d'un Historien que d'un compilateur de Mémoires. Plus de choix dans les faits, & une critique plus sévère; plus d'ordre & d'exactitude dans la narration; plus d'attention à se renfermer dans son objet, & à en lier toutes les parties; surtout plus de noblesse, de précision, & d'agrément dans le style.
    Une vie assujettie aux loix de l'histoire, doit avoir une marche régulière, & il n'est pas permis à celui qui l'écrit de faire de trop grands écarts. Quand on écrit des Mémoires, on a les coudées plus franches; on peut faire de petites excursions, appuyer sur quelques détails, saisir certains objets qui paroissent étrangers, & qui n'entreroient pas dans une histoire faite avec soin. Je crains qu'on ne m'accuse d'avoir abusé de cette liberté: tout ce que je puis dire, c'est que mes intentions étoient bonnes. Personne n'ignore qu'il faut plus d'esprit & de talens pour écrire une vie, que pour compiler des

Mémoires. La compilation est un travail presque méchanique [*sic*], qui donne plus de peine & fait moins d'honneur."

24. *Ibid.*, 1: lxvii (lxxv).

25. *Ibid.*, 1: cxiv.

26. *Ibid.*, 1: lxvii (lxxv).

27. A later biography, Susanna Dobson's *The Life of Petrarch. Collected from Mémoires pour la vie de Petrarch* [*sic*] (London, 1805), actually does put the abbé's "materials" to use, although readers might well feel that the ultimate *Vie* remained elsewhere. Originally published in 1775, this two-volume version of the *Mémoires* was in a sixth edition in 1805. Dobson cut Sade's prefaces, notes, and *pièces justificatives*, and substantially condensed the narrative, omitting all "tedious and minute discussions" (Dobson, *Life*, 1: xi). For Dobson, the chief point to Petrarch's life is its warning to anyone tempted by adulterous affections "to check every unhappy inclination in its birth" (*Ibid.*, 1: xii).

28. [Abbé de Sade], *Mémoires*, 1: lxvi.

29. *Ibid.*, 1: lxvii (lxxv).

30. *Ibid.*, 1: viii.

31. *Ibid.*, 1: lxvii (lxxv); "une bonne vie de Pétrarque, qui vous fasse enfin connoître cet homme célèbre que vous admirez depuis si long-temps, & dont vous n'avez qu'une connoissance très-superficielle."

32. Sade's effrontery is thrown all the more sharply into relief when one considers the immense energies and cultural-political investments that Petrarch represented in Florentine self-imagining. See Jay Tribby, "Florence: The Cultural Capital of Cultural Capital," *The Eighteenth Century: Theory and Interpretation* 35 (1994): 223–40.

33. [Abbé de Sade], *Mémoires*, 1: lxx–lxxi.

34. Homi K. Bhabha, "DissemiNation," in *The Location of Culture* (London: Routledge, 1994), 162–63.

35. It would be interesting to explore the persistence of Provençal identity through the abbé and his compatriot Peiresc during the century of state-building that separates them. See Peter N. Miller's chapter in this volume.

36. The abbé discusses Provençal literature at some length and seeks to establish its preeminence among Romance literatures ([Abbé de Sade], *Mémoires*, 1: 74–80, 153–54). Provençal was also highly significant for the marquis de Sade, who expanded his interest in the language while corresponding with a childhood friend, "Milli" Rousset, from prison. Part of the interest is nostalgia for the past, part literary pleasure, part a strategy of self-preservation, as he and Rousset occasionally use Provençal as a code to taunt the French-speaking prison censors. See J. Hayes, "Writing to the Divine Marquis," in *Writing the Female Voice*, ed. E. Goldsmith (Boston: Northeastern University Press, 1989), 203–18.

37. Laborde, *Les Infortunes*, 10–11; "Mon intention n'est pas de faire du Marquis un ange mais de m'en tenir aux textes et documents d'époque et autant que faire se peut éviter de boursoufler ces textes avec des passage repris aux œuvres les plus sadiques du Marquis pour pallier à l'absence de documents."

38. Carolyn J. Dean provides a sharply critical account of the heroic mythologizing of Sade by Lely and earlier generations of French intellectuals (Apollinaire, the Surrealists, Bataille, Klossowsky, etc.) in *The Self and Its Pleasures: Bataille, Lacan, and the History of the Decentered Subject* (Ithaca, N.Y.: Cornell University Press, 1992), 133–99. Jane Gallop, however, maintains a distinction between Sade and the "libertine fraternity," in *Intersections: A Reading of Sade with Bataille, Blanchot, and Klossowsky* (Lincoln: University of Nebraska Press, 1981).

39. Jacques Derrida, *Memoirs of the Blind*, trans. Pascale-Anne Brault and Michael Naas (Chicago: University of Chicago Press, 1993), 65. Derrida discusses the autographic dimensions of the Louvre project that resulted in *Mémoires d'aveugle*, 31–39.

40. For a discussion of several efforts of this sort, an elaboration of "autography" as non-narrative self-writing, and a useful bibliography, see H. Porter Abbott, "Autobiography, Autography, Fiction," *New Literary History* 19 (1988): 597–615.

41. Jane Tompkins, "Me and My Shadow," *New Literary History* 19 (1987): 169; revised and reprinted in *Gender and Theory: Dialogues on Feminist Criticism*, ed. Linda Kauffman (New York: Basil Blackwell, 1989). Nancy K. Miller discusses Tompkins's essay in *Getting Personal: Feminist Occasions and Other Autobiographical Acts* (New York: Routledge, 1991), 1–30.

42. Miller, *Getting Personal*, 5.

43. Iain Chambers, *Migrancy, Culture, Identity* (London: Routledge, 1994), 25.

44. "One could argue that the fundamental subject of the *Canzoniere* is not so much or not only the psychology of the speaker as the *ontology* of his selfhood, the struggle to discern a self or compose a self which could stand as a fixed and knowable substance." Thomas M. Greene, *The Light in Troy: Imitation and Discovery in Renaissance Poetry* (New Haven: Yale University Press, 1982), 136.

45. [Abbé de Sade], *Mémoires*, II: v–xii.

46. Sade was not altogether unaware that his friend took some topics less seriously than he. Upon receipt of the first volume, Voltaire wrote, "je vous crois allié de Pétrarque non seulement par le goût et par les grâces, mais parce que je ne crois point du tout que Pétrarque ait été assez sot pour aimer vingt ans une ingrate" (12 February 1764, D11694; Voltaire, *Correspondance*, ed. Theodore Besterman, 10 vols. [Paris: Gallimard, 1964–], VII: 564.). Voltaire was in the habit of teasing the abbé and his brother the comte (father of the marquis) about their legendary lineage. As he wrote to the comte in 1758:

> Ou vous êtes fils de putain
> Ou vous êtes fils d'une ingrate;
> Voyez ce qui le plus vous flatte.
> Le premier me rendrait trop vain.

(Unpublished letter in *Bibliothèque Sade: Papiers de famille*, ed. Maurice Lever [Paris: Fayard, 1993], I: 784.)

47. Sade, 12 February 1779 in *O. C.*, XII: 181 (original emphasis and ellipses); "Il était environ minuit. Je venais de m'endormir, ses mémoires à la main. Tout d'un coup, elle m'a apparu . . . Je la voyais! L'horreur du tombeau n'avait point altéré l'éclat de ses charmes, et ses yeux avaient encore autant de feux que quand Pétrarque les célébrait. Un crêpe noir l'enveloppait en entier, et ses beaux cheveux blonds flottaient négligemment dessus. Il semblait que l'amour, pour la rendre encore belle, voulût adoucir tout l'appareil lugubre dans lequel elle s'offrait à mes yeux. 'Pourquoi gémis-tu sur la terre?' m'a-t-elle dit. 'Viens te rejoindre à moi. Plus de maux, plus de chagrins, plus de trouble, dans l'espace immense que j'habite. Aie le courage de m'y suivre.' A ces mots, je me suis prosterné à ses pieds, je lui ai dit: 'O ma Mère! . . . ' Et les sanglots ont étouffé ma voix. Elle m'a tendu une main que j'ai couverte de mes pleurs; elle en versait aussi. 'Je me plaisais, a-t-elle ajouté, à porter mes regards dans l'avenir, lorsque j'habitais ce monde que tu détestes; je multipliais ma postérité jusqu'à toi *et ne te voyais pas si malheureux.*'" The marquis has rewritten Petrarch's vision of Laura following her death, recounted in the *Trionfo della morte*, part II, a passage which had been translated by the abbé as: "Elle me dit: reconnoissez celle qui vous retira de la voie commune, lorsque votre jeune coeur s'attacha à elle. En disant cela d'un air sérieux & modeste, elle s'assit sur le bord d'un ruisseau, à l'ombre d'un laurier & d'un hêtre, & elle m'ordonna de m'asseoir auprès d'elle. J'obéis, & je lui dis:

"Comment ne reconnoîtrois-je pas ma Déesse. Mais, ajoutai-je en pleurant, dites-moi vîte, je vous prie, si vous êtes morte ou en vie. Je suis en vie, reprit-elle, vous êtes mort. Vous le serez jusqu'au moment où vous quitterez la terre"; [Abbé de Sade], *Mémoires* II: 448.

48. Lever, *Sade*, 19; Raymond Jean, *Un portrait de Sade* (Arles: Actes Sud, 1989), 20; Chantal Thomas, *Sade: L'Oeil de la lettre* (Paris: Payot, 1978), 41–42.

49. Echoing (and nearly parodying) his predecessor, Lever recounts a pilgrimage to the murky underground chambers of the abbé's residence at Saumane, during which a couple of tourists who are there with him manage to lose their daughter in the dark . . . And the panicked mother cries out: "Justine!!!": Lely in *O. C.*, I: 638; Lever, *Sade*, 672, n. 12.

50. Sade, *O. C.*, II: 638 (original emphasis and ellipses).

CHAPTER SEVEN

A comic life: Diderot and le récit de vie

Stephen Werner

"Other fellow did it, other me . . . Lui, c'est moi."

James Joyce, *Ulysses*[1]

Diderot's collected works contain no *Confessions* and the chances of a lost writing with a title of this kind turning up in the catalogue of a Parisian bookseller could not be more remote. Yet the concerns with self-portraiture and the recounting of experience in a vein of intimacy and personal revelation were deeply felt by Diderot, as central to his outlook as they were to Rousseau.[2]

He uses an essay on a favorite dressing gown worn throughout his youth and then unaccountably lost, for example, as an occasion not only to meditate on the passing of time and the onset of middle age, but also to give readers a tour of his apartment in a behind-the-scenes manner familiar to many of the writings of the *philosophe*, describing its features, inventorying contents and, in general, opening up a private and closed-off space to public gaze.[3] Diderot appears in La Préface-Annexe or second half of *La Religieuse* where, speaking in his own name, he tells readers how this ironic addition or hoax to the first story of Suzanne Simonin's enforced stay in a convent came into being and relates the pleasure he took in devising it (a commentary that gives this story, only outwardly related in a vein of gothic somberness, clear qualities of black humor and ironic dissociation).[4]

With the series of plates devoted to the cutler's trade in the pictorial volumes of the *Encyclopédie*, Diderot brings family history to the pages of this great compendium of Enlightenment knowledge. He selected these engravings, as he did virtually all of the other prints in the text, and used them not only to validate key interests in the dignity of labor but also the artistic potential of his own past. Scenes of cutlers at work are set against the background of *ateliers* where his father, a famous regional cutler, worked and which Diderot would often visit as a young man.[5] Other examples of self-depiction abound in the *oeuvre*: the use of Monsieur Hardouin (a barely concealed version of Diderot) in the play *Est-il bon? Est-il méchant?*, incidental reminiscences in the *Correspondance*, and the presence in *Le Rêve de d'Alembert* of a character named "Diderot," the last, a clear example of the self-parody to which *le philosophe* was so often attracted.[6]

Diderot's most creative technique of self-description, however, came in a more forceful manner than the occasional anecdote. It occurs in writings specifically devoted to the study of self (or the "autobiographical"). Texts such as these allowed Diderot to present readers with a full portrait of himself, and to do so through use of a device of narration so deeply ingrained in the *oeuvre* as to be virtually synonymous with it. The device is that of "speaking through others."[7] As his great anti-novel *Jacques le fataliste* takes shape through a critical reading of Sterne's *Tristram Shandy*[8] or *Le Supplément au voyage de Bougainville* as the result of a rewriting of Bougainville's original travel narrative *Voyage autour du monde*,[9] so, too, will Diderot's self-portrait emerge through similar strategies of irony and displacement. The story of his life will not be told directly or even in the first person. It will emerge through a commentary on the experience of someone else as part of a technique of *altérité*. Personal narrative, in the unorthodox and loose manner of what has come to be known as "life-writing" or *récit de vie* rather than the more formal one of "autobiography," holds the key to two exemplary contributions to the genre: *L'Essai sur les règnes de Claude et de Néron*, an essay in the heroic or exemplary mode about a celebrated philosopher and dramatist of classical antiquity, and *Le Neveu de Rameau*, a comic writing whose setting is a day of carnival or Saturnalia in eighteenth-century Paris and whose subject is a contemporary of Diderot's, a bohemian musician and immoralist named "Rameau's Nephew."[10]

The *Essai sur les règnes de Claude et de Néron* was first published in 1778 under the complete title *Essai sur la vie de Sénèque le philosophe, sur ses écrits, et sur les règnes de Claude et de Néron*. The work was conceived as the final volume of a six-volume edition of Seneca's works edited by Joseph-Louis La Grange, Diderot's friend and fellow Latin enthusiast. It is a long text (four hundred pages in the recent Hermann edition)[11] and afforded Diderot ample room to celebrate the life of the thinker who, along with Horace and Lucretius, stood as one of the central classical influences on his thought.[12]

Diderot recounts, in the early pages of the essay, the facts of Seneca's

education and family history. He reflects on the circumstances surround-
ing the Roman philosopher's ties with his former pupil Nero; speaks of
the connection, problematical in the extreme but seemingly universal in
application, between a life of learning and a devotion to worldliness.
Commentaries on individual passages of texts such as the *Letters to
Lucilius* take up a good part of the essay and allow Diderot to engage in
the close textual readings in which he excelled. *L'Essai sur les règnes de
Claude et de Néron* reaches its point of greatest density with an account of
Seneca's final days. Diderot here describes how Seneca was forced to
commit suicide at the command of Nero, an act to be taken as proof of
Stoic resolve: a heroic death in the manner of Socrates.

As Diderot evokes the memory of the man he was to call an "honnête
païen"[13] or expatiates on the value of any one of Seneca's philosophical
maxims, he is drawn by instinct to the digressions that are the rule of the
essay,[14] a diffuse and open genre, given to asides, free-wheeling dialogue,
and the casualness summed up in the phrase "Je ne prononce pas, j'in-
terroge" (I form no final answers; I only ask questions).[15]

Comparisons between Roman emperors and French kings are very
much on Diderot's mind as he surveys the Silver Period of Roman literature. Ancient customs supply contrasts with contemporary or modern
ones. Differences between Rome and Paris are also to be noted and
studied with respect to their influence on the themes of imperial gran-
deur and *mondanité*. The deeper association brought into play by the
account of Seneca is more personal. Diderot has used the Roman's life-
story as a sounding board for reflections on his own life experience, a
procedure to which he was to draw attention when he spoke of Seneca
as a second self or alter ego: "C'est autant mon âme que je peins" (I paint
a portrait of my own inner being as much as I do his).[16]

The approach allows Diderot room for a variety of intimate observations and remarks. He describes, for example, his reading habits and
favorite authors. In the margins of his essay he speaks of a meeting with
Voltaire, evokes the wiles of Parisian editors, offers praise of the saving
grace of work. A section in the middle part of the text opens up a digres-
sion on Rousseau, his former boon companion and friend, now
deceased:

Rousseau is no more. He basely and in cowardly fashion insulted me. Yet I never
hated nor sought vengeance from a man who, over the long years of his life,
readily accepted all of the comforts and benefits of friendship (and indeed
openly proclaimed my innocence). I deeply admired Rousseau the writer,
though I had little regard for Rousseau the human being. Scorn is a cold feeling

and does not lead to acts of violence. What I felt only was a desire to rebuff his many efforts at rekindling our friendship. Any confidence I might have had in him had totally vanished.[17]

Diderot's most revealing comments come in the earliest pages of the *Essai*. They are indeed conceived as a preface. But the mood they convey is not that of an impersonal introduction or the cool analysis of an editor. Diderot speaks here of his private feelings and in a style almost confessional in nature. His career (and life) are drawing to a close. The tone evoked is one of wistfulness and melancholy, that of a *philosophe* reflecting on his past in a vein of unburdening and (surely the appropriate term) lyrical confession:

This essay, expanded by successive readings from a small number of pages to the length of the present volume, is the fruit of my labor (or, to put it better, free time) during one of the most pleasant moments of my life. I was in the country, virtually alone, freed from care and worry, able to let the hours slip by with no other goal than communion with myself in the evening when the day had come to an end, as one arises in the morning after a restful evening's dream. The passage of time freed me from the torment of passion and the boredom that comes in its train. I had lost the taste for the frivolities to which pleasure attaches such importance. Approaching as I was the point where life was about to become extinct, I sought only the approval of my conscience and that of a few friends. More interested in what would happen "after my death" than in any praise that I might be granted "while still alive" I said this to myself: What would the human race lose when the little I wrote and the few words I still intended to write perished? What would I myself have lost? I did not seek to entertain; still less was I desirous of applause. My goal was a far more substantial one. I sought to study as impartially as possible the life and works of Seneca, to defend a great man, to weep at his weaknesses, and to profit from his strong and abiding philosophy. Such was my state of mind when I began to write this essay; such is the state of mind in which I wish my text to be read.[18]

Diderot's account of Seneca is one of many tributes by eighteenth-century French authors to their Latin heritage. It allowed those who purchased the volume ample room for appraisal of Seneca's belief, transmitted to posterity by Tacitus, that his epistles presented the portrait of a life lived fully in accordance with virtue (an *imago vitae suae*) and, in addition, provided a good deal of information about the life experience and sensibility of Diderot.

Yet it is to *Le Neveu de Rameau*, a satire in the vein of Roman carnival, that one turns for evidence of Diderot's most significant commitment to self-portraiture. This text (by universal admission Diderot's most celebrated literary achievement) is a work of fiction and thus endowed with a largeness of scope denied the essay. More to the point, it is conceived in an openly autobiographical vein. One is to take *Rameau's Nephew*, in fact, as the exemplary statement of Diderot's encounter with his inner self.[19]

The first or "outer" subject of this narrative could not be more at odds with the earlier portrait of Seneca. In a manner vaguely reminiscent of Johnson's *Life of Savage*, it recounts the life of Lui (He), the "nephew" of the celebrated composer of French grand operas, Jean-Philippe Rameau. Unlike Seneca, Lui is not a celebrated figure of classical antiquity whose activities provided material for sober histories of the ancient past; rather, he is a contemporary of Diderot's about whom little was known to those who first bought the text.[20] If Diderot's one venture into *récit de vie* studies a philosopher whose life took shape against the pomp of imperial Rome, the other examines the career of a musical hack whose existence evoked the banal facts of a workman's Paris (the latter city described with a vividness of detail and sense of topography that makes *Le Neveu de Rameau* a key urban fiction of the period.)[21] Far from supplying an exemplary instance of Stoic sacrifice or the quest for wisdom, Lui was, quite the contrary, an immoralist, a shameless disciple of luxury and power, the spokesman for a philosophy of resentment and class inequity that made him into a French version of the English Pirate Jenny.

But it is the color or tone of *Le Neveu de Rameau* that provides the more forceful contrast between the Roman biography and the life of Diderot's contemporary. The story of Lui's career is not told as a sober literary document or meditation on philosophy. Only comedy, the touch of humor, could do justice to so bizarre a creature (and so curious a career). *Le Neveu de Rameau* is, indeed, a satire. Its impulse derives, as clearly stated in the Horatian epigraph that adorns the first page of the text, from the Saturnalia: the Roman feast day when the normal constraints of society were turned upside-down and a period of mayhem and license allowed to reign.[22]

Diderot's narrator is fully alive to the literary potential of this Parisian oddity thrown into contact with "M. le philosophe" (Mr. Philosopher), or "Moi" (Myself), through one of those chance encounters that are the stuff of Saturnalia.[23] His portrait of Lui is a brief one. Yet it provides an unforgettably vivid picture of the man described as:

one of the weirdest characters in this land of ours where God has not been sparing of them. He is a compound of the highest and the lowest, good sense and folly. The notions of good and evil must be strangely muddled in his head, for the good qualities nature has given him he displays without ostentation, and the bad ones without shame.[24]

The text of *Le Neveu de Rameau* details the eccentricities of deportment of this bohemian straggler, whose fate it was to spend his Mondays at a table of elegant bankers and his Wednesdays skulking about Paris, looking for handouts with the dejected mien which would make one think he had just come from a long stay with the Trappists and who accomplishes all of this in a realistic and breezy manner clearly inherited from La Bruyère:

Nothing is less like him than himself. At times he is thin and gaunt like somebody in the last stages of consumption; you could count his teeth through his cheeks and it is as though he had had nothing to eat for days on end or had just come out of a Trappist monastery. A month later he is sleek and plump as though he had never left some millionaire's table or had been shut up in a Cistercian house.[25]

Page after page of close reporting on Lui's dialogue with "Moi" about ethics, philosophy, and – the more central interest – Italian opera, draws attention to the *dialogue de sourds* technique called for by *philosophe* satire and the naive questions, repetitions, and blank answers that are its stock in trade.

With scenes that show Lui imitating his wife's walk, head held high, playing with a fan, wiggling his behind in a most amusing and ridiculous caricature of "our little tarts" or doing a take-off of a miser hugging golden ducats, pantomime is introduced to the story of Lui and "Moi" and with it a comic vein of gesture and low bodily intent.

In the one-man band scene, pantomime takes on even greater force. Lui is shown imitating an entire orchestra (or opera) in a passage to be taken as an illustration of the moment of transcendence at the heart of Diderot's satire and as a style of comic prose attuned to the broken sentences, emphatic interjections, parataxis, and other examples of passionate writing meant to reveal a mode of *philosophe* prose stripped of its patrician balance and poise and, as the narrator says, "set to music."[26]

That Diderot – himself a *mélomane* and lover of the theatre – would be sensitive to connections of a personal kind conveyed by Lui is certain and put into sharp relief in a variety of passages of *Le Neveu de Rameau*, all designed to emphasize comparisons between "Rameau's nephew" and the former editor-in-chief of the *Encyclopédie*. The nephew's life as a

Parisian *marginal* or out-of-work fiddler prods Diderot into psychological associations about his own early years as an impecunious scribbler in the French capital on the lookout for the odd translation job, and it leads to a description of Lui whose resemblance to Diderot on one of his bad days could hardly be accidental:

HE: That's very true, good Lord, very true. Now, Mr. Philosopher, put your hand on your heart and tell the truth. Time was when you weren't as well off as you are today.

MYSELF: I'm not that well off even now.

HE: But you wouldn't still be going to the Luxembourg in summer, you remember –

MYSELF: That'll do, yes, I remember.

HE: In a gray plush coat.

MYSELF: Yes, yes.

HE: Threadbare on one side, with a frayed cuff, and black woolen stockings darned up the back with white thread.

MYSELF: All right, all right, have it your own way.

HE: What did you do in those days in the Allée des Soupirs?

MYSELF: Look pretty silly.

HE: After that you used to trot along the road.

MYSELF: Quite right.

HE: You used to give mathematics lessons.

MYSELF: Without knowing a word about it myself – isn't that what you're driving at?

HE: Exactly.[27]

Dialogue between Lui and "Moi," though designed to pit the morally subversive views of Lui against the conservatism of "Moi" and thus further the topsy-turvy world of carnival, also allows Diderot to conduct a conversation with his own consciousness or innermost self as though in sympathy with the confessional mood established by Rameau.[28]

"Moi" presents a view of Diderot in his most amiable and avuncular guise. "Moi" is a devoted father and friend. A stable fellow, conventional enough in outward manner, he enjoys coming down from his apartment to partake of the carnival atmosphere of the day. The outing is a bit of slumming. It allows "Moi" to seek information about points of culture that have passed him by and to have a bit of fun (though never, of course, to be deeply changed by carnival). For "Moi" is a man of great solidity. His allegiances are to the absolutes of the French culture into which he was born and to the condition of a *père de famille*. If "Moi" can be called, in the inevitable Hegelian formulation, "the happy self," it is not because he seeks pleasure or mindless enjoyment. Happiness means self-control, stability, recognition of the need to subordinate the individual to community will.

Lui, at first the target of "Moi's" condescension but later revealed as his philosophical mentor, brings to Diderot's *examen de conscience* a perspective of a radically different kind. For Lui is not only an exponent of hedonism or the resentments later to be evoked by Max Scheler. He is endowed with a prophetic streak fully outside genteel philosophizing in the manner of "Moi." The subject of Lui's study is the fragility of the society into which he too was born and to which he brings a strangely visionary lens. Norms of understanding, hierarchies of value and meaning are not, as "Moi" would have it, absolute or necessary but relative and contingent. They undergo stress, submit to change, modulate, in a way Diderot was to term a kind of "musicalizing," into new conditions and beliefs.[29] The latter are recognizable to those possessed of visionary imagination and foresight, those who, like Lui, can stand aside from their historical or "passport" condition and gaze into the future.[30]

But it is Lui's condition as a philosophical clown that is most revealing of Diderot's personal involvement. Describing Lui in this manner not only allowed Diderot to give a Socratic (or *buffa*) ancestry to his outlaw musician and, thus, to deepen the value of commentaries on his character and ideas, it also encouraged the self-parody to which Diderot was so frequently to turn.[31] The clown's mask allowed him to poke fun at, indeed to mock, his own artistic condition as a satirist or novelist: the creator of genres unrecognized by the classical past, genres thought trivial or unworthy.[32]

The temptation of authors to depict themselves in this fallen or debased manner was, as Jean Starobinski has shown, a leading motif of an ironic sensibility put into practice, with varying degrees of emphasis, by Flaubert, Musset, and Jarry.[33] The topos allowed for a transcendence, through fiction, of an actual (and painful) historical condition. More to the point, the clown's condition sponsored a key variation on the "auto-biographical." Diderot has not only been able to bring comic portraiture in line with a general analysis of problems of genre or art, he has also made it into a privileged vehicle for the theme (essential to the modern temper) of a "portrait of the artist":

What is soon apparent is that the clown is not only a poetic or illustrative motif but a way of dramatizing, through parody and indirection, first questions of art. From early romanticism (and before) artists often relied on clowns to convey an exaggerated and off-centered image of themselves and indeed the purpose of

art. Clowns stand for self-portraiture in a mode of parody. Nor is the parody
only maudlin or sarcastic. Musset's account of himself as Fantasio, Flaubert's
line that his essential nature was that of a circus acrobat, Jarry crying out on his
deathbed, "Father Ubu will now try to sleep a bit," Joyce's "I am but an Irish
clown, a great joker at the universe": here are not only bits of ironic self-analysis but epiphanies of the artist viewed through the lens of laughter. Analysis of
the bourgeois order is now backed up by the kind of self-criticism targeted at
the very purpose of aesthetic creation. The approach is a central feature of
modernity, understood as such for well over one hundred years.[34]

Diderot's self-portraits gain in intensity through the economy and con-
cision of his text (a mere eighty pages or so, the acting-out of which
would require less than an hour) and through his use of the technique
of "carnival"[35] as a framing structure: the *philosophe* having brought
together in the pages of his satire a vast array of literary influences and
sources, from La Bruyère,[36] Horace, and Petronius, to the popular
outdoor theatre known as *le théâtre de la foire* (pantomime and ballet), all
mixed at will and treated with the disdain of parody.

It is the more compelling as a personal document (and instance of *récit
de vie*) because of the circumstances of its publication. *Le Neveu de Rameau*
is not only a lost work of Diderot's, published first in a German translation of a manuscript sent to Catherine the Great and only, in 1821,
brought out in French. Rameau's narrative is also, as Charles Asselineau
was surely the first to point out, a secret text. The story was not meant
to be published or to see the light of day. Its place was in Diderot's desk,
a writing to be taken out now and then for private reading and enjoyment:

Generous, well-intentioned and humane as he was, Diderot often gave himself
over to self-examination. His ardent temperament doubtless caused many an
intemperate or violent public outburst. Yet one cannot but assume that his
private bouts of self-analysis were a good deal less impassioned. Is *Le Neveu de
Rameau* a pamphlet directed at the morals and opinions of Diderot's own time?
Is it a confession of skepticism bequeathed to future generations? I incline to
the later view. For the dialogue between Lui and "Moi" was not only unpublished during Diderot's lifetime but kept secret. It was only through the translation by a foreigner in possession of a copy of the original manuscript that its
existence was revealed to the French reading public for the first time.[37]

Publishing *Le Neveu de Rameau* violates Diderot's wishes but is a necessary
act of literacy. It rescues a document of a unique kind without which
French literature would be immeasurably the poorer. The story is that of
an outing in Paris at the time of Saturnalia, an account of a meeting

between a philosopher and a failed musical virtuoso. It is also, of course, a tale of Diderot and "Diderot": his secret and unpublished confession.

A portrait of Diderot framed through the lens of classical antiquity whose casual style bears the clear impress of Montaigne; a portrait set against the experience of Lui, a Socratic clown and hunger artist at a time of Saturnalia: here are Diderot's most vivid efforts at bequeathing to posterity an image of himself. Both accounts offer keen evidence of his interest in "speaking through others" and endorse the value of *récit de vie*. But it is surely *Le Neveu de Rameau*, the more extended and modern version of the mode, that enjoys pride of place. For this is the exemplary instance of "life-writing."

The text's importance is due in no small measure to the way it violates the impersonality and reserve of *philosophe* satire in the manner of *Candide* or *Les Lettres persanes* (writings of great comic momentum where the face of their author is always absent) and to its general associations with Rousseau – a figure who shadows many a page of Diderot's narrative, assonance of whose name with that of "Rameau" is surely more than accidental.[38] But it is even more so because of the relationship of *Le Neveu de Rameau* to the history of narration in the first-person intimate mode of the "autobiographical." With his account of himself as Rameau's nephew, Diderot has now challenged and to no small extent undermined the belief, taken for granted in all earlier French writings from those of the sixteenth- and seventeenth-century *mémorialistes* to Rousseau, that self-portraiture could not but be an exercise of an earnest kind, given to decorous appraisals of the past, a sober scrutiny of motive.[39]

Comedy, the representation of self through satiric exaggeration and ironic fantasy, has now come to be understood as enjoying the properties of authenticity and truth formerly ascribed to more serious efforts at selfstudy. For comedy has, in the pages of *Le Neveu de Rameau*, been divested of its traditional role as a medium of intellectual satire or the casual study of manias and *tics*. Through its Socratic connections, comedy is now a mode of extraordinary critical insight and revelation. Its presence points satire in the direction of new interests in self-consciousness, subjectivity, and what Rousseau had earlier termed knowledge "underneath the skin." Comedy shapes and gives life to a style of dialogue rescued from the deaf and dumb conversations of *Candide* or *Les Lettres anglaises* and, because opened to dramatic pacing, fast questioning, and pantomime, allowed to breathe the air of theatre. In the scene of the one-man band, for example, its influence allows for one of those syntheses of form and content to which Diderot was so often attracted and which offers an example of *philosophe* prose endowed with passion and a spirit of lyricism.

Ultimately comedy dramatizes (and, in the Socratic manner, "births"[40]) the sensibility that stands over *Le Neveu de Rameau* in so many ways as its defining subject and its fresh version of the genre as well (two literary discoveries that could not offer greater contrast to the other "autobiographical" study of Seneca). The sensibility is that of the performing or ironic self; the genre that of *récit de vie* in a revised and comic shape. Diderot has, in *Le Neveu de Rameau*, created a text which, although written in the middle years of the eighteenth century, already contains within it the seeds of Céline's *Trilogy* or (by far the more revealing intertextuality) Dostoevsky's *Notes from Underground*.

NOTES

1. James Joyce, *Ulysses* (London: Penguin, 1986), 37.
2. In addition to *Les Confessions*, Rousseau was also the author of other works of an autobiographical stripe. Among the most prominent are *Rousseau Juge de Jean-Jacques*, *Les Rêveries du promeneur solitaire*, and the "fragments" published in volume 1 of the Pléiade edition of his works, Bibliothèque de la Pléiade, ed. Bernard Gagnebin and Marcel Raymond, 5 vols. (Paris: Gallimard, 1959–95). Other practitioners of the mode in the French eighteenth century include (in addition to Diderot) Rétif de la Brétonne, the author of *Monsieur Nicolas*, and Sade, many of whose novels have a distinctly confessional side.
3. Denis Diderot, *Œuvres complètes*, ed. Assézat-Tourneux, 20 vols. (Paris: Garnier, 1875–77), IV: 6.
4. Diderot, *Œuvres complètes*, ed. Jean Varloot et al., vol. XI (Paris: Hermann, 1975).
5. For Diderot's role in the *Encyclopédie* plates (and an analysis of their place in the great war-machine against ignorance and intolerance) see Stephen Werner, *Blueprint: A Study of Diderot and the "Encyclopédie" Plates* (Birmingham, Ala.: Summa, 1993).
6. Diderot also appears as Ariste in *La Promenade du sceptique*. His role in the *Discours sur la poésie dramatique* is also to be emphasized. The theme is studied by Otis Fellows in *Diderot* (Boston: Twayne, 1977), 159.
7. "Speaking through others" is a translation of "la parole des autres," the phrase used by Jean Starobinski in a landmark article entitled "Diderot et la parole des autres," *Critique* 28 (1972): 3–22.

8. The transformation of *Tristram Shandy* into *Jacques le fataliste* is the subject of chapter 4 of Stephen Werner's *Diderot's Great Scroll: Narrative Art in "Jacques le fataliste,"* Studies on Voltaire and the Eighteenth Century 128 (Banbury: Voltaire Foundation, 1975).

9. Bougainville's travel journal was published in 1771. Diderot's vastly more sophisticated commentary, owing to the subtlety of the *philosophe's* views on primitivism and his use of techniques of literary self-reflection, was completed the next year. It had to wait until 1796 to be published.

10. "Récit de vie" is the French equivalent of "life-writing." The phrase takes into its purview both autobiography, a genre that has been the subject of a good deal of recent critical study, from Philippe Lejeune's *Le Pacte autobiographique* (Paris: Seuil, 1975), Michael Sheringham's *French Autobiography* (Oxford: Clarendon Press, 1993), to John Sturrock's *The Language of Autobiography* (Cambridge and New York: Cambridge University Press, 1993), and documents of a more unorthodox and problematical nature. Among them are (speaking only of France) Montaigne's *Essais*, Saint-Simon's *Mémoires*, Proust's *Jean Santeuil* and – works with special relevance to Diderot because of their doubled authorship – *Roland Barthes par Roland Barthes* and the three-volume study of Flaubert published by Sartre under the title *L'Idiot de la famille*. There is as yet no one definitive study of this "baggy monster."

11. Diderot, "Essai sur les règnes de Claude et de Néron," in *Œuvres complètes*, ed. Jean Varloot et al., vol. xxv (Paris: Hermann, 1986), cited hereafter as Diderot, "Essai."

12. The most thoughtful study of the connection between Diderot and Seneca is that of Fritz Schalk, *Diderot's "Essai über Claudius und Nero"* (Köln and Opladen: Westdeutcher Verlag, 1956).

13. Diderot, "Essai," 8.

14. For study of the essay as a literary genre, see Georg Lukács, *Die Seele und die Formen* (Berlin: Luchterhand Hermann, 1971), 27. Lukács speaks of the genre as an "occasional matter." Comments on the form can also be found in Theodor W. Adorno, "Der Essay als Form," in *Noten zur Literatur*, 4 vols. (Frankfurt am Main: Suhrkamp, 1958–74), 1: 25.

15. Diderot, "Essai," 36.

16. *Ibid*.

17. *Ibid*. All translations into English are my own; "Rousseau n'est plus. Quoiqu'il eût accepté de la plupart d'entre nous, pendant de longues années, tous les secours de la bienfaisance et tous les services de l'amitié, et qu'après avoir reconnu et confessé mon innocence, il m'ait perfidement et lâchement insulté, je ne l'ai ni persécuté ni haï. J'estimais l'écrivain, mais je n'estimais pas l'homme, et le mépris est un sentiment froid qui ne pousse à aucun procédé violent. Tout mon ressentiment s'est réduit à repousser les avances réitérées qu'il a faites pour se rapprocher de moi: la confiance n'y était plus."

18. *Ibid*., 35; "Cet essai, que les mêmes lectures multipliées ont porté successive-

ment d'un très petit nombre de pages à l'étendue de ce volume, est le fruit de mon travail, ou pour mieux dire, de mon loisir pendant un des plus doux intervalles de ma vie. J'étais à la campagne, presque seul, libre de soins et d'inquiétudes, laissant couler les heures sans autre dessein que de me trouver le soir, à la fin de la journée, comme on se trouve quelquefois le matin après une nuit occupée d'un rêve agréable. Les années ne m'avaient laissé aucune de ces passions qui tourmentent, rien de l'ennui qui leur succède: j'avais perdu le goût de ces frivolités auxquelles l'espoir d'en jouir longtemps donne tant d'importance. Assez voisin du terme où tout s'évanouit, je n'ambitionnais que l'approbation de ma conscience et le suffrage de quelques amis. Plus jaloux de préparer des regrets [après ma mort] que d'obtenir des éloges [de mon vivant], je m'étais dit: 'Quand le peu que j'ai fait et le peu qui me reste à faire périraient avec moi, qu'est-ce que le genre humain y perdrait? Qu'y perdrais-je moi-même?' Je ne voulais point amuser; je voulais moins encore être applaudi: j'avais un plus digne objet, celui d'examiner sans partialité la vie et les ouvrages de Sénèque, de venger un grand homme, s'il était calomnié; ou s'il me paraissait coupable, de gémir de ses faiblesses, et de profiter de ses sages et fortes leçons. Telles étaient les dispositions dans lesquelles j'écrivais, et telles sont les dispositions dans lesquelles il serait à souhaiter qu'on me lût."

19. Diderot, *Le Neveu de Rameau*, ed. Jean Fabre (Geneva: Droz, 1950).
20. For an account of Rameau's known activities in eighteenth-century France, see "Cinq Témoignages sur Jean-François Rameau," appendix to *Le Neveu de Rameau*, ed. Fabre, 243–54. J. F. Falvey, *Le Neveu de Rameau* (London: Grant and Cutler, 1985), 22, records the following: "He was born in Dijon on 31 January 1716, and was still alive in 1766 when he was authorized to publish his autobiographical mock-poem, *La Raméide*, a publication briefly reviewed by Grimm in his *Correspondance Littéraire* of June–September 1766. He was married at Saint-Séverin, the parish church for a large area of the Left Bank, on 3 February 1757; in January 1761 his wife died, and in June 1761 his son died." The police incident in which he insulted the Directors of the Opera happened in 1748.
21. For a reading of *Le Neveu de Rameau* as a celebration of ordinary Parisian life see Stephen Werner, *Socratic Satire* (Birmingham, Ala.: Summa Press, 1987), 47–52.
22. Diderot's specific indebtedness to Horace and the carnival topos is underscored in the epigraph: "Vertumnis, quotquot sunt, natus iniquis" (Born under the baleful influence of Vertumnis). The line comes from the *Satires* II, vii. Its subject is the Saturnalia, the Roman feast day where, as James Frazer has written, "the distinction between the free and the servile classes was abolished; slaves changed places with masters, convicts with judges, and the entire society of Rome was turned into a crazy-quilt or upside-down republic" (*The Golden Bough* [New York: Doubleday, 1961], 319).
23. Diderot's narrator uses the term "Moi" (Myself) when he is describing himself. "Moi" and Lui (Rameau's nephew), of course, stand in a dialectical

relationship to one another. "M. le philosophe" is a derogatory term used by Lui to refer to "Moi," his dialectical counterpart. The quotation marks around "Moi" are a means of highlighting the doubling back on self (dédoublement) which is Diderot's favored mode of self-presentation.

24. Diderot, *Le Neveu*, 3; "un des plus bizarres personnages de ce païs ou Dieu n'en a pas laissé manquer. C'est un composé de hauteur et de bassesse, de bon sens et de déraison. Il faut que les notions de l'honnête et du déshonnête soient bien étrangement brouillées dans sa tête; car il montre ce que la nature lui a donné de bonnes qualités, sans ostentation, et ce qu'il en a reçu de mauvaises, sans pudeur."

25. *Ibid.*, 4; "Rien ne dissemble plus de lui que lui même. Quelquefois, il est maigre et hâve, comme un malade au dernier degré de la consomption; on compteroit ses dents a travers ses joues; on diroit qu'il a passé plusieurs jours sans manger, ou qu'il sort de la Trappe. Le mois suivant, il est gras et replet, comme s'il n'avoit pas quitté la table d'un financier, ou qu'il eut été renfermé dans un couvent de Bernardins."

26. *Ibid.*, 82–85.

27. *Ibid.*, 28–29.

> LUI. Cela est juste, morbleu! et très juste. Là, monsieur le philosophe, la main sur la conscience, parlez net; il y eut un temps où vous n'étiez pas cossu comme aujourd'hui.
> "MOI". Je ne le suis pas encore trop.
> LUI. Mais vous n'iriez plus au Luxembourg en été . . . Vous vous en souvenez? . . .
> "MOI". Laissons cela; oui, je m'en souviens.
> LUI. En redingote de peluche grise . . .
> "MOI". Oui, oui.
> LUI. Ereintée et les bas de laine noirs et recousus par derrière avec du fil blanc.
> "MOI". Oui, oui, tout comme il vous plaira.
> LUI. Que faisiez-vous alors dans l'allée des Soupirs?
> "MOI". Une assez triste figure.
> LUI. Au sortir de là, vous trottiez sur le pavé.
> "MOI". D'accord.
> LUI. Vous donniez des leçons de mathématiques.
> "MOI". Sans en savoir un mot; n'est-ce pas là que vous en vouliez venir?
> LUI. Justement.

28. With the exception of the opening or overture passage about the Café de la Régence and stage directions introduced every now and then, the entire text of *Le Neveu de Rameau* is conceived in the form of dialogue. See, for study of the mode, Werner, *Socratic Satire*, 59–61.

29. "Musiquer" (to set to music) is a neologism. Diderot uses it three times in *Le Neveu*: "Il n'y a pas six vers de suite . . . qu'on puisse musiquer" (86); "J'aimerais autant avoir à musiquer les maximes de La Rochefoucauld" (86); "Je musiquais comme il plaît à Dieu" (10).

30. The recent study by Hans-Robert Jauss, *The Dialogical and the Dialectical "Neveu de Rameau": How Diderot Adopted Socrates and Hegel Adopted Diderot* (Berkeley: Center for Hermeneutical Studies in Hellenistic and Modern Culture, 1983), is by far the most exhaustive analysis of the Diderot–Hegel relationship. Cf. Lionel Trilling, "The Sentiment of Being and the Sentiments of Art," in *Sincerity and Authenticity* (Cambridge, Mass.: Harvard University Press, 1971), ch. 3.

31. Rameau's nephew (Lui) and Socrates are physically unattractive, even ugly. Their lives symbolize ties between inner subjective truth and outer appearance. Both men also share a problematical social origin (the one the son of a midwife, the other, a mere "nephew" of the great French composer Jean-Philippe Rameau). Both the *daimon* and *la maudite molécule paternelle* are voices of an irrational kind.

32. Georges May, *Le Dilemme du roman au dix-huitième siècle* (Paris: Presses universitaires de France, 1963).

33. Jean Starobinski, "Portrait de l'artiste en Saltimbanque," *Critique* 25:2 (December 1969): 1034.

34. *Ibid.*, 1035; "L'on . . . s'aperçoit en effet que le choix de l'image du clown n'est pas seulement l'élection d'un *motif* pictural ou poétique, mais une façon détournée et parodique de poser la question de l'art. Depuis le romantisme (mais non certes sans quelque prodrome), le bouffon, le saltimbanque et le clown ont été les images hyperboliques et volontairement *déformantes* que les artistes se sont plu à donner d'eux-mêmes et de la condition de l'art. Il s'agit là d'un autoportrait travesti, dont la portée ne se limite pas à la caricature sarcastique ou douloureuse. Musset se dessinant sous les traits de Fantasio; Flaubert déclarant, 'Le fond de ma nature est, quoi qu'on dise, le saltimbanque'; Jarry, au moment de mourir, s'identifiant à sa créature parodique: 'Le père Ubu va essayer de dormir'; Joyce déclarant: 'je ne suis qu'un clown irlandais, *a great joker at the universe*' . . . Le jeu ironique a la valeur d'une interprétation de soi par soi: c'est une épiphanie dérisoire de l'art de l'artiste. La critique de l'honorabilité bourgeoise s'y double d'une autocritique dirigée contre la vocation esthétique elle-même. Nous devons y reconnaître une des composantes caractéristiques de la modernité, depuis un peu plus d'une centaine d'années."

35. Mikhail Bakhtin, *Rabelais and His World* (Cambridge, Mass.: MIT Press, 1968). The mode is also discussed in Bakhtin's *Problems of Dostoevsky's Poetics* (Ann Arbor, Mich.: Ardis, 1973).

36. La Bruyère's *Les Caractères* is a central (though generally overlooked) influence on Diderot's text. The connection is made clear through a common interest in portraits as well as the use, in the one-man band scene, of the device of anaphora (the pronoun "il").

37. Diderot, *Le Neveu de Rameau*, ed. Charles Asselineau (Paris: Poulet-Malassis, 1862), xxi–xxii; "Cet homme sincère, honnête, humain, devait s'interroger souvent, et si la mobilité de ses nerfs irritables, si la contradiction et l'ardeur de son tempérament le provoquèrent en public à des affirmations violentes, il est à supposer que dans le secret il était vis-à-vis de lui-même moins

intrépide et moins absolu. Est-ce un pamphlet qu'il a voulu écrire contre les mœurs et les opinions de son temps? Est-ce sa confession de sceptique découragé qu'il a voulu laisser? Je serais tenté de le croire quand je songe que ce dialogue est resté jusqu'à la fin de sa vie non seulement inédit, mais secret, et que ce n'est que par la version d'un étranger, à qui une copie en avait été communiquée, que son existence nous a été révélée pour la première fois."

38. For the Rousseau–Rameau relationship see Werner, *Socratic Satire*, 58.
39. Retz and Saint-Simon are the most significant influences in this regard.
40. The word is indeed used in Diderot's text as a symbol of the Socratic or midwifing function of comic irony: "Puis il ajoutoit: C'est cela, je crois. Voilà que cela vient; voilà ce que c'est que de trouver un accoucheur qui scait irriter, precipiter les douleurs et faire sortir l'enfant." (98).

CHAPTER EIGHT

Letters, diary, and autobiography in eighteenth-century France

Benoît Melançon

In July 1762, Diderot wrote Sophie Volland about a project he was undertaking in his letters.

My letters are a more or less faithful history of my life. Without meaning to, I am doing what I have so often wished for. Why, I said, an astronomer will spend thirty years of his life on top of an observatory, his eye glued day and night to the end of a telescope, simply to determine the movement of a star, and no one makes a study of himself, no one has the courage to keep an accurate record of all the thoughts that come into his mind, all the feelings that agitate his heart, all his sorrows and joys. In this way century after century will go past without anyone knowing whether life is a good or a bad thing, whether human nature is good or evil, and what makes up happiness and unhappiness. But it would need a lot of courage to reveal everything. One might find it easier to accuse oneself of planning a great crime than to admit harbouring petty or low or despicable feelings . . . This sort of self-analysis would have its uses for the writer too. I am sure that in the long run one would be anxious to have nothing but good things to enter in the record each evening. But what about you, would you reveal everything? Try asking Uranie the same question, for there is absolutely no point in committing yourself to a plan of sincerity which frightens you.[1]

Letters, suggested Diderot, should transform themselves into a diary: one should write every day, confide in a text one's most intimate thoughts, and force oneself to say the truth, nothing but the truth. This new breed of text, part letter, part diary, would serve as a moral guide for others as well as for oneself. If this project were to succeed, it would solve a problem which Diderot had been dealing with for a while. With regard to the history of personal narratives, two dimensions of Diderot's project ought to be stressed: first, that the text he wished to write was intended not only for its author, but also for an external reader, in this case Sophie Volland; second, that this project appeared at a time when the diary genre did not yet exist in French literature, at least publicly.

Three years later, again in a letter to Sophie Volland, Diderot wrote about a different type of personal narrative and a different endeavor –

autobiography: "Since my project was to continue the story of my life as soon as the completion of my work left me free, I had jotted down brief notes on a piece of paper that became a logogriph after a while. I don't understand them any more."[2] Instead of writing daily, Diderot would take notes, and then assemble them into a narrative. This new project would be as difficult as the earlier one. In November 1765, as in July 1762, still years before Rousseau's *Confessions* were to popularize the genre that we now know as autobiography, the writer would address himself to an external reader (Sophie Volland).[3]

Both of Diderot's projects failed: he neither kept a diary nor wrote the story of his life from childhood to his latter days.[4] The reasons for Diderot's lack of action – whether because of a lack of courage, in the first case, or because of a poor memory, in the second – matter little here. What should interest the contemporary critic is, rather, the need that Diderot felt as a letter writer to venture into new directions in the 1760s. One question that arises from his two life-writing projects is particularly important in the history of correspondence, diary, and autobiography: what are the effects of each genre's poetics on the construction of the others? This chapter will investigate the relations between correspondence, diary, and autobiography in eighteenth-century French literature, in order to help understand the so-called advent of the two latter genres at the end of the century and its importance with regard to what could be called the invention of individuality during that period. Three texts, or sets of texts, will be studied: not only Diderot's letters of the 1760s, but also Elisabeth Bégon's writings of the 1740s and 1750s, and Rousseau's *Confessions*.[5] For each set of texts, formal characteristics and the role of the reader will be specifically addressed. In the conclusion, after some methodological remarks, these authors' treatments of time will be compared with those of Restif de la Bretonne and Beaumarchais, for this particular question seems central to the history of personal genres.

Marie-Isabelle-Elisabeth Rocbert de la Morandière was born in Montréal in 1696, and she married, in 1718, Claude-Michel Bégon (d. 1748), a Frenchman who would rise from *major de Québec* (in 1726) to *gouverneur de Trois-Rivières* (in 1743). In 1737, their daughter Marie-Catherine-Elisabeth (b. 1719) was married to another Frenchman, Michel de Villebois de La Rouvillière, and they had two children, Honoré-Henri (b. 1738), educated in France, and Marie-Catherine (b. 1739). This second child was raised by her grandmother, Madame Bégon, after the death of her mother in 1740, and her father's departure for France and then Louisiana. In 1748, after she was widowed, Elisabeth Bégon began a correspondence with her son-in-law, Michel de Villebois de La Rouvillière, Marie-Catherine's father. The published texts all date between 1748 and 1753, the latter year marking the point at which she learned of La Rouvillière's earlier (1752) passing. Some letters were written from Montréal, others from what is now known as Charente-Maritime, where Madame Bégon moved in 1749, hence acquiring her nickname "l'Iroquoise."[6] She died there in 1753. Traditionally, her texts have been read either as a source of information about the last decade of New France or as a kind of epistolary novel in which Madame Bégon's affection for her son-in-law soon turns – or so it is said – into love. One could argue that historians and psychoanalysts have not sufficiently considered the formal characteristics of the texts that constitute the volume entitled by its latest publisher *Lettres au cher fils* – that "cher fils" being Michel de Villebois de La Rouvillière,[7] – and that these formal characteristics are of interest in a study of the relations between the personal genres throughout the eighteenth century.

Bégon's corpus, originally edited in 1935 by Claude de Bonnault and Pierre-Georges Roy, then in 1972 and 1994 by Nicole Deschamps, consists of 432 texts. These texts are of two different types. Most of them are labeled "journal" by their author: between 12 November 1748 and 26 February 1751, Madame Bégon filled nine *cahiers* that she would send to her son-in-law as soon as a ship left Montréal bound either for France or Louisiana. Since maritime traffic was stopped many months a year in New France due to the rigors of winter, she decided to write daily but to send out her letters only when she was sure that they could reach their destination. All of those *cahiers* seem to have been preserved. The rest of the texts published in *Lettres au cher fils* are more traditional letters, sent out as soon as written; sixty-one of these letters, written on loose leafs, and mostly dated after 26 February 1751, have survived, but many others were lost. The two components of *Lettres au cher fils* differ not only in their means of transmission and state of conservation but also formally, in at least four ways.

First, the letters from the journal are explicitly part of a continuous text. The incipit of Madame Bégon's writings reads: "My dear son, now that I'm done with a series of letters that burdened me, I will chat with you daily, with the everlasting pleasure I feel when I do so, and I will repeat over and over that this correspondence is the only consolation I am left with."[8] From day to day, Madame Bégon reminds her addressee of what she had told him previously, she comments on her own writing, she corrects or develops certain of her stories. On 13 November 1748, in the second of the texts preserved, she writes: "Je te disais hier, cher fils . . ." (I was telling you yesterday, dear son), thus inserting her text in a series.[9] A few days later, she stresses the fact that, contrary to the day before, she now has something new to say: "Si je n'avais rien de nouveau hier, cher fils, à te dire, en voilà aujourd'hui."[10] By the end of the exchange, she still uses the same device, when she tells her son-in-law that her irate letter of the previous day must not worry him: "Tu vois, cher fils, que je ne suis pas plus capable aujourd'hui de garder de rancune contre toi que je ne l'ai fait par le passé."[11] The texts in Elisabeth Bégon's journal are thus linked one to the other, and this creates a sense of continuity that is not to be found in the loose-leaf letters. As she states very clearly, Madame Bégon refuses to interrupt her writing: "C'est seulement, cher fils, pour ne point dérouter mon journal, ayant écrit beaucoup aujourd'hui à Québec," she writes her son-in-law on 30 May 1749, apologizing for the brevity of that day's entry, but, at the same time, reiterating the necessity of not skipping a day.[12]

Second, the length of the texts varies considerably. Those of the journal are generally very short, but together in the *cahiers*, they create a longer text than the loose-leaf letters. Each of these loose-leaf letters is longer than the texts of the journal, but they are not part of a larger text as explicitly as the *cahiers*. They remain independent from one another, even though they are included serially in *Lettres au cher fils*. This difference in length is not only material; it changes the temporal frame of Madame Bégon's writing. Time, the material of which correspondence, diary, and autobiography are all made, is not the same in every type of writing. In the case of the loose-leaf letters, time is fragmented, discontinuous, segmented by mail deliveries and the expectation of letters to come; in the case of the journal, it is still fragmented – Madame Bégon dates all of her entries, – but the fact that she writes every day and that she collects all daily entries in *cahiers* alleviates the fragmentation effects.

The content of the two types of texts is also different. For example, in the journal, Madame Bégon writes continually that she is afraid to bore her correspondent, and she admits quite openly that she repeats herself: "Je crains de t'ennuyer, n'ayant rien d'intéressant à te dire et n'aurais à te répéter que la peine que j'ai toujours de ton absence à laquelle je ne puis m'accoutumer," she writes on 7 June 1749.[13] Conversely, what Geneviève Haroche-Bouzinac dubs the "thème postal"[14] – the concrete conditions of epistolary exchange as they are expressed explicitly in letter writing – seems to worry Madame Bégon mostly in her loose-leaf

letters. Once again, these differences in subject matter have to be interpreted with regard to the poetics of the diary and of the correspondence.
In the first case, the sense of continuity created by the daily entries of
the journal puts the writer in a position to comment on and evaluate her
previous entries, and this rereading is one of the characteristics of the
diary genre: each day's experience is similar to the previous one, argues
Madame Bégon. In the second case, it is the poetics of the correspondence which imposes – up to a point – the subject matter: letter writers
tend to be easily obsessed with the whereabouts of their texts, and every
mail delivery reinforces that obsession. While the differences between
the two poetics cannot solely account for each and every difference in
subject matter, it should be stressed that poetics do have that kind of
effect on writing.

The last difference between the two series of texts in *Lettres au cher fils*
is to be found in the use of the letters sent to Madame Bégon by Michel
de Villebois de La Rouvillière. Whereas the journal is mostly oblivious
to these letters, the loose-leaf letters are clearly structured in relation to
them – they are answers. The author of the journal is forced by the
circumstances to rely entirely on her own writing when she addresses her
son-in-law; for long periods of time she cannot receive letters. The *épis-
tolière*, on the other hand, claims that she never leaves letters unanswered.
Since Michel de Villebois de La Rouvillière is not a prolific letter writer,
to say the least, Madame Bégon always answers the letters she receives,
if only to show her correspondent that she really cares about his letters
and to require more of them. Moreover, she often states in the earliest
cahier of her journal that she does not know whether her son-in-law is in
France or Louisiana when she writes to him: "mais où t'écrire, cher
fils?," asks Madame Bégon on 12 March 1749.[15] This ignorance
differentiates further the journal from the loose-leaf letters, since the
latter always remind Madame Bégon where her "cher fils" is located.

What are the consequences of these four differences for the study of
the relations between the personal genres in eighteenth-century France?
They reveal the limits of each genre and they explain – at least partially
– Diderot's failure in trying to write letters that would form a diary.
When Madame Bégon is forced by external circumstances to write her
journal, she proposes to her reader a text that is (comparatively) continuous, has its own subject matter, and stands partially autonomous. On
the other hand, when she is able to send letters out on a regular basis,
she writes texts that are discontinuous, clearly fragmented, and overtly
reader-oriented. In the first case, the formal characteristics of the texts

are determined by the diary's poetics, its specific relation to time and
unity; in the second case, the poetics of epistolarity – the fact that letters
are, by necessity, part of a "chain of dialogue"[16] – explains the central
role of the reader. In Diderot's case, when he intends to send Sophie
Volland his diary he tries to integrate into one genre – the correspondence – the formal characteristics of another – the diary. He would have
liked to blend continuity and discontinuity, unity and fragmentation,
self-centered investigation and dialogue, the image he had of himself
and the one he created for Sophie Volland, self-imposed introspection
and selfless reactions. In this project Diderot failed, but the questions
raised by his attempt are important with regard to the history of life-
writing.

One question still remains to be addressed: is Madame Bégon's
journal a true *journal intime*, a diary, as the genre is defined today?
Although the previous analysis would seem to lead to a positive answer,
one has to stress the fact that things are not that clear. On the one hand,
Madame Bégon writes every day, confides her love – whether maternal
or not – for her son-in-law, recounts her activities, tells of the "nou-
veautés" that concern the people who surround her, depicts her ail-
ments.[17] On the other, she does not venture into her most intimate
thoughts – even about Michel de Villebois de La Rouvillière – nor recall
her past; her dead husband, to take but one example, is mentioned only
twice in *Lettres au cher fils*.[18] One should not make too much of sentences
like "I feel at peace when I can find the time to tell you that I love you"[19]
or "But I'm afraid to confide in anyone. My experience teaches me to
keep everything inside."[20] It must not be forgotten that neither Madame
Bégon nor Diderot knew of a genre named the *journal intime* that would
foster and be defined by self-centered expression. To address a text to
someone else is something quite different from writing a *journal intime*.

In the decade that followed Madame Bégon's *Lettres au cher fils*, Jean-
Jacques Rousseau started to write his *Confessions*. Even though they were
published only after their author's death, the initial stages of their
writing coincide precisely with Diderot's attempts at life-writing in his
correspondence. Since Rousseau uses letters in the *Confessions*, their analysis should prove fruitful for the historical interpretation of life-writing
in the French Enlightenment. The only aspect of the problem addressed
here is the status and role of the reader in Rousseau's use of his own correspondence.[21]

Rousseau's goal in writing the *Confessions* is made clear on numerous
occasions, notably in the fifth paragraph of the seventh book: "The real
object of my confessions is, to contribute to an accurate knowledge of

my inner being in all the different situations of my life. What I have promised to relate, is the history of my soul; I need no other memoirs in order to write it faithfully; it is sufficient for me to enter again into my inner self as I have hitherto done."[22] This statement is only partially true. If Rousseau repeats over and again that he wishes to present posterity with his *vérité*, he does not rely only on his memory to do so. Throughout the tenth book of the *Confessions*, he admits that he perused what remained of his correspondence while preparing his autobiography: "I accordingly determined to devote my leisure to carrying out this undertaking, and I commenced to collect the letters and papers which might guide or assist my memory, greatly regretting all that I had torn up, burned, or lost, up to this time."[23] In writing one's life, memory alone is insufficient. Texts are needed.

The problem Rousseau faces in reading the papers he collected for his *Confessions* is the same he faced whenever writing was involved. For Rousseau, is it not the essence of writing to lie, or at least to create too great a distance between the self and the world? In his autobiography Rousseau does not reflect on this issue *per se*, but he is forced to deal with it each and every time he wants to use or quote a letter: the truth he seeks seems to elude him the moment he alludes to a letter. One example is the exchange of letters that took place between Rousseau and the maréchale de Luxembourg at the time of *La Nouvelle Héloïse*.

Madame de Luxembourg had asked Rousseau to send her a manuscript copy of his epistolary novel. Rousseau himself judged his answer to her request to be polite and honest, and he was astonished that his intended message was misinterpreted: "je lui écrivis quelque chose d'obligeant et d'honnête à ce sujet; du moins telle était mon intention. Voici sa réponse, qui me fit tomber des nues."[24] Surprised, and wondering what he had done wrong, Rousseau wrote Madame de Luxembourg to correct any misunderstanding.

On receiving this letter [by Madame de Luxembourg], I hastened to reply to it before examining it more fully, in order to protest against any impolite interpretation; and, after having devoted several days to this examination with a feeling of uneasiness which may be imagined, without being able to understand what was the matter, I wrote the following note as a final answer on the subject . . . It is now ten years since these letters were written. I have often thought of them since then: and, even to this day, I am so stupid on this point, that I have not been able to understand what she could find in the passage in question that was, I will not say offensive, but even calculated to cause her displeasure.[25]

Ten years afterward, Rousseau still could not fathom what he had said to stir such a reaction from his former patron.

Whether or not Rousseau's lack of understanding of this matter was due, as he says, to his "stupidité" is irrelevant here. What matters in this episode is the discovery – not fully acknowledged by Rousseau – of the fact that a letter has many meanings, as many meanings as it has readers. Letters are not merely witnesses to events past. As texts, they can be interpreted. Not only their writers but also their readers make them what they are. Their formal characteristics might be different from those of the autobiography, but their nature is not. In ascertaining this phenomenon, Rousseau puts himself into a paradoxical situation: if one can interpret a letter, then one is surely justified in interpreting an autobiography. If the truth of the self lies neither in the letters Rousseau collects, rereads, and quotes, nor in his finished autobiography, where, then, does it lie?

When, in the very same year (1765), Diderot attempted to mold his correspondence into an autobiography, he encountered difficulties similar to those faced by Rousseau. Both wanted to write a life narrative at a time when models for that type of writing did not yet exist. Both relied on letters, which for Rousseau were artifacts and for Diderot were a means of communication. Both knew that their projects were novel – or so they believed. Rousseau stated in the opening sentences of his book that he was the first person ever (and the last, as well) to undertake such a task: "Je forme une entreprise qui n'eut jamais d'exemple et dont l'exécution n'aura point d'imitateur."[26] Diderot was not quite so conceited, but he confided to his correspondent that she was to decide whether or not this type of writing was worth continuing: "Voilà, mon amie, une petite ébauche de nos causeries; si elles vous conviennent, je continuerai."[27]

Why is it, then, that Diderot did not manage to write an autobiography in his letters, when Rousseau succeeded in doing so in his *Confessions*? One could argue that the specific relations between letter writers and their first readers are such that they preclude the writing of an autobiography in the form of letters.[28] Diderot addressed his narrative to a very specific person – his lover Sophie Volland. Rousseau, in contrast, was not so specific about his readers – he addresses a vaguely defined posterity. Both Diderot and Rousseau were confronted with the writer's inevitable implied definition of his or her readers. Critics such as Charles A. Porter have already shown that this "implied reader" varies according to the different types of personal narratives: "the address differentiates it [the letter] both from the diary, 'addressed' normally to its author alone, and from the autobiography, which usually does not have an identifiable – at least a single – addressee and is not ordinarily a 'private' communication."[29] Since Diderot addresses Sophie Volland in what, for the sake of the argument, can be considered a "private communication," is it possible for him to write his autobiography through his correspondence?

Arguably, the poetics of correspondence forces one to answer this question in the negative. In choosing to write a letter, Diderot chooses to draw of himself a portrait that is defined by the very fact that he writes to one addressee, and not to some faceless posterity. Furthermore, this portrait necessarily evolves over the course of the correspondence, for the letter writer and the addressee change over time, and the conditions in which they write and read the letters are almost as important as the letters themselves. Whereas the autobiographical writer tries to give some coherence to the different episodes of his life after these episodes occurred – or when he claims that these episodes are over – the *épistolier* often writes about events that are still happening by virtue of their retelling and their commenting by the addressee. Since he will not discuss his autobiography with actual readers, Rousseau is not tied as closely as Diderot to the possibility of a reader's reaction. While it is true that every reader is supposed to make sense of the texts he or she reads – this is one of the lessons of the *Confessions* – an implied reader's response is not to be confused with the actual dialogue between letter writer and letter reader that characterizes correspondence. Rousseau may have had conflicts with Madame de Luxembourg, but they were not the same as those he had with posterity, and what the *Confessions* recall is to be distinguished from what they provoked. *Tout dire* – which is the root of his lifewriting – does not have the same implications for Rousseau as it does for Diderot.

Relations between the personal genres in eighteenth-century literature are too complex to draw any definitive conclusions from the comparison of only three sets of texts, for several other contemporaneous developments helped shape the nature of these relations, among them: the growing cultural appeal of solitude; the new emphasis placed on feeling, sentiment, and sensation; the influence of the first-person novel; shifts in social activities such as conversation; the apparent decline in religious belief with its concomitant impact on confession; changes in traditional forms of self-expression – travelogues, memoirs, collections of sayings (*ana*); the rise of the *fonction auteur*; and the history of both handwriting techniques and the paraphernalia associated with diary-keeping.[30] Nonetheless, the study of Diderot, Bégon, and Rousseau can lead to at least three general problems concerning the history of these relations and to a new contextualization of personal genres.

The first of these questions deals specifically with French literature
within the general context of European literatures, and it concerns the
rise of personal narratives. What are the comparisons that can be made,
for example, between Samuel Pepys's diary and those of his French
counterparts of the next century? What is the place of Casanova's
Histoire de ma vie in the evolution of the autobiographical genre? Surely
it is unlikely that the transformations of the personal genres can be
restricted to one country or one language. The problem here stems from
the fact that scholars of the French Enlightenment seem to be oblivious
to this European context. In fact, to take but one example (that of autobiography), one could argue that these scholars have accepted at face
value Rousseau's initial statement in the *Confessions* that he was creating
a new genre, distinct from the spiritual tradition that followed the
Augustinian model; they have failed to take note of the many forms of
autobiography that were developing concurrently throughout Europe.[31]
This ignorance of non-French traditions doubly reflects the state of literary studies in the French world. On the one hand, most specialists of
French literature are not in the habit of reading foreign corpora alongside their own, although they often manage to quote briefly some Locke,
Newton, Hume, or Richardson. On the other hand, Anglo-Saxon scholars seem to be more willing than the Francophones to review texts and
practices outside of the mainstream and to distance themselves from the
cult of great men, thus allowing themselves to open their inquiry to new
objects, regardless of their origins. Did the French *livre de comptes* and
various *carnets* lead to early forms of autobiography, as they did in
England at the beginning of the seventeenth century? Critics of French
literature would be hard-pressed to answer this question, for they would
have to contest Rousseau's opening lines in order to do so.

Indeed – and this is the second general problem – it does not seem
likely that the development of personal narrative can be appreciated
only by studying "professional" writers of just one national culture. If
Diderot and Rousseau – as well as Casanova – are known for other types
of writing, such is not the case with Madame Bégon and Pepys. Texts by
non-professional writers, or by writers of less fame than the canonical
ones, should also be considered if one is to understand how the diary
and the autobiography were born, and how the epistolary genre evolved
at the same time. Among them, one would have to scrutinize the
Jansenist writers of the *Nouvelles ecclésiastiques* (1728–1803): the victims of
persecution one hears from or reads about in this clandestine periodical
are not faceless – they tell their individual stories, very often in the form

of letters or diaries. Such is the case of Canon Roussel, from Châlons-sur-Marne: according to a letter sent to the *Nouvelles* on 4 April 1728, he was a "man of great order, and . . . he kept a daily journal of everything he did."[32] Similarly, but in the non-ecclesiastical world, Jean M. Goulemot and Didier Masseau have recently argued that a major change in reading practices occurred at the end of the *Siècle des lumières*, and that this change had important consequences for self-expression. Their analysis of the hundreds of letters received by Bernardin de Saint-Pierre after the publication of his novel *Paul et Virginie* (1788) reveals that the novelist's readers not only recognized themselves in his characters, but that they felt compelled to tell him in writing how the characters' lives matched their own. To Rolf Engelsing's dual model of reading – the German historian distinguishes intensive reading (few books, often read) from extensive reading (many books and periodicals, read once) – Goulemot and Masseau add a new relationship of the reader to the book which they call "lecture intimiste" (one book, often read, in which the reader recognizes himself and feels forced to write to its author).[33] Life-stories from artisans and skilled workers also command particular interest with regard to the birth of life-writing. Whether librarians like Valentin Jamerey-Duval, glaziers like Jacques-Louis Ménétra, or printers like Nicolas Contat, such non-professional writers seem to be less concerned with the canons of literary genres than their professional counterparts.[34] Marie-Claire Grassi has demonstrated how formal aspects of letters written by another group of non-professional writers at the opposite end of the social spectrum – members of the nobility – combine to produce what she calls "seuils d'intimité": the complex inter-twining of personal pronouns (*tu/vous*), confidences, and proxemics. For Grassi, the period during which these writers changed their modes of self-expression is located between 1780 and 1830.[35]

Even an eccentric such as Jean-Marie Chassaignon (1735–95) and a minor poet such as the chevalier de Bonnard (1744–84) are of interest here. The first one, in his *Cataractes de l'imagination* (1779), insists on the uniqueness both of his personality and of the genre he uses. In his "Avis essentiel" he writes that

neither Voltaire, J. Jacques, Corneille nor Montesquieu have felt what I feel. I prefer *my self* to all these tiresome characters. I prefer *my self* to everything that exists; the sweetest moments of my life I have spent by *my self*; that solitary *self*, surrounded by graves, and invoking the Supreme Being, would suffice to make me happy even on the remains of the universe . . . A friend's treachery saddens me less than his importunity when he forces *my self* to re-enter the world . . . In the streets where I like to walk alone, I go through the same crisis as that of a man lost in a forest full of murderers or ferocious animals; the slightest thing alarms me; my eye fastens on the gaze of the first person that I come into contact with: if he stares at me, I back away; he plans an attack on me; he's going after my delight in *my self*; if he comes up to me, his sole purpose is to harm me; by talking with me, he will put an end to my conversation with a genius; and his conversation cannot compensate for that loss . . . O how I would love to be taken to a barbarous land where no one would know me, where no friend would interrupt me, where *my self* would belong entirely to me; half an hour taken away from me, is a glass of blood drawn from me, is a piece of my heart stripped away from me.[36]

Three years before Rousseau's *Confessions* and *Rêveries du promeneur solitaire* were to be published, Chassaignon asserts himself in no ambivalent way. Not only does he stress the fact that his *moi* is without equivalent – not even Voltaire, Rousseau, Corneille, or Montesquieu, those "fastidieux personnages" compare – but he also depicts himself as the victim of others, friend and foe alike, eager to divert his attention away from the real genius with whom he wishes to converse – himself. This solitary *moi*, obsessed with his death and the loss of time, could have tried to write the story of his life, but he did not, with the exception of a short text called "Ma confession; mon horoscope; scenes inouies."[37] Instead he chose to defend his aesthetic conceptions against those of several contemporary critics. In order to do so, he needed "a genre unknown to our times."[38] Chassaignon thus linked explicitly the limits of the genres and the possibility of self-expression: "Just as my way of thinking is opposed to that of other men, so does the form of my book differ from all other books."[39] To express his "way of thinking," Chassaignon had to create a "literary monster" (monstre littéraire) mixing erudite collage and dissertation, poetry and prose, French and Latin, testimony and mysticism. Montaigne, whom he names as his model, – as did both Diderot and Rousseau – is clearly not enough.

On a more traditional note the chevalier de Bonnard recorded "nearly everyday," his "impressions" and "memories." His editor, Alexandre Piedagnel, quotes a few of them:

I was saying yesterday that I'd gladly trade my life for money, if the amount was large, if I could dispose of it freely to benefit individuals as well as the public, to build helpful institutions, to enrich my friends and to relieve the underprivileged, in a word to be helpful: people laughed at me; nobody believed me . . . What! I could die lowly and unknown to anybody, and I would not swap my death for the glory of being helpful for a long time! . . .[40]

More than the unsurprising presence of "bienfaisance" achieved through things "utiles," what should concern the reader in this entry is the apparent absence of fear in the face of death, and the author's treatment of time. Not only does he evoke his immediate past, but he positions himself in the future, first by discussing his place within posterity, second by creating the standard by which he would later be judged.

The treatment of time is crucial in all forms of life-writing. The diary postulates daily writing. The autobiography asks for retrospective linear writing. The letter has the power to mix different kinds of temporal representation: the present of the writing, an idealized past, a much-expected future. If one is to understand the appearance of new personal genres, or of modifications to existing ones, then one should study the temporal possibilities any given genre provides at any given moment in history; this is the third of the three general problems raised in this conclusion. With regard to the personal genres in eighteenth-century France, it could be argued that the need for new ways to handle time manifested itself early in the century (Jamerey-Duval, Bégon, Diderot, Contat), but that it gained momentum, so to speak, in its last twenty-five years (Rousseau, Chassaignon, Bonnard, Ménétra, the diaries selected by Pierre Pachet in *Les Baromètres de l'âme*). Then, what appeared to be new genres (the autobiography, the diary) offered themselves as answers to a long-standing quest (as found in many correspondences or lesser-known texts). One could go so far as to say that genres that did not yet exist publicly or on a large-scale, nonetheless imposed their rules and modes of representation on genres that already had a long history. This would suggest that genres are not only concretizations of formal characteristics but that they are answers to questions not yet clearly formulated by society.

But is there really a need for such a differentiating of genres at the end of the eighteenth century in France? Two well-known texts made public at the very same time tend to show that such was the case at the beginning of the 1780s – the very period that saw the publication of the *Rêveries du promeneur solitaire* (1782) and the *Confessions* (books I to VI were published in 1782, books VII to XII in 1789). Restif de la Bretonne's *Sara ou la dernière aventure d'un homme de quarante-cinq ans* dates from 1783. It recalls one year in the life of Monsieur Nicolas, Restif's alter ego, that of his tormented affair with Sara, the young daughter of his landlady. This autobiographical novel shows its narrator obsessed not only with the interpretation of his actions at a particular point in time, but also with the comparison of

these actions to previous ones. Monsieur Nicolas's eagerness to com-
memorate all aspects of his past, his thirst for anniversaries, his lament
for days gone by, is everywhere evident in the book:

After the mother and the daughter left, I began to write the continuation of this
Story, which I put down faithfully day by day; what I've added to it since
amounts to the causes of events, mostly unknown then . . . I had another odd
habit: for a few years I had fancied strolling round the Île Saint-Louis; even
before I met Sara, I used to engrave on its stones the dates of the main events
of my life. One year later, the same day, I went back to them: then, moved by
some kind of exhilaration, to be still alive, I kissed them, and I drew them over,
adding *twice* or *thrice*. When I met Sara, I started to write my dates daily; I went
to sigh on my beloved island, I wrote every event in shorthand, whether my situation was gay or my soul was suffering, once I was unfortunate. This is how,
without knowing it, I sustained my affection for Sara, while fostering my sensibility. May that help others; as for me, I nurse solely my pain! . . .[41]

At a time when there is no such thing in France as an autobiography or
a diary – if one is to believe most literary histories – here is a character
who engraves his diary entries on city walls and tells of this activity in a
linear *récit* blending day-to-day writing with subsequent additions. The
passage of time pervades every aspect of the narration, from the cult of
anniversaries to the retrospective sorrow.

The year after Restif published *Sara*, permission was granted
Beaumarchais to stage his *Mariage de Figaro*. Often read as a prelude to
the Revolution, Figaro's long monologue in the play's fifth act is as much
about the self and its relation to time:

What an incredible series of events! How did it happen to me? Why these things
and not others? Who drew them down on my head? Forcibly set on the road of
life, not knowing where it leads, and bound to leave it against my will, I've tried
to keep it as rosy as my natural cheerfulness permits. Here again I say *my* cheerfulness without knowing if it belongs to me any more than those other things;
nor do I know who this *I* may be with which I am so concerned – it's a shape-
less collection of unknown parts, then a helpless puny thing, then a lively little
animal, then a young man thirsting for pleasure, with a full capacity to enjoy
and ready to use any shifts to live – master here and valet there, at the whim of
fortune; ambitious from vanity, industrious from need – and lazy . . . with
delight! An orator in tight spots, a poet for relaxation, a musician from time to
time, a lover in hot fits: I have seen everything, done everything, worn out everything. At last my illusion is shattered, and I'm now wholly disabused . . . blasé
. . .![42]

The *moi* which eludes Figaro is clearly set in time: the character does not
comprehend the reasons why he had to live such and such an event, but

he tries to organize the story of his life in a coherent *récit* moving from his conception and his early years, to his youth and his numerous *métiers*. In the context of the *Mariage*, Figaro's soliloquy will soon be followed by his long-awaited, and much-threatened, wedding, and the dark over-tones of his narrative will make room for the final "Vaudeville." Figaro's *désabusement* is firmly rooted in time, as is Restif's, but it does not lead to the same resentment.

Throughout the eighteenth century, in France as elsewhere in Europe, people tried to make sense of their lives in writing. Be they the readers-turned-contributors of the *Nouvelles ecclésiastiques*, a widow leaving New France for France, Bernardin de Saint-Pierre's audience, members of the French provincial nobility, artisans and skilled workers, minor figures such as the abbé de Sade, Chassaignon, and Bonnard, or famous *hommes de lettres* such as Voltaire, Rousseau, and Diderot, they all looked for new tools to express themselves. Since they knew of no formal model for such self-expression, they molded older personal genres – correspondence and memoirs – into more appropriate ones for their needs. Their endeavor, in its slow evolution from the 1740s to the 1780s, paralleled that of novelists such as Restif de la Bretonne and dramatists such as Beaumarchais. They would soon be heard in the political arena, most forcefully in the various "Déclarations des droits de l'homme et du citoyen." Still, their will to fuse personal narratives with new treatments of time did not go unopposed: Morellet, in his *Mémoires . . . sur le dix-huitième siècle et sur la Révolution*, and Bernardin de Saint-Pierre's old man, in *Paul et Virginie*, kept warding off self-expression, even after Rousseau's *Confessions*.[43] The tensions between the genres were still very much alive: individuality was not yet what it was eventually to become – the founda-tion of modern life.

NOTES

1. Denis Diderot, *Diderot's Letters to Sophie Volland: A Selection*, trans. Peter France (London: Oxford University Press, 1972), 17; "Mes lettres sont une histoire assez fidèle de la vie. J'exécute sans m'en apercevoir ce que j'ai désiré cent fois. Comment, ai-je dit, un astronome passe trente ans de sa vie au haut d'un observatoire, l'œil appliqué le jour et la nuit à l'extrémité d'un télé-scope pour déterminer le mouvement d'un astre, et personne ne s'étudiera soi-même, n'aura le courage de nous tenir un registre exact de toutes les pensées de son esprit, de tous les mouvements de son cœur, de toutes ses pensées, de tous ses plaisirs; et des siècles innombrables se passeront sans qu'on sache si la vie est une bonne ou une mauvaise chose, si la nature humaine est bonne ou méchante, ce qui fait naître notre bonheur et notre

malheur. Mais il faudroit bien du courage pour rien céler. On s'accuseroit peut-être plus aisément du projet d'un grand crime, que d'un petit sentiment obscur, vil et bas . . . Cette espèce d'examen ne seroit pas non plus sans utilité pour soi. Je suis sûr qu'on seroit jaloux à la longue de n'avoir à porter en compte le soir que des choses honnêtes. Je vous demanderois, à vous: 'Diriez-vous tout?' Faites un peu la même question à Uranie; car il faudroit absolument renoncer à un projet de sincérité qui vous effrayeroit"; Denis Diderot, *Correspondance*, ed. Georges Roth and Jean Varloot, 16 vols. (Paris: Editions de Minuit, 1955–70), IV: 39. Original French texts and their sources will be cited in the notes immediately after the reference for the English translation. I would like to thank the Conseil de recherches en sciences humaines du Canada and the Fonds pour la formation de chercheurs et l'aide à la recherche du gouvernement du Québec for their funding of my research on "La naissance de l'intimité au Siècle des lumières."

2. My translation; "Comme mon projet étoit de reprendre l'histoire de ma vie aussitôt que la fin de ma tâche m'en laisseroit la liberté, j'avois jeté des petites notes sur un feuillet volant qui est devenu par lapse de tems un logogriphe à déchiffrer. Je n'y entens plus rien"; Diderot, *Correspondance*, V: 169–70.

3. On the history of autobiography in France, see Philippe Lejeune, *Le Pacte autobiographique* (Paris: Seuil, 1975). On Diderot's odd autobiographical writings, see Pierre Lepape, *Diderot* (Paris: Flammarion, 1991), 167, 223–24, 288–90; Jean-Claude Bonnet, "L'Ecrit amoureux ou le fou de Sophie," in *Colloque international Diderot (1713–1784)*, ed. Anne-Marie Chouillet (Paris: Aux amateurs de livres, 1985), 105–14; and Yoichi Sumi, "L'Eté 1762: A propos des lettres à Sophie Volland," *Europe* 661 (May 1984): 113–19.

4. François Laforge has studied this failure in "Diderot et le 'journal intime'," *Revue d'histoire littéraire de la France* 87:6 (November–December 1987): 1015–22. For his part, Stephen Werner argues that Diderot, instead of writing his own autobiography, resorted to other people's *récit de vie*; see here his "A comic life: Diderot and *le récit de vie*."

5. From a similar perspective, I have already discussed Rousseau's *Rêveries du promeneur solitaire* and Voltaire's *Carnets* and *Mémoires* in the "Conclusion" of my *Diderot épistolier: Contribution à une poétique de la lettre familière au XVIIIᵉ siècle*, (Montréal: Fides, 1996), 423–28. See also Julie Candler Hayes's chapter, in which she shows how biography, autobiography, memoirs, and family romance are intertwined in the abbé de Sade's *Mémoires pour la vie de François Pétrarque*.

6. Elisabeth Bégon, *Lettres au cher fils: Correspondance d'Elisabeth Bégon avec son gendre, 1748–1753*, ed. Nicole Deschamps (Montréal: Boréal, 1994), 205. All references in the essay are to this edition.

7. No letters by Michel de Villebois de La Rouvillière to his mother-in-law have been preserved. *Lettres au cher fils* also includes, besides Madame Bégon's writings, two letters by one of her sons, Claude-Michel-Jérôme Bégon, and a dozen letters by Marie-Catherine de Villebois, Madame

Bégon's granddaughter, either full letters or complements to Madame Bégon's letters. For a reading inspired by Norbert Elias's sociological thought, see my "La Configuration épistolaire: Lecture sociale de la correspondance d'Elisabeth Bégon," *Lumen* 16 (1997).

8. My translation; "A présent, mon cher fils, que je me vois débarrassée de tant d'écrits qui m'ont beaucoup coûté, je pourrai, avec la même satisfaction que j'ai toujours eue à m'entretenir avec toi, le faire tous les jours, et te répéter cent fois que c'est tout ce qui me reste de consolation"; Bégon, *Lettres*, 43.

9. *Ibid.*, 44.

10. *Ibid.*, 56.

11. *Ibid.*, 336.

12. *Ibid.*, 182.

13. *Ibid.*, 186

14. Geneviève Haroche-Bouzinac, *Voltaire dans ses lettres de jeunesse, 1711–1733* (Paris: Klincksieck, 1992), 183–87.

15. Bégon, *Lettres*, 129.

16. Janet Gurkin Altman, *Epistolarity: Approaches to a Form* (Columbus: Ohio State University Press, 1982), 187.

17. Bégon, *Lettres*, 44.

18. *Ibid.*, 161, 221.

19. My translation; "Je me trouve en mon centre lorsque je peux avoir un moment à te dire que je t'aime"; *ibid.*, 313.

20. My translation; "Mais je n'ose me confier à personne. L'expérience m'apprend à tout garder en moi-même"; *ibid.*, 139.

21. For a more elaborate study of this aspect of the *Confessions*, see my "Le Malentendu épistolaire: Note sur le statut de la lettre dans *Les Confessions*," *Littérales* 17 (1995): 77–89.

22. Jean-Jacques Rousseau, *Confessions*, Everyman's Library: Biography, 2 vols. (London and New York: J.M. Dent and E. P. Dutton, 1931), 1: 252; "L'objet propre de mes confessions est de faire connaître exactement mon intérieur dans toutes les situations de ma vie. C'est l'histoire de mon âme que j'ai promise, et pour l'écrire fidèlement je n'ai pas besoin d'autres mémoires; il me suffit, comme j'ai fait jusqu'ici, de rentrer au dedans de moi"; Jean-Jacques Rousseau, *Les Confessions*, ed. Jacques Voisine (Paris: Garnier, 1980), 322.

23. Rousseau, *Confessions*, II: 161; "Je résolus donc de consacrer mes loisirs à bien exécuter cette entreprise, et je me mis à recueillir les lettres et papiers qui pouvaient guider ou réveiller ma mémoire, regrettant fort tout ce que j'avais déchiré, brûlé, perdu jusqu'alors"; Rousseau, *Les Confessions*, 609.

24. Rousseau, *Les Confessions*, 617.

25. Rousseau, *Confessions*, II: 167; "En recevant cette lettre [by Madame de Luxembourg], je me hâtai d'y répondre, en attendant plus ample examen, pour protester contre toute interprétation désobligeante, et après m'être occupé quelques jours à cet examen, avec l'inquiétude qu'on peut concevoir, et toujours sans y rien comprendre, voici quelle fut enfin ma dernière

réponse à ce sujet . . . Il y a maintenant dix ans que ces lettres ont été écrites. J'y ai souvent repensé depuis ce temps-là, et telle est encore aujourd'hui ma stupidité sur cet article, que je n'ai pu parvenir à sentir ce qu'elle avait pu trouver dans ce passage, je ne dis pas d'offensant, mais même qui pût lui déplaire"; Rousseau, *Les Confessions*, 617–18.

26. Rousseau, *Les Confessions*, 3.
27. Diderot, *Correspondance*, V: 173.
28. Reasons other than formal, notably philosophical or psychological ones, have been advanced to explain Diderot's attitude toward autobiography. Michel Delon has suggested both types of explanation: see "La Circulation de l'écriture dans les *Lettres à Sophie*," in *Diderot: Autographes, manuscrits, éditions*, ed. Béatrice Didier and Jacques Neefs (Paris: Presses universitaires de Vincennes, 1986), 131, and "La Faute à Rousseau," *Le Magazine littéraire* 252–53 (April 1988): 23.
29. Charles A. Porter, "Foreword," *Yale French Studies* 71 (1986): 2. See also Altman, *Epistolarity*, 84–89, 112.
30. Pierre Pachet has studied both in *Les Baromètres de l'âme: Naissance du journal intime* (Paris: Hatier, 1990), 45, and in "Vers une sténographie de l'intime: Entre Fénelon et Constant: Karl Philipp Moritz," *Littérales* 17 (1995): 41–56. On collections of *ana*, see Francine Wild, "Les Ana et la divulgation de l'intimité," in *Ordre et contestation au temps des classiques*, ed. Roger Duchêne and Pierre Ronzeaud, 2 vols. (Paris–Seattle–Tübingen: Papers on French Seventeenth-Century Literature, 1992), II: 33–42. On the *fonction auteur*, see Didier Masseau, *L'Invention de l'intellectuel dans l'Europe du XVIIIᵉ siècle* (Paris: Presses universitaires de France, 1994), 17–44.
31. For instance, what is the relationship between Rousseau's *Confessions* and the "secular autobiography" Paul Delany describes in the second part of his *British Autobiography in the Seventeenth Century* (London and New York: Routledge & Kegan Paul, and Columbia University Press, 1969), 107–66?
32. My translation; "[un] homme d'un grand ordre, & . . . il tenoit Regître jour par jour de tout ce qu'il faisoit"; *Nouvelles ecclésiastiques, ou Mémoires pour servir à l'histoire de la constitution Unigenitus: Tome premier Qui contient les années 1728, 1729 & 1730*, 3rd edn. (Utrecht: Aux dépens de la Compagnie, 1735), multiple paginations, 57.
33. See Jean M. Goulemot, "Tensions et contradictions de l'intime dans la pratique des Lumières," *Littérales* 17 (1995): 13–21. Also, see Jean M. Goulemot and Didier Masseau: "Lettres au grand homme ou Quand les lecteurs écrivent," in *La Lettre à la croisée de l'individuel et du social*, ed. Mireille Bossis (Paris: Kimé, 1994), 39–47; and "Naissance des lettres adressées à l'écrivain," *Textuel* 27 (February 1994): 1–12. Engelsing's model is exposed in *Der Bürger als Leser: Lesergeschichte in Deutschland, 1500–1800* (Stuttgart: Metzler, 1974).
34. Valentin Jamerey-Duval, *Mémoires: Enfance et éducation d'un paysan au XVIIIᵉ siècle*, ed. Jean M. Goulemot (Paris: Le Sycomore, 1981); Jacques-Louis Ménétra, *Journal de ma vie: Jacques-Louis Ménétra, compagnon vitrier au 18e siècle*,

ed. Daniel Roche (Paris: Montalba, 1982). There are two modern editions of Contat's *Anecdotes typographiques* (1762): Nicolas Contat, *Anecdotes typographiques, où l'on voit la description des coutumes, mœurs et usages singuliers des compagnons imprimeurs*, ed. Giles Barber (Oxford: Oxford Bibliographical Society, 1980); and Philippe Minard, *Typographes des lumières suivi des "Anecdotes typographiques" de Nicolas Contat, 1762* (Seyssel: Champ Vallon, 1989).

35. Grassi has numerous articles on this topic: see, for example, "Friends and Lovers (or The Codification of Intimacy)," trans. Neil Gordon, *Yale French Studies* 71 (1986): 77–92.

36. My translation; "Voltaire, J. Jacques, Corneille ni Montesquieu n'ont pas senti ce que je sens. Je préfère *moi* à tous ces fastidieux personnages. Je préfère *moi* à tout ce qui existe; c'est avec ce *moi* seul que j'ai passé les plus doux moments de ma vie; ce *moi* isolé, entouré de tombeaux, & invoquant le grand être, suffiroit à mon bonheur sur les décombres de l'univers. . . . La perfidie d'un ami m'eût fait moins de peine, que son importunité, lorsqu'il est venu m'arracher à *moi-même* . . . Dans les rues où je me plais à marcher seul, je suis dans la crise d'un homme égaré dans un bois rempli d'assassins ou de bêtes féroces: le moindre objet m'allarme; l'éclair de mon œil va saisir le regard du premier qui me coudoie: s'il m'envisage, je recule; c'est un attentat qu'il médite; il en veut à la jouissance de *moi-même*; il ne m'aborde que pour me nuire; il va supplanter en me parlant, le génie avec lequel je converse; & dont son entretien ne peut me dédommager . . . que ne suis-je transporté dans une contrée barbare où personne ne me connoisse, où je ne sois interrompu par aucun ami, où *moi* m'appartienne tout entier; une demi-heure qu'on m'enleve, est une verrée de sang qu'on me tire, est un lambeau de mon cœur qu'on m'arrache"; [Jean-Marie Chassaignon], *Cataractes de l'imagination, déluge de la scribomanie, vomissement littéraire, hémorragie encyclopédique, monstre des monstres: Par Épiménide l'inspiré, Dans l'antre de Trophonius, au pays des visions*, 4 vols. (n.p., 1779), I: 79–81. With his strange use of *moi* (my self), Chassaignon clearly wishes to distinguish himself from all other men, even in his grammar.

37. *Ibid.*, III: 81–89.

38. My translation; "Un genre inconnu à ce siècle"; *ibid.*, I: 6.

39. My translation; "Ma façon de penser est aussi opposée à celle des autres hommes, que mon ouvrage diffère par la forme des autres ouvrages"; *ibid.*, I: 76.

40. My translation; "Je disois hier que je donnerois volontiers ma vie pour de l'argent, si la somme étoit forte, si j'avois la liberté d'en disposer en actes de bienfaisance générale et particulière, en établissemens utiles, ou pour enrichir mes amis et soulager un grand nombre de malheureux, enfin pour être utile: on se moquoit de moi; on ne me croyoit pas . . . Eh quoi! je m'expose à mourir obscur et ignoré, et je n'achèterois pas de ma mort la gloire d'être longtemps utile"; quoted in *Œuvres choisies du chevalier de Bonnard publiées avec une introduction par Alexandre Piedagnel* (Paris: Librairie des bibliophiles, 1891), x–xi.

41. My translation; "Après le départ de la mère et de la fille, je me mis à écrire la suite de ce Récit, que j'ai fidèlement tracé jour par jour; ce que j'y ai depuis ajouté se réduit aux causes des événements, alors ignorées pour la plupart . . . J'avais encore une autre manie: je me sentais depuis quelques années un goût décidé pour me promener sur l'Ile Saint-Louis; avant même de connaître Sara, j'y gravais sur la pierre les dates des principaux événements de ma vie. L'année suivante, au même jour, je les revoyais: alors, transporté d'une sorte d'ivresse, d'exister encore, je les baisais, et je les retraçais de nouveau, ajoutant *bis* ou *ter*. Quand je connus Sara, mes dates devinrent journalières; j'allais soupirer sur mon île chérie, j'y écrivais chaque événement en abrégé, la situation gaie ou douloureuse de mon âme lorsque je fus malheureux. C'est ainsi que, sans le savoir, je prolongeais mon attachement pour Sara, en entretenant ma sensibilité. Que tout cela serve aux autres; car, pour moi, je ne me nourris plus que de douleur! . . ."; Restif de la Bretonne, *Sara ou la dernière aventure d'un homme de quarante-cinq ans* (Paris: Stock, 1949), 150. To contextualize Monsieur Nicolas's moral stance, one should turn to Michel Condé's book, *La Genèse sociale de l'individualisme romantique* (Tübingen: Niemeyer, 1989).

42. *Six French Plays*, vol. IV of *The Classic Theatre*, ed. Eric Bentley, trans. Jacques Barzun (New York: Doubleday Anchor, 1961), 448–49; "O bizarre suite d'événements! Comment cela m'est-il arrivé? Pourquoi ces choses et non pas d'autres? Qui les a fixées sur ma tête? Forcé de parcourir la route où je suis entré sans le savoir, comme j'en sortirai sans le vouloir, je l'ai jonchée d'autant de fleurs que ma gaieté me l'a permis: encore je dis ma gaieté sans savoir si elle est à moi plus que le reste, ni même quel est ce *moi* dont je m'occupe: un assemblage informe de parties inconnues; puis un chétif être imbécile; un petit animal folâtre; un jeune homme ardent au plaisir, ayant tous les goûts pour jouir, faisant tous les métiers pour vivre; maître ici, valet là, selon qu'il plaît à la fortune; ambitieux par vanité, laborieux par nécessité; mais paresseux . . . avec délices! orateur selon le danger; poète par délassement; musicien par occasion; amoureux par folles bouffées, j'ai tout vu, tout fait, tout usé. Puis l'illusion s'est détruite, et, trop désabusé . . . Désabusé"; Beaumarchais, *Le Mariage de Figaro*, in *Théâtre*, ed. Jean-Pierre de Beaumarchais, Act 5, scene 3 (Paris: Garnier, 1980), 306–07.

43. See André Morellet, *Mémoires de l'abbé Morellet de l'Académie française sur le dix-huitième siècle et sur la Révolution*, ed. Jean-Pierre Guicciardi (Paris: Mercure de France, 1988), 39, and Bernardin de Saint-Pierre, *Paul et Virginie*, ed. Robert Mauzi (Paris: G. F. Flammarion, 1966), 143. Morellet's *Mémoires* were written in 1805 and published in 1821.

CHAPTER NINE

Portrait of the object of love in Rousseau's Confessions

Felicity Baker

Rousseau's portrayal of Madame de Warens in his *Confessions* far exceeds the theory of women which he had previously set out in the fifth book of *Emile*. How can we fail to see this as a progress, a maturation? The theory in *Emile* and the reflective dimension of *La Nouvelle Héloïse* were surely a stage on the way to the liberation of the autobiographical object of love. So the portrayal of Madame de Warens can provide readers with the starting point of a more constructive response to the theory than mere disappointment at its conventionality, its stereotyping of women, and its advocacy of the double standard. Rousseau himself, in his *Confessions*, recognizes his relationship to that in many ways transgressive woman as a matrix of his thinking. The potential implications of the portrait could be far-reaching for our understanding of the theoretical writings; particularly for our interpretation of the fact that those who are integrated as citizens in *Du contrat social* are not theorized *as male*.[1] The figure of Sophie alone arises out of a theoretical construction: that of sexual complementarity, at the point of Emile's initiation into the legitimate social pact. But attentive readers who would not want merely to project their own wishful meanings into Rousseau's texts, but would like to think that women could legitimately feel designated by his inspiring philosophy of freedom and equality, have a right to ask whether an inexorable *logical* complementarity compromises the pact of association with the theorizing of the veiled woman. It seems to me that there is not any such rigidifying complementarity across those contemporaneous texts, for the reason just stated: that the citizens, and even Emile, are not theorized as male. I would like to propose that this fact liberates *Du contrat social* from systematic interdependency with the theoretical side of the other works of 1756 to 1762, and it entitles us to take *Du contrat social* forward with its author to the point where the portrayal of Madame de Warens, the most constant object of Rousseau's love, supersedes the earlier theorizing of women. Entailed in this move is the proposition that portraiture, whatever it may owe to theories, constitutes in itself a major advance over theory, or at least, over the theory of sexual difference which is in question here. All the details of the way in which this portrait of a woman is constructed could contribute to transformations on the theoretical level, thanks to Rousseau's perception of her character and personality as proffering to him, from the time of their first meeting, a kind of key to the gates of the city: much more than a presentiment of true community; rather, real evidence of the communion of all humanity.

In the theoretical dimension of the potentially possible good society, the question of women constitutes, in Rousseau's works, a major gap which is probably not meant to be resolved. His theory of women located in the *Lettre à d'Alembert*, *La Nouvelle Héloïse*, and Book v of *Emile*, disappoints us for two reasons: its grounding in a now thoroughly obsolete eighteenth-century conception of women's biological destiny and its exclusive orientation toward an empowering integration of women (still necessarily submissive) into the non-egalitarian European society of his own lifetime. His reforming ambitions, in that contemporary context, do not go beyond his contention that if women gave all their moral liberty and creative energy to the private sphere and conformed to the principle of pudicity, they could become a force for social improvement. But, when he confronts the questions of the just society and of education for major change in *Du contrat social* and *Considérations sur le gouvernement de Pologne*, he does not mention women at all. We know only that he disagrees, in that area, with Plato, who would treat the female Guardians of the Republic in exactly the same way as the males. We know, therefore, that Rousseau considers women too different from men to prosper with the self-same education and social integration.[2]

Today, when the non-differentiating of women and men has not yet proven either easy to achieve in our society or always positive in its effects when apparently achieved, we can hardly say with certainty how Rousseau should have filled the gap left by his rejection of Plato's solution. Many recent feminist critics of Rousseau have felt justified in concluding that he himself filled that gap with the same theory of women's place as we find in the works mentioned above. Is it likely that, while all else changes in the shift of perspective from societies based on oppression to the society of the fundamental pact, Rousseau would think that the condition of women alone should remain the same? If he did think that, it is important that he did not say it; that alone would endow his silence with an emancipatory meaning, alongside his somewhat too explicit remonstrations about women's behavior in the corrupt society of his day. I am disposed to interpret the silence of *Du contrat social* on women in the following way: in the society of free citizens, theory cannot prescribe how women "should" voluntarily live their difference. It is only in an empty space so defined that the fact that the citizens are not theorized as male can begin to signify. This reflection opens the space for Rousseau's portrait of the woman he seems to have known best.

THE PORTRAITIST'S TELESCOPIC VISION

Rousseau radically transforms literary traditions to show that Madame de Warens was not like other people. Like Diderot, who insists in *Sur les femmes* that any man writing about women must write with passion, he recognizes that objective knowledge of the human does not exist as such; he knows the loved woman not as a separate being but only in her relationship with himself and others. Her portrait winds in and out of most of the books of the *Confessions* and emerges again in the last "Promenade." He looks back in memory, not just at her, but at her world; the writing combines subjectivity with distance. The sequence of successive approaches to her portrayal reminds me of Saint-Preux, the young hero of *La Nouvelle Héloïse*, who, when separated from his beloved Julie by the width of Lake Geneva, gazes toward her house through that new invention, the telescope, recalling and imagining one detail after another of her daily life, thanks to the distant visibility of her familiar places.[3] Each point of focus of the telescope, each remembered activity of the woman depicts her moral character. Preserving her separateness without attempting to be impartial, he does justice to her.

The successive quality of the series of points of telescopic focus on the woman does not fragment the portrait but rather progressively trains the eye on its diverse facets, bringing to the surface the light contained within each one. At twenty-seven, Françoise-Louise-Eléonore de la Tour, baronne de Warens, the orphaned, educated daughter of noble Protestants of the Pays de Vaud, abandoned her husband and country to convert to Catholicism in Savoy, then part of the kingdom of Sardinia. There, the church and King kept her and expected her to give hospitality to other new converts from across the border; one of these was the sixteen-year-old Rousseau, thirteen years her junior. She was a marginal figure, known (not only through Rousseau's testimony) for her exceptional intelligence, grace, and sincerity, whose marred reputation in no way prevented her from representing fundamental values in a cultural milieu itself largely discredited. Her unorthodox transmission to Jean-Jacques of cultural values and of that sense of the real possibility of community which gave him hope forever, a hope which his works still transmit to us, must be conveyed by the writer without infidelity to either the transmitted values or the unconventional modes of the transmission. She is both the social and the loss of the social. The portrayal therefore contains much ritual, and yet the rituals are unique, created for the exceptional occasion. Each major point of focus of the telescopic vision becomes the pretext for a short essay or discourse, rather than a narrative, analyzing in depth an aspect of her character and its value for him.

Rousseau's autobiographical writing was so innovative in its rejection of memoir form and static classical portraiture (based on binary morality and the characterology of humoralism), that he hardly felt it to be writing at all, just self-expression.[4] We can discern a patchwork of earlier literary modes; certainly Marivaux provided a basic model in *La Vie de Marianne*, where, as Peter Brooks shows, reflective commentaries and moral analyses follow anecdotes to constitute the fictional represented self in a framework of social interaction.[5] We find the alternating styles of pastoral and picaresque novels, and we hear echoes of La Bruyère's characters, or portraits, amid maxims in the manner of La Rochefoucauld. But Rousseau's self-portrayal takes off in a new direction, governed by the mobility of a developing self, changed by travel, and dynamized by multidetermined and morally complex modifications and influences. The outcome was to inspire Michel Leiris, who saw it as exemplary of the heterogeneous writing needed to "grasp the human," which he himself espoused in his ethnopoetic combination of anthropology and autobiography.[6] But the mobile, flowing self-portrait depends on the classical portrait genre adopted for the work's other characters. The portrait of Madame de Warens lies between the stable portraits (sometimes caricatures) of small-part players whom the first-person subject does not know long enough to see them change (or of whom he is certain they will never change) and his *portrait-fleuve* of himself. Hers is a classical portrait audaciously prolonged, transformed, extended, and deepened, in which the author takes her, as he takes himself, outside the codifiability expected by the theory of the four humors, which, just like himself, she radically contradicts. For example, he presents as a kind of riddle her combination of warm sensibility and "cold temperament," or lack of emotional need for sex. Scholars have inferred that he was seduced by a tall story on her part, thereby showing themselves more susceptible to anti-feminine prejudice than the allegedly misogynist writer and entirely missing Rousseau's rhetorical point: that humoralism was as inadequate to explain the woman as it was to explain himself. Her reappearance throughout the *Confessions* represents her constancy as Rousseau's most deeply internalized object. The reader may feel wonderment but can hardly be surprised when she reappears in the last "Promenade": "I was free, and better than free, because, subjected by my attachments alone, I just did what I wanted to do."[7]

The following pages pause at the first three major telescopic focal points in this great portrait, not summarizing Rousseau's whole account of each aspect but exploring the figures of thought which identify and express, in each case, a unique aspect of Eléonore de Warens: the experience of meeting her; what it was like to live in her little community; his involvement in her precarious social and political situation; her unconventional forming, through the gift of her own sexuality, of Rousseau's heart and mind in combination. The limits of space oblige me to explore elsewhere their shared musical and religious sensibility. I will conclude with some remarks about the psycho-social qualities of this portrait viewed as a whole.

THE FIRST MEETING

Rousseau introduces the reader to Madame de Warens in Book II, amid the shock of his exclusion from Geneva, his almost hallucinatory daydreams of freedom after running away from the brutality of the master to whom he was apprenticed, and the harsh reality of encountering from others, not the adult solicitude he needed but the self-interest of older people ready to use him for their own ends. The writer initially sets the woman against that context, using simple linguistic opposition and all the hyperbole of mythic binarism. In a world conceived (uncharacteristically, for Rousseau) as Manichean, she brings salvation.

This theological imagery functions in a secular dimension, "sacralizing" the purely human event of the first meeting and presenting the woman to the reader in a ceremony which makes the meeting a rite of passage – contrasted, however, with conventional ritual by the absence of hierarchical elements. Rousseau announces three times his first sight of her. The first "I *see* Madame de Warens" is followed by a depiction of his own appearance at the moment she first saw him: hers is a face whose gaze reflects him back to himself; he receives an adequate self-image as an immediate gift from her. He has to explain this to us because he was at that age (of which we learn much more in *Emile*, Book IV) when his character was about to take on its full coherence, as it now does; surrounded by none but negative influences, he would have turned out badly, but her presence saves him. The second "I *see* her, reach her, speak to her" produces a memory of the place where she stood: "Can I not surround that happy place with a golden rail! Draw to it the whole world's reverence! Whosoever loves to honor the memory of men's salvation should approach it on his knees." The woman in that place turns on hearing his voice: "*What became of me at the sight of her!*" The ritual third utterance brings us into her presence: "I *see* a countenance full of grace, fine blue eyes full of gentleness, a dazzling complexion, the contours of an enchanting bosom."[8] Sensual femininity suffuses the ceremonial. She reads his letter, pities his plight, invites him to dine with her, listens to his story. Such is the quality of this noblewoman's presence that she puts the timid youth at ease, at once and forever; she spontaneously creates equality.

This elaborate ceremony rejects all external forms of religious authority to instate a subjective form of the sacred in the relationship of Rousseau with the loved woman. Throughout Book II, everything turns on apparently unmarked uses of the word *grâce*. As soon as Jean-Jacques has met Madame de Warens, he is sent off to Turin to be converted to Catholicism at the Catechumens' Hospice, where they enjoin him, on arrival and departure, to be faithful to the gift of grace, but where he feels spiritually and homosexually abused. Fortunately, he can remember those who cared for his body and soul in childhood, especially his young aunt, "full of grace, intelligence and sense,"[9] and he now carries within him the graceful image of Madame de Warens. After he leaves the hospice, he is welcomed with grace by a beautiful stranger, Madame Basile. On one level, a clear opposition is set up between a misused theological doctrine of grace and the notion of a feminine grace in which the woman's unstinting gift of her self and her love to the boy child and to the man preserves his place within the social realm and ensures its continuance. But a sacralization of womanly grace, which is meant to be taken seriously, immediately supersedes this opposition of the womanly and the divine. In social life, "grace" designates the threefold movement constitutive of social exchange – giving, receiving, and returning the gift – without which community would not be possible, and it was once thought so important as to be depicted (so some believed) in the Three Graces on a wall in Pompeii.[10] "Grace" designates the profound acquiescence of the woman in the kinship systems of traditional societies, when she is herself the gift exchanged between families; in modern societies, it expresses her free gift of herself to her husband's family. Rousseau's transformation of feminine grace already epitomizes an open attitude to the social, one in which the grace of women can take effect outside matrimonial rites, in unformalized relationships which can save the soul of a young man making his way alone in a derelict society whose continuance is not at all certain.

There is more. At a deeper level, Rousseau is writing against St. Augustine's *Confessions*, which his own choice of title might at first suggest he wanted to follow. The ritualized, threefold approach to the lovable woman, described above, comments on St. Augustine's account of his gradual progress toward the light of salvation, which, for him, took the path of a turning-away in disgust from woman, who represents the flesh and the devil. Several times, the church father accompanies this movement with incantatory biblical quotations, a number of which come from the first chapter of St. John's Gospel. In violent contrast with Augustine's approach, we can hear the music of Rousseau's evocations of women "full of grace, intelligence and sense" as a poetically treacherous translation of St. John, chapter 1, verse 14: "And the Word was made flesh, and dwelt among us (and we beheld his glory . . .), full of grace and truth."

To the modern autobiographer's mind, placing the sacred squarely in a man's encounter with the fully incarnate and sociable woman entails no desecration. Thanks to Bayle, Rousseau can confidently make himself the authority on the location of the sacred as seen from his own subjective viewpoint; going much further than Bayle, he does away with the doctrine of Christ's mediation, finding the good news of men's salvation in a woman's generosity and discovering that pity comes not from outside the world but from living nature, and that it can emerge within society, in fleshly passion itself. Thus the near-absence of the figure of Christ in Rousseau's work is not a silence; rather, his poetic figures, which are clarified further in *Emile*, Book IV, intentionally express a repudiation of the central doctrine of Christian theology: "We are born twice, as it were: the first time for existence, and the second time for life; once for the species, another time for sex . . . This is the second birth," the crisis of adolescence, whereby a "man is truly born unto life and nothing is foreign to him."[11] The sixteen-year-old Jean-Jacques, who has just undergone that other "second birth," namely conversion, declines its invitation to a religiosity which turns us away from "this life" and, instead, lovingly embraces the whole experience of living.

With the collapse of paternal authority, an eighteenth-century phenomenon already a fact of life for Jean-Jacques, we can expect the sacred
to come to the surface in other places. Rousseau's experiences displace
it, not simply to womanly grace and subjectivity but to a marginal
woman, an outcast, abject in the eyes of her family. Such a radical displacement could appear to subvert and pervert the social law by putting
the human object of taboo right in the sacred center of social life, but
Rousseau's portrait undermines that meaning, illuminating Eléonore de
Warens's genius for upholding the fundamental laws of community even
while the larger society, which excluded her, betrayed those laws.
Leaving for Turin after their first meeting, Jean-Jacques already knew
she was adequate to his emotional needs; he felt himself to be "son
ouvrage," her creation; borrowing psychoanalytical imagery, we might
say he contained within him a woman who could contain him. It was the
dreaming adolescent's "unheard-of privilege" to have met in Madame
de Warens the object of his desire.[12]

THE PLEASURE OF HER COMPANY

Rousseau expands thrice on life in Madame de Warens's small community: in Books III, V, and VI. I will explore only once his figures of feminine grace, focusing mainly on the first description in Book III, even
while appreciating his reasons for recurring to the theme of her environment: to convey the precious gift of duration in time, the perseverance,
for long enough to meet his needs, of his belonging to her world and of
her attachment to him; to show how her skills and interests diversified in
different places and how his educational pursuits responded, both
mimetically and in already original ways, to her variations.

Her lifestyle of modest abundance became Rousseau's permanent
ideal, as evidenced in his later works.[13] Whatever she had, she shared, in
hospitality and beneficence: customs of the nobility in the hierarchical
society of the day, customs in which she had been reared. But she performed them entirely differently, not only because her own financial
dependence on the church entirely transformed the meaning of her
giving, but also because, although she had little to give, she gave it all.
And, as we gradually learn, even more than all of it. Her early fascination with business now responded to her need to supply the gap between
her resources and what she gave to others' need. In Book III, Rousseau
scarcely mentions the money problem, because he wants readers first to
revel, as he had done, in a picture of plentiful simplicity, as yet

untouched by the anxiety of knowing that it was not sustained by sufficient funds. Once he starts to relate that anxiety, however, his panicking incomprehension becomes clear. Or perhaps he comprehends but still sees her spending and her extravagant attempts to invest and make profits as a failing in her, rather than a marvelous performance on the part of a woman who could not know – any more than he could, because such facts did not yet have the status of knowledge – what gigantic social forces worked against her slightest hope. Even today, scholars seem all too ready to concur with Rousseau's dismay, and they go further than he, referring to her financial imagination and creative projects as pathological, and worse. This becomes her ugly aspect; in artistic creation, however, the feeling of ugliness may characterize the heights. It may be maladjusted to be far ahead of one's time, but what if there were no way of realizing that she was out of line with socio-economic reality? Sifting through Rousseau's expressions of anguish, to pause, instead, at the places where he praises her flair for business, her gift for extending her vision beyond her tiny and seemingly circumscribed world, and her commitment to the goal of profit only in the location of human need, that is to say, only at the furthest extreme from the accumulation of capital "enclosed from the common" (to borrow John Locke's phrase), I would propose that, through her dreams and schemes, and regardless of the fact that she could never succeed, she represents *par excellence* the principle of self-management extended into every small domain of social life. Is this not, today, one of the best hopes of new life for the thinking of the Left and for the emerging resistance to excesses in institutional power? And are many, today, very much closer to realizing such a hope than Eléonore de Warens ever was? Rousseau compares her to political intriguers like Madame de Longueville, saying that in the latter's place, Madame de Warens "would have governed the State."[14] Her destiny as a subject, however, did not take the shape of the large society and of power. But she certainly espoused the personal principles of freedom and responsibility.

She was fully aware of the political dimension, presenting herself regularly at court and deftly retaining royal approval, as well as her pension, for as long as she was physically strong enough to negotiate the diplomatic labyrinth which was the path to it: no small feat of skill and daring, in a milieu where she had not only friends but also enemies, critics of her unorthodox conduct and her debts.[15] She put her social experience to intellectual and moral profit, reflecting on it and passing on the fruits of her experience to Rousseau.

The possibility of social rejection and loss of patronage never left her, because she had indeed marked herself out as a transgressor; she was, in fact, permanently put in the wrong by society. It was this "error of her ways" that the church reversed into its opposite: namely, into her compulsory exemplariness to other, younger errant souls. She depended for social as well as financial survival on the beneficence of church and King, which, being far from disinterested, ceased to be bestowed once she became too frail with age to be an asset, a star convert. She transgressed, not only in her youthful actions but in their lifelong consequences and through certain essential characteristics which she never suppressed: through being a woman on her own, having abandoned husband, family, religion; through her business ambitions; through her practice of making her own decisions about her sexual life and initiating, to a degree that astonishes, her own relationships with men, from the gardener's nephew to the bishop and the King. Her very transgressions bespeak her gifts, which can come as no surprise; Laclos affirms that the gifted and ambitious woman has no path open to her that is not transgressive; in the world of action, she can only be dangerous.[16] But Madame de Warens departs from his criteria, inventing for herself an alternative path, away from evil. Rousseau writes that she would have shone in the best social circles. She was cultured, well-read, and attractive to intelligent men who wished to attract her in return, but she did not make a career of that attractiveness. She had fine judgment in literature and perceived Jean-Jacques's gifts before they could find expression. Intellectual and sensual freedom of expression went hand in hand for her, and for him as well, without launching either one of them on a career of sexual–intellectual conquest and possession. He desired her without wishing to possess her; they freely caressed each other and received each other's kisses.

Her domestic atmosphere was of benign laughter, equal sharing, cooperative work. Boring tasks performed with her became pleasurable. These often entailed the brewing of herbal medicines, a lifelong activity for her and one of her never-to-succeed business concerns. Rousseau mocked that interest relentlessly, not only because all medicines were better avoided and plants were not for use, but also because he considered the work it involved unladylike. She was impervious to male mockery and claimed she had secrets. So true-to-life do I find the portrait that I feel I can take issue with the portraitist's critical distance in this area. How can he object to that use of plants when he ate fruits and vegetables himself? How can he not see in her herbal remedies a form of those popular and useful arts, which, he was among the first to see, distinguished any indigenous culture exercising them, arts which only flourish through that same respectful attention to natural things that he himself accorded to plants? I wish he did not have a blind spot in relation to her creative role in the very quality of the life he here describes. He understood, as well as anyone, the value of meaningful work. Perhaps I should not blame him for lacking our concept of the food supplement or the notion of "use without mistreatment" that is so appealing in the present political climate to some on the Left. I would wish Rousseau to be in every way as advanced as Madame de Warens, but his mocking way of portraying this aspect of her indicates that he was not. He admits, however, that her example taught him the art of sustained attention to any detail of the living world – a bird, a bee, a leaf – and he goes on to say that he loved to teach animals to trust him, to attach themselves to him knowing that he would let them leave him at any time: the secret, in fact, of the way that Madame de Warens attached him so happily to herself. Here he sees the link between close attention to everything that lives and the social values of freedom and equality. Despite his disrespect for herbalism, this picture of their shared existence, and even the man's identification with women's work, can undoubtedly strike us as an essential forerunner of the socialism espoused by William Morris 150 years later. Their inseparability from close observation of the living universe, and the place they give to a transformed art as the paradigm of meaningful experience, lie at the heart of both Rousseau's and Morris's projects.[17] These pages show us that with Madame de Warens, Rousseau acquired the gift of attention, an essential psychical and cultural development opening the way to learning and to knowledge. Attention provides the link between the completeness of that self–other relationship and – at the furthest extreme – the whole of the living world, the only unity.

As soon as Rousseau moved into her house, Madame de Warens began to launch him from the world of dreams upon the path of ways and means to an independent existence. With her guidance and unfailing support, he began to outgrow unreal ambitions, retaining only the wish to live with her always. He tried learning Latin, after someone had told her that he was too dim-witted to be anything but a priest. Latin did not flourish, but music did, because Madame de Warens sang and gave him some lessons. Through its association with her, music was to be a new and lasting passion for him. Around 1730, he felt his first impulse to write. The men whose teaching he links to hers in those years became his models for a pedagogical relationship in which the "natural inequality" of the learner becomes accessible to a development toward equality through learning, by dint of the teacher's positioning of himself on the same level as the pupil: of one of these, the young Abbé Gâtier, he writes that "he seemed rather to study with me than to instruct me."[18] Rousseau's new, non-authoritarian pedagogy was already germinating in Madame de Warens's atmosphere: "My heart was forming my reason."[19] He adds, however, that this predominance of the heart impeded some aspects of his learning: a significant observation about a certain incompatibility of teaching with sexual relationships. The remark exemplifies a rare quality of this story of love: its combination of passionate appreciation with freedom from idealization. The defect he perceives can be referred to without fear of disfiguring the portrait: after all, Madame de Warens was not his teacher or his lover; she was everything, his salvation. What he received from her usually comes to us (if at all) from many different people; it cannot surprise us if he consequently had to live some contradictions inside the one relationship, but he knows better than to criticize the woman on that account. She was simply responsive to his needs, and he had many needs; loving one woman was his unconventional way of loving and learning in a long, continuous pairing. We can see the extremism of his choices (his impatience with others who interrupted their shared solitude, for example), and even the price he paid for that extremism, the obstacle to some kinds of learning; yet our normative awareness of his unusual sentimental-intellectual education should certainly not blind us to his fabulous good fortune, his incredible luck in finding a woman who let him do so many things in his own way. What did he lose, after all? The price paid, in his case, was small. While he could not yet acquire mental and technical skills efficiently, his energies were absorbed in what would later prove to have been a valuable gestation: the slow formation within him of a dependable object relation, without which later learning and extraordinarily innovative thinking might not have been possible.

BREACHES OF THE SOCIAL CONTRACT

Madame de Warens may well strike us as exemplary in her spontaneous egalitarianism, as well as in her determination to be herself; that is, not to be merely an exemplary woman for all women. This is a problematic area for women who may find that the social constraints of conforming to prescribed good feminine models or of setting examples for others can mean the death of originality, can condemn them to idealization, and can also, through a confusion with the feminine stereotype, radically devalue womanly grace – whereas this latter must itself be a work of creative originality, or else it is not grace at all.[20] Rousseau brings out the complexity and originality of the dimension of exemplariness in Madame de Warens's character by representing her as an example for him. That implies a notion of an exemplariness destined not to be merely imitated but transformed in indirect and original ways. With a comparable complexity in the fictional mode, Rousseau confers the same significance on Julie in her relationship with Saint-Preux. Nevertheless, this fictional heroine counts among the problematic instances of feminine exemplariness, not so much through his characterization of her (where originality certainly has priority over example and over the temptation of stereotype), as through the other characters' discourse about her. Julie herself admits that she suffers from this treatment by others until, finally, she is glad to die: evidence enough of Rousseau's acute awareness of the critical obstacles to women's selfhood contained in the social requirement of exemplariness. Yet the theoretical substructure of the narrative viewpoint of *La Nouvelle Héloïse* adheres to that requirement; in fact, in all Rousseau's works, only the portrayal of Madame de Warens wholly transcends it.

The truth-to-life of the portrait of Madame de Warens actually depends on her not being an ideal model for general application. The woman in the portrait is indubitably a subject, although depicted primarily as an object of male desire, a position which Rousseau lets us know partly empowered her as a force of alternative socialization in some initially, partially disoriented men's lives. In this context, where the difficulty of the man's portrayal of the woman determines its extreme value for modern readers, we must give particular attention to an area that Rousseau himself leaves in relative shadow. At the end of Book III, he alludes briefly to activities of hers that we are least likely to find exemplary: her secret journey to Paris, carrying (on this Rousseau is silent, but the historical documents are not) plans of revolution, apparently not so much because her people were oppressed (although we should take care not to overinterpret our very incomplete information), as because her present lords and masters wished to extend their empire into the land of her birth.

The picture of Madame de Warens's beneficent community would be incomplete without a consideration of this aspect of her conduct. We are first obliged to locate it in relation to Rousseau's portrait of her, since

he claims not to know about it. Perhaps we could bring some suspicion
to bear on that assertion. We may be dealing with some kind of gentle-
manly discretion, since he must have known the secret mission of
Madame de Warens would have been exhaustively documented in
official places. But this discretion is highly selective; bearing in mind
what he does recount of her private life, how can we understand this
area of scruple? A hard look at the text might answer this question and
might also show whether the claim of ignorance is not belied elsewhere.
Suspicion alights first on the comparison with Madame de Longueville,
the political intriguer; Madame de Warens would not have resembled
the famous *frondeuse*, but would have governed the state. The key to
Rousseau's meaning lies in his words, "in her place"; he argues that
Madame de Warens engaged in plotting rather than affairs of state only
because she did not occupy Madame de Longueville's privileged place.
Real insecurity drove her to intrigue.

Rousseau was absent for a year after Madame de Warens's mission to
Paris, but on his return, she instantly had him placed in the office of the
Royal Survey, a project directly linked to Sardinia's political plans. She
had not lost all contacts, then, after the idea of annexing the Pays de
Vaud came to nothing. She set store by his position there, although,
when Rousseau casually abandoned it after eight months to become a
music teacher, she had not the heart to be angry. Later, in Book v of the
Confessions, he recounts an event which he attaches retrospectively to his
time in the Survey, excusing himself for having forgotten to include it
where it belonged. The story has obvious relevance to our present
search, and the still suspicious reader can detect that Rousseau has,
uncharacteristically, deliberately fudged the dates.[21]

Recounting various journeys he made from Chambéry, Rousseau
mentions finding himself in Geneva in 1737, at the time when civil strife
began there, and he describes his horror and subsequent resolve never
to be involved in any civil war and never, if his Genevan citizenship were
ever restored to him, to defend freedom, in fact or in thought, by force
of arms. He then goes on to say that he was not always so patriotic and
must recount a very grave deed "imputable to me" (à ma charge). Just
after he left the Survey (1732), he had visited his aunt in Geneva and had
been invited by her to make what use he wished of the papers left by his
deceased uncle. He had taken away a critical analysis of the weaknesses
detected in a plan for fortifications which had been carried out in
Geneva. Back in Chambéry, he had sought, at an unspecified time, to
cut an impressive figure with Coccelli, his recent employer in charge of

the Survey, by showing him the critical report, which was a rarity as it
had been banned and all copies seized before it had been distributed (his
uncle, in an official capacity, had written a commentary on the report).
Coccelli had borrowed it and had never returned it. Rousseau concludes
his story with expressions of relief that Sardinia was entirely unlikely to
lay siege to Geneva, but he also reproaches himself for having, through
such foolish vanity, revealed to the republic's oldest enemy the defects of
its fortifications.

This constitutes a clear point of intersection between the autobiographical narrative and archival documents, and, by combining the two,
we can establish the strong probability that Madame de Warens and
Rousseau collaborated, in fact, in seeking to assist any imperialist intentions Sardinia might have entertained in respect of Geneva. Rousseau
seems to predict that certain readers will make the link; the specification
"imputable to me" suggests that the deed might otherwise be laid at
the door of his benefactress, as scholars have previously noted.
Furthermore, this collaboration was not as limited in time as Rousseau
seems to suggest. If he handed over the report a short time after he left
the Survey, around 1732, it was not so long after Madame de Warens's
journey of 1730. But he mentions that he showed it to Coccelli at the
time when they both attended a baptism, which can be dated with certainty: 23 April 1737, that is, exactly two days after civil hostilities broke
out in Geneva. Rousseau's visit to Geneva came three months later, in
July. His patriotic fervor, therefore, followed by a mere three months his
treacherous action. Scholars conclude that Madame de Warens incited
him to this action, since she alone had pressing reasons to persuade the
court of Sardinia of her assiduous loyalty. This assumption may be accurate, but it should not justify placing blame upon her as if Rousseau were
a mere child; he was, after all, twenty-five years old. To blame either or
both is beside the point; we need only recognize that he would not have
become involved in the machinations if her interests had not been at
stake.

What an extraordinary complication this brings, however, to
Rousseau's portrait of his object of love! He locates the account of his
own treachery, in fact, exactly where it chronologically belongs, but he
gives us to understand that it belongs earlier; actually about five years
earlier but only some thirty pages earlier in the text of Book v, just before
his account of the beginning of his sexual relationship with Madame de
Warens, instead of after it. The impact on chronology does not matter
much, since Rousseau does not guarantee chronological accuracy, and

precise time notations can be few and far between. His focus on the
"chain of his secret affections"[22] fully validates his tendency to write a
short discourse on any important topic that he introduces, and such discourses tend to contain their own historical depth, with the result that
the dates sometimes jump backwards and forwards. Yet the subterfuge
is rather devious: he wants to underplay the extent to which he and
Madame de Warens involved themselves in political intrigue that, on at
least two occasions, led them as mature adults to try to betray their native
lands.

He writes, I believe, as the author of *Du contrat social* and as a Genevan,
constrained to admit that he and the woman who provided a matrix of
his thinking had broken their own social contracts. The fact remains that
he acknowledges this, in his own case, leaving just a clue or two embedded in the text to suggest to curious readers that she was involved as well.
The major disturbance thereby generated in the portrait of Madame de
Warens can thus appear to the beholder as an ill-lit, murky area, imputable to the painter rather than to his subject and somehow marginal to
her. Rousseau succeeds in preserving our positive impression of her and
her compassionate community, without really lying about her action.
After all, it is true that she would not have needed intrigue if her situation had been more favorable. Nevertheless, having sorted out what the
writer is doing, we are at liberty to put the attempted breaches of contract together with the life of the small pre-political community that
made the theory of the just contract possible. We can then see (even if
we lack, in her case, detailed knowledge) that the shared experience of
truly terrible relationships with their origins helped to tie these two
together. But the writer's literary genius prefers to associate the experience of love with his most idyllic childhood memories, "le vert paradis
des amours enfantines." We lose none of our affection or respect for the
lovers (far from it, since the writer has not previously induced us to ideal-
ize them), but we gain, perhaps, a tangential light on Rousseau's sense
that his sexual possession of Madame de Warens felt something like
incest.

Our reading must, therefore, not merely embrace the negative aspects
of this couple together with their positive aspects but also aspire to an
understanding of the co-involvement of the good with the bad.
Rousseau's positive vision of anthropological hope, his trust in the
human species's potential, finds, here, its corresponding psychical reality
in the good object of love, but, at the same time, his almost equally powerful historical pessimism is brought to the fore in his avowal that both

he and Madame de Warens had acted unworthily under duress. Although they were never morally abased, both descended to political intrigue against their native land, in reaction against social injustices undergone. *Du contrat social* had already explained that when a people, having been constrained to obey, can throw off the yoke, it is right to do so and to return to its natural independence; individuals may react in the same way, as both Madame de Warens and Rousseau had done, taking flight from the contracts (of marriage, of apprenticeship) which bound them to their homeland and which both, we may assume, experienced in some way as violent. But their attempted collusion with the King of Sardinia's imperialist disposition toward their native Pays de Vaud and Geneva can only be excused, not justified, by reference to the state of oppression in which the Sardinian King and the church then held Madame de Warens (keeping her under constant surveillance, forbidding her to leave Savoy without royal approval, requiring her to be "ever more exemplary and withdrawn").[23] The passages in which Rousseau deals with these outcomes of their negative relation to their origins and his careful maneuvers to avoid incriminating the loved woman constitute that major disturbance in the portrait without which it would not have been a work of truth. We have to embrace the whole picture and the small distortion Rousseau introduces into it. This distortion lies not in his protection of her name, but, rather, in his inciting us to think that his own breach of his original social contract took place before he became her lover, when, in fact, it occurred after that major rite of passage and, even more significantly, after she had taught him – an integral part of their conversational lovemaking – how to think and to compare. Embracing the whole of the portrait of Madame de Warens, we embrace that distortion also; recognizing the distortion as such, we grasp the portrait's truth and also the force of the reference to the feeling of incest.

  Guy Rosolato interprets the law prohibiting incest as the symbolic pact between child, parents, and society; a truly bilateral pact obliging the child to renounce its first object of love but guaranteeing in return the child's later freedom to choose an external love object. As such, the taboo simultaneously symbolizes the law in its entirety and inaugurates the child's social integration through his/her acceptance of it.[24] If we accept Rosolato's hypothesis, then the image of *a feeling of incest*, occurring where it does in the *Confessions*, reveals the taboo functioning successfully; the feeling of incest metaphorically expresses for Rousseau and Madame de Warens the simultaneity of sexual consummation and

attempted betrayal of the societies of their birth. The textual contiguity
of the themes of the breach of the social pact and the woman's sexual
gift of herself to the young man has often triggered a primary-process
operation in readers, awakening their fantasies of the evil woman and
tempting them to project blame on to her. In the writing, however, it is
the primary-process contiguity that marks the presence of a causal link
between the half-admitted betrayal and the feeling of incest, with the
emotional meaning of sharing a wound rather than of blaming the
woman. In the distortion of chronology, the taboo leaves its trace, which
is to say that its socially integrative power is perfectly efficacious; the
woman's gift of her sexual love turns out, after all, to be in keeping with
her extreme sociability and not with betrayal of the sense of community.
We are in the presence of the structure Rousseau describes in *Emile* and
identifies in his own childhood experience: that of the innate feeling of
justice and injustice, innate in the sense not of the instinctual but of the
spontaneous effect, whereby an injustice suffered (in this case, that of
being induced to do wrong) can inaugurate the love of justice.[25] The
creative achievements of these two people – her benevolent little community, his works – are to be measured against their bad beginnings in
their birthplaces and the resulting breaches of their social contracts, in
the midst of which they found each other.

These observations began with my suggestion that we could carry *Du
contrat social* forward in time with its author to the point where his portrayal of Madame de Warens in the *Confessions* supersedes his earlier theorizing of women. Rousseau's disturbed and partial account of those
shared breaches of the social contract, the most obscure moment of the
portrait, may mark the most extreme advance for *Du contrat social*, beyond
the confines of its own immediate text to a point where we can see the
fundamental social pact emerging from the shared wound of a painfully
initiated but miraculously reparative sexual relationship. I am somewhat
hesitant about using Leiris's metaphor of the shared wound, which
could very easily attract inappropriate connotations. Leiris finds in
certain drawings of André Masson a new, more hope-inspiring, mythi-
cal primal scene, in which the man does not merely rape the woman, but
the wound is shared.[26] If the shared wound is relevant to Rousseau, and
even if we may identify it as another of his secularizations of the biblical story of the Fall, it nevertheless must not be assimilated to the doctrine of guilt and redemption that he so explicitly and lucidly discards.
The value of the metaphor of the shared wound lies in its potential,
noted by Leiris, for rendering explicit (by giving it a name) a collective

effort in our culture to constitute a new mythological representation of the man–woman relationship; a collective effort in which these works of Rousseau deserve to be recognized as an important moment. It might begin to emerge that the silence of *Du contrat social* about women does not imply that they are absent from the contract but rather suggests that *les citoyennes* are not, theoretically speaking, a separate group from *les citoyens*. That inference entails no very great interpretative leap on my part, any more than my supposition that Rousseau, approaching the contractually problematic material of the attempted betrayals of birthplace, writes the *Confessions* as the author of *Du contrat social*. After all, given the theoretical coherence of the many episodes of the *Confessions*, if he had considered women not to be parties to the fundamental pact, the story of the attempted betrayals would not have been difficult for him to tell. He could then have relied implicitly on his reader's assumption that the woman stepped out of line as women do – the very assumption of those who would exclude women from the free contractual society. That Rousseau does not tell the story that way permits us to infer that women are citizens in the society of the egalitarian pact.

The subsequent facets of the portrait present the enrichments of sexual experience: the young man's discovery of the woman's inner self and of her moral depth, and his resultant experiences of liberation, including the one brought by the *feeling* of incest.

SEXUAL EXPERIENCE

Rousseau's writing, as we noted earlier, never pretends to separate the subjective from the objective; the autobiography analyzes the subjective origins of the theory, and his social theory permeates the writing of the self, even the portrait of the beloved other. Conversely, he clearly states that that love relationship was the matrix of his relation to reality: "It was she who taught me how to think, how to compare."[27]

The eighteenth century, generally speaking, gave precedence to the social over the emotional. Even Rousseau, who differed from his contemporaries in valuing solitude and daydream very highly, nevertheless depicts himself throughout most of the *Confessions* as giving priority to social considerations, so making this work a quintessentially eighteenth-century text. Most importantly for my topic, he relates that when Madame de Warens, after five or more years of shared existence, offered him her sexual intimacy, he knew that it was not right for him emotionally, but he needed it socially, and so he took the plunge.[28] Far from a superficial or a negative decision, this entails a complex understanding of the sexual which helps, I believe, to define their whole relationship in the very positive terms in which he meant us to comprehend it.

We have explored the social function of the notion of incest, the way it expresses in the mythological dimension the highly significant grounding of this couple's bond of love in a shared bad relationship to birthplace. Now we can turn to the autobiographer's way of identifying subjectively with that mythic meaning, his fantasy elaboration of the "feeling of incest," which becomes, through the magic of his pen, a creative individual translation of the collective symbol. We do not leave the domain of "ethnopoetic" portraiture, but here it follows a new path, deep into his experience of both the woman's sexuality and his own.

The most detailed development of the portrait of Madame de Warens focuses on her sexual life. The light Rousseau sheds necessarily leaves shadow. For him, there is a mystery in her saying she was a woman without desire, because he knew her to have a warm sensibility and deep attachments to men. As readers with two centuries' greater distance from the theory of the four humors, we should be able to attempt an understanding of both her claim and his sense of her mystery, without simply disbelieving her as modern scholars tend to do. He does not share at all her free-thinking views on sexual morality, but he does affirm that they do not make her promiscuous, and he defends her free gift of herself in her most meaningful relationship to a man, whoever he may be. In representing thus her apparently fearless crossing of caste barriers, he sheds light on a "non-incestuous" quality of her loves,[29] a preference for the outside and for egalitarian bonds. This pronounced preference, in which we might think we recognize our own modern world, is not accompanied, however, by the superficialization to which we seem to feel condemned by our democratic sensibilities. On the contrary, Rousseau indicates in the loves of Eléonore de Warens an enriched, more flexible form of the moral code of beneficence and gratitude, which we ill-advisedly assume to be the now obsolete appurtenance of a hierarchical society put behind us. That is not to say that any social stability is claimed for this extremely modern love by the author of *Du contrat social*, who was so acutely conscious of the fragility of egalitarian political relations. The loves of Madame de Warens are as modern in this as in other respects.[30]

Jean-Jacques's sexual initiation began (after some five years of desiring her, kissing and caressing her) with serious talks, in which Madame de Warens put to him the emotional and social advantages of experience and gave him time to think it over. At least one woman in the small local society of Chambéry had designs on him, combining sexual and other ulterior motives. Rousseau, as we have already seen, did not feel right about making love with his beloved and desirable benefactress, but he describes a situation in which it was the only, or the best possible, path away from a possibly imminent initiation into negative sexual entanglements motivated by social competitiveness: "dangerous liaisons," as he himself calls them in *La Nouvelle Héloïse*.[31] Madame de Warens did not merely offer a safety net to a young man about to fall anyway, whatever the circumstances. She offered the opportunity for him to choose between two paths. I would suggest that he felt she was the right path, both because he really loved and trusted her (and not the other woman) and because she was not right for him sexually. It seems he needed a first relationship which he would have to leave behind. He goes on to describe his sadness on first possessing her, "as if I had committed incest."[32] The aspect of sadness always, thereafter, accompanied his possession of her. That fact notwithstanding, he recounts at length his enjoyment of their deepened intimacy and the privilege of being treated now as even more fully her equal – as her confidant. What she told him about herself he applied to himself, and he learned how to think and to compare.

Despite the space and emphasis Rousseau gives to it, the wonderful success of the sexual relationship can become eclipsed in the mind of the reader by the sheer complexity of his analyses of his profound experiences upon entering and leaving the sexual dimension of his love of Madame de Warens. I think this is explained by the relative simplicity of the narrative of fulfillment; by its perhaps unexpected reliance on the surface of discourse; by its focus on the conversations after lovemaking, on the level where the two people took an extreme social and intellectual interest in each other, which is the conscious subjective level of culturally developed preference furthest removed from the undifferentiated physical impulse of Rousseau's man in nature and from those unconscious drives for which Freud tells us the choice of the object of desire is a matter of absolute indifference. In contrast, all our intellectual efforts are required to structure our reading of the approach to sexual realization through breaches of the social contract and feelings of incest and, again, to grasp the sense of the ending of the sexual phase. However, the major reality function of their intimacy, the fact that she taught him how to think and to compare, binds the sexual experience to both its mythic beginning and its end.

In Book v, Rousseau writes about a period of serious illness, which required Madame de Warens to nurse him back to health and also put an end to their lovemaking. Modern scholarship cannot add to the lucidity of Rousseau's self-analysis. He tells us that he needed a mistress; while making love he had been imagining a sexual partner with whom he could feel free. Then he adds that he was burning with "love without an object" and threw himself into one passionate commitment after another: a journey, a novel, a concert, a supper, a walk.[33] Finally, from that state, he swung over into melancholy and thought he would die.

It is as if Rousseau's choice of Madame de Warens as a sexual partner were simultaneously determined by a psychical fidelity to loving as distinct from competitive relations, and by a complex, apparently unconscious psycho-social knowledge that he needed an object of some vague taboo whose renunciation would guarantee him the freedom to choose another woman. The presence of an unconscious force taking him in the right direction seems attested by the body's recourse to illness to obtain the needed outcome. The ensuing movement of the portrait of Madame de Warens passes rapidly from her tender ministrations during his illness to his departure for Montpellier to consult a famous physician; both journey and life-threatening illness were abruptly interrupted and transformed by a chance encounter with another lovely woman, with whose help he found himself sexually completely free. To this jubilant encounter with Madame de Larnage, which lasted only six days or so, Rousseau gives disproportionate space in Book VI. The details of this episode fall outside my topic, but both the fact of its insertion and the importance given to it within the space of the portrait of Madame de Warens are entirely relevant here. Primary-process effects of contiguity, already observed in relation to the breach of the social contract, can make sense of the inclusion of the Madame de Larnage episode in this context. It is, in fact, part of the portrait; Rousseau's spectacular liberation with his attractive traveling companion dramatically enacts the very *freedom within attachment* by which he always defines his relationship to the woman who has unconstrainingly nurtured his development for many years. Rousseau, although he could not know about unconscious processes as such, was not unaware of these effects of contiguity; they are part of what he calls "the chain of secret affections," and he knows how to let them speak for themselves in his writing. So he makes no excuses for the placing and importance of what might seem a minor episode in his autobiography. In fact, the whole portrait of Madame de Warens has prepared the presence of this window looking out on a scene of erotic freedom with another woman.

Between the beginning and the ending, both heavily invested with unconscious psycho-social meaning which reaches the reader through disturbances in the surface of the narrative, the young lover has learned how to think and compare. He has learned that a woman's – as well as a man's – sexual behavior can be for a purpose of attachment even when free of conventional bonds; that sexual love expresses the lovers' meanings and can create a sense of true community in a paralyzing social context. Keeping together, in the person of Madame de Warens, his object of love and his sexual choice, even in the face of anxiety about incest, he has been entirely emotionally successful. Accepting her offer of sex, he accepted with it the sense of prohibition which would free him for another woman. He calls the breach of the taboo "near-incest," not because they were close kin, which they obviously were not, but because her role as benefactress and educator could serve the needed function of imposing the missing taboo which permits freedom elsewhere. In this light, his sense of "incest" permits an extension into the rest of his life of the freedom afforded by his attachment to Madame de Warens.

No contradiction should be felt when, recounting his return to Madame de Warens after the adventure with Madame de Larnage, Rousseau describes as loss his discovery that she had taken another lover, her farm manager Wintzenried. Of course Rousseau wanted to retain his first, freely chosen love object for himself, forever; he wanted emotional growth without giving anything up, and it is touching, perhaps, that scholars' reactions to this part of the text suggest that they, too, feel he should have had that. Even she suggests that he need not leave or give her up. But he cannot share her with that unworthy man and so he has to go. Rousseau's unique gift for a mode of writing which relives uncritically in its entirety the original emotion (surely the fundamental mode of autobiographical writing, however rarely emulated) gives us first the whole of his urge for liberation, which was the very gift of maturation that he received from Madame de Warens herself and enacted with Madame de Larnage, and then the whole of his hurt and loss. It is left to the reader to supply the interpretation, simultaneously psychoanalytical and anthropological, to weigh the sense of loss against the need for freedom, and to observe that the sadness he likens to a sense of incest, in fact, integrates the oedipal pact into his sexual life: one renunciation promising the freedom to choose among other women. These and other important aspects of the portrait of Madame de Warens by the man who loved her have been thought by some readers to call for their judgment upon her, even their blame, and so a quite other picture has grown up in the scholarly editions, an unjust caricature of the real woman; whereas Rousseau explicitly included these aspects in the portrait because they were inseparable from his irreplaceable experience of loving her and for their important function in an unusual, and yet true, social integration.

The modern theory of incest that could help us to articulate for ourselves the feeling of "near-incestuousness" related by Rousseau would be the one which locates the social function of incest in the establishing of identity and difference as the basis of thought.[34] The man, in this account, must not mingle the same with the same. Not only can this prohibition be felt to apply between family members, as literal incest; but also, though distinct from literal incest, *l'inceste approché* (near-incest) can be felt equally proscribed, as it was by Rousseau, who describes so precisely the nourishing, nurturing, rearing, and educating by Madame de Warens from which his vague, incest-like anxiety arose. Not every man need experience such things as proximity to incest, but the possibility of doing so is there if needed, as it was for Rousseau: to which we can add that the feeling was all the more readily available for this psychical and intellectual use, since it was already suggested in the atmosphere by the founding of the couple's emotional bond in a symbolic sense of betrayal of birthplace. The feeling, the possibility of using it, and the need to use it all came together for Rousseau, precisely because Madame de Warens taught him how to think and to compare, to judge: "Comparer, c'est juger," notes an eighteenth-century dictionary.[35] Her gift of herself, her confidences, also enabled him to compare himself to her and taught him how to differentiate himself from her. Rousseau was more intensely aware than most that thought-process and object-relation are one: "My heart was forming my reason." His love structures his mind. For that reason, he feels a certain wrongness in sexual realization. The theory of near-incest allows us to conceive that, if Madame de Warens constituted the space that could contain him, in which his emotional and intellectual linking was free to evolve, he might, for that reason, have felt that he and she were in a certain sense identical and that he would, therefore, have to leave her in order to find the sexual freedom that only comes with the perception of difference. Or, perhaps he felt that there was a risk of their being identical and that he should, consequently, maintain a distance between them. It hardly matters which; once the feeling and idea of incest have occurred, the painful logic of growth structures the narrative: sadness in intimacy, distance, liberation with a new object of desire; then, the unhappy realization that the first intimacy is in the past.

The birth of reflection and comparison has that price, and, in Rousseau's case, the huge claims of reflection would later be balanced by compromises in real relationships, while the persevering first attachment worked itself out in the poetic apotheosis of the novel. Even at the end of his life, that attachment still lives in the tenth "Promenade," and the pain of loss is still fresh. But without the autobiographical portrait of Madame de Warens, the life study, we would be in the dark about the woman and the relationship from which a gift of freedom could be relayed to the future, to the brief erotic adventure with Madame de Larnage, and to mature creative work.[36]

"I was free, and better than free, because, subjected by my attachments alone, I just did what I wanted to do": so the tenth "Promenade" distils the happiness of Rousseau's life with Madame de Warens. His great works all maintain that trust of freedom within attachment, with its variable balance between the freedom to leave – like that of the birds whom he taught to trust him and like his own freedom to enjoy the favors of Madame de Larnage, the freedom to stay – like that of Saint-Preux at Clarens, or the freedom to share – as he, for so many years, had shared the life of Madame de Warens. In *La Nouvelle Héloïse*, Julie's Elysium, her symbolic garden at Clarens, offers a haven for birds which gives them the freedom to stay or to leave, a figure of her womanly grace and of her husband's generosity. With his habitual sense of reality Rousseau adds a pool from which, as Saint-Preux observes, the fish are not free to leave; Julie responds that the pool is their relative freedom, since they had been destined for the oven. A fine illustrator of a 1788 edition of the novel made that scene beside the pool the subject of his frontispiece to the whole of Part IV, with Saint-Preux's words as the caption: "Here are prisoners, nonetheless."[37] In the pre-Revolutionary social moment, the engraver's exacerbated sense of the immobilization of human relationships carries to extremes the figure of freedom to stay or leave: any compromise of that freedom, even in a compassionate cause, becomes unbearable. At that moment, the potential contractual tension contained within the figure expresses a demand, a protest. But Rousseau, writing the portrait of Madame de Warens in what was already that pre-Revolutionary moment, but just a little earlier, can so wholeheartedly expand on the spontaneous freedom of doing only what he wanted to do that the regulatory idea of contract probably does not occur to us as we read about his love. That freedom in attachment was her gift to him, which he passes on to us through his art of the life study.

I would propose, however, as suggested above, that this portrait reveals the germinating stage of the Rousseauian transformation of the idea of contract. Madame de Warens turned her back on her own marriage promises, but she could not be further removed from Diderot's famous image of lovers as having "returned to the state of nature,"[38] an image meant to expose the promise of duration as pure illusion. Responding to that image, Rousseau's image of deeply conversational lovemaking conjoins the instant of the body's pleasure with the moral involvement of a verbal exchange articulated in time. Without her inaugural violation of the marriage contract, what would we know of her power to contribute to the formation of a new idea of the dependable community fostering psychical, moral, and intellectual growth? A woman whose life, seen from a conventionally judgmental or frankly misogynist distance, might appear to correspond to the stereotype of anti-contractual erotic license, epitomizes for Rousseau the perfection of the moral and social codes of hospitality and beneficence: apparently spontaneous (therein lies the art, which has nothing to do with mystification) social graces imbued with that love of the fundamental law without which there would never be citizens worthy of the egalitarian pact. His portrait of her is wholly structured on that reversal from appearance to psychical and social truth.

NOTES

1. The point that the citizenry cannot be said to exclude women since the citizens are not theorized as male, is owed to a comment by David Lee on an earlier version of this chapter, in the context of my Enlightenment and Postmodernism Research Discussion Group (French Department, University College, London).

2. For the textual facts concerning women's potential as citizens, and especially for the incompleteness of Rousseau's proposals for women's place in society, seen in relation to the education of girls, see Jean Bloch, "Rousseau et l'éducation nationale et patriotique des filles," in *IIe colloque international de Montmorency: J.-J. Rousseau, politique et nation. 27 septembre–4 octobre 1995* (forthcoming, 1999).

3. J. J. Rousseau, *La Nouvelle Héloïse*, in *Œuvres complètes*, ed. Bernard Gagnebin and Marcel Raymond, 5 vols. (Paris: Gallimard, Bibliothèque de la Pléiade, 1959–95), II: pt. I, letter 26. The *Œuvres complètes* hereafter cited as *O. C.*

4. For a vivid description of the accidental birth of Rousseau's revolutionary, lyrical autobiographical writing style see the editors' introduction to *Les Confessions* in Rousseau, *O. C.*, I: xix–xxi.

5. Peter Brooks, *The Novel of Worldliness* (Princeton: Princeton University Press, 1969).

6. Michel Leiris, *Cinq études d'ethnologie* (Paris: Denoël/Gonthier, 1969), 114, as quoted in Anna Warby, *The Ethnographic Subject: Reflexivity in the Works of Michel Leiris* (University of London, thesis in progress). I borrow from Anna Warby the adjective "ethnopoetic."

7. Rousseau, *Rêveries du promeneur solitaire*, in *O. C.*, I: 1099.

8. Rousseau, *Les Confessions*, in *O. C.*, I: 48–49.

9. *Ibid.*, I: 61.

10. Marcel Mauss's classic essay of social anthropology, *The Gift*, describes the threefold movement of giving, receiving, and returning good services which perpetuates the social: "Essai sur le don," *Année sociologique* (1923–24): 30–186; English translation by I. Cunnison, *The Gift* (London: Cohen and West, 1954). Edgar O. Wind, interpreting the Three Graces in *Pagan Mysteries in the Renaissance* (London: Faber and Faber, 1958), treats divine grace apart from social grace. For womanly grace, see Shakespeare, *The Winter's Tale*, I: 2. Playing on the word "grace," this scene establishes the drama's action as the violation by jealous Leontes of his wife's grace, necessitating her "death" until her final redemption and return to life become possible. I owe this reference to Marion Trousdale.

11. Rousseau, *Emile*, in *O. C.*, IV: 489–90.

12. See Jean Starobinski, *Jean-Jacques Rousseau: La transparence et l'obstacle* (Paris: Gallimard, 1971), 401.

13. See, for example, *Lettre à d'Alembert, La Nouvelle Héloïse, Emile*, and *Du contrat social*.

14. Rousseau, *Les Confessions*, in *O. C.*, I: 51.

15. *Ibid.*, I: 111.

16. Pierre-Ambroise Choderlos de Laclos, "Des femmes et de leur éducation," in *Œuvres complètes* (Paris: Gallimard, Bibliothèque de la Pléiade, 1979).

17. See Fiona MacCarthy, *William Morris, A Life for Our Time* (London: Faber and Faber, 1994).

18. Rousseau, *Les Confessions*, in *O. C.*, I: 119.

19. *Ibid.*, I: 123. My translation of "mon coeur formait mon jugement."

20. In *The Winter's Tale*, Shakespeare figures Hermione's grace – and perhaps Leontes's perverse misconstrual of it – in the attribution of a statue of the "dead" woman to Giulio Romano, the great Mantuan artist who interpreted both the true and the aberrant forms of sensual love. Hermione is not dead, and the "statue" beheld is Hermione herself. We can conclude that Shakespeare likens his own art to Romano's. The reference to the work of Romano enables today's readers to measure the distance separating womanly grace from stereotypical femininity.

21. Rousseau, *Les Confessions*, in *O. C.*, I: 216–18.

22. Rousseau, *O. C.*, I: 1149. This version is a draft of the *Confessions*. In the final text, Rousseau explains that "the chain of feelings" is his guide to the chain of events which caused the feeling (*Les Confessions*, in *O. C.*, I: 278).

23. François Coppier to the Bishop of Geneva-Annecy, 31 July 1730, Rousseau, *Correspondance complète*, ed. R. A. Leigh (Les Délices, Geneva: Institut et

Musée Voltaire, 1965), 1: 304–05. Communications between Madame de Warens and the King of Sardinia were mediated by the Sardinian Ambassador to Versailles and (as here) by the King's chaplain in Turin, François Coppier. The letter cited contains the king's instruction to Madame de Warens, conveyed by his chaplain (Coppier) to her local bishop, who, in turn, was expected to convey it to her. This volume (pp. 292–311) contains all the letters relating to Madame de Warens's journey and the plans of revolution.

24. Guy Rosolato, "Le Symbolique," in *Essais sur le symbolique* (Paris: Gallimard, 1969), 112–18.

25. Rousseau, *Emile*, bk. 1, in *O. C.*, IV: 286; *Emile*, bk. 2, in *O. C.*, IV: 329; Rousseau, *Les Confessions*, bk. 1, in *O. C.* 1: 18–21 (the episode of the broken comb).

26. Leiris's point about a drawing entitled "Rape" is that, in representing the wound as shared, Masson invents a new myth (differentiated from the usual representation of sexual coupling common to our culture's mythological system). The sharing of the wound can be associated with the anthropological theory of sacrifice (cf. Georges Bataille) which stresses that for authenticity, the sacrificer must be himself the sacrifice. In Leiris's thinking, the shared wound is also connected to the requirement of sexual equality. In Rousseau, a quality of sacrifice characterizes artistic communication; see Patrick Coleman, *Rousseau's Political Imagination: Rule and Representation in the Lettre à d'Alembert* (Geneva: Droz, 1984) and his "Rousseau and Preromanticism: Anticipation and Oeuvre," *Yale French Studies* 66 (1984): 67–82.

27. Rousseau, *Les Confessions*, in *O. C.*, 1: 260. My translation of the original: "C'était elle qui m'avait appris à réfléchir, à comparer."

28. *Ibid.*, 1: 196.

29. "Non-incestuous" seems the right expression here; however, another possible reading emerges in Tijana Miletic's *Literary Emigrations* (University of London, thesis in progress), on the French-language writing of Milan Kundera, Jorge Semprun, and Agota Kristof, in whose works the incest motif articulates the relation to the new language with the mourning of the lost one. Miletic finds this link briefly confirmed in George Steiner's comment that the incest motif represents Nabokov's relation to his adopted language (referred to in Elizabeth Klosty-Beaujour, *Alien Tongues: Bilingual Russian Writers of the "First" Emigration* [Ithaca, N.Y.: Cornell University Press, 1989]). Despite the continuity of French for Madame de Warens and Rousseau, we should explore the possibility that Rousseau's reference to incest may partake of this modern structure.

30. For Rousseau's assessment of the chances of democracy, see Luigi Luporini, "'Se ci fosse un popolo di dei . . .': una eco di Platone nel *Contrat social*," in Università di Firenze, Facoltà di Filosofia, *Annali dell'Istituto di Filosofia* 6 (1984): 115–27.

31. For Rousseau's use of the idea of "dangerous liaisons," which presumably

inspired the title of Laclos's novel, see Ronald Rosbottom, "Roman et secret: Le Cas des *Liaisons dangereuses*," *Revue d'histoire littéraire de la France* 82 (1982): 588–99.

32. Rousseau, *Les Confessions*, in *O. C.*, 1: 197.

33. *Ibid.*, 1: 219–22.

34. See Françoise Héritier, *Les Deux Soeurs et leur mère: Anthropologie de l'inceste* (Paris: Odile Jacob, 1994).

35. *Dictionnaire de l'Académie* (Paris, 1740).

36. Jean Starobinski comments in "L'Ecart romanesque," in *Jean-Jacques Rousseau*, 401, that "the whole episode of Les Charmettes, with its very saddening end, but also with its extension in the distant future of his success in Paris, stands as proof of the fertility of the *romanesque* [novelistic imagination and daydream], of its aptitude for finding an outlet in 'real life,' even at the cost of a conversion and of a disciplined mutation of the goal of desire." My reading differs from this one but the two are not mutually exclusive; the difference is one of perspective and emphasis. My aim has been to foreground Rousseau's remarkable tribute to Madame de Warens and, therefore, to focus on all he recounts as having really happened (whether for good or for ill) and on what he tells us she gave him anyway, regardless of the final gap between the real situation and his dream of having her to himself.

37. C.-P. Marillier, one of the engravers of Rousseau, *La Nouvelle Héloïse* (Paris: Poinçot, 1788).

38. Denis Diderot, "Indécent," in vol. VIII, *Encyclopédie* (Neufchâtel: Samuel Faulche, 1765), 667.

CHAPTER TEN

Fichte's road to Kant

Anthony J. La Vopa

In August of 1790, Johann Gottlieb Fichte, aged twenty-eight, found himself at the first of several low ebbs in his fortunes. Two months earlier he had returned from Zürich to Leipzig in search of "prospects," but nothing had materialized. The friends he had expected to rejoin in Leipzig had moved on. He considered himself too old to consort with students, and he was too poor and obscure to mingle in the polite society that gave the city its reputation for elegance. Writing popular novels, he had discovered, was neither a financially rewarding nor a personally satisfying way to make a living.

Fichte's letters from this period convey a palpable sense of loneliness and self-pity. In early August, in the course of requesting a loan from Dietrich von Miltitz, his deceased patron's son, he reported that he had just pawned all his clothes except what he was wearing. He had needed the money, he explained, to stay alive and to maintain his "honor" by paying debts promptly. If he did not receive the loan within a few days, it would be too late to save him from "going under."[1]

In fact Fichte was at the threshold of the great turning point of his adult life. In the letter to Miltitz, he noted that he had found an opportunity to earn some cash by giving a student private lessons in Kant's philosophy. It was this "mere accident" occasioned by "need," he would soon recall, that led him to Kant's *Critique of Pure Reason*. Within a few days, as he advanced to the *Critique of Practical Reason*, he "threw [himself] entirely into Kantian philosophy . . . out of true taste."[2] He recalled the resulting transformation in a letter to his friend Henrich Nikolaus Achelis in November 1790:

I came to Leipzig with a head that swarmed with great plans. Everything failed, and from so many soap bubbles all that was left over was the light foam from which they had formed . . . it was half in despair that I seized a *Partie* that I should have seized earlier. Since I could change nothing outside myself, I resolved to change what was inside me. I threw myself into philosophy, and indeed – and this is self-evident – into Kantianism. Here I found the antidote to the true source of my ill, and joy enough beyond that. The influence that this philosophy, and especially the moral part of it . . . has on the entire system of thought of a person, the revolution that has arisen through it especially in my own way of thinking, is inconceivable.[3]

In the late 1780s and the 1790s, Kantian philosophy made a good number of converts among Germany's educated youth. It was not the first time that an eighteenth-century author had struck a chord in a generation coming of age. From the mid-1770s onward, a veritable youth cult had developed around Goethe's *Die Leiden des Jungen Werthers*.[4] Even to today's readers, Goethe's novel conveys an extraordinary sense of emotional immediacy. Kant is quite another matter. He was building an awesomely abstract and intricate philosophical system, and he made no pretence to being able to explain it in layperson's language. The new philosophy was, in Fichte's apt description, "head-breaking."[5]

The revolution Fichte described to Achelis and others has striking resemblances with the conversion experience (Bekehrung) that had figured centrally in Pietist preaching and autobiographical testimony since the late seventeenth century. This is not to say that Fichte experienced his discovery of Kant's "reason" as a reception of grace in the evangelical sense; he was too much the eighteenth-century rationalist to make that explicit analogy. But the young Lutherans who discovered Kant needed a cultural precedent – a grid which, with suitable adjustments, would give their transformative experience a recognizable structure – and conversion was readily available. That they experienced something like the emotional intensity of conversion is perhaps obvious. But there is also the same dramatic sequence that begins with the piercing insight, perhaps occasioned by an apparent accident, but revealing the total corruption of the person's life to date; that progresses to the experience of rebirth, with its feeling of enormous relief from the burdens of self-delusion; that culminates in an eagerness to bear witness, to rescue others from the wrong path.[6]

These affinities are particularly striking in Fichte's "conversion." He brought to his reading of Kant an emphatically Protestant set of religious beliefs and ethical values, and the *Critiques* can be said to have reaffirmed them. His Kantianism was in that sense much simpler than Wilhelm von Humboldt's or Friedrich Schiller's. Their aesthetic ideal of an unconditionally free *Individualität* was grounded in Kant's ethics; but it also drew on the new Hellenism, which exhibited a pagan reverence for sensual expression that was hard to reconcile with Kant's eminently

Lutheran tendency to equate fulfillment of duty with the repression, not the channeling, of sensuality. They had to detach the emancipatory thrust of Kant's individualism from the iron constraints of his asceticism.[7] Fichte had no such ambivalence; Kant allowed him to reaffirm the commitment to duty, and to a freedom exercised in and through duty, with which he had entered adulthood.

While the analogy with conversion suggests the religious resonances of Fichte's encounter with the *Critiques*, it does not explain why he was so powerfully gripped by Kant's thought. If we assume instead a philosophical standpoint, Fichte's Kantianism can be taken as an example of "radical reflexivity," the turn inward in which Charles Taylor finds the grounding of modern Western conceptions of selfhood; but that approach, though helpful, is also insufficient.[8] What needs explaining is why Kantian reflexivity seemed to cut through the field of tensions Fichte had been trying to resolve. The young man who discovered the *Critiques* was a marginal intellectual trying to justify himself. He was pulled between his need for public openness and the imperatives of place-seeking, between his reluctance to cut himself off from the popular world of his origins as a village weaver's son – the emotionally vibrant and comforting world of his father's piety – and his eagerness to win full-fledged membership in an educated elite. He had to reformulate a paradox central to Lutheranism. How could he ground his freedom in an inner, emotional spontaneity, and, at the same time, transmute that spontaneity into an outer-directed imperative to control oneself and, through self-mastery, to change the world?

Honor, duty, struggle: within this triad the young Fichte sought to fashion an identity and define a purpose. Put simply, the road to honor (*Ehre*) lay through fulfillment of duty (*Pflicht*), and meeting the imperatives of duty required a relentless struggle (*Kampf*) against both inner demons and external obstacles. An impulse to struggle – an eager combativeness – already marks Fichte's way of confronting the world and himself when he enters the historical record as a private tutor in the mid-1780s, several years before discovering Kant.[9] In his unpublished writings and his correspondence we see the forms the impulse assumed, the idioms it employed, the outlets it sought.

In a homiletic exercise from the mid-1780s, Fichte evoked the Christian's relentless "struggle against sinful desires." He confided to his fiancée from Leipzig in late December 1790, that, rather than attend church services, he devoted his Sundays to the "sacred duty" of "self-examination" (*Selbstprüfung*) and prayer.[10] "The voice of duty is worthy of honor to you above all else," his précis of the "Rules for Self-Examination" (*Regeln der Selbstprüfung*) for 1791 began; and a "main examination" every evening would make that voice still "louder." This was followed by a litany of mea culpas, attributing an impressive list of faults – his "vanity," his "inflexibility," his "hardness," his "reckless openness and talkativeness" – to "pride." The first failure to conduct this "impartially strict" examination, he warned himself, "will throw you back into your previous total corruption" and "will make you forever unimprovable."[11]

For Fichte's generation, as for earlier generations of German Lutherans, duty and honor were inconceivable without an internal struggle, a willed mastery over the "nature" within. However secular their idealism might become, it was still driven by the ethic of self-denial that had inspired Lutheranism from its inception and that, since the late seventeenth century, had received a powerful new stimulus from the Pietist revival. Fichte's education had imbued him with the eighteenth-century rationalist's skepticism toward the "enthusiasm" (*Schwärmerei*) – the unbridled emotionalism and mystical pretensions – of Pietist religiosity. Likewise he had come of age with a rationalist's distaste for Lutheran orthodoxy. By the time he drafted his "Rules," his asceticism no longer operated within the economy of salvation that Luther's *sola fide* had evoked. And yet, there was still the assumption of a fundamental human corruption, inherent in sensual gratifications, passionate impulses, and social vanities. Moral development was still a victory of the spirit over the flesh, a self-denying advance toward purely spiritual transcendence. In the absence of grace, the only antidote to corruption was a rational act of the will within the natural man, an exercise in self-discipline that achieved self-mastery. Like many other *Gelehrten* of his generation, Fichte was driven by a this-worldly asceticism, an ethos that made inner self-mastery the means to efficacious service *in* the world. Though the world was not to be resanctified in the Pietist sense, within a traditional Christian eschatology, reform still aimed at a thorough going moral regeneration. It was this outer-directed struggle – the self-sacrificing devotion to service – that the self-discipline achieved in inner-directed struggle made possible.

Fichte was well aware that it was a short step from honor to pride. The insistence on self-mastery became pride when it prevented him from admitting need even to his friends, for fear that they would offer him help merely "*out of pity for need*" rather than out of respect for his person.[12]

One of his reactions in conflicts with employers – one way he sought to
assert a self-disciplined will – was to force others to be as open as he liked
to think he was. Struggle, here, meant breaking through the inhibitions
imposed by the tutor's inferior rank and financial dependence. He could
will a mutual frankness that would in effect negate the reality of his
employers' power and his own vulnerability. But, as these conflicts esca-
lated, Fichte sought invulnerability in a tactic that was anything but
frank. Bent on victory in a battle of wills, he resorted to a calculated, self-
contained withdrawal – and thus made self-discipline a weapon in a
power struggle.

In the long run, of course, these were the petty skirmishes of a tran-
sitional phase; the road to duty and honor lay through the practice of a
calling (Beruf) in the world. It was above all in his struggle to find a
calling and, in more modern terms, to launch a career that Fichte's commitment to openness collided with the realities of his situation. "I do not
want merely *to think*," he wrote to his fiancée in March of 1790, "I want
to act" (*handeln*). At the close of the letter he expanded on this aspiration;
"I have only one passion, only one need, only a fullness of feeling of
myself; to have an effect outside myself" (*ausser mir zu würken*).[13] Fichte
was *not* voicing an intellectual's frustration with a life devoted to words
and theory to the exclusion of practical deeds. What he rejected was the
self-enclosed world of pure scholarship; the alternative – the life of
action he sought – was the communicative action in which words had a
real impact. For his generation the determination to escape the corporate ghetto of the traditional *Gelehrtenstand* (learned order) was, in positive terms, an aspiration to have an effect on the larger society and polity
by asserting a truly public voice. Ultimately it was in this sense – as intellectuals addressing a public audience – that they sought to break through
the walls and inhibitions of the old-regime hierarchy with "purely
human" forms of communication.[14]

Fichte's very choice of verb recalls Goethe's famous diagnosis of the
educated commoner's dilemma in *Wilhelm Meisters Lehrjahre*. What makes
the theatre so alluring to Wilhelm is the impossibility of breaking
through, the lack of a viable public outlet for the commoner's aspiration
to "have an effect." "A *Bürger* can achieve merit and even develop his
spirit in extreme necessity," Goethe has Wilhelm lament in a much-
quoted passage, "but his personality gets lost [*geht verloren*], however he
may present himself." Unlike the nobleman, who "gives everything
through the presentation of personality," the Bürger "gives nothing."
Whereas the essence of the nobleman is "to perform and have an effect"

(*tun und wirken*), the function of the *Bürger* is merely "to achieve and produce" (*leisten und schaffen*).[15]

Goethe was asking the bourgeois moralists among his readers to admit that the courtly tradition could not be dismissed out of hand as corrupt (and corrupting) formalism. In his person, as in his physical setting, the ideal nobleman embodied the "representative publicness" with which his order exhibited its unique fusion of social preeminence and public authority. Performing the conventions of rank with inbred ease, the nobleman conveyed a public presence on all occasions and in all situations. The implication of this ideal was that the commoner, no matter how educated he might be, was condemned to a truncated private existence. In a sense, however, young intellectuals of Fichte's plebeian background had a way of mitigating this dilemma. They grew up with the expectation that they would enter the clergy, perhaps as schoolmen but preferably as pastors. It was because they *were* disadvantaged and lacked alternatives, of course, that they had to accept the shabby financial rewards that most pastorates offered. But the office nonetheless exercised a strong appeal, and that was because it represented the only public platform accessible to young men of their background.

The focal point was the sermon. Particularly in villages and small towns, the Sunday sermon in the local church was likely to be the only regular public event witnessed by boys from uneducated families. It was public not simply because it embodied the institutional authority of church and state, but also because – and this dimension of public status was much more rare in a corporate society – its audience was drawn from all levels of the social hierarchy. What enthralled the audience was a rhetorical performance; the eloquent sermon represented a supreme display of the same verbal prowess with which the exceptional poor boy excelled in school and won his teachers' approval. It was the lure of the pulpit in all these senses that Karl Philipp Moritz – a contemporary of Fichte, and, like him, a former poor student (armer Student) from an uneducated family – recalled in his autobiographical novel *Anton Reiser*. As a young boy, Anton was mesmerized by a local preacher who "carr[ied] away" his audience "irresistibly," and who even dared chastise leading citizens by name for their opulence and their indifference to "injustice and oppression."[16]

This exalted vision of the pulpit retained a hold on Fichte well beyond his university years. What had prompted a visiting baron to sponsor his education for the clergy in 1770, after all, was his ability to recite the Sunday sermon verbatim. Preaching had figured centrally in the turning

point of his life. To Fichte, as to Moritz, the heroism of the pastorate lay
not in the daily rounds of pastoral care, but in feats of pulpit oratory. He
grew up with the expectation that the pulpit would offer him a platform
from which to assert a public voice. It is a measure of the tenacity of this
expectation that, in the late 1780s and early 1790s, Fichte's hopes
remained fastened on a pastoral appointment, though he no longer
thought of himself as an orthodox Lutheran and in principle disdained
to stoop to the "hypocrisy" that an appointment would probably require.

His goal, Fichte reported to his friend Friedrich August Weisshuhn
from Leipzig in May 1790, was still to become "a preacher not without
renown."[17] A few weeks later, in search of a pastorate in Saxony, he trav-
eled to Dresden to win the sponsorship of Christoph Gottlob von
Burgsdorff, the President of the High Consistory. When von Burgsdorff
tried to steer him into an academic career in classical studies, Fichte pro-
tested that the subject was "too unimportant to fill a human life," and
would not allow him "to effect [*würken*] as much as he could effect." He
would be a mediocrity at the lectern, he dared inform his potential
patron, but could "excel" in the pulpit. In Leipzig in the summer of 1790,
despite his chronic lack of money, he took private lessons with a *Gelehrter*
who trained actors in "declamation." The instructor "sits in darkness
and unknown," he wrote to his fiancée, because he lacks "a spirit of
initiative" and, in any case, "is no preacher." He himself aspired to be
"the first in the art"; that is how he would "make [his] reputation, or
there would no longer be any justice in the world."[18]

But could this ambition really be satisfied in a pastorate? The clerical
journals of the late eighteenth century were filled with complaints about
the stultifying remoteness and obscurity that so many young theology
candidates had to endure in rural parishes.[19] Even as he looked to the
pulpit for a public platform, Fichte was aware of this dilemma. He could
not "slink in the usual way," he informed his parents in June 1790, merely
to "place [himself] in a village pastorate."[20] For the moment, at least, he
was captivated by the possibility of finding employment at a court, as a
preacher, or as the tutor to a young prince. Responding to his fiancée's
objection that he was too inflexible and "too open" to do well in the
vipers' nest of court life, he insisted that this was precisely the opportunity he needed to learn "to accommodate [himself] to others sometimes,
to deal with false people or people entirely contrary to [his] character."
What really attracted him was the prospect of "effect[ing] something
greater" in "a larger theatre."[21]

But this was fantasy; in the late 1780s and early 1790s, Fichte confronted the real threats to his integrity in his efforts to secure a pastorate. The very conditions for clerical preferment were bound to frustrate his aspiration to assert a voice that would be truly human in substance and truly public in scope and impact. The pastorate was one of the many offices distributed through the multi-tiered patronage networks of old-regime society. In Saxony, the highest tier was formed by the great noble households – the preeminent families, which had virtually hereditary rights to the highest ecclesiastical offices and which controlled many pastoral appointments directly or through relatives and clients. Well-positioned patrons were especially important for theology candidates of Fichte's obscure background, since they lacked the family connections that oiled the careers of young men from clerical dynasties and educated bourgeois families.

By the late 1780s Fichte was in danger of becoming a client *manqué*, condemned to watch his former schoolmates advance while he languished on the tutoring circuit.[22] His original patron, Baron von Miltitz, had died in 1774, and roughly a decade later the baroness, reacting against disturbing reports about his conduct as a student, had washed her hands of him. The patronage chain had snapped at its key link, and it could not be repaired. At von Burgsdorff's insistence, he wrote to the baroness, begging her "complete forgiveness," but to no avail. She had probably been too alarmed by rumors of his religious heterodoxy, though she did not bother to tell him exactly what had displeased her.[23]

By 1790, a government-sponsored crackdown on the Lutheran clerical Enlightenment was radiating from Prussia to the other North German states, including Saxony. Nonetheless, Fichte still hoped to become a preacher in Saxony if an "*honest* opportunity" arose.[24] But that was the issue; in the very effort to secure an appointment, he might have to compromise the openness and hence the integrity he hoped to bring to the pulpit. In his combative posture Fichte prided himself on defying this temptation. Unlike other young clergymen in Saxony, who adopted a "slavish, light-shy, hypocritical way of thinking" in the face of "a more than Spanish Inquisition," he was stimulated by the prospect of "battling through all the entrenchments and still making a [clerical] career."[25]

If Fichte would not stoop to blatant falsification to win a new patron, however, he could not entirely avoid self-degradation.[26] As personal, informal, and scattered as the eighteenth-century workings of patronage were by modern bureaucratic standards, they were not random. The overall effect was a controlled selection of recruits for the clergy. Control was exercised not simply by weeding out the openly heterodox, but also by requiring proof of the deference that outsiders – i.e., recruits from uneducated families – were expected to have absorbed. In private, of course, clients could censure individual patrons for abuse of power; but there was little room to ask whether patronage as an institution made for an unjust distribution of life chances. In a relationship pervaded by paternalist norms, the client was expected to confide in his patron as a novice in search of the mentor's advice; as a supplicant in need of a sponsor; and perhaps as a penitent seeking the forgiveness needed to retain or to regain sponsorship.[27]

This was the posture Fichte had to assume if he was to have any hope of preferment in the Saxon clergy. On one level he blamed himself for his predicament. There was an element of genuine self-reproach in his admission to potential sponsors that as a student he had failed to learn how to make himself "agreeable" and "accommodating." But at a deeper level the imperatives of clientage cut against the grain of Fichte's self-construction, and his efforts to comply with them make painful reading. He was not above sounding the religious chord, and indeed he pounded it when the occasion demanded. So long as he was disdained by someone he revered, he wrote Baroness von Miltitz in the effort to secure her pardon, he could not regain "confidence in [himself] and others" and once again approach God "with joy." All the more devastating, he added, was the disdain of those "who were for him in place of God on the earth."[28]

Even in his more obsequious moments, Fichte's omissions hedged his self-degradation. In refusing to make excuses for the "final sad events" that had provoked the baroness, he also avoided a specific admission of fault. More often, though, he took pains to offset the client's conventional language of reverential gratitude with the moralistic idiom of merit and service that came so much more naturally to him. If von Burgsdorff passed him over for an appointment, he would accept his fate in all humility; he had no doubt that the president considered only "merits" and the "capacities" to acquire them.[29] In the initial version of his first letter to Marie Christiane von Koppenfels, the *grande dame* through whom he hoped to secure an appointment at the Weimar court, he praised her "kind condescension" and her "friendliness" (*Freundschaftlichkeit*). In the second draft he deemed friendliness too bold a term, but assured the lady that he did not revere in her the providentially assigned "rank" she "[had] in common with many," since "that would only fill [him] with mute respect and recall [to him] the duty to withdraw." It was reverence for "the woman of spirit, of taste, of heart, of broad knowledge" that "expand[ed] [his] heart" and spurred him to "everything noble and good."[30]

With this kind of pseudo-intimacy Fichte tried to spare himself the conventional forms of obsequiousness, even as he acknowledged the legitimacy of his potential sponsor's vastly superior rank. But he also played the game – and in a way that put the language of merit in the service of flattery. The manipulation of language offered a kind of protective shield, but he still had to contend with the voice of duty within. It told him that true honor lay not in social calculation, but in the honest assertion of an inner self.

While Fichte was searching for a place, he was also confronting the issues that preoccupied intellectuals of his generation and made so many of them receptive to Kant's philosophy. Two draft sermons written sometime in the mid-1780s, when he was still a tutor in rural Saxony and was preparing to make his reputation in the pulpit, provide our first glimpse of his struggle on this front. The surviving record then leaps across several years to a highly condensed meditation entitled "Some Aphorisms on Religion and Deism," written in Leipzig toward the end of that depressing summer of 1790.[31]

In Fichte's passage from the beliefs and doubts of his boyhood to his Kantian resolution of a spiritual crisis, the draft sermons and the aphorisms are scattered moments. And yet they form the two parts of a whole; they record the opposed voices in a young man's internal argument. While one voice insisted on the freedom of the will, the other dismissed our subjective experience of freedom as an illusion needed to endure the iron constraints of our condition. It was this argument that Fichte thought he had resolved, albeit reluctantly and painfully, in the summer of 1790, on the eve of his engagement with Kant's *Critiques*.

Like Karl Leonhard Reinhold, the first of the celebrated figures among Kant's disciples,[32] the young Fichte sought to reconcile "head" and "heart," to avoid having to choose between critical rationality and emotional spontaneity. Unlike Reinhold, however, he approached Kant's *Critiques* as a philosophical neophyte of markedly parochial background. Until 1788, when he took an employment in Zürich, he had never left his native Saxony. If we can believe his self-advertisement to a potential patroness, his favorite authors included Montaigne and Rousseau as well as Lessing, Wieland, Goethe, and Schiller.[33] By 1790, he had probably read Rousseau's *La Nouvelle Héloïse*. But it is safe to assume that, when he and his friends argued philosophy, they drew on an eclectic fund of largely second-hand knowledge.

Fichte was, in his way, an eighteenth-century rationalist, but he was largely a product of the religious culture of German Lutheranism. In Germany, it was Lutheran clergymen, including professors in the theology faculties of the many universities, who had set the tone for the Enlightenment since the middle decades of the century. The key figures – Friedrich Wilhelm Jerusalem, Johann Salomo Semler, Johann Joachim Spalding, and others – were known as the Neologists. By the 1780s, they were presiding over a broad movement for renewal of the established churches. Eager to learn from the English and French varieties of rationalism, the Neologists had also been adept at weakening the corrosive impact of imported thought as it was absorbed into a native religious tradition.[34] It was this cautious eclecticism that had made Lessing, the intellectual hero of Fichte's school days, contemptuous of academic theologians. Lutheran orthodoxy was "foul water," Lessing had confided to his brother in 1774, but the "new-fashioned theology" wanted to replace it with "liquid manure." "Under the pretext of making us rational Christians," a new breed of "bunglers and half-philosophers" was "mak[ing] us extreme irrational philosophers."[35]

In a sense Lessing's derision was undeserved. If there was a single stance that defined the Neologists as a group, it was their rejection of the doctrine of original sin, with its categorical refusal to concede any efficacy to human agency. They regarded Christian virtue, to be sure, as a triumph over sensuality, and to that extent they remained faithful to the ascetic impulse in Lutheranism. But they also insisted that the triumph did not require a supernatural intervention, a wrenching turn effected by grace, since the moral nature of the natural man had inherently good impulses. Human nature was "incomplete," not corrupt to the core; with the proper training and guidance, it was "perfectible."

The Neologists were, in fact, redefining the very grounding of Christian truth. Once the orthodox belief in an inherited natural corruption was discarded, the view of Christ's suffering and death as a redemptive sacrifice – a vicarious atonement for a corrupted humanity, unable to atone for itself – could be reinterpreted in the light of the new confidence in man's inherent capacity for ethical perfectibility. To orthodox Lutherans the authority of dogmatic tradition was unimpeachable because it rested on the transcendent objectivity of revelation, proven by the Gospel miracles. What emerges from the Neologists' writings is an emphatically subjective criterion for the truth-value of the Christian tradition; the uniqueness of revelation lay in its capacity to awaken the inner impulses and fulfill the inner needs of the human personality, not in the disclosure of a supernatural objectivity otherwise beyond human grasp. In keeping with this new subjectivism, the Neologists' biblical scholarship interpreted much in the Gospel narratives as the historically contingent expressions of a specific culture.

And yet the Neologists might be said to have deserved Lessing's epithet. They are perhaps best described as rational theists – which is to say that, if a truly philosophical position required a thoroughgoing skepticism, they were indeed "half-philosophers." While the French *philosophes* were waging war *à outrance* against Christianity as such, the Neologists were quietly trying to rationalize Protestantism from within. Though they were more than willing to acknowledge that the legacy of the Reformation had been corrupted, they did not share the radical skeptic's view that all religions, including Protestantism, were variations on mankind's penchant for superstition. In its essence, Protestantism was distinguished from other religions by its unique rationality; it represented the most advanced stage that mankind's understanding of its relationship with God had reached. The Gospels were not literally inspired in their every word, but in their distilled core they were the depository of a revelation. They recorded the eminently rational moral truths that God had sent Christ to teach. Not all biblical miracles were to be explained as cultural metaphor; some were historical facts needed to reinforce the moral authority of Christ's teaching by demonstrating the divine source of his mandate. Chief among the latter, of course, was the Resurrection.[36]

By the 1780s, the Neologists were the reigning elders of an Enlightenment establishment. As illusory as it soon proved to be, their confidence in the inevitable demise of Lutheran orthodoxy made sense in Prussia and several other North German states, where they enjoyed the sponsorship of "enlightened" governments. But new threats were gaining momentum, and, in the face of them, the Neologists felt compelled to maintain a middle ground – a rationally defensible but emotionally grounded religious belief, holding head and heart in a delicate balance. Since the *Sturm und Drang* movement of the early 1770s, educated youth had shown a marked susceptibility to the allure of irrationalism, whether it took the form of a Wertherian cult of inspired genius or a Rousseauian reverence for the truth of authentic feeling. To the Neologists, all this was suspiciously reminiscent of the Pietist enthusiasm they had rejected as young men; there was the same unbridled

emotionalism, and the same tendency to mistake emotional abnormal-
ity for privileged lucidity about spiritual truths, if not for direct inspira-
tion. In this direction, the Neologists emphasized that, as emotive as
religious experience might legitimately be, there was no substitute for
rational understanding.

From the other direction the threat was posed by advocates of a purely
"natural" religion – the modern variety of deism, with God reduced to
an objective principle of pure rationality, manifested to the human intellect in the harmonious regularity of natural laws. There was no room
here at all for imaginative feeling; religion – if the word still applied –
became purely a matter of cold deliberation and judicious consent. As
disdainful as they were of the excesses and self-delusions of Pietist fervor,
the Neologists were not rationalists in this exclusive sense; they could not
repudiate the feelings of awe and solace that had suffused their own
childhoods in pious Lutheran homes. They knew from experience that
religion, if it were to have existential depth, had to offer consolation and
hope, and that, on both counts, it had to address quintessentially human
emotional needs. As Spalding put it in 1784, the human being deprived
of "stirrings" (*Rührungen*) of the heart "feel[s] the most painful loss";
human beings have an inherent need "not merely *to understand, but also to
feel; not merely to be enlightened, but also to be warmed.*"[37]

Fichte's exercises in homiletics from the mid-1780s record a young
man's efforts to find his bearings within this field of multivalent tensions.
For all their philosophical resonances, Fichte's questions and answers
were still firmly embedded in Lutheran theology and biblical exegesis. It
was not simply that the format required this idiom. As he imagined
himself addressing the spiritual needs of a hypothetical audience, Fichte
used the idiom to construct a personal identity, with space for the autonomous exercise of will within a larger framework of constraints.

It had been roughly seven years since Lessing had conducted his
Fragmenten-controversy, but in "On the Intentions of Jesus' Death," the
longer of the draft sermons, Fichte was still taking up the gauntlet that
Lessing (via Reimarus) had thrown down. In addition to pointing out
inconsistencies in the Gospel narratives, Reimarus had appealed to
common-sense logic to expose the Resurrection as a hoax.[38] Christ could
have proved his divinity, after all, simply by not dying. Better still, the
Resurrection could have been arranged as a public demonstration
before the Jewish nation. In Fichte's counterargument, it was precisely
its reliance on "demonstrations . . . wrapped in a certain dark light" that
made Christianity (by which he meant Protestantism) "unique" among

religions. If Jesus had simply disappeared, the resulting confusion would have destroyed his work. On the other hand, a public demonstration would have produced a "coerced" certainty about the Resurrection, a "persuasion" limited to the "understanding" and hence "too strong, too forceful." While Christian "proofs" were "*correct* and *satisfying* to the sharpest spirit of research," they did not "impose themselves" because they were not merely a matter of "sharpening our understanding." By "activat[ing] inner feeling of the true and the good" – by satisfying the emotional needs of a "pure heart" – Christian belief "warm[ed]" and "correct[ed] our understanding" and thereby "perfect[ed] our entire nature."[39]

The belief in the uniqueness of Christianity, the grounding of the truth of Christian revelation in human subjectivity, the explanation of Jesus' divine mission in terms of his moral teaching and example rather than his redemptive sacrifice: all this places the Resurrection sermon on the Neologists' middle ground. On closer inspection, though, Fichte's version of the "friendship" between reason and emotion in Christian belief has different terms of reciprocity. To the Neologists it was the exercise of critical judgment that grounded the autonomy of the enlightened Christian. However vital emotion might be, it had to remain subordinate to the governing power of reason. Fichte's emphasis reversed the dynamic; it was emotion that grounded autonomy and purely rational persuasion that threatened it. His language is often borrowed from the eighteenth-century aesthetic and literary cult of sensibility (*Empfindsamkeit*), but in its deepest resonances it points to an antecedent impulse.

Fichte's conception of human autonomy was still structured by the set of oppositions – between the faith of the reborn Christian and the "fleshly" reason of the Old Adam, and between the inner depth of true spirituality and the externality of mere legalism – that Luther had made central to Protestantism from its inception. To be gripped by faith meant, of course, to discard the illusion of human freedom; receptivity to the supernatural gift came with the realization of total helplessness. But faith penetrated through the heart, and that was to say that the force of its grip lay in activating emotional predispositions and satisfying emotional needs at the irreducible core of the human personality. Hence the Christian paradox of freedom in slavery; faith – even as it made the believer a passive instrument in the hands of the Lord – was experienced as an act of spontaneity, an immediate, self-generated grasp of truth. By itself, rational comprehension, with its reliance on logic and the evidence

of the senses, was the vehicle of external coercion in merely human (or
fleshly) modes of intersubjectivity.

It was this opposition between an external coercion, exercised in and
through rational argument, and an inner freedom grounded in emotion
that Fichte applied to his defense of the Resurrection. In a sense, he
remained entirely within the conventions of his chosen idiom. He did
not confront, much less explain, the constraints imposed by his origins,
his poverty, his precarious dependence on patronage. Focusing on how
revelation mediated the relationship between the individual believer and
his God, he acknowledged social factors only as instruments of, or as
obstacles to, that mediation. In his economy of salvation, the collective
middle term was a spiritual community of believers, not a society with
a discernable social structure and a causal role in its own right. And yet,
in an oblique but important sense, Fichte's personal agenda had a social
dimension. As a "scholar" of plebeian origins, on the margin of the educated elite and facing the possibility of remaining there, he had two
inseparable concerns: to justify himself as an exceptional case, and to
remain integrated into a socially inclusive Christian community despite
his critical distance on the world he had left. If he thought of himself as
in some sense deserving of privilege, he also sought bonds with a larger
public – with the audience on which he aspired to have an effect. In his
projection of a rhetorical community, and in the way he envisioned
freedom *in* community, Fichte asked how a society dichotomized into an
educated elite and an uneducated mass could also form an integrated
public.

At issue in the Resurrection sermon was the nature of religious community and the place Fichte sought to assume within it. If Christianity
had relied solely on "sharp, deeply thought considerations and strict
proofs" it would have been a "mere *Wissenschaft*" for "*a few good heads*,"
exercising "less influence on practical life" and contributing less to "the
happiness [*Beglückseeligung*] of its individual members and the whole." Or
it would have been merely a political movement, a mass blindly following a head (*Haupt*), like the "monarchy" under which Mohammed
welded "fantastic, unimproved men" into a "revolutionary" movement.[40] Again Fichte reversed the usual associations; it was an exclusive
reliance on reason – and not an excess of emotion – that made for mass
manipulation.

Fichte did not bother to reconcile his oddly paired images of scholarly exclusiveness and revolutionary mobilization. What the combined
images make clear is the appeal of an emotionally grounded community

of belief to a young scholar of his background and aspirations. Such a community promised a kind of subjective autonomy that allowed and indeed required participation in a socially inclusive religious culture; and in that sense, it reconciled the private and the public, inner freedom and membership in a collective body. Fichte's Christianity was a genuinely popular religion, in the sense that its foundation lay in the universal needs and impulses of the human heart. It did not necessarily exclude sharp scholars like himself, but it required them to keep their rationalism warmed and thereby continually revitalized by a living knowledge shared with their less intelligent, or at least less educated, brethren. The "few good heads" could experience the inner freedom of Christian belief, but only if they remained bonded with the larger community as good hearts.

In the other draft sermon, the immediate subject – the Annunciation – occasioned an exploration of the meaning of Christian election. Fichte reminded his hypothetical audience that ultimately it was not Mary's "outstanding merits" and "purity of heart" that explained her selection as the mother of Jesus. Rather God, in the completely free exercise of his "mercy" (*Gnade*), gave her "the most advantageous opportunity to become one of the most excellent people on the earth." The implication was not that most people were beyond the pale of God's mercy; every human being, even among the pagans and the Jews, was given "some opportunity *to become good*."[41] But, just as God singled out Christianity to achieve a higher degree of moral perfection than other religions, so, too, within the larger community of Christians, he guided a select few to greater heights. Fichte's personal stake in this view of providential election became obvious as he elaborated:

He [God] gives some a *better natural* understanding to recognize the truth and a *better, softer, more pliant* heart to succeed in loving it and obeying it. He gives them *better education* [*Erziehung*], *better instruction in youth* . . . He surrounds them *with more virtuous society*. The world that surrounds us, especially in youth, does much to give our soul its direction . . . *He unites all circumstances of their life, all the earthly destinies they encounter in the world, for the purpose of improving their souls* . . . Fortunate is he who the Divinity educates with a loving strictness, who is reminded of His existence through sufferings and pain at every stupidity, every thoughtlessness, every neglect of his duty, every forgetting of the God watching over its exercise.[42]

For the "unfortunate" and the "fortunate," Fichte went on to explain, "struggles" against corruption were waged with very different prospects for victory. The unfortunate – individuals whose "poor understanding" and "*unfeeling* heart" were reinforced by a corrupt upbringing – could emerge victorious if they wanted to "win through the power of religion"; but the odds were against them. Providence arranged the life of the fortunate – through natural gifts of head and heart, through an advantageous education and intercourse with "the most virtuous people" – to make the struggle "easier" and allow them to "climb higher" in virtue. But this was a privilege that had to be justified according to unusually strict rules of accountability. The fortunate had to fulfill their potential in their innermost subjectivity, in the interior realm of motives visible only to God.[43]

We are reminded that Fichte's religiosity, for all its roots in the Lutheran subsoil, no longer operated within the orthodox economy of salvation. Conspicuously absent is any dichotomy between an Old Adam mired in human corruption and a reborn Christian in the grip of God's saving grace. Instead, following the route the Neologists had taken, Fichte found the structuring principle of spiritual biography in an ideal of self-development (*Bildung*). God did not intervene in the individual life by wreaking a sudden and dramatic turn (Bekehrung) from nature to grace. Sanctification was now an inner, organic process in which the individual, under the guiding hand of providence, developed his innate natural capacity for moral perfectibility. By the 1780s, the Neologists were using this concept of the individual's biography – what Semler called "the moral history" of the "more capable human beings" – to recast the Lutheran distinction between an elect and a visible church, and to give it a social dimension Luther had not intended. The elect were those Christians who, by virtue of their natural capacities, were more "morally alert" and "capable" than the mass of "external Christians." In its essential content, their profession of faith was no different from that of the mass, and in that sense they remained integrated into a larger public community of belief; but whereas the mass passively accepted a public dogma, "thinking Christians" came at truth in their own ways and grasped it in a process of active comprehension. The underlying implication was clear enough; if the educated elite were to remain within a Christian public community, it had to be granted the inner freedom, the right to pursue a "moral private religion," that its privileged insight warranted.[44]

It was this conception that Fichte applied in the Annunciation sermon. If he was clearly indebted to the Neologists, he was also more personal in his emphases. The Neologists had resolved the tension between free will and providential necessity more or less implicitly; the external life plot – its formative events and circumstances – at once made the "elected" Christian an instrument of providence and promoted a process of inner self-determination. Fichte was more self-conscious about this resolution, and more explicit about reconciling the imperatives of duty with a felt need for willed "action." He remained too securely anchored in the Lutheran ethical tradition, of course, to entertain the possibility of moral relativism. The elected Christian was not free to decide what his duty was; he could simply seize or neglect opportunities to fulfill a higher standard of duty. But in this latter sense – in the assertion of will in the face of God-given opportunities – the elected Christian enjoyed a kind of privileged freedom, the corollary to his active grasp of religious truth.

Most of the Neologists were sons of educated officials, and most notably of pastors; they regarded their membership in the learned estate as a birthright. It was Fichte's very different social experience that underlay his insistence that the elect meet a higher standard of perfectibility. By the very rigor of that standard he sought to justify his exceptional social ascent. At the same time, though, the Neologists' confident assumption that this higher perfectibility could be achieved *within* a larger public community of belief had special importance for Fichte. It addressed his countervailing aspiration to membership in an inclusive collectivity, preserving some kind of connection between elite and mass. In the providential economy of life chances, the elect, in its new image, was not a breed apart, the chosen few in a predestined dichotomy; it occupied a higher level of spirituality in a hierarchical continuum.

The draft sermons may have been meant to impress potential patrons, but they were not exercises in hypocrisy. Tentatively, and with highly selective exegeses, Fichte made the sermon format serve his need for self-definition and self-justification. And yet, even as he was developing these personal variations on the themes of rational theism, Fichte was playing devil's advocate for a radical alternative. As early as 1784, a year or two before the sermon drafts, he argued the case for uncompromising determinism in discussions with friends; and in 1788 and 1789, he tried to persuade friends in Zürich to the same position.[45]

Determinism applied to human behavior the mechanistic principle of causation with which modern science was constructing a physical universe of regular, predictable laws. Its operating assumption was that the processes of human subjectivity, like the workings of the physical universe, were reducible to actions and reactions within a chain of sufficient causes. The result was an uncompromising environmentalism, applied to ideas as well as to actions; the sense experience that produced thought was, itself, caused by external stimuli. All this was the standard fare of French materialist psychology, but Fichte had probably first encountered the full-blown case for determinism in the crudely popularized version published in 1770, by Karl Ferdinand Hommel, a law professor at Leipzig. To Hommel, modern scientific determinism was entirely compatible with the Lutheran doctrine of predestination, and, indeed, was simply another way of stating it. Conveniently, the feeling of being free – a feeling inherent in human nature – was also testimony to the higher wisdom of providence; without that feeling individuals could not be held accountable for their actions, and, hence, the state would have no moral ground for using the threat of punishment and the prospect of reward to maintain order. This was to say that, from a rigorously philosophical standpoint, freedom of the will was no more than an illusion – though, in an eminently utilitarian corollary, the illusion was socially and politically indispensable.[46]

The specter of this mechanistic reductionism and fatalism haunted the German debate about Spinoza and "pantheism" in the 1780s. In 1785, Friedrich Jacobi's published version of a conversation with Lessing – a conversation in which Lessing was alleged to have admitted that he had always been a Spinozist – sent shudders through the Enlightenment establishment.[47] Jacobi was wielding the revered figure of Lessing in an assault on the Neologists' compromise between head and heart. If Lessing had, indeed, been a Spinozist, as Jacobi defined that persuasion, then "rational" theologians were deluding themselves and misleading the public. Lessing's secret was dramatic proof that rationalism inevitably led to materialist determinism and, thence, to atheism. The only escape from this inherently nihilistic momentum was the blind "leap of faith" with which the Christian admitted the impotence of reason in the face of religious mystery.

Fichte certainly was aware of this controversy, but he neither accepted Jacobi's *ad ultra* implication about rationalism nor embraced his alternative. Instead he made determinism the ground for what he called a "pure deistic system," with God retained as "the eternal and necessary being," the "first cause" in the chain of sufficient causes. To put it another way, he stopped short of atheism, but only by stripping away all traces of theistic anthropomorphism and reducing the concept of a Divinity to a purely logical necessity.

It was with a commitment to this deistic (i.e., determinist) alternative that Fichte thought he had resolved his internal argument in the summer of 1790. His "Aphorisms" record his abandonment of the Neologists' middle ground. The eighteen entries have none of the tentative repetitiveness of the sermon drafts; they are a series of concisely formulated definitions and conclusions, advanced in strict logical sequence. In a sense, they take us back to our point of departure; Fichte was still arguing that a public Resurrection would have been too "forceful" for a religion "grounded more on feelings [*Empfindungen*] than on convictions [*Überzeugungen*]." But, on one level, he had finally applied the lesson that Lessing's two-front polemic had been designed to drive home. "Religion" could and should be an internally self-sufficient system of beliefs proceeding from emotionally self-evident principles; the effort to purify it with philosophical rationality – "to unite as far as possible speculation with the claims of religion" – resulted in "a deism that [did] not even work as deism" and that made its advocates "suspect of not going to work very honorably." The advantage of his own, consequential deism was that it left the Christian religion "its entire subjective validity," since "it never [came] into collision with it."[48]

Through most of the aphorisms, the very impersonality of the format conveys a sense of relief and even of liberation. The young "speculator" had used rigorous logic to purge himself of his elders' need to unite head and heart in a workable marriage. Using the distinction between religion and speculation, he opted for an epistemological division of labor between cleanly different kinds of knowledge. But he also assigned himself to one side of that division, and, in the last two aphorisms, this self-definition turned an impersonal exercise in logic into a personal lament. The speculator faced "moments when the heart takes revenge on speculation," when "the entire [deterministic] system" is thrown into "disorder," when "a pressing desire [*Sehnsucht*] for reconciliation arises." But there were no "means of escape," since it was too late to "cut himself off from those speculations beyond the boundary." A compulsion for rational speculation that "proceeds straight ahead," without regard for consequences, had become "natural to him"; it was "interwoven with the entire turn of his spirit."[49]

In the light of Fichte's theological preoccupations, it is not hard to understand the sense of loss and embitterment that surfaces in the aphorisms. In the very act of repudiating his earlier vision of Christian freedom, Fichte magnified what he had lost. The believing Christian not only aspired to seize God-given opportunities; "his heart demands a God who lets Himself be entreated, who feels sympathy, friendship . . . [and] with whom [he can] enter a relationship of mutual modification."

In his intensely personal relation with his God, in other words, the Christian asserted his will in the hope of changing his assigned life course, even as he allowed himself to be changed by it. But if the rational theist had found ways to ground freedom in an inner reality of human experience, the pure deist had concluded that freedom was an illusion. Speculation revealed "a Being that has no point of contact whatsoever" with any human being. Since "any change in this world [was] necessarily determined by a sufficient cause," Fichte reasoned in the fifteenth aphorism, both the "activity" and the "suffering" of "each thinking and feeling being" was what it must be. What believers called "sin" was simply a product of this necessity; and it, in turn, produced results which were "just as necessary as the existence of the Divinity" and hence were "ineradicable."[50]

The deistic alternative was emphatically secular, and in that sense modern; but it too lacked an explanation of justice and injustice in terms of social structure. Society was still subsumed under an extra-social abstraction. The difference is that providence had been replaced by a mechanistic law of causation – a law that, in contrast to the believer's imagined relationship with his God, was forbiddingly impersonal as well as inflexible. In the absence of freedom and hence of responsibility, the individual could neither justify himself morally nor identify injustice in the constraints that faced him.

The pain of disillusionment was reinforced by another realization; in facing up to his impotence, Fichte had acquired a new sense of his social isolation. The epistemological division of labor implied a cultural and social segregation. Whereas in the draft sermons the "few good heads" had remained bonded to the mass in a larger community of belief, there was now a watertight dichotomy between the speculators and "non-speculating mankind." Christianity was "the best popular religion" (*Volksreligion*) – which was to say that belief in Christ's mediation had a unique power to satisfy human "need," transcending historical and cultural differences, but also that such belief was limited to "good and simple souls."[51] The latter phrase was ambivalent; it evoked emotional spontaneity and innocence, but it also connoted ignorance and weakness. The speculator could recommend such a religion "with the inner-most warmth" to "those who need it"; but his own deism effected "a certain inflexibility," which "prevent[ed] participation in the pleasant feelings [*Empfindungen*] that flow from religion."[52]

There was something intensely personal about Fichte's commitment to an impersonal determinism. It was not simply that he had sacrificed his moral self-justification, his God-given right to rise above the social world of his origins; he had also lost his conviction of a bonding with that world through emotive symbols and metaphors. Reluctantly, but with the iron grip of logic, Fichte accepted the conclusion the draft sermons had avoided: that the zone of privileged insight – the zone occupied by intellectuals like himself – had no common ground of subjectivity with the religious culture of the masses. If the voice of speculation had public resonance, it was within that caste-like zone; the same critical distance that allowed its occupants to proceed straight ahead also prevented them from participating in and having a direct impact on a public community of belief.

The final irony is that, in taking this painful step, Fichte did *not* commit himself unreservedly to critical rationality over emotional belief. The aphorisms conveyed a heightened ambivalence about *both* head and heart. In a sense, as the antipode to the rationalist's submission to persuasion, the spontaneity of the believer's emotional commitment was still a kind of freedom. But to satisfy emotional "need" was also to admit dependence, to succumb to human weakness; in that sense, Christian belief was not for "the strong," but for "the sick, who need the doctor."[53] Speculators, of course, were free precisely in the sense that they had transcended need. They had the intellectual fortitude required to proceed straight ahead without flinching in the face of personal loss. But there was a high price for the exercise of this kind of privileged freedom. Whereas the elect of the sermon drafts had been endowed with "softer" and "more pliant" hearts, as well as with superior natural intelligence, the new intellectual elite was burdened with a certain "inflexibility," an inability to respond to the inner stirrings of the heart. Fichte had confronted a kind of coercion inherent in rational autonomy, the inverse of the Christian paradox of freedom in slavery. The person who seemed "invincible in the field of speculation" experienced his intellectual freedom as a grim but irreversible fate – and he could not release himself from its grip even when he felt the "pressing desire" to escape back into an eminently human satisfaction. If his rationality was his strength, it was also an inhuman compulsion; its freedom had to be endured.

When Fichte's tutoring responsibilities led him to Kant's *Critique of Pure Reason*, in the late summer of 1790, he confronted the text as a reluctant but unflinching determinist. Not surprisingly he focused on Kant's third antinomy and gave it a markedly one-sided reading. In this exercise in transcendental dialectic, the thesis demonstrated the necessity of

assuming transcendental freedom. The antithesis demonstrated, with
equally rigorous logic, that everything in the world takes place solely in
accordance with the laws of nature and, hence, was subject to the law of
causality. It was the thesis that clinched the issue for Fichte. He concluded from it that even "the most sharp-witted defender of freedom
who ever was" (i.e., the voice of the thesis) had been unable to provide
a rational proof; the concept of freedom had simply been inserted from
"somewhere else," and probably from "sensibility" (*Empfindung*).[54]

Taken by itself, the thesis might be said to yield this interpretation; but
in his search for confirmation of his pure deism, Fichte had wrenched
the antinomy out of the larger context of Kant's argument. Kant's aim
was not to prove or disprove either position, but to demonstrate that, in
their claims to knowledge beyond sense experience, both could be true
or false. What he claimed to have identified were the ordering structures
inherent in our "theoretical" understanding of the natural world – or, to
put it another way, the innate concepts that imposed order on the "sensible manifold of perceptions" and, hence, were the condition of any
knowledge of nature, including human psychology.

Fichte had concluded from his selective reading of the *Critique of Pure
Reason* that his deterministic system was unassailable. Hence, it was all
the more wrenching to find his conviction being demolished as he read
the next treatise, the *Critique of Practical Reason*. To his amazement, he
reported to his friend Weisshuhn, "the concept of absolute freedom"
had been "proven" to him. Suddenly, and quite unexpectedly, he had a
compelling justification for the conviction of moral meaning and
responsibility he had recently abandoned. By limiting "theoretical"
knowledge to the phenomenal world of sense experience, Kant had
opened the way to a radically new moral theory, premised on the claim
that "practical" (i.e., moral) knowledge was grounded in the noumenal
self, the "I" as pure rational "intelligence." When the rational intellect
turned inward – when it reflected on itself – it became aware of the
Moral Law, the law of its unconditional autonomy. This idea of
transcendental freedom could not be "understood" (in the way that
physical causation, for example, was understood), but it was nonetheless
an unavoidable "fact of reason," self-evident in our inner awareness of
our spontaneity.

Fichte was exhilarated by the sheer cogency of Kant's argument,
which liberated him from the compulsion of his own logic. The self-
styled determinist now felt justified in abandoning conclusions he
had come to reluctantly, with a deep sense of loss, and in embracing the

conviction of freedom that his combative personality craved. Rather than choosing between mutually exclusive alternatives, as he had felt compelled to do in the aphorisms, he could now resolve his internal argument within a Kantian set of dualisms. In the second *Critique*, Kant had "proven" the possibility he had raised toward the close of the first one: that the human being was morally free in his "intelligible character" *at the same time* that he was determined by natural causation in his "empirical" (or phenomenal) character.

If Kant's logical cogency gripped Fichte with unusual force, that was because it resolved his internal argument between head and heart. The personal wholeness Fichte had sought as a Protestant believer and had despaired of as a determinist, now seemed within reach. The radicalism of Kant's theory, of course, lay in its uncompromising insistence on the rational purity of morality. Kant took pains to distinguish knowledge of the Moral Law from the emotional embrace of supernatural truth that grace was said to induce, and from the innate emotional preference for the good that some eighteenth-century moral theorists (including some Neologists) had attributed to human nature. But Kant also acknowledged that, in the sense world, a moral intention, like any other, must be impelled by a desire and an "interest" in satisfying it. A "good will," he argued, was a "higher faculty of desire." While other interests subjected the will to heteronomy, the paradox of the interest that motivated moral action was that it was disinterested. This was because the moral law induced a feeling of reverence for itself, as an imperative that overrode all empirical desires.[55]

Ultimately Fichte found Kant's argument for "absolute moral freedom" so compelling because it made this inner spontaneity the source of a fundamentally Protestant ethos. If "nature" was consigned to the realm of appearance, it was also the resistant substance against which the will had to struggle as it sought to realize its moral potential. Only on the assumption of "the freedom of the human being," Fichte wrote to his friend Achelis in November 1790, "[were] duty, virtue and in general morality possible." The "categorical imperative" required a relentless "strengthening for further effort," and hence the same ascetic self-mastery – the same struggle within – with which the Protestant believer sought to suppress natural corruption. This was, in fact, the first way in which Fichte's conversion changed his daily life in the late summer and fall of 1790. In early September, he reported to his fiancée that, though he had previously been "too unsteady to follow a fixed course," he was now observing a strict regimen. Accustomed to rising late, he was getting up at five every morning to "force [himself] to self-overcoming." His tutoring responsibilities were sandwiched between mornings and evenings devoted to study. In a parallel effort to "become completely master over [himself]," he had taken to depriving himself of "something [he] would have liked to have." The point was to "declare war on every emerging passion as soon as it reveal[ed] itself."[56]

When Fichte spoke of the new "peace" his conversion had brought him, he was not referring simply to his restored sense of personal wholeness. He had learned to "concern [himself] more with [himself]," he assured his fiancée, and not to bother with "things outside [himself]."[57] He did not retreat into monastic seclusion, but his ascetic turn inward at least brought a temporary respite from ambition and the attendant threats to his honor. Having fretted for months about his penury, Fichte now faced his "shaky external situation" with equanimity. Having risked his precious integrity in the quest for new patrons, he was now determined to preserve his "independence" and indeed to shun worldly power by refusing to be either "lord" or "servant." For this marginal intellectual, it would seem, Kant's epistemological dualism – his distinction between noumenon and phenomenon – had an immediately relevant social corollary. It clarified the choice between self-contained integrity and dissimulation in the pursuit of prospects. Indifferent to "all brilliance of the World," he now strove "not to appear, but to be."[58]

But what would this Kantian convert actually *do*? His sights were still fastened on preaching, though he had no practical strategy for securing access to a pulpit without sacrificing his integrity. Here again he had found a promise of self-justification in the *Critiques*. Kant insisted repeatedly that, as abstract as the several formulations of the categorical imperative were, neither extraordinary intelligence nor formal education was needed to grasp their essential moral truth. This was because the moral criterion of universality (or non-contradiction) was rationally self-evident, and because its self-evident rationality induced an emotional response – the feeling of reverence – that powerfully reinforced it. For Fichte, this conception of the spontaneity of moral knowledge had two momentous implications. In his Kantian persona, the rationalist was not exercising the coercive persuasion that had violated Fichte's Lutheran ideal of inner freedom; clarification of the moral law activated listeners' latent capacities for moral insight and hence induced them to *emancipate themselves* from the illusions of heteronomy. And, in this kind of communication, the communion of hearts had a perfectly legitimate and, indeed, necessary role. For this latter reason, Fichte counseled his

fiancée that it was only misguided "reasoners" (*Vernünftler*) like himself
who needed Kant's head-breaking antidote. She should "believe only in
[her] own feeling," since she was one of the "honorable people" who
had always "felt" (but had not "thought") the truth of Kant's message.[59]

All this is to say that Kant's moral theory offered Fichte a symbolic
route out of his social isolation. Having numbered himself among the
coldly logical speculators, cut off from the emotionally satisfying beliefs
of the masses, he had found a way to reconnect. The categorical imperative promised to be the grounding for the inclusive public community,
at once cognitive and emotional, that he had originally sought in his
elders' half-philosophical Lutheranism. If the Kantian turn inward was
to regenerate an age "rotten to its roots," it required a new mode of communicative action. The uprooted intellectual had found a rhetorical
mission and with it, a moral justification. As a Kantian preacher he
would make philosophy "popular" (*populär*) and "effective in the human
heart through eloquence."[60] His vocation was to "imprint (Kant's) moral
principles on the heart of the public with energy and fire, in a popular
form of presentation."[61]

Fichte would soon try to achieve such a rhetoric – to give the public
voice of the philosopher a truly popular form – in his Kantian defense
of the principles of the French Revolution.

NOTES

1. J. G. Fichte, *Gesamtausgabe der Bayerischen Akademie der Wissenschaften*, ed.
Reinhard Lauth, Hans Jacob, and Hans Gliwitsky, 9 vols. (Stuttgart-Bad
Cannstatt: Frommann-Holzboog, 1964–95), III: pt. 1, 163–66. The
Gesamtausgabe includes Fichte's early unpublished writings as well as his correspondence. It will be referred to hereafter as GA. All English translations
are my own. Footnotes for offset extracts display the original German texts
and spellings. Unless otherwise specified, all italics within quotations are
present in the original German text.
2. GA, III:1, 167–68.
3. *Ibid.*, 193–94. Italics are mine, added to indicate that this word is the
German as in the original quote. "Ich kam mit einem Kopfe der von großen
Plänen wimmelte, nach Leipzig. Alles scheiterte, u. von soviel Seifenblasen
blieb mir nicht der leichte Schaum übrig, daraus sie zusammengesezt waren
. . . es war halbe Verzweiflung, daß ich eine Partie ergrif, die ich eher hätte
ergreifen sollen. Da ich das außer mir nicht ändern konnte, so beschloß ich
das in mir zu ändern. Ich warf mich in die Philosophie, und das zwar – wie
es sich versteht – in die Kantische. Hier fand ich die Gegenmittel für die
wahre Quelle meines Uebels, u. Freude genug obendrein. Der Einfluß den
diese Philosophie, besonders der Moralische Theil derselben . . . auf das

ganze Denksystem eines Menschen hat, die Revolution, die durch sie besonders in meiner ganzen Denkungsart entstanden ist, ist unbegreiflich."

4. See especially Klaus R. Scherpe, *Werther und Wertherwirkung: Zum Syndrom bürgerlicher Gesellschaftsordnung im 18. Jahrhundert* (Bad Homburg: Gehlen, 1970).

5. GA, III:1, 171.

6. On the Pietist conversion experience see Wolf Oschlies, *Die Arbeits- und Berufspädagogik A. H. Franckes, 1663–1727*, Arbeiten zur Geschichte des Pietismus, vol. VI (Witen: Luther-Verlag, 1969), 184–92; Erhard Peschke, *Bekehrung und Reform: Ansatz und Wurzeln der Theologie August Hermann Franckes*, Arbeiten zur Geschichte des Pietismus, vol. XV (Bielefeld: Luther-Verlag, 1977), 111–14; Anthony J. La Vopa, *Grace, Talent, and Merit: Poor Students, Clerical Careers, and Professional Ideology in Eighteenth-Century Germany* (Cambridge: Cambridge University Press, 1988), 145–64.

7. On Humboldt's reception of Kant see esp. Christina M. Sauter, *Wilhelm von Humboldt und die deutsche Aufklärung* (Berlin: Duncker & Humblot, 1989), 294–309. On Schiller see Josef Chytry, *The Aesthetic State: A Quest in Modern German Thought* (Berkeley: University of California Press, 1989), 77–90.

8. Charles Taylor, *Sources of the Self: The Making of the Modern Identity* (Cambridge, Mass.: Harvard University Press, 1989), esp. 143–367.

9. Looking back on his tutoring employment in Zürich, he recalled a "ceaseless war" against "a host of prejudices, obstructions, and insolences of all sorts," a war he "wanted to win" while guaranteeing himself "an honorable retreat." Fichte to Weisshuhn, 20 May 1790, GA, III:1, 120. On tutoring, see especially the introductory essay in Ludwig Fertig, *Die Hofmeister: Ein Beitrag zur Geschichte des Lehrerstandes und der bürgerlichen Intelligenz* (Stuttgart: J. B. Metzler, 1979); La Vopa, *Grace, Talent, and Merit*, 111–33. Fichte's combativeness may derive from his formative experiences as an eldest son made conscious of his exceptionality by his father's favoritism, and already pitting his will against a resistant mother.

10. GA, III:1, 203.

11. "Die Stimme der Pflicht sei Dir über alles ehrwürdig. Damit sie lauter in dir werde, so sei es jeden Abend eine Deiner Hauptprüfungen, ob du dich wohl den Tag über gegen dieselbe vergangen habest ... Rotte den Stolz aus, und auch die gefährliche Frucht deßelben, die Eitelkeit, wird verschwinden. Bis dahin – su[/]che nie zu glänzen, und sei nie weiser, als die, mit denen Du lebst. Suche in der Gesellschaft weniger Deine Vorzüge, als andrer ihre geltend zu machen. Wenn Du geschmeichelt wirst, so denke schnell an Deine Fehler ... Auch Deine Unbiegsamkeit, und Härte gründet sich auf Stolz. Bestreite wenigstens die Früchte, bis Du die Wurzel ausgerottet hast. Uebe Dich in Sanftmuth und Geduld ... Deine unbesonnene Offenheit, und Geschwäzigkeit ist ein Zweig Deiner Eitelkeit ... Diese Prüfung sei unpartheiisch strenge. Du bist versichert, daß die erste Unterlaßung derselben Dich dahin bringt es auf immer zu unterlaßen; Dich in Dein ganzes voriges Verderben zurückstürzt; und Dich dann auf immer unverbeßerlich macht"; "Regeln der Selbstprüfung für das Jahr 1791," GA, II:1, 379–80.

12. Fichte to Johanne Rahn, 15–16 March 1790, GA, III:1, 83.

13. *Ibid.*, 72–73.

14. On efforts to break through the corporate shell of the *Gelehrtenstand*, see especially *Bürger und Bürgerlichkeit im Zeitalter der Aufklärung*, ed. Rudolf Vierhaus, Wolfenbütteler Studien zur Aufklärung, vol. VII (Heidelberg: Lamberg Schneider, 1981).

15. Dieter Borchmeyer, *Höfische Gesellschaft und französische Revolution bei Goethe* (Kronberg/Ts.: Athenaeum-Verlag, 1977), 30–53.

16. Karl Philipp Moritz, *Anton Reiser: Ein psychologischer Roman* (Frankfurt am Main: Insel, 1979; orig. pub, 1785–90), 66–76. See also La Vopa, *Grace, Talent, and Merit*, 70–71.

17. GA, III:1, 120.

18. *Ibid.*, 130.

19. La Vopa, *Grace, Talent, and Merit*, 326–35.

20. GA, III:1, 139.

21. In an earlier letter he had taken a different tack; he could continue to develop his "character" at a court because "uprightness and directness have the most effect where they are most seldom found." *Ibid.*, 69–73, 81–87. On bourgeois perceptions of court life, see esp. Borchmeyer, *Höfische Gesellschaft*; Paul Mog, *Ratio und Gefühlskultur: Studien zur Psychogenese und Literatur im 18. Jahrhundert* (Tübingen: Niemeyer, 1976), 36–46.

22. La Vopa, *Grace, Talent, and Merit*, 83–110.

23. GA, III:1, 131, 140–43, 145–47, 149–51.

24. Fichte to Johanne Rahn, 17 March 1790, in *ibid.*, 89.

25. *Ibid.*, 131, 158.

26. *Ibid.*, 149–51, 157–61.

27. La Vopa, *Grace, Talent, and Merit*, 85–97. On paternalist ideology see also Bengt Algot Sørensen, *Herrschaft und Zärtlichkeit: Der Patriarchalismus und das Drama im 18. Jahrhundert* (Munich: Beck, 1984).

28. GA, III:1, 145–47.

29. *Ibid.*, 150. See also Fichte's letter to Graf Georg Alexander Heinrich Hermann von Callenberg, 27 December 1789, in *ibid.*, 41–42.

30. Fichte to Marie Christiane von Koppenfels, 11 June 1790, in *ibid.*, 137.

31. The two sermon drafts, "An Mariae Verkündung" (delivered 25 March 1786), and "Über die Absichten des Todes Jesu" (probably also written in 1786), are in GA, II:1, 53–66, 75–98. "Einige Aphorismen über Religion und Deismus" is in *ibid.*, 287–97. My analysis of these texts has been greatly aided by Reiner Preul, *Reflexion und Gefühl: Die Theologie Fichtes in seiner vorkantischen Zeit* (Berlin: De Gruyter, 1969).

32. Karl Leonhard Reinhold, *Versuch einer neuen Theorie des menschlichen Vorstellungsvermögen* (Prague: C. Widtmann und I. M. Mauke, 1789), 51–56. On Reinhold see especially Frederick C. Beiser, *The Fate of Reason: German Philosophy from Kant to Fichte* (Cambridge, Mass.: Harvard University Press, 1987), 226–65.

33. Fichte to Marie Christiane von Koppenfels, 11 November 1790, in GA, III:1, 134. In Zürich, in his evening translation exercises, he had also made himself

familiar with at least part of Montesquieu's *L'Esprit des lois*. See the "Tagebuch Zürich," in *ibid.*, 212.

34. See Walter Sparn, "Vernünftiges Christentum: Über die geschichtliche Aufgabe der theologischen Aufklärung im 18. Jahrhundert in Deutschland," in *Wissenschaften im Zeitalter der Aufklärung*, ed. Rudolf Vierhaus (Göttingen: Vandenhoeck und Ruprecht, 1985); Hans Erich Bödeker, "Die Religiosität der Gebildeten," in *Religionskritik und Religiosität in der deutschen Aufklärung*, Wolfenbütteler Studien zur Aufklärung, vol. XI (Wolfenbüttel: L. Schneider), 145–95. Still useful for biographical detail and for succinct expositions of theological issues, is Karl Aner, *Die Theologie der Lessingzeit* (Halle/Saale: M. Niemeyer, 1929).

35. Quoted in Klaus Epstein, *The Genesis of German Conservatism* (Princeton: Princeton University Press, 1966), 134. On Lessing's theology, see Leonard P. Wessel, *G. E. Lessing's Theology: A Reinterpretation* (The Hague: Mouton, 1977).

36. Typically Jerusalem – the man who had openly rejected the doctrine of original sin as early as the 1740s – defended the historical facticity of the Resurrection in his *Betrachtungen über die vornehmsten Wahrheiten der Religion* (Braunschweig: Waisenhaus, 1778). See Aner, *Theologie*, 302–03.

37. Johann Joachim Spalding, *Vertraute Briefe die Religion betreffend*, 2nd rev. edn. (Breslau: G. Lowe, 1785), 219, and his *Gedenken über den Werth der Gefühle in dem Christentum*, 5th edn. (Leipzig: M. G. Weidmanns Erben und Reich, 1784).

38. See esp. "Über die Auferstehungsgeschichte" (Fünftes Fragment) and Lessing's commentary, in G. E. Lessing, *Gesammelte Werke*, ed. Paul Rille, vol. VII (Berlin: Aufbau-Verlag, 1956), 778–816.

39. GA, II:1, 79–80.

40. GA, III:1, 87–90.

41. *Ibid.*, 55–57.

42. *Ibid.*, 59–60; "Er [Gott] giebt einigen einen *beßeren natürl*[ichen] Verstand die Wahrheit zu erkennen, u. ein *beßeres weichres folgsameres* Herz sie lieb zu gewinnen u. ihr zu gehorchen. Er giebt ihnen *eine beßre Erziehung, beßren Unterricht in der Jugend . . . Er* umgiebt sie *mit tugendhafter Gesellschaft.* Die Welt die uns umgiebt, besonders in der Jugend umgiebt, thut viel unsrer Seele ihre Richtung zu geben . . . *Er vereinigt alle Umstände ihres Lebens, alle die irrdischen Schicksaale, die sie auf der Welt treffen zu dem großen Zwecke der Verbeßerung ihrer Seele.* . . . Glüklich ist der, den die Gottheit mit einer liebreichen Strenge erzieht, den sie bei jeder Thorheit, bei jeder Unbedachtsamkeit, bei jeder Vernachläßigung seiner Pflicht, bei jeder Vergeßenheit eines [/] über ihre Ausübung wachenden Gottes, durch Leiden u. Schmerz an ihr Daseyn erinnert . . . " (original italics).

43. *Ibid.*, 60–62.

44. See Johann Salomo Semler, *Über historische, gesellschaftliche und moralische Religion der Christen* (Leipzig: Georg Emanuel Beer, 1786), esp. 226–47, and *Abhandlungen von freier Untersuchung des Canon*, ed. Heinz Scheible (Gütersloh: Mohn, 1971). See also Bödeker, "Religiosität," 151–53, 175–76, 180–81; Peter

Hanns Reill, *The German Enlightenment and the Rise of Historicism* (Berkeley: University of California Press, 1975); Gottfried Hornig, "Die Freiheit der christlichen Privatreligion: Semlers Begründung des religiösen Individualismus in der protestantischen Aufklärungstheologie," *Neue Zeitschrift für systematische Theologie und Religionsphilosophie* 21 (1979): 198–211; Trutz Rendtorff, *Kirche und Theologie: Die Systematische Funktion des Kirchenbegriffs in der neuen Theologie* (Gütersloh: G. Mohn, 1966), 36–56.

45. See esp. Preul, *Reflexion*, 94–130.
46. Alexander von Joch [Karl Ferdinand Hommel], *Über Belohnung und Strafen nach Türkischen Gesetzen* (2nd edn., 1772; reprinted, Berlin: E. Schmidt, 1970).
47. F. H. Jacobi, "Über seine Gespräche mit Lessing," in G. E. Lessing, *Gesammelte Werke*, ed. Paul Rille, vol. VIII (Berlin: Aufbau-Verlag, 1956), 616–34. On the Spinoza controversy, see especially Beiser, *The Fate of Reason*, 44–108; Hermann Timm, *Gott und die Freiheit: Studien zur religionsphilosophie der Goethezeit* (Frankfurt am Main: Vittorio Klostermann, 1974).
48. GA, II:1, 288.
49. *Ibid.*, 291.
50. *Ibid.*, 287–90.
51. *Ibid.*, 289–90.
52. *Ibid.*, 290.
53. *Ibid.*, 289.
54. *Ibid.*, 290.
55. This aspect of Kant's thought is emphasized in Roger J. Sullivan, *Immanuel Kant's Moral Theory* (Cambridge: Cambridge University Press, 1989).
56. GA, III:1, 172–73.
57. *Ibid.*, 186–87.
58. *Ibid.*, 194.
59. *Ibid.*, 171.
60. *Ibid.*, 170–72.
61. *Ibid.*, 195.

CHAPTER ELEVEN

Mary Robinson and the scripts of female sexuality

Anne K. Mellor

Who – or what – was Mary Robinson? What can we learn from an exploration of the life and writings of this almost forgotten female author of the English Romantic period? I turn our attention to Mary Robinson because she poses what I think is a fascinating problem, both about our current intellectual constructions of subjectivity and about the ways in which women – and in particular female sexuality – were understood in Europe between 1780 and 1830. The career of Mary Robinson forces us to confront the question: How could the story of female sexuality in the late eighteenth-century be told? This question implies two prior questions. First, *who* got to tell the story? The person who performed the sexual act? Or the people who observed the act, from near or afar? Whose voice carried more credibility, the autobiographer's or the biographer's? And secondly, *how* was the story of female sexuality told? What generic conventions or narrative plots were available in the culture of eighteenth-century England to make a particular story of female sexuality comprehensible and credible?[1]

Let me begin with a few uncontested historical facts concerning Mary Darby Robinson, celebrated actress, writer, autobiographer, and the first lover of the Prince of Wales and future King of England, George IV. Mary Darby was born on 27 November 1758, in Bristol, the daughter of Mary Seys, a respectable Welsh woman, and John Darby, an adventurous and financially successful American merchant-seaman. When Mary was eleven, John Darby left his family to sail to Labrador to set up a whale-fishing industry, taking along a mistress; the industry failed and he never returned to his family. On 12 April 1773, at the age of fifteen, Mary Darby married Thomas Robinson, an articled law-clerk. Her first daughter, Maria Elizabeth, was born on 18 November 1774; a second daughter, Sophia, who lived only six weeks, was born in the summer of 1778.

A year after Maria's birth, in 1775, Thomas Robinson was confined to the Kings Bench Prison for debtors; his wife and daughter stayed there with him for nine months, during which time Mary Robinson began publishing poetry to earn money. In 1776, she returned to the career she had abandoned at the time of her marriage, that of actress. She made her debut as Juliet on 10 December 1776, at the Drury Lane Theatre and was an immediate success. She quickly became one of the leading actresses of the day, excelling in female *ingénue* roles in both tragedy and comedy – her most famous performances were as Cordelia, Juliet, Perdita, and Amanda in Sheridan's adaptation of Vanbrugh's *The Relapse*. On 3 December 1779, she gave a command performance as Perdita in *The Winter's Tale* for the Royal Family; six months later, she and the eighteen-year-old Prince of Wales became lovers and she separated from her husband. By August 1781, the affair was over and in October, Mary Robinson went to Paris where she was fêted as "la Belle Anglaise." In December she returned to London, resumed her acting career, and by May 1782, had begun an affair with Colonel Banastre Tarleton, a particularly ruthless leader of the British troops in the War against the Colonies; known as the "Swamp Devil," Tarleton was the officer who, a year before, had forced Thomas Jefferson to flee from Monticello. In June 1783, traveling overnight to Dover while pregnant, in order to pay off Tarleton's creditors and thus prevent him from having to leave England, Mary Robinson had a miscarriage which left her partially paralyzed in her hands and legs. She and Tarleton remained lovers for sixteen years, until he left her at his mother's insistence in 1798. Robinson supported them both with her 500 pound annuity from the Prince and the income from her substantial publication of poetry, novels, plays, and political tracts. She died on 26 December 1800, in her daughter's arms, after completing the first half of her *Memoirs*.

To understand better how both female sexuality and female subjectivity were constructed in the eighteenth century, we must first look at the ways in which Mary Robinson's life-story was told in texts and images. There were four very different, competing versions of the sexual nature of this "fair celebrity." Crudely summarized, she was either (1) a whore; (2) an "unprotected" and abused wife; (3) a star-crossed lover; or (4) a talented performer and a successful artist. I will discuss each of these versions in greater detail.

THE ACTRESS AS WHORE

In this account, Mary Robinson is represented as the seducer of an overprotected, naive, impressionable, and entirely sincere young man. She is

11.1 *Florizel and Perdita*, anonymous print published 18 October 1783.

a scheming, manipulative older woman (she was three years older than
the Prince) out for fame, fortune, and power. This was the narrative of
Robinson's life favored by the popular press. The Prince's lovenote to his
"Perdita," signed (in blood) "Florizel" and accompanied by a cut-out
heart in which he had written, "Unalterable to my Perdita through life"
on one side, and on the other, "Je ne change qu'en mourant," was visu-
ally displayed in an anonymous print *Florizel and Perdita*, published 18
October 1783 (Figure 11.1). Here, George III laments his son's fall before
the Circean charms of the flagrantly bare-breasted Perdita, while her
husband, the "King of Cuckolds," supports her other putative lovers
(Lords North and Fox and Tarleton) on his horns. James Gillray's scur-
rilous print, *The Thunderer* (Figure 11.2), published on 20 August 1782,
portrays her lover Tarleton as the boastful, cowardly soldier Bobadill in
Ben Jonson's *Every Man in his Humour*, triumphing over his headless three-
plumed rival Prince George. As Tarleton claims,

11.2 James Gillray, *The Thunderer*, published 20 August 1782.

often in a mere frolic I have challeng'd 20 of them, kill'd them; – challeng'd 20 more, kill'd them; 20 more, kill'd them too; & thus in a day have I kill'd 20 score; 20 score, that's 200; 200 a day, 5 days a 1000; that's – a – Zounds, I can't number them half; & all civilly & fairly with this one poor Toledo!

To which the Prince ironically replies, "I'd as lief as 20 Crowns I could *talk* as fine as you, Capt." Their exchange takes place at the Sign of the Whirligig, over which the bare-breasted Robinson spins, sexually impaled, singing out "This is the Lad'll kiss most sweet/ Who'd not love a soldier?," and tempting all who so desire to "Alamode Beef-hot every night." The whirligig, by the way, was a commonly used punishment for *army* prostitutes.

This caricature version of Mary Robinson is summed up in another anonymous print, *Scrub and Archer* (Figure 11.3), published on 25 April 1783, in which two characters from Farquhar's *The Beaux' Stratagem*, Scrub – here, as Charles Fox, the liberal Whig who befriended Robinson after the Prince rejected her and interceded with the Prince on her behalf – and Archer – here, as the Prime Minister Lord North – in the scene in which they become "sworn brothers," discuss the lady's maid Gypsey, or Mrs. Robinson, who stands beside Joshua Reynolds's portrait of Banastre Tarleton. Archer comments: "And this Col: I am afraid has Converted the Affection of your Perdita." Scrub responds: "Converted, ay perverted my dear Friend, for I am Afraid he has made her a Whore . . ."

Such representations of Mary Robinson were by no means limited to satirical cartoons. The anonymous author of the verse-epistle, *The Vis-A-Vis of Berkeley-Square*, published in London on 14 June 1783, opened with the following Dedication to "Florizel": "This poem, / on the matchless Phryne Perdita, / is most respectfully dedicated and applied, / to the great, the gay, the good, and gallant / Florizel; / as / testimony of the author's abilities, / the heroes' powers,/ and the lady's parts. / May the poet's continue to mend, / the Florizel's to propend, / and the lady's to extend . . ." The Epitaph begins:

> *Phryne* had Talents for Mankind,
> Open she was, and unconfin'd.
>   Like some free port of Trade.
> Merchants unloaded here their freight,
> And agents from each foreign state
>   Their *diff'rent Entries* made.[2]

It was not only the popular press that endorsed this reading of Perdita Robinson as a temptress or whore. The poet Peter Pindar, who later became her close friend, introduced the classical courtesan Lais thus:

11.3 *Scrub and Archer*, anonymous print published 25 April 1783.

Think of the sage who wanted a fine piece:
  Who went, in vain, five hundred miles at least,
    On Lais, a sweet *fille de joie*, to feast -
The Mrs. Robinson of Greece.[3]

If Mary Robinson was a whore, what was her husband? A cuckold obviously, but also, in the eyes of the popular press, a pimp and even a blackmailer. The anonymous "editor" (in fact, the author, now identified as Jacob Rey, a.k.a. John King or "Jew" King) of *Letters from Perdita to a Certain Israelite, and His Answers to Them* accused Thomas

Robinson of aiding his wife in fabricating her epistolary correspondence with the Prince in order to sell the letters to King George III for
a handsome sum.[4] As the Preface asserts, "The general Object of this
Publication" – which purports to be a series of love and blackmailing
letters from Perdita to her young, wealthy Jewish lover (Jacob Rey) – "is
the same as was the *original* Intent of the *Society for checking and prosecuting
Swindlers*. This species of Imposture has long infested Trade . . . it has
furnished Parliament both with ministerial Tools and patriotic
Declaimers; but it remained for Mr. and Mrs. R ———— to introduce it
into the Traffic of Love."[5] This view of Thomas Robinson as the pimp
of his young wife was incorporated by Thomas Rowlandson into his
widely disseminated aquatint of Vauxhall Gardens, in which he portrays Mary Robinson holding her husband's arm while she flirts with
the Prince beside her.

The painters of some of the most accomplished portraits of Mary
Robinson subtly convey the same interpretation. We should keep in
mind that there were many portraits of Mary Robinson – she may have
been the most often painted woman of her day, the other contender for
that honor being, not the Queen, but Lady Hamilton, who began her
career as a professional courtesan. I turn first to the most distinguished
of all the portraits of Mary Robinson, the full-length study done by
Thomas Gainsborough for the Prince of Wales in 1781 (figure 11.4).
Paying homage to Mary Robinson's widely acclaimed beauty,
Gainsborough represents Mrs. Robinson as Perdita in the eighteenth-
century rococo conception of a shepherdess's attire popularized by
Marie-Antoinette.

It is the details that communicate Gainsborough's subtle criticism of
Perdita Robinson. Her eyes are half-closed in the calculating gaze of a
professional coquette. Her skin-tone is, uniquely among her portraits, a
tawny yellow, suggesting a stereotyped "oriental" licentiousness. Her
foot seems to swing or beckon seductively. Her right hand holds a fluffy,
gauze handkerchief, a simulacrum for the pubic hair which it strategi-
cally covers, while her left hand assertively displays an open miniature.
Although the subject of this miniature was not defined by
Gainsborough, it was widely assumed to be the miniature of the Prince
of Wales by Jeremiah Meyer which, encased in diamonds and containing the infamous valentine, had been sent by Florizel to his Perdita in
1780. By flaunting this miniature, a traditional emblem of fidelity,
Gainsborough's Perdita implicitly claims to have "possessed" the young
Prince. Most suggestive, the faithful dog beside her, whose panting

11.4 Thomas Gainsborough, *Mrs. Robinson* (1781).

11.5 Sir Joshua Reynolds, *Mrs. Robinson* (1782).

tongue is exactly the same color as Perdita's lips, subtly implies her
bestial sexuality. This implication is reinforced by the rural setting in
which she sits, a nature unconstrained by those works of art – urns,
sculptures – which Gainsborough frequently includes in his portraits of
aristocratic women. Mrs. Robinson's uncivilized or immoral sexual
desire is further suggested by the snaky vine coiling among the fig leaves
on the lower right.

Other artists also portrayed Mrs. Robinson as a coquette or courtesan, although none in so highly finished a full-length portrait as Gainsborough's. Sir Joshua Reynolds, in the first of several portraits (figure 11.5), depicts Robinson in the pose and costume utilized by Rubens in his portrait of his wife. This costume functions in contradictory ways. It suggests an attempt to establish a respectable lineage for a woman now fallen on hard times, a frequent practice used by dispossessed or alienated family-members in eighteenth-century portraiture, as Marcia Pointon has reminded us.[6] At the same time, this dress is a subtle reminder – along with her half-closed, calculating eyes and slightly pursed lips – of Mary Robinson's infidelity.

This view of Mary Robinson as a woman no better than she should have been was endorsed by several of her later biographers. Even as he celebrated her acting skills, Edward Robins, the author of *Twelve Great Actresses* (1900), commented that her liaison with the Prince of Wales was a "disaster – that unsuspected catastrophe that begins with the roses of unhallowed romance, and ends with the rank weeds of folly and neglect."[7] And Lily Adams Beck, in *The Exquisite Perdita*, in 1926 summed up her career thus: "Though no courtesan in soul she had made the courtesan's choice, and must now play the part as successfully as in her lay, for from henceforth retreat there would be none."[8]

This version of Mary Robinson's life-story conformed to the preexisting social construction of actresses as, by profession, whores. As Kristina Straub has argued in *Sexual Suspects*, the cultural discourse of this period – invoking the famous example of Nell Gwyn – frequently conflated the professional actress with the professional courtesan. Because both display their female bodies in public for the arousal and gratification of male specular desire, actresses, like whores, became sexually commodified.[9] As soon as Mary Robinson went on the stage, she began to receive numerous and increasingly remunerative propositions: the Duke of Rutland offered her 600 pounds a year to become his mistress, while the Prince of Wales gave her a bond for 20,000 pounds to be paid when he came of age.

THE UNPROTECTED WIFE

The second version of Mary Robinson's life represents her as an innocent young wife whose husband fails to meet his legal, moral, and social obligations, thereby leaving her exposed to the abuses of royal power and privilege. In this narrative, the fifteen-year-old Mary Darby was "sold" into marriage by her impoverished mother to a man who took advantage of her beauty and innocence. Thomas Robinson first deceived her and her mother by claiming that he was the legal heir of his extremely wealthy "uncle," James Harris. In fact, Harris was his natural father who had no intention of supporting his impecunious, bastard son. Moreover, Thomas Robinson was an inveterate gambler and womanizer, who deceived his wife with numerous mistresses and finally led them both to financial ruin and the debtors' prison. Virtually abandoned by her husband to the predations of his libertine friends, Lord Lyttleton and Edward Fitzgerald, Mary Robinson fell easy prey, in this narrative construction of her life, to the charms of the handsome young Prince of Wales. But the Prince was no better than the other men who had taken advantage of Mary Robinson's extraordinary beauty: he promised to pay her 20,000 pounds for giving up her stage career and becoming his permanent mistress, if not his wife, but then reneged on this debt, abandoning her after a year and leaving her 5,600 pounds in debt.[10]

This is the version of Robinson's life promoted by her daughter Maria Elizabeth, who, in her preface to her mother's *Memoirs*, characterized her as "an unprotected and persecuted woman . . . the victim of calumny and misrepresentation."[11] This version was endorsed by some of Robinson's contemporaries, one of whom summed up her relationship with the Prince thus: "she attracted the notice of an illustrious character; and, being peculiarly unfortunate, as has been generally reported, in her matrimonial alliance, after a long series of such attentions from a lover such as, we apprehend, few hearts could resist, whether we consider his rank, his figure, or his accomplishments, she, in an unhappy hour of deep resentment, quitted her profession in favour of one so armed at all points to captivate and conquer."[12] And Mary Robinson herself, in a letter to John Taylor written over a decade later, on 5 October 1794, blamed both the Prince and her publishers and public for her misfortunes:

My mental labours have failed through the dishonest conduct of my publishers. My works have sold handsomely, but the profits have been theirs.

Have I not reason to be disgusted when I see him [the Prince Regent] to whom I ought to look for better fortune lavishing favours on unworthy objects, gratifying the *avarice of ignorance* and *dulness*, while I, who sacrificed reputation, an advantageous profession, friends, patronage, the brilliant hours of youth, and the conscious delight of correct conduct, am condemned to the scanty pittance bestowed on every indifferent page who holds up his ermined train of ceremony?[13]

11.6 Sir Joshua Reynolds, *Mrs. Robinson* (1784).

This is the narrative of Robinson's life followed by Sir Joshua Reynolds in his second and most sympathetic portrait of Mrs. Robinson, painted in 1784 (figure 11.6). In this image, Mary Robinson is the abandoned woman, filled with melancholy, gazing with sorrow upon a tempestuous sea and a horizon where the sun sinks and no ships appear. She is clearly an eighteenth-century Ariadne, confined upon a rock, waiting for a lover who never comes. The ghostly white pallor of her skin and powdered white hair suggest a premature aging, even oncoming death. And the striking black ribbon at her neck subtly suggests a garrote or strangling rope, even decapitation, while the exfoliating reddish ribbons at her waist suggest a deep and bleeding wound to her heart. Significantly, this particular pose of the turned-away head was technically known in the eighteenth-century painting trade as a "lost profile."

Reynolds's vision of Mary Robinson as Ariadne was endorsed by other painters of the time. Both George Englehart and Thomas Lawrence portrayed her with a brooding, slightly melancholic air. Englehart, further, posed her against Ariadne's rock, while Lawrence gave her a bandage-like headdress that suggests a woman with a wounded mind.

This sympathetic view of Robinson was adopted by many of her later biographers. J. Fitzgerald Molloy insisted that the facts of her life "show the exposed situation . . . of a female of great personal and natural attraction, exposed to the gaze of libertine rank and fashion, under the mere nominal guardianship of a neglectful and profligate husband."[14] Joseph Grego consistently condemned the Prince Regent as a Don Juan, a "heartless dissembler" with a "fickle breast."[15] And Edward Robins attacked the Prince as a "royal blackguard" who, in his treatment of his Perdita, "generally qualified himself for the vices which he was soon to possess in such abundant perfection."[16]

The Prince of Wales was further identified with the irresponsible Prince Hal of Shakespeare's *Henry IV*, first by the printmaker S. Boyne in 1784 (figure 11.7): here, "Prince Pretty-Man," boosted by Falstaff (as Charles Fox), robs the Exchequer to pay his mistresses, the foremost of whom is Mary Robinson. An anonymous novel titled *The Royal Legend: A Tale*, published in 1808, only three years before the Prince of Wales assumed the Regency, also displaces the Prince's affair with Mary Robinson onto wild Harry, the future King Henry V, and in extremely critical terms: "from the moment that the prince beheld the lovely Perdita, from that moment did he, in imagination, trample on the laws of honour and of virtue, mark her for his prey, and fix on her, though a wife and mother, as the object of sating his dawning unruly passions."[17] Moreover, the author insists, the Prince never intended to pay his bond to Perdita, since "Princes are not like other men; for in these days they seem to trample on the rules of justice and honour, and instead of becoming obedient to the laws, they make them subservient to their own purposes."[18]

The Royal Legend and Boyne's print powerfully uncover the political

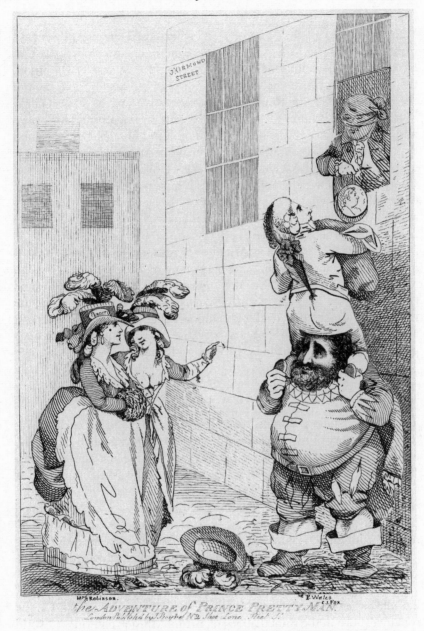

Figure 11.7 S. Boyne, *The Adventure of Prince Pretty-Man*, published 24 March 1784.

issues at stake in the narration of Robinson's affair with the Prince of
Wales. The story of the "unprotected" wife abused by royal power pro-
motes a Jacobin narrative denouncing a monarchy or *ancien régime* that
has abused its constitutionally limited powers. In the case of Robinson,
this political narrative was employed by educated professional men of
the middle classes – by Reynolds and other artists such as James Gillray
in his satiric caricatures of the Prince Regent, by lawyers and historians
and businessmen – to denounce the moral and financial excesses and
depredations of aristocratic men, of such libertines as Lords Lyttleton
and Fitzgerald and Malden, the Prince's emissary, as well as of the
Prince himself. Here the political attack is mounted in the putative name
of female innocence and vulnerability – the "unprotected" damsel in
distress, Britannia herself – but it functions as a claim for the rights of
middle-class professional men.

The image of Robinson as Ariadne suggests, however, that this political script can also be employed by women against the class of men.
Modern feminist readers of the narrative of Robinson's life could
equally well see it as the script of patriarchal privilege, in which the
husband as well as the royal lover impoverishes, deceives, betrays, and
abandons his wife. In this political narrative, then, sexual as well as class
politics are written over the body of Mary Robinson.

TRUE LOVE

The third version of Robinson's sexuality available during her day was
the oft-told story of two "starcrossed" lovers. In this version, both Perdita
and Florizel are deeply in love. For Florizel, it is his first and most passionate love; for Perdita, it is her first true love (since she claimed never
to have loved her husband). And their love would have endured, so this
version goes, had not the Prince's uncle, the Duke of Cumberland, led
him astray, first by insisting that he could never "permanently" ally
himself with an actress and a commoner, and secondly by introducing
him to the even more seductive wiles of an eminent courtesan, Mrs.
Armstead, who tempted him away from his unsuspecting Perdita.

This is the version of her sexual desire constructed by Mary Robinson
herself, in her *Memoirs*. She portrays herself as the victim of a Gothic
romance, born in the ruined abbey of Bristol Minster, entering a "world
of duplicity and sorrow" with a "sensitive and perpetually aching heart,"
destined by fate to love and to suffer through no fault of her own.[19]
Despite her husband's infidelities and the numerous propositions, even

the attempted rape, of the libertine Lords Lyttleton and Fitzgerald, she swears, "God can bear witness of the purity of my soul; even surrounded by temptations, and mortified by neglect."[20]

Not until Fate intervenes – for as she says, "we cannot command our affections" – does her loyalty to her husband waver. But when the Prince relentlessly pursues her through his agent Lord Malden, when she is finally convinced of his "inviolable affection," when she finds it impossible to be "insensible to all his powers of attraction," then she is finally overwhelmed by sincere and passionate love.[21] The Prince's love, she insists, was equally sincere; "the public avowal of our mutual attachment" was, therefore, inevitable. Only "destiny" could end such a love: as she insists, "the tones of his voice, breaking on the silence of the night, have often appeared to my entranced senses like more than mortal melody. Often have I lamented the distance which destiny had placed between us: how would my soul have idolized such a *husband*!"[22] She adamantly denies any motive other than disinterested love; her story, she insists, is that of "romantic credulity" in which both she and the Prince are finally betrayed.[23] She is the victim of "female malice," of "calumny and persecution";[24] the Prince is the "victim" of the "delusive visions" that "betray" royalty into believing they can set aside their royal obligations in order to fulfill their private desires. As she sums up her view of the Prince after he has abruptly ended their relationship:

Heaven can witness the truth of my assertion, even in this moment of complete despair, when oppression bowed me to the earth, I blamed not the Prince. I did then, and ever shall, consider his mind as nobly and honourably organized, nor could I teach myself to believe, that a heart the seat of so many virtues, could possibly become inhuman and unjust. I had been taught from my infancy to believe that elevated stations are surrounded by delusive visions, which glitter but to dazzle, like an unsubstantial meteor, and flatter to betray. With legions of these phantoms it has been my fate to encounter; I have been unceasingly marked by their persecutions, and shall at length become their victim.[25]

As early as the summer of 1781, Mary Robinson had insisted upon this interpretation of her affair. As Lord Malden wrote to the Prince of Wales during his negotiations with Mrs. Robinson for the return of the Prince's letters and bond in August 1781:

Mrs. R. delivered to Lord Malden in trust all letters written to her by the P. of Wales. She is shocked by the idea in Col. Hotham's letter that the money mentioned is in consideration of return of these papers. Her great inducement in delivering up the letters is to restore H. R. H.'s [His Royal Highness George III] peace of mind, and Ld. Malden wd. like this to be acknowledged in writing to make it clear that Mrs. R. has not sold papers so dear to her.[26]

11.8 George Romney, *Mrs. Robinson* (1781).

This construction of Robinson's story was endorsed by other writers and painters of the day. Peter Pindar, in his "Elegy on Mrs. Robinson," hailed her as the "DAUGHTER OF LOVE." The painter George Romney portrayed her in 1781 as a widow (figure 11.8), a woman of sincere convictions fated to survive without love. Here, she appears in demure dress, as a much older, self-confident woman, her skin still a pure white, her cheeks still suffused with the blush of innocence, her breast and hair modestly covered, a muff discreetly concealing her hands. The parallel image of the Prince as a sincere and innocent young man capable of loving truly was widely disseminated in a series of miniatures of the young Prince by Richard Cosway.

Later biographers have, on the whole, favored this version of Mary Robinson's life. Stanley Makower, in *Perdita – A Romance in Biography* (1908), described the Prince as "a nature all romance and poetry," "a youth in the first glow of manly folly," while Mary Robinson was "no desperate adventuress, but an ill-starred lady" who felt "an unconquerable love" for the Prince and whose apparent "hardness" was but "a thin layer set by experience upon the unfathomable depths of her romantic nature."[27]

The most extreme version of this narrative of two "star-crossed lovers" originally appeared in 1814, in Pierce Egan's *The Mistress of Royalty; or, The Loves of Florizel and Perdita*. Egan first praises the Prince in hyperbolic terms: "the overwhelming, dazzling splendor of her impassioned, illustrious admirer, unhackneyed in the ways of intrigue, breathing forth the sentiments of genuine affection . . . united with a taste superlatively grand, not only rendered him confident, but eloquent and persuasive."[28] He then justifies Perdita's love for this Prince:

Flattered to the very utmost in obtaining the conquest of the distinguished F[lorizel], a conquest exciting envy in most of the female breasts in the kingdom, who were sighing to entangle him in their chains – the too susceptible Perdita was placed in no common situation. *PROPRIETY* was at length lulled off its guard by insinuating palliatives. *FORTITUDE* was decoyed from its post, by the opening splendour and fascination of the scene, *REFLECTION* was at too great a distance to come up in time to offer any advice upon this critical occasion. So that the formal *WIFE* was soon forgotten in the elevated *MISTRESS* . . .[29]

Egan ends with a poem, from which I quote only a few lines:

> The trav'ller, if *HE* chance to stray,
> May turn uncensur'd to his way;
> Polluted streams again are pure,
> And deepest wounds admit a cure;
> But woman! no redemption knows,
> The wounds of honour never close.[30]
> . . .
> Shall vertue's flame no more return?
> No more the virgin splendour burn?
> No more the ravag'd garden blow
> With spring's succeeding blossom? – No.
> Pity may mourn, but not restore,
> And woman falls to rise no more.[31]

I quote Egan's rather feeble poetic efforts to remind us of the generic convention that finally controls this narrative of Robinson's sexuality. In her *Memoirs*, Mary Robinson set out to retell the tale of Tristan and Isolde or of Romeo and Juliet, but the story she actually tells is that of a loving female whose lover, although initially devoted to her, nonetheless voluntarily deserted her. This narrative thus echoes the two poems Mary Robinson tells us she memorized in her childhood – John Gay's ballad of a maid "all melancholy lying, / Thus wail'd she for her Dear" ("'Twas when the Seas were roaring") and Alexander Pope's *Elegy to the Memory of an Unfortunate Lady*. This is also, of course, the plot of such later works as *Anna Karenina* and *Emma Bovary*. As these parallel narratives forcefully remind us, the pre-scripted narrative conclusion of the story Mary Robinson intended to write of her sexuality – the sincerely loving but cruelly rejected woman – always ends with the death of the fallen woman. But Mary Robinson did not die, at least not till twenty years later, which brings me to the fourth and last version of her life-story.

THE FEMALE ARTIST

In this narrative, Mary Robinson transforms her suffering into enduring art. Robinson was a writer before she was an actress: she published her first volume, *Poems*, in 1775 and a long poem, *Captivity*, in 1778, on her experiences in a debtors' prison. In these literary works, as in the poems she admired as a youth, especially William Mason's "Elegy on the Death of Lady Coventry," female poetic sensibility is constructed in the way that Burke had recommended in his essay on *The Sublime and the Beautiful* (1757). Burke equates the "beautiful" with a female voice of soft, delicate melancholy, of gentle suffering, and patient resignation.[32] Female poetic creation is identical with the expression of emotional pain.

In her career as a writer, Mary Robinson deliberately exploited this image of the female poetess as one who has loved, suffered, lost, yet lived to tell the tale in notes of melancholic sweetness. She publicly identified herself with Sappho. In 1796, she published a sequence of love-sonnets from *Sappho to Phaon* (note that Robinson directs *her* Sappho's love poems to a male lover). As one of her contemporary readers insisted, Robinson "is entitled to be considered as a *legitimate* poetic daughter of the Lesbian Muse, whose loves and sorrows she has so sweetly sung to the British lyre. Nor shall we have one reader, gifted with a poetic spirit, or good taste, who will not hold him or herself indebted to us for thus confirming Mrs. Robinson's claims, and daring to place her on the Sapphic throne even

11.9 Engraving after Angelica Kauffmann, *The British Sappho*.

with a [Charlotte] Smith or a [Anna] Seward."[33] And Coleridge hailed
her as a poet and woman "of undoubted genius," singling out for praise
the "fascinating metre" and "new and very distinct" images of her poem
The Haunted Beach.[34]

This is the version of Robinson painted by the only woman who did
a portrait of her, Angelica Kauffmann, the leading female artist of
the day (figure 11.9). Titling her portrait *The British Sappho*, Kauffmann

portrayed Robinson as the icon of female classical beauty: austere, pure, garbed in Greek peasant robes. Robinson here becomes what her early poetry constructs: a classically idealized image of the female artist as the conveyor of beauty and truth. Her piercing eyes look outward at the viewer in cool assessment. She is the owner, not the object, of the gaze.

The representation of herself as above all an artist is also the self Robinson chose to project in her *Memoirs*. In contrast to a masculine Romantic myth of authorship, a myth of original genius, the *Memoirs* develop a myth of female authorship as maternal creation, an authorship that combines intense feminine sensibility with biological motherhood. Robinson tells us that she began her literary efforts in order to support her newborn daughter. She continued them in a room where "my table was spread with papers, and everything around me presented the mixed confusion of a study and a nursery."[35] Throughout the first half of her *Memoirs*, she argues that it was her destiny to love too credulously, to be deceived and betrayed, to suffer; but equally, it was her maternal responsibility to translate that suffering into poems and novels that provided "solace."[36]

Robinson's *Memoirs* are themselves a self-conscious artistic creation, one that translates the genre of Sappho's love-poetry into the genre of prose-autobiography. Robinson deliberately represents her life as a repetition of Sappho's, of the female artist who loves and loses her lover to a rival. At the same time she employs the genre of the gothic romance, with its plot of the tortured, long-suffering heroine who is at last enabled to speak her own story to a sympathetic listener, in this case her own daughter. Imitating the gothic novels of Sophia Lee, Ann Radcliffe, and Charlotte Dacre Byrne, Robinson constructs her own life as that of a persecuted heroine, born and raised in a stormy world of terrifying torments, destined to end, as her daughter concludes this narrative, where she began, "a prisoner in her own house . . . deprived of every solace but that which could be obtained by the activity of her mind, which at length sunk under excessive exertion and inquietude."[37]

But, when Maria Elizabeth completes her mother's *Memoirs*, taking up the narrative halfway through, at the moment when Robinson's affair with the Prince is consummated, she replaces the image of her mother as a loving and lovelorn Sappho with the image of the female artist as exclusively a mother. She reduces Mary Robinson's sixteen-year affair with Banastre Tarleton to a single footnote. She insists that Robinson's writing career was always secondary to her maternal duties, fitted into the interstices of household management and childcare. It began in earnest, Maria records, only as a relief from the anxieties aroused by her daughter's illness and the cares of daily nursing:

Every device which a kind and skilful nurse could invent to cheer and amuse her charge, was practised by this affectionate mother, during the melancholy period of her daughter's confinement. In the intervals of more active exertion, the silence of a sick chamber proving favourable to the muse, Mrs. Robinson poured forth those poetic effusions, which have done so much honour to her genius and decked her tomb with unfading laurels.[38]

Not only does Maria Robinson re-situate the origin of her mother's creative writing in maternal solicitude and domestic duty, but she also develops an aesthetic theory which values certain kinds of poetry over others. She condemns Mary Robinson's earlier poems as an "error" because they adhered to the "false metaphors and rhapsodical extravagance" popularized by the Della Cruscan poets Robert Merry and Hannah Cowley, who celebrated the refinements of an extreme erotic sensibility, while she praises those poems which show a maternal concern for the sufferings of the unfortunate. She singles out as especially "admirable" Mary Robinson's *The Maniac*, which was based on an incident in which a homeless and crazed old man, "*mad Jemmy*," was hounded by a crowd of people: "The situation of this miserable being seized her imagination and became the subject of her attention . . . She would gaze upon his venerable but emaciated countenance with sensations of awe almost reverential, while the barbarous persecutions of the thoughtless crowd never failed to agonize her feelings."[39]

After summarizing her mother's extensive publications, year by year, Maria Robinson ends the *Memoirs* by subsuming the female artist completely into the mother, concluding that "the benevolent temper, the filial piety and the *maternal tenderness of Mrs. Robinson* are exemplified in the preceding pages, as her genius, her talents, the fertility of her imagination and the powers of her mind, are displayed in her productions, the popularity of which at least affords a presumption of their merit."[40] Situating her mother entirely within a family circle, Maria Elizabeth focuses the second half of the *Memoirs* on Mary Robinson's loyalty to *her* mother, Mary Seys Darby, who died in 1793, in the house of that daughter "who, though by far the *least wealthy* of her children, had proved herself through life the most *attentive* and *affectionate*."[41] So insistent is Maria Elizabeth on this theme that she devotes the last page of the *Memoirs* to a poem by Mary Robinson written on her brother's death, a brother who is elsewhere ignored in the history of Robinson's life. Not to be outdone, Maria Elizabeth repeatedly stresses her *own* loyalty to

Mary Robinson, a filial duty so complete that – as she twice tells us – she gave up a handsome fortune to remain with her mother.

Mary Robinson had represented the female artist as both lover and mother. Her daughter transformed that narrative into a construction of the female artist as only a devoted mother. In thus rewriting her mother's life as that of a devoted daughter, sister, and mother, as Linda Peterson has suggested, Maria Elizabeth imposed on her mother's life the new middle-class ideal of woman as an angel in the house.

CONCLUSIONS

If we turn to Mary Robinson's own poetry and fiction in an effort better to understand her subjectivity, we find an equally diverse and contradictory series of authorial self-images. Robinson's writings range over an enormous range of genres, subjects, and authorial stances. At one moment she is "Laura Maria," the Della Cruscan poet of refined sensibility, weeping for her lost lover in a language of calculated artifice. At another, she is the voice of Rousseau, the man of feeling and revolutionary sympathies, as in her 1797 novel *Walsingham*, in which the protagonist is the victim both of an overly intense and often paranoid imagination and of the cruel deceptions of a malicious enemy, who draws on the powers of aristocratic privilege to deny him his birthright. In her *Lyrical Tales* of 1800, her answer to the *Lyrical Ballads* of Wordsworth and Coleridge, she employs the voice of perceptive social satire and the mock-heroic, as well as that of sympathy for the sufferings of the oppressed. In her self-idealizing autobiographical novel of 1799, *The Natural Daughter*, she takes up the moderate feminist position of rational common sense and female independence, enabling her protagonist Martha both to escape her tyrannical husband and to preserve her reputation for chastity. And in her militantly feminist tract, *Thoughts on the Condition of Women* of 1798, she assumes the voice of Mary Wollstonecraft, angrily attacking the sexual double standard and demanding equality for women.

Not only does her authorial stance shift, so does her name. Mary Robinson adopted at least nine different pseudonyms during her writing career, ranging from the Della Cruscan "Laura Maria" and the feminine "Julia" and "Portia," through the eroticized "Sappho" and "Lesbia" and the cross-dressed "Oberon," to the feminist "Ann Randall" and the old crone of the *Morning Post*, "Tabitha Bramble." As Judith Pascoe has observed, this practice of using widely disparate pseudonyms publicly produced an authorial self "constructed from a mélange of antithetical cultural forces" rather than the sequential, coherently developing authorial self represented by Wordsworth in *The Prelude.*[42]

What are we finally to make of this bewilderingly diverse exhibition of contradictory poetic personae and texts? Here I can offer only a few speculative conclusions. First, we might think of Mary Robinson as initiating that particular conception of the poetical character later so well defined by Keats: of the poet as a chameleon, as one who "has no identity" but is "continually informing and filling some other Body."[43] I would, therefore, argue against Linda Peterson's assertion that Robinson, in her *Memoirs*, initially embraced a masculine Romantic myth of authorship as produced by a solitary, originating genius.[44] I would suggest instead that Robinson, drawing on the etymological association of genius with genial, associates "genius" with sensibility or the empathic capacity to enter into the feelings and character of other people, a capacity that she genders as feminine.

From a historical perspective, we might argue that Mary Robinson embodies what Foucault would call a product of a set of pre-existing master-narratives. In other words, her subjectivity is always already an interpellation (to use Althusser's formulation) into already written ideological texts. From this perspective, Mary Robinson becomes a vivid example of the way in which individual agency, and especially female agency, is necessarily subsumed into pre-scripted sexual and gender narratives (such as "the woman as whore," "the woman as angel in the house," etc.). This historicist reading is supported by Robinson's *Memoirs*, in which she inscribes herself as a victim, a victim of her innate temperament, her "too acute sensibility";[45] her appearance; and above all of social circumstances beyond her control. Or we might argue, instead, that Mary Robinson's production of her self as a set of written and visual texts was a conscious and calculated process of self-commodification – that Mary Robinson, much like the poet and novelist Letitia Landon who followed her, was producing what she knew would sell in the cultural marketplace of her day.

Whether she commodified herself deliberately or not, the one conclusion we can safely draw, I think, is that Mary Robinson consciously created what we now call a "postmodernist subjectivity," a concept of the self as entirely fluid, unstable, and performative.[46] Going far beyond the "double-self" of Renaissance self-fashioners who distinguished between their public and private personae, Mary Robinson introduced to her time the possibility that a knowable self, and especially that coherent, stable, and predictable subjectivity so insistently (and anxiously) promoted by William Wordsworth and the school of developmental psychology he heralded, does not exist. This possibility was shrewdly – if spitefully – recognized by Laetitia Matilda Hawkins, who, in 1824, insisted that Robinson's entire life was a performance:

> Our Perdita . . . acquired a remarkable facility in adapting her deportment to her dress . . . Today she was a *paysanne*, with her straw hat tied at the back of her head, looking as if too new to what she passed, to know what she looked at. Yesterday she, perhaps, had been the dressed *belle* of Hyde Park, trimmed, powdered, patched, painted to the utmost power of rouge and white lead; tomorrow, she would be the cravatted Amazon of the riding house: but be she what she might, the hats of the fashionable promenaders swept to the ground as she passed.[47]

That Robinson was aware of the possibility that any self is *only* a performance is vividly recorded in her novel *Walsingham*. Here she originated the idea that a person is a "polygraph." The polygraph was a late eighteenth-century invention, a mechanical device consisting of two pencils or pens connected by an adjustable rod, which enabled one to make an exact copy of whatever one was writing or drawing. In *Walsingham*, Lord Kencarth, an idle young man of fashion, boasts that he has not one but two polygraphs, explaining that

> a polygraph is a fellow that apes one's dress and manners as close as one's shadow: one that is up to all our gossip; is sick, lame, blind, gay, grave, in and out of condition, in imitation of his prototype. Why, a true polygraph would break an arm, fracture a leg, knock out an eye, or starve himself into a decline, rather than lose a single trait of his noble original. . . .[48]

As Sharon Setzer has noted, Robinson then carries this notion of the self-as-mere-copy one step further: the self that the polygraph copies may itself be a fiction.[49] Lord Kencarth's "best polygraph," we learn, has perished because he aped a lie. As Kencarth explains,

> News arrived from Bath that I was down of a fever with little hopes of getting about again. Queer my sconce, if my polygraph didn't get drunk five nights following, till his pulse was up to a physician's . . . poor graphy was taken in, kept his bed three days, and hopped the twig on the fourth, queer my nobility! . . . I was obliged to bury my ghost, lest he should continue to frighten the Dowagers, and set me down as a dead letter on the list of knowing ones.[50]

Kencarth fears, and rightly, that a living self may be only a letter, a cipher, a fictive script, and a dead one at that!

If, in Mary Robinson's view, the very self is a copy, a performance, a simulacrum, then her authentic sexuality and subjectivity are as "lost"

11.10 John Downman, drawing, *Mrs. "Perdita" Robinson.*

to us as her culturally assigned name, "Perdita" – "the lost one" – would suggest. Her identity – personal and authorial – can be nothing more nor less than the sum total of the scripts she performed both in public and in private, in her own narratives and in those of others. We must therefore think of Mary Robinson as Biddy Martin thinks of Lou Andreas-Salome, as comprised of a "concrete historical site and a set of texts," rather than as a person or an author.[51] In the case of Mary Robinson, I would argue, any distinction between the self *as* art and the self *in* art collapses. Robinson was to her day what Madonna perhaps is to ours, nothing more nor less than "The Fair Celebrity" – a set of visual and verbal public texts. I, therefore, end with this drawing by John Downman (figure 11.10), which gives us Mrs. Mary Robinson as the remote, alluring, fashionable, but forever inaccessible "Perdita" – the woman who is always already constructed by the gaze of her admirers and the gendered scripts of eighteenth-century England.

NOTES

1. On the general subject of representation, whether of self or other, I have consulted the following works: Bella Brodzki and Celeste Schenck, eds., *Life/Lines: Theorizing Women's Autobiography* (Ithaca, N.Y.: Cornell University Press, 1988); Nancy Chodorow, *The Reproduction of Mothering* (Berkeley: University of California Press, 1978); Joan DeJean, *Fictions of Sappho, 1546–1937* (Chicago: University of Chicago Press, 1989); Paul John Eakin, *Touching the World: Reference in Autobiography* (Princeton: Princeton University Press, 1992), and *Fictions in Autobiography: Studies in the Art of Self-Invention* (Princeton: Princeton University Press, 1985); Jan Fergus and Janice Farrar Thaddeus, "Women, Publishers, and Money, 1790–1820," *Studies in Eighteenth Century Culture* 17 (1987): 191–207; Georges Gusdorf, "Conditions and Limits of Autobiography," in *Autobiography: Essays Theoretical and Critical*, ed. James Olney (Princeton: Princeton University Press, 1980); Estelle Jelinek, ed., *Women's Autobiography: Essays in Criticism* (Bloomington: Indiana University Press, 1980); Philippe Lejeune, *On Autobiography*, trans. Katherine Leary (Minneapolis: University of Minnesota Press, 1989); Mary G. Mason, "The Other Voice: Autobiographies of Women Writers," in *Life/Lines*, ed. Brodzki and Schenck, 19–44; Felicity Nussbaum, *The Autobiographical Subject: Gender and Ideology in Eighteenth Century England* (Baltimore: Johns Hopkins University Press, 1989); James Olney, *Metaphors of Self: The Meaning of Autobiography* (Princeton: Princeton University Press, 1972); Gill Perry, "'The British Sappho': Borrowed Identities and the Representation of Women Artists in Late Eighteenth-Century British Art," *Oxford Art Journal* 18:1 (1995): 44–57; Sidonie Smith, *A Poetics of Women's Autobiography: Marginality and the Fictions of Self-Representation* (Bloomington: Indiana University Press,

1987); Donna C. Stanton, ed., *The Female Autograph* (Chicago: University of Chicago Press, 1984). On Mary Robinson, I have consulted: Robert D. Bass, *The Green Dragoon: The Lives of Banastre Tarleton and Mary Robinson* (New York: Henry Holt, 1957); Chris Cullens, "Mrs. Robinson and the Masquerade of Womanliness," in *Body and Text in the Eighteenth Century*, ed. Veronica Kelly and Dorothea Von Mucke (Stanford, Calif.: Stanford University Press, 1994), 266–341; John Ingamells, *Mrs. Robinson and Her Portraits* (London: Wallace Collection, 1978); John C. Mendenhall, "Mary Robinson (1758–1800)," *The University of Pennsylvania Library Chronicle* (March 1936): 2–10; Marguerite Steen, *The Lost One: A Biography of Mary (Perdita) Robinson* (London: Methuen, 1937).

2. *The Vis-A-Vis of Berkeley-Square: or, A Wheel off Mrs. W**T**N's Carriage. / Inscribed to Florizel* (London, 14 June 1783).

3. Peter Pindar, "More Lyric Odes to the Royal Academicians," Ode VI, lines 49–52; in *The Works of Peter Pindar*, ed. John Wolcot, vol. 1 (London, 1830), 48.

4. *Letters from Perdita to a Certain Israelite, and His Answers to Them* (London: Printed for J. Fielding, W. Kent, J. Stockdale and J. Sewell, 1781). In private conversation, 29 October 1996, Iain McCalman identified the author of this work as the "Al Capone of London," the notorious Jewish blackmailer and radical publisher Jacob Rey, better known as John or "Jew" King.

5. *Letters from Perdita*, Preface.

6. Marcia Pointon, *Hanging the Head: Portraiture and Social Formation in Eighteenth-Century England* (New Haven and London: Yale University Press, 1993), 62.

7. Edward Robins, *Twelve Great Actresses* (New York and London: G. P. Putnam's Sons, 1900), 245.

8. Lily Moresby Adams Beck [E. Barrington, pseud.], *The Exquisite Perdita* (New York: Dodd, Mead and Co., 1926), 363.

9. Kristina Straub, *Sexual Suspects: Eighteenth-Century Players and Sexual Ideology* (Princeton: Princeton University Press, 1992), 89–108.

10. Although Mary Robinson later claimed that her debts amounted to over 7,000 pounds, at the time the Prince ended their affair, she told his emissary Lord Malden that her debts amounted to "5,600 and odd pounds": Lord Malden to Lord Southampton, 24 August 1781, letters from and to the Prince of Wales and Viscount Malden, and correspondence between Viscount Malden, Lord Southampton, and Colonel Hotham concerning Mrs. Robinson and the Prince of Wales, 31 July–5 September 1781, Hertfordshire Record Office, nos. 294–312, National Register of Archives, no. 7244 (cited hereafter N.R.A. 7244). The Prince paid her 5000 pounds for the return of all his letters (Colonel Hotham to Lord Malden, 5 September 1781, N.R.A. 7244: 310), but her request for a 500 pound annuity in lieu of the Prince's bond for 20,000 pounds was not granted until after the Prince came of age in 1783 and Charles Fox interceded on her behalf.

11. Mary Robinson, *Memoirs of the Late Mrs. Robinson Written by Herself* (1801), ed. Walter Lewis (London: Cobden-Sanderson, 1930), v, cited hereafter as Robinson, *Memoirs*.

12. Cited by Walter Lewis in his introduction to *ibid.*, vii–viii.

13. Cited by J. Fitzgerald Molloy in his introduction to *Memoirs of Mary Robinson* (London and Philadelphia, 1895), xii–xiii.

14. *Ibid.*, v.

15. Joseph Grego, "'Perdita' and Her Painters: Portraits of Mrs. Mary Robinson," *The Connoisseur* 5 (1903): 107, 99.

16. Robins, *Twelve Great Actresses*, 250.

17. *The Royal Legend: A Tale* (London, 1808), 42.

18. *Ibid.*, 59.

19. Robinson, *Memoirs*, 2.

20. *Ibid.*, 58.

21. *Ibid.*, 128, 127.

22. *Ibid.*, 138, 137.

23. *Ibid.*, 146.

24. *Ibid.*, 155.

25. *Ibid.*, 148.

26. Lord Malden to the Prince of Wales, August 1781, N. R. A. 7244: 296.

27. Stanley V. Makower, *Perdita: A Romance in Biography* (London: Hutchinson & Co., 1908), 208, 237, 270, 285, 187.

28. *The Mistress of Royalty; or, the Loves of Florizel and Perdita*, ed. Pierce Egan (London, 1814), 14.

29. *Ibid.*, 16–17.

30. *Ibid.*, 13.

31. *Ibid.*, 18, lines 1–2, 7–12

32. On Burke's construction of female beauty and the adoption of Burke's category by the female poets of the Romantic period, see Anne K. Mellor, *Romanticism and Gender* (New York: Routledge, 1993), ch. 6.

33. Cited by Lewis in the introduction to Robinson, *Memoirs*, viii.

34. Samuel Taylor Coleridge to Southey, 25 January 1800, in *Collected Letters of Samuel Taylor Coleridge*, ed. Earl Leslie Griggs (Oxford: Clarendon Press, 1956).

35. Robinson, *Memoirs*, 107.

36. *Ibid.*, 168.

37. *Ibid.*, 181.

38. *Ibid.*, 165.

39. *Ibid.*, 173.

40. *Ibid.*, 194 (my italics).

41. *Ibid.*, 179.

42. Judith Pascoe, "Mary Robinson and the Literary Marketplace," in *Romantic Women Writers: Voices and Countervoices*, ed. Paula R. Feldman and Theresa M. Kelley (Hanover, N.H., and London: University Press of New England, 1995), 264.

43. John Keats to Richard Woodhouse, 27 October 1818, in *The Letters of John Keats*, ed. Maurice Buxton Forman (London: Oxford University Press, 4th edn., 1931; 1952).

44. Linda H. Peterson, "Becoming an Author: Mary Robinson's *Memoirs* and the Origins of the Woman Artist's Autobiography," in *Revisioning Romanticism: British Women Writers, 1776–1837*, ed. Carol Shiner Wilson and Joel Haefner (Philadelphia: University of Pennsylvania Press, 1994), 37.
45. Robinson, *Memoirs*, 6.
46. Eleanor Ty has compared Mary Robinson's subjectivity to Julia Kristeva's concept of the "questionable subject-in-process" in an article that came to my attention after this essay was first given as a lecture at the Clark Library, UCLA, on 11 February 1995. See Eleanor Ty, "Engendering a Female Subject: Mary Robinson's (Re)Presentations of the Self," *English Studies in Canada* 21:4 (December 1995): 407–31, here, 414.
47. Laetitia Matilda Hawkins, *Memoirs, Anecdotes, Facts, and Opinions*, 2 vols. (London: Longman and Rivington, 1824), II: 24.
48. Mary G. Robinson, *Walsingham; or, the Pupil of Nature*, 4 vols. (London, 1798; 2nd edn., London: Lane, Newman and Co., 1805), IV: 10.
49. Sharon Setzer, "The Dying Game: Crossdressing in Mary Robinson's *Walsingham*," paper delivered at the 1996 Interdisciplinary Nineteenth-Century Studies Conference.
50. Robinson, *Walsingham*, 4: 280
51. Biddy Martin, *Woman and Modernity: The (Life)-Styles of Lou Andreas-Salome* (Ithaca and London: Cornell University Press, 1991), 2.

CHAPTER TWELVE

After Sir Joshua

Richard Wendorf

What happens when a painter dies? This is a simple and, I think, a fundamental question that is rarely posed and even less frequently answered. "When Sr Joshua Reynolds died," William Blake wrote in his edition of Reynolds's collected works,

> All Nature was degraded:
> The King dropd a tear into the Queens Ear:
> And all his Pictures Faded.[1]

Blake's sly response, to which I shall return later in this chapter, betrays envy and covetousness even though Blake himself anticipated such a charge in a squib he entered in his notebook:

> These Verses were written by a very Envious Man
> Who whatever likeness he may have to Michael Angelo
> Never can have any to Sir Jehoshuan.[2]

Blake took no pains, however, to conceal his anger and righteous indignation and, in his marginal commentary, as Lawrence Lipking has noted, he exorcizes the demon of Sir Joshua "with magic and art," thereby taking possession of his book:[3]

While Sr Joshua was rolling in Riches Barry was Poor & Unemployd except by his own Energy[,] Mortimer was calld a Madman & only Portrait Painting applauded & rewarded by the Rich & Great. Reynolds & Gainsborough Blotted & Blurred One against the other & Divided all the English World between them[.] Fuseli Indignant almost hid himself – I am hid.[4]

Not quite. Death is a compelling, even liberating psychological and cultural force, and the simple fact of death often discharges latent criticism (and even admiration) from the closet. Blake's marginal commentary was written roughly fifteen years following Reynolds's death, in response to Edmond Malone's sympathetic and ideologically conservative memoir: "A Mock! . . . A Mock! . . . A Lie! . . . Villainy! a Lie! . . . This Whole Book was Written to Serve Political Purposes."[5] But in the so-called Rossetti Manuscript (the notebook in which Blake sketched at the

12.1 William Blake, "The Rossetti Manuscript," MS. p. 74.

time of Reynolds's death in 1792) the amiable visage of the President of the Royal Academy appears at the top of a page strewn with characteristic Blakean figures (figure 12.1).[6] It seems that even the iconoclastic Blake could not entirely suppress Reynolds's countenance: Sir Joshua's image has an eerie afterlife, surrounded by the mythic figures of Blake's imagination, including a Job-like head to which his own portrait is intriguingly attached.

Even Reynolds's closest friends and admirers discovered that his death
provided them with the emotional distance to write fully and carefully
about their colleague's failings. Only a few minutes following Reynolds's
death, Edmund Burke noted that his friend's humility, modesty, and
candor never forsook him, "even on surprise or provocation, nor was the
least degree of arrogance or assumption visible to the most scrutinizing
eye, in any part of his Conduct or discourse."[7] Burke wrote these lines
as he sat in Reynolds's house in Leicester Square with one of the
painter's nieces sitting at his side. Several years later, however, he would
remember that Sir Joshua was timid in society, and that – in his intellectual life – he betrayed a propensity for generalizing that could not be supported by what Burke called "the variety of principles which operate . . .
in the human mind and in every human Work."[8]

Burke wrote as a close friend, but also as one of the three executors of
Reynolds's will. Burke served as the public voice of the deceased
painter's family and as guardian to Mary Palmer, the niece who served
as Reynolds's principal housekeeper and companion during his later
years and who, following her uncle's death, married an Irish peer, the
fifth Earl of Inchiquin (later created Marquess of Thomond). Edmond
Malone, the Shakespearean editor who had been involved in the
Herculean task of keeping Boswell sober enough to complete his life of
Johnson, would also serve as Reynolds's literary executor. Philip
Metcalfe, a brewer, handled the financial aspects of Reynolds's will and
estate, and it is principally his cache of documents, now preserved in the
Hyde Collection at Four Oaks Farm, that provides us with an unparalleled view of the political maneuvering, attention to detail, and
financial considerations concerning one of the most important funerals
of late eighteenth-century London.

In taking these various duties upon themselves, Reynolds's executors
were responding to their friend's role not just as a painter, but as the head
of a household, as a man of letters, and as a public figure who had pre-
sided over – and often dominated – the artistic life of the nation for
almost thirty years. Much of what they were called upon to do, in other
words, would have been consistent with their responsibilities as executors of the estate of any prominent cultural figure, particularly that of a
writer. And literary estates (unlike the remains of a painter's studio) have
received a good deal of scholarly attention, most recently by Michael
Millgate in *Testamentary Acts* and by Ian Hamilton in *Keepers of the Flame*.[9]

The focus of Millgate's fine book, for instance, is on "the ways in
which writers famous in their own time have sought in old age to exert

some degree of posthumous control over their personal and literary rep-
utations – over the extent and nature of future biographical investigation and exposure, and over the interpretation and textual integrity of
their published works." Millgate skillfully shows how the longevity of an
author makes not only *self*-reappraisal possible, but also affords writers
the opportunity to "enforce such a reappraisal and seek to ensure its continuation beyond their own lifetimes – to reconstruct, in short, the entire
self-construct known as, say, Robert Browning."[10] Millgate therefore
argues with some eloquence for the significance of the years immediately preceding a writer's death, which, although they have often been

dismissed as periods of passive fame, physical decay, and unelected creative
silence, may in fact deserve rigorous scrutiny as the locations of deliberate, comprehensive, and effectual rewritings of both texts and lives – as well as of testamentary acts with profound and often unanticipated consequences both for
future scholarship and for the long-term prosperity of the author's own work
and reputation.[11]

But the moral of Millgate's instructive tales (he examines the late careers
of Tennyson, Hardy, and Henry James in addition to Browning's) – and
of Ian Hamilton's as well – is that no amount of personal intention,
careful planning, or sympathetic collaboration can guarantee that an
author's wishes will finally be honored or realized. Millgate points out,
in fact, that none of his four subjects "proved to possess any special gift
for foreseeing the subsequent pattern of events, or any privileged immu-
nity to the always tragi-comic ironies of human mischancing."[12]

The examination of testamentary acts also suggests the close affinities
that bind together an author's literary remains (unfinished or unpublished work in particular), his or her personal papers (the raw stuff of
biography), and the existing literary corpus (which might be augmented
and/or revised in a collected, "standard" edition). It is therefore not
unusual to find a close friend or relative acting as legal trustee, literary
executor, editor, and biographer consecutively – or even simultaneously
– and Millgate provides the shrewd admonition that modern biographers and editors often find themselves confronting the same dilemmas
(and shouldering the same responsibilities) as their author's original
designees.

Why should such affairs be any different for a painter's friends, relatives, and legal representatives? In the case of Reynolds there was – on
the surface, at least – little difference indeed, for he was both an author
and an important public figure. Malone could therefore follow his
service as legal executor by gathering Reynolds's principal writings

together for a collected edition in 1797, writing the first substantial memoir of his friend, and deciding to suppress a portion of the painter's *Nachlaß*, particularly his virulent and unfinished "Ironical Discourse," which Malone presumably believed would diminish rather than enhance Reynolds's posthumous reputation.[13] The phenomenon of Sir Joshua's afterlife is complicated, however, by several factors, the most important of which is the manner in which painting – which was a business as well as an art, the work of the hand as well as the mind or imagination – had evolved in England during the eighteenth century.

When I wrote in *The Elements of Life* about the issue of biographical authority and therefore the importance (for aspiring biographers) of legitimate succession, I pointed out how significant a role predetermined succession played both in the careers of biographers and in the more firmly established profession of portrait-painting.[14] But there is a crucial difference between friends and relatives who serve as biographers or literary executors and those who serve within (and sometimes inherit) another painter's studio. William Hogarth, for example, was Sir James Thornhill's son-in-law as well as his former student. His marriage to Jane Thornhill secured him both a wife and a substantial patron: the industrious apprentice simultaneously gained a surrogate father, an artistic master, and a living representative of the English baroque, especially as it emerged in the most esteemed of contemporary genres, secular history painting. Another tradition of English painters and apprentices, moreover, extended in an unbroken line from John Riley to Jonathan Richardson, Richardson to Thomas Hudson, Hudson to Reynolds, and Reynolds to James Northcote, who wrote, as we shall see, the most substantial and influential early biography of his master.

The life (or death) of the artist thus differs from that of the writer to the extent that painting – and portrait-painting in particular – exists as a business, as a practice, as an enterprise grounded in specific sites, figures, and rituals: the waiting room, the viewing gallery, the studio (with its props and backdrops), the common lectures and demonstrations, the life classes, the commerce with paint-grinders, picture-framers, and engravers, the assistance and collaboration of assistants, the training of pupils, the apprenticeship system itself. It was rarely a solitary life, and often not an artistic endeavor that could easily stake its claims – as literature increasingly began to do – to the integrity of original composition.

Reynolds's uncomfortable awareness of the tensions embedded within his choice of career can be detected throughout his *Discourses on*

Art, which quickly move from directives concerning the importance of imitating the works of the classical and Italian masters to the necessity of approaching one's work in intellectual as well as manual terms. Every person whose business is description, he cautioned his audience in the seventh discourse, "ought to know *something* concerning the mind, as well as *a great deal* concerning the body of man."[15] Success in your art, he told his youthful listeners, "depends almost entirely on your own industry; but the industry which I principally recommended, is not the industry of the *hands*, but of the *mind*."[16] And yet the act of painting is so visibly and symbolically tied to the physical world that it is difficult to extricate it from the work of the hand.

An arresting reminder of the diurnal as well as the more exalted nature of the painter's existence has survived in a particularly interesting form. One of Reynolds's spade-shaped palettes, slightly cracked but otherwise in good repair (figure 12.2),[17] provides us with an intriguing example of artistic filiation, for it bears the still-legible marks of its varied ownership. The first inscription, at the top of the palette, reads as follows: "Calling on Mr. Northcote I found him holding this Pallet & he told me Sir Jos. Reynolds gave it him – after his Decease I called on his Sister & she gave it me." The second inscription is more specific, and tells us who wrote the first: "This Pallet belonged to James Northcote R.A. & was given me by his sister Sunday Evening May 11th 1834. his Principal Pictures Painted off it. J Cawse." The final inscription curtly informs us that "I bought this Pallette of John Cawse Charles Roberson" (Roberson was a supplier of painter's materials, with premises in Long Acre and Piccadilly). Reynolds's palette has thus literally been handed down from one generation to another. Associated, by definition, with the mechanical business of painting, the palette has become an icon with its own inscriptions and its own aura, eventually becoming a commodity to be bought and sold in the marketplace of art.

Northcote's heirloom, with the various inscriptions that finally displaced the painter's pigments, figures both the physicality of an artist's work and the hand-me-down nature of Reynolds's legacy. No other artist got to know Reynolds better than Northcote did, but the former apprentice never entirely outgrew the mixture of admiration, servility, resentment, and disapproval that he had harbored earlier in his career. His emotional response to Reynolds was therefore not unlike that of Sir Joshua's sisters Frances and Elizabeth, whose relationships with their brother were often stormy indeed, as I have elsewhere shown.[18] Northcote's was an insider's view, but a restricted one all the same:

12.2 Sir Joshua Reynolds's palette.

neither talented enough to excite Sir Joshua's professional jealousy nor sufficiently lacking in talent to lose him his master's attention, Northcote commanded a liminal listening post in a small room apart from the studio itself. He dined with Reynolds, and more frequently with Frances, but he "never in his life dined at Sir Joshua's table, when there was a *grand party*."[19]

If Northcote's voice appears to ring too loudly in the memoirs and scholarship devoted to Reynolds, it is principally by default, for Reynolds firmly broke the *domestic* line of succession among British painters by refusing to marry and by leaving no children. There was no Lady Reynolds with whom to collaborate (as Blake did with his wife Catherine), nor to continue to produce copies of her husband's prints after his death (as Jane Hogarth did), nor to write a combative biography of her husband (as Amelia Opie did). The painter's nieces, Mary Palmer and Theophila (Offy) Palmer (later Mrs. Gwatkin), remained keepers of the flame following their uncle's death – and formidable gate-keepers as well – but we discover little sense of professional continuity in the roles they played.[20] Reynolds's estate and his artistic legacy were placed firmly in the hands of his closest male friends at the time of his death (Boswell, Burke, and Malone). The fact that so much of that legacy finally devolved upon James Northcote tells us as much about Reynolds as it does about his potential biographers.

There was active speculation, both during and after Reynolds's lifetime, about who would write his biography – or write it best.[21] Boswell was the logical candidate, but he soon realized how difficult it would be to characterize someone who lacked the "prominent features" that make biography successful.[22] Burke found himself in the same predicament, and thus the task fell to Malone, who proceeded as best he could, drawing upon several autobiographical fragments in Reynolds's hand, polishing them in the process,[23] and eventually producing a reverential memoir that is long on generalization and short on actual documentation. It is, moreover, the work of a literary scholar, someone who – like Boswell – knew very little about the texture and business of a painter's life. This Northcote knew well, and it is precisely the focus on Reynolds's domestic and professional existence that makes his awkward, unfocused, and repetitive narrative so valuable. Part of the biography's disjointedness derives from the fact that it attempted to digest a compilation of notices culled from old newspapers by a team of researchers employed by the publisher, Henry Colburn.[24] Of more interest to us, I think, is the fact that it represents one stage in a series of essentially autobiographical acts in Northcote's lifetime. Northcote and his brother wrote frequently to one other once the aspiring painter left his native Plymouth for apprenticeship within Sir Joshua's household. Northcote later wove these and other documents into the draft of an autobiography, and it is this narrative that he used as the basis for his biography of Reynolds – literally abandoning his own autobiography in order to resurrect the life of his master in 1813.[25]

This complicated act of self-effacement begins (paradoxically) to explain the presence of Northcote himself within a narrative devoted to someone else, and to explain, at the same time, the competing emotions that Reynolds's biographer still nurtured. Northcote's biography is more critical than Malone's, but not (as Martin Postle has shown) as critical as the sometimes acidulous notes upon which it was based.[26] And even though Northcote revised the narrative so that it could be published in two handsome volumes in 1818, he was never, really, finished with Reynolds himself. His table-talk was often Reynoldsian in subject as well as character, and it was eagerly collected by James Ward as well as Hazlitt. Sometimes the conversations Northcote held with Hazlitt ("Boswell Redivivus") appear to corroborate facts and opinions in the biography, but often they are difficult to pin down, as an exasperated Benjamin Robert Haydon noted in his diary: "The whole conduct in the abominable Boswell Redivivus of Northcote's Hazlitt is a disgrace. One talks & the other writes. If you accuse Northcote, he swears Hazlitt has put down what he [did] not say, and if you go to Hazlitt, he says, 'Am I answerable for what Northcote says?'"[27]

It is surely not unusual that Reynolds lived on, often with such vitality, in the pages of other painters' works. The years following Reynolds's death in 1792 were filled with various and interesting acts of appropriation: not just Blake's marginalia, but Haydon's and Hazlitt's as well.[28] Horace Walpole noted in his *Miscellany* that "Sr Josh. Reynolds's models, casts & duplicate Prints Sold by auction at Greenwood's Leic. fields April 16–17. 1792."[29] Lord and Lady Inchiquin presented Reynolds's sitter's chair to James Barry, once Reynolds's antagonist but now one of his posthumous supporters.[30] Sir Thomas Lawrence, who would succeed Benjamin West as president of the Academy, later acquired the famous chair at auction, and it was sold to each succeeding president until Lord Leighton presented it to the Academy in 1879. Lawrence also purchased several of Reynolds's unfinished portraits of George III, completing them himself in yet another act of appropriation. Both Lawrence and Joseph Farington, moreover, are thought to have owned an unusual self-portrait by Reynolds in which he displays himself in front of a canvas on an easel, and it is undoubtedly the focus on Reynolds *as* a painter that attracted these two academicians to a picture in which the paraphernalia of the studio was almost certainly introduced, posthumously, by another hand.[31]

The most active keepers of the flame, however, were the reproductive engravers who had flourished long before Reynolds's death. William Richardson published a full catalogue of prints in 1794, and Valentine Green issued a series of posthumous beauties as well.[32] Reynolds once remarked of James McArdell that "by this man, I shall be immortalized."[33] The irony, of course, was that Reynolds's paintings had faded so dramatically – and so quickly – that he was in desperate need of the reproductive printmakers in order to document his original tonal values for posterity. Malone had mentioned the fate of many of Reynolds's paintings in a footnote to his memoir, which was later given a characteristic twist by Blake in his marginal comment: "I do not think that the Change is so much in the Pictures as in the Opinions of the Public."[34]

But Blake also noted the actual fading of the colors (the result of Reynolds's incessant and dangerous pursuit of more dramatic effects), even if, as we have seen, his response was both fanciful and quite telling:

> When Sr Joshua Reynolds died
> All Nature was degraded:
> The King dropd a tear into the Queens Ear:
> And all his Pictures Faded.

By "degraded" Blake literally means that nature was debased – lowered in rank or quality – which parries Malone's emphasis on the number of noble pallbearers at Reynolds's funeral. Blake would later remark, in another marginal aside, that "I always considerd True Art & True Artists to be particularly Insulted & Degraded by the Reputation of these Discourses[,] As much as they were Degraded by the Reputation of Reynolds's Paintings, & that Such Artists as Reynolds, are at all times Hired by the Satans, for the Depression of Art[.] A Pretence of Art: To Destroy Art."[35] Blake's point in his first couplet is that just as Reynolds's paintings had debased art during his lifetime, so his physical dissolution now debased nature at his death. Nature is not saddened, not brought low, by his death; far from invoking the pathetic fallacy, Blake in fact violates poetical decorum in order to put his subject in his proper place. The King, moreover, would have been one of the last Englishmen to shed a tear at the death of his Principal Painter, for George III and the artist he had knighted got on notoriously badly: Allan Ramsay, the King insisted, "is my painter."[36] But the King's opinion did not count for much in the world of art. One of the marks of Reynolds's reputation was that it could withstand even the ignorance and indifference of a sovereign who had been persuaded to found a national academy. Blake's deliciously ironic image of the connubial monarch shedding and sharing crocodile tears insists not only on the cause and effect of the King's response but also on the simultaneity – and consequently the finality – of these two activities. Blake wants a death, an end to the debasement he believes Reynolds had dealt to generations of young British artists.

The final words (and images) among the Romantics belong not to William Blake, poet and painter, however, but to Wordsworth and Constable. In a poem written during the fall of 1811, Wordsworth provided an inscription to be engraved on a cenotaph that Sir George Beaumont raised a year later in Reynolds's honor at the end of an avenue of trees on his country estate at Coleorton. It is an interesting act of ventriloquism in which the poet resuscitates Reynolds's memory and reputation precisely by invoking the natural cycle of generation that Blake would deny the painter:

> Ye Lime-trees, ranged before this hallowed Urn,
> Shoot forth with lively power at Spring's return;
> And be not slow a stately growth to rear
> Of pillars, branching off from year to year,
> Till they have learned to frame a darksome aisle; –
> That may recall to mind that awful Pile
> Where Reynolds, 'mid our country's noblest dead,
> In the last sanctity of fame is laid.
> – There, though by right the excelling Painter sleep
> Where Death and Glory a joint sabbath keep,
> Yet not the less his Spirit would hold dear
> Self-hidden praise, and Friendship's private tear:
> Hence, on my patrimonial grounds, have I
> Raised this frail memorial to his memory;
> From youth a zealous follower of the Art
> That he professed; attached to him in heart;
> Admiring, loving, and with grief and pride
> Feeling what England lost when Reynolds died.[37]

Wordsworth's Beaumont will shed the "private tear" that George III could drop only in Blake's unconventional ear. The lime-tree aisle points to the darkened interior of St. Paul's, where the painter's body had been interred, but the ambition of the poem is to transplant the spirit of an absent friend to the patrimonial grounds of his disciple, a connoisseur and amateur painter. Reynolds, the quintessentially urban artist, the painter who told Charles James Fox that "the human face was *his* landscape,"[38] has been inscribed within the grounds of Beaumont's ancestral estate, claimed not just by "England" but by a particularly powerful rural vision of that country's greatness.

When John Constable was a guest of Sir George and Lady Beaumont in the fall of 1823, he noted that, "in the dark recesses of these gardens, and at the end of one of the walks, I saw an urn – & bust of Sir Joshua Reynolds – & under it some beautifull verses, by Wordsworth."[39] Constable sketched Beaumont's memorial to Reynolds in pencil and gray wash on 28 November, the last day of his visit to Coleorton, transcribing Wordsworth's poem on the back of his drawing (figure 12.3).[40] The sketch is unusual in two respects, for Constable has placed both Reynolds and Wordsworth under erasure here, suppressing the image of the bust of Sir Joshua while also rendering the inscription in such a loosely suggestive and therefore illegible manner that neither the author nor the subject can be identified.

The impromptu sketchiness of this drawing would seem to speak for itself, of course, were it not for Constable's careful transcription of the poem (which he took pains to correct)[41] and – more importantly – his lingering anxiety concerning the legibility of the monument when he began to paint this subject a decade later. When Constable shared his worries about the inscription with Charles Leslie in 1836, Leslie replied by sketching his own design for the cenotaph, with "REYNOLDS" firmly printed on the monument's plinth. "How will something like this do for your inscription," Leslie wrote to his friend; "to my mind the name is so much better."[42] So much better than what? Better than Constable's undulating lines? Better than a painted transcription? Better than nothing?

Constable's difficulty in representing Wordsworth's poem was in part technical (because of the difference between paint and incised stone), in part aesthetic (because of the large number of lines that *could* be painstakingly transcribed, a strategy that would inevitably turn his viewers into readers), in part stylistic (because of the difference between precise verbal transcription and his normally loose manner of handling paint), and in part psychological, for the dilemma of rendering these lines of verse was clearly linked with the relationship Constable was forging between himself and his artistic precursor, between himself and his poetical contemporary.

Constable sent his painted version of the scene at Coleorton, now known as *The Cenotaph* (figure 12.4), to the Royal Academy's annual

12.3 John Constable, *The Cenotaph*. Graphite and grey wash (1823).

12.4 John Constable, *The Cenotaph*. Oil on canvas (1836).

exhibition later in 1836, the last to be held at Somerset House. Constable entitled the painting *Cenotaph to the Memory of Sir Joshua Reynolds, Erected in the Grounds of Coleorton Hall, Leicestershire, by the Late Sir George Beaumont*, remarking to a friend that he "preferred to see Sir Joshua Reynolds's name and Sir George Beaumont's once more in the catalogue, for the last time in the old house."[43] The finished painting shows that Constable agreed with Leslie's suggestion, although Constable corrected the place-ment of the letters on the monument: "REYNOLDS" is legibly rendered within the text of Wordsworth's poem, which finally serves as the vehicle for a tribute whose tenor now resides in the artist's hands alone.

This is not to say, however, that Constable is unfaithful to the argu-ment of Wordsworth's text, for the autumnal setting of the poem is care-fully orchestrated in the mellow brown modulations of the canvas (both the poet and the painter had visited the Beaumonts, years apart, in November). In the painting, moreover, Constable's dramatic introduc-tion of the stag – a creature whose vitality and nobility contrast sharply with the melancholy topos that Constable had introduced in another picture, *Jacques and the Wounded Stag*[44] – surely represents yet another movement in Beaumont and Wordsworth's attempt to naturalize the ele-gance and urbanity that Reynolds and his work personified. The stag has been at leisure, and we – as spectators, as amblers – have disturbed him. His imminent departure reminds us, however, that the carefully designed walks and gardens of Coleorton, with their contrived perspectives and literary shrines, are still intimately linked with the even more natural world that surrounds them.

When Constable completed his painted version of the cenotaph in the 1830s, moreover, something characteristically interesting happened as he worried over the inscription, unveiled the busts of Michelangelo and Raphael framing the monument, and introduced the strong, somewhat disturbing figure of the stag. Ronald Paulson has put the case most force-fully by arguing that the painting is primarily an elegy to Reynolds, and to the end of an era. Paulson sees the stag as a symbol of "majesty trapped – dying because of man's hounding him to death." The perse-cuted stag is "at bay," representing "not Reynolds but Constable himself, standing in the ambience of Reynolds, Raphael, and Michelangelo."[45] In an extended footnote, Paulson pushes this argument even further by suggesting that the painting is "full of ambivalence," that it is the one "explicit expression" in Constable's work as a painter of the ambiva-lence he felt toward those friendly, mentoring presences (Beaumont,

John Fisher, Joseph Farington) who were "utterly uncomprehending of what he was trying to do" in his landscapes.[46]

Not everyone will agree with Paulson's interpretation. James Heffernan, for example, is right to point out that Constable's stag is neither pursued nor persecuted, for by the time Constable painted this canvas he had been a full member of the Academy for seven years, successful both as an artist and as a lecturer. If the stag does represent Constable, Heffernan concludes, "it expresses not a plaintive appeal to a hostile public but the confidence of one who had long since – in his own words – 'found an original style'." Michelangelo, Raphael, and Reynolds (the two great practitioners of history painting, and its most recent exponent) are thus invoked here "to witness the fact that Constable has decisively cleared a space for his own kind of landscape painting in the history of art." The three monuments to the history of art that remain in the painting must compete for our attention with the natural elements that work to "displace history" at Coleorton.[47]

I think that Heffernan is essentially correct in his reading of this enigmatic painting, but I am not entirely comfortable with the terms of his engagement. *The Cenotaph* is not so much a work of displacement, or suppression, or ambivalence (as Paulson put it) as it is an exercise in appropriation and reinscription.[48] The bust of Reynolds may have disappeared from the head of the monument, but it has been *doubled* through artistic association. Wordsworth, whose poem Constable had inserted in the catalogue entry for his picture, had called upon the lime trees to "frame a darksome aisle" that would "recall to mind" the urban cathedral in which Reynolds's body was buried. As I have already suggested, this is an act of transplantation – perhaps figuratively of disinterment – on Wordsworth's part, as the poet puts us in mind of St. Paul's only to ask us to reinscribe Reynolds here, in the serenity of this cultivated rural setting.

Constable takes this process a step further as he places the cenotaph and matching terms within a natural cathedral in which they have their place, but in which they no longer represent a dominant force. The monument to Reynolds is painted in a relatively flat manner, with only occasional impasto, whereas the natural elements in the foreground of the painting are vigorously – almost startlingly – accentuated by the painter's extensive use of the palette knife (a practice we find in several contemporary paintings, including *Salisbury Cathedral from the Meadows*). The stag has just emerged from a small pool of water that has collected in front of the cenotaph. The branches of the trees on the left-hand side of the canvas, moreover, closely echo the color and form of the stag's antlers, above which they tower.

Constable offers us, finally, a view of art that generously (and literally) reinscribes the monuments of the past rather than suppressing or forcibly displacing them. A cenotaph is, after all, an empty tomb (*kenos taphos*), a sepulchral monument marking what is absent, what is to be found elsewhere. In Constable's painting, however, it draws attention to a presence that is celebrated and appropriated at the same time. The point is not, simply, that Constable must clear a space for his own art, for as early as 1802, in his letter to John Dunthorne, he realized that "there is room enough for a natural painture."[49] What matters in *The Cenotaph* – and in Reynolds's complicated legacy as a painter and public figure – is that the aesthetic tradition Constable inherited from Reynolds has a place within the natural landscape (and the natural painture) that now encompasses it. Surely Constable's gesture – and particularly his allusive inclusion of the two statues that frame the darksome aisle – would have been appreciated by Reynolds, who opened his first discourse by invoking Raphael, and who closed his final address by stating that "I should desire that the last words which I should pronounce in this Academy, and from this place, might be the name of – MICHAEL ANGELO."[50]

NOTES

1. *William Blake's Writings*, ed. G. E. Bentley, Jr., 2 vols. (Oxford: Clarendon Press, 1978), II:1459. Blake annotated the first volume of *The Works of Sir Joshua Reynolds*, 3 vols. (London, 1798), now in the British Library. For the fullest analysis of the problem of dating Blake's famous pen-and-pencil commentary, see G. E. Bentley, Jr., *Blake Books* (Oxford: Clarendon Press, 1977), 691–93.
2. *William Blake's Writings*, II:943. These lines are associated with – and may even form the conclusion to – a poem entitled "Florentine Ingratitude" in which Blake vents his anger at Reynolds's politeness, his Uffizi self-portrait, and his veneration of Michelangelo.
3. Lawrence Lipking, *The Ordering of the Arts in Eighteenth-Century England* (Princeton: Princeton University Press, 1970), 165.
4. *William Blake's Writings*, II:1450.
5. *Ibid.*, II:1454–59.
6. See *The Notebook of William Blake*, ed. David V. Erdman with Donald K. Moore (1973; 2nd edn., n.p.: Readex Books, 1977), N74. The dating of individual pages within the Rossetti Manuscript – let alone the various images on each page – is extremely complicated, as Erdman demonstrates in his

introduction. Page 74 appears to fall within the period 1788–93, in which
"Blake was using the Notebook for various overlapping projects"; Erdman
also notes that this page may have been started early and filled up later (p.
12 and n. 2). Erdman does not identify what I believe to be the head of
Reynolds, nor does Martin Butlin, *The Paintings and Drawings of William Blake*,
2 vols. (New Haven and London: Yale University Press for the Paul Mellon
Centre for Studies in British Art, 1981), 1:99 (No. 201 79[d]). Butlin suggests
that the male profile to the right is "something like Blake's own"; see
Geoffrey Keynes, *The Complete Portraiture of William & Catherine Blake*
(London: Trianon Press for the William Blake Trust, 1977), 21 and pl. 19, for
Blake's own head in full profile.

7. *The Correspondence of Edmund Burke*, ed. Thomas W. Copeland et al., 10 vols.
(Cambridge: Cambridge University Press; Chicago: University of Chicago
Press, 1958–78), VII:75–76.

8. *Ibid.*, IX:329.

9. Michael Millgate, *Testamentary Acts: Browning, Tennyson, James, Hardy* (Oxford:
Clarendon Press, 1992); Ian Hamilton, *Keepers of the Flame: Literary Estates and
the Rise of Biography from Shakespeare to Plath* (London: Hutchinson, 1992;
Boston and London: Faber and Faber, 1994).

10. Millgate, *Testamentary Acts*, 2–3.

11. *Ibid.*, 205.

12. *Ibid.*

13. See Reynolds, *Portraits*, ed. Frederick W. Hilles (London: Heinemann; New
York: McGrawHill, 1952), 123–26, and Richard Wendorf, *Sir Joshua Reynolds:
The Painter in Society* (Cambridge, Mass.: Harvard University Press; London:
National Portrait Gallery, 1996), ch. 5.

14. Wendorf, *The Elements of Life: Biography and Portrait-Painting in Stuart and
Georgian England* (Oxford: Clarendon Press, 1990; corrected edn., 1991),
273–74.

15. Reynolds, *Discourses on Art*, ed. Robert R. Wark (1959; 2nd edn., New Haven
and London: Yale University Press for the Paul Mellon Centre for Studies
in British Art, 1975), 118.

16. *Ibid.*, 117.

17. The property of Hazlitt, Gooden, & Fox (London). I am grateful to Lindsay
Stainton for providing me with a photograph and with a transcription of
the various legends on the palette (there is a fourth on the handle).

18. See Wendorf, *Sir Joshua Reynolds*, ch. 2.

19. *The Diary of Benjamin Robert Haydon*, ed. Willard Bissell Pope, 5 vols.
(Cambridge, Mass.: Harvard University Press, 1960–63), V:487.

20. It was, however, an artistic household, as Theophila Gwatkin told Haydon
very late in her life: "Everybody in the house painted. Lady Thomond &
herself, the coachman & the man servant Ralph & his daughter, all painted,
copied & talked about Pictures" (*ibid.*, V:487).

21. See, for example, James Northcote, *The Life of Sir Joshua Reynolds*, 2nd edn.,
2 vols. (London, 1818), II:210–11.

22. Reynolds, *Portraits*, 20.

23. See Frederick W. Hilles, *The Literary Career of Sir Joshua Reynolds* (Cambridge: Cambridge University Press, 1936; reprinted. Hamden, Conn.: Archon, 1967), 195–96.

24. See Ronald Lightbown's introduction to the facsimile edition as well as Martin Postle, *Sir Joshua Reynolds: The Subject Pictures* (Cambridge: Cambridge University Press, 1995), 301–02, and William Hazlitt, *Complete Works*, ed. P. P. Howe, 21 vols. (London and Toronto: J. M. Dent, 1930–34), XI: 269–70 (on seeing it through the press).

25. See Stephen Gwynn, *Memorials of an Eighteenth Century Painter (James Northcote)* (London, 1898), 4–5. Northcote actually wrote his autobiography in the third person: "James Northcote, whose life I am to write . . ." (5).

26. See Postle, *Sir Joshua Reynolds: The Subject Pictures*, 302.

27. Haydon, *Diary*, III:464.

28. See Frederick W. Hilles, "Reynolds among the Romantics," in *Literary Theory and Structure*, ed. Frank Brady, John Palmer, and Martin Price (New Haven: Yale University Press, 1973), 267–83.

29. *Horace Walpole's "Miscellany" 1786–1795*, ed. Lars E. Troide (New Haven: Yale University Press, 1978), 131.

30. *Reynolds*, ed. Nicholas Penny (London: Royal Academy of Arts, and Weidenfeld and Nicolson; New York: Abrams, 1986), no. 163. Lady Thomond eventually sold several paintings to George IV; see Martin Postle, "A Taste for History: Reynolds, West, George III, and George IV," *Apollo* 138 (1993): 186–91.

31. See Wendorf, *Sir Joshua Reynolds*, ch. 1, where I cite the authority of David Mannings.

32. Noted, for instance, by Edward Edwards, *Anecdotes of Painters Who Have Resided or Been Born in England; with Critical Remarks on their Productions* (London, 1808), 210; see also Penny, *Reynolds*, 36. The standard general study is David Alexander and Richard T. Godfrey, *Painters and Engraving: The Reproductive Print from Hogarth to Wilke* (New Haven: Yale Center for British Art, 1980).

33. Quoted by Robin Simon, *The Portrait in Britain and America with a Biographical Dictionary of Portrait Painters 1680–1914* (Oxford: Phaidon Press; Boston: G. K. Hall, 1987), 129.

34. *William Blake's Writings*, II:1457.

35. *Ibid.*, II:1460.

36. See Wendorf, *Sir Joshua Reynolds*, ch. 5.

37. Wordsworth, *The Poems*, ed. John O. Hayden, vol. 1 (Harmondsworth: Penguin, 1977; New Haven: Yale University Press, 1981), 853.

38. *Reminiscences and Table Talk of Samuel Rogers: Banker, Poet, & Patron of the Arts, 1763–1855*, ed. G. H. Powell (London: R. Brimley Johnson, 1903), 53.

39. John Constable to John Fisher, 2 November 1823, in *John Constable's Correspondence*, ed. R. B. Beckett, 6 vols. (Ipswich: Suffolk Records Society, 1962–68), VI:143.

40. Graham Reynolds, *The Later Paintings and Drawings of John Constable*, 2 vols.

(New Haven and London: Yale University Press for the Paul Mellon Centre for Studies in British Art, 1984), 1:126 (no. 23.31). Constable's transcription includes several variant readings from the published version of Wordsworth's poem I quote in my text.

41. *Ibid.*

42. *John Constable: Further Documents and Correspondence*, ed. Leslie Parris, Conal Shields, and Ian Fleming-Williams (London and Ipswich: Tate Gallery and Suffolk Records Society, 1975), 244.

43. *John Constable's Correspondence*, v:32.

44. See Felicity Owen and David Blayney Brown, *Collector of Genius: A Life of Sir George Beaumont* (New Haven and London: Yale University Press for the Paul Mellon Centre for Studies in British Art, 1988), 222, who also discuss the genesis of Wordsworth's poem (136).

45. Ronald Paulson, *Literary Landscape: Turner and Constable* (New Haven and London: Yale University Press, 1982), 137.

46. *Ibid.*, 194, n. 15.

47. James A. W. Heffernan, *The Re-Creation of Landscape: A Study of Wordsworth, Coleridge, Constable, and Turner* (Hanover, N. H., and London: University Press of New England for Dartmouth College, 1984), 79.

48. For an influential analysis of how Constable appropriated the familiar sites of his native country and family home in his early landscape paintings, see Ann Bermingham, "Mapping the Self: Constable/Country," ch. 3 in *Landscape and Ideology: The English Rustic Tradition, 1740–1860* (Berkeley and Los Angeles: University of California Press, 1986).

49. *John Constable's Correspondence*, ii:32.

50. Reynolds, *Discourses*, 15, 282. Graham Reynolds, *The Later Paintings and Drawings of John Constable*, 1:286, is right to point out, by the way, that Reynolds had painted himself with a bust of Michelangelo when he presented his self-portrait to the Royal Academy, and that Joseph Wilton's bust of Michelangelo was placed above the entrance doorway to the Academy's rooms in Somerset House.

Index

280